PRAISE

EVERY DAY Is GAME DAY

"The pro sportsman (Pat) and the die-hard fan (Mark) have all the bases covered in *Every Day Is Game Day*. They'll make you laugh and think and, ultimately, want to do better in your walk with God."

David Steele,
Orlando Magic broadcaster

"The market is filled with all kinds of devotionals, but *Every Day Is Game Day* stands out as being both insightful and enjoyable. If you're a sports fan who loves God, you owe it to yourself to make this one a part of your daily walk."

Bob Boone,
Former MLB player and manager and four-time All-Star

"Who knew that so much fun and insight could be packed into a 350-word devotion? Mark and Pat have given Christian sports lovers a real gift."

Tommy Sheppard,
Washington Wizards general manager

"If you love sports and God, this devotional is just what you're looking for."

Chet Walker,
NBA Hall of Famer

"Would you rather be entertained or challenged? With *Every Day Is Game Day*, you don't have to choose! You'll be both, thanks to Mark and Pat's knowledge and wit and passion for spiritual growth."

Vince Nauss,
President of Baseball Chapel

"Even people who think they know a lot about sports will be amazed at the sports stories in this book. But it's the spiritual insights that make *Every Day Is Game Day* so strong."

Norm Sonju,
Dallas Mavericks cofounder, former president and general manager

"Important things, like pursuing a deeper relationship with God, don't have to be difficult and unpleasant. Mark and Pat prove it with *Every Day Is Game Day*."

Dickie Noles,
Former Major League pitcher

"How many times have you wished you could find a devotional that you would look forward to picking up every day? Well, you found it. *Every Day Is Game Day* will light a fire in your spiritual life."

Jon McGlocklin,
NBA champion, All-Star, and Milwaukee Bucks broadcaster

"Sports is a great metaphor for the Christian life, which means a sports devotional is bound to be an effective tool for spiritual growth … especially when it's written by Pat Williams and Mark Atteberry."

Jeff Turner,

NBA player, Olympic gold medalist, and Orlando Magic broadcaster

"The Christian life is a day-by-day challenge, which means a day-by-day source of inspiration is a tremendous help. Thanks to Pat and Mark for giving us *Every Day Is Game Day*, a perfect day-by-day resource."

Ernie Accorsi,

Former general manager of the Baltimore Colts, Cleveland Browns, and New York Giants

"A strong devotional life is key if you want to walk faithfully with God. I am always thrilled to find books that make devotions easier and more meaningful, and *Every Day Is Game Day* is certainly one of those."

Dr. Jay Strack,

Founder and president of Student Leadership University

PAT WILLIAMS
MARK ATTEBERRY

EVERY DAY
— IS —
GAME DAY

A 365-Day
Sports Devotional

Published by Advantage, Charleston, South Carolina.
Member of Advantage Media Group.

ADVANTAGE is a registered trademark, and the Advantage colophon is a trademark of Advantage Media Group, Inc.

Printed in the United States of America.

10 9 8 7 6 5 4 3 2 1

ISBN: 978-1-64225-314-6
LCCN: 2021919517

Cover design by Carly Blake.
Layout design by Wesley Strickland.

This publication is designed to provide accurate and authoritative information in regard to the subject matter covered. It is sold with the understanding that the publisher is not engaged in rendering legal, accounting, or other professional services. If legal advice or other expert assistance is required, the services of a competent professional person should be sought.

 Advantage Media Group is proud to be a part of the Tree Neutral® program. Tree Neutral offsets the number of trees consumed in the production and printing of this book by taking proactive steps such as planting trees in direct proportion to the number of trees used to print books. To learn more about Tree Neutral, please visit www.treeneutral.com.

Advantage Media Group is a publisher of business, self-improvement, and professional development books and online learning. We help entrepreneurs, business leaders, and professionals share their Stories, Passion, and Knowledge to help others Learn & Grow. Do you have a manuscript or book idea that you would like us to consider for publishing? Please visit advantagefamily.com.

PAT'S DEDICATION:

For Bobby Bowden, A dear friend
and incomparable witness for Christ.

MARK'S DEDICATION:

For my mother, Barbara Atteberry,
At eighty-seven, there are two things
she never misses: a St. Louis Cardinals
game and her daily devotions.

CONTENTS

FOREWORD

DURING MY TWELVE-YEAR NBA career, one of the challenges I faced was keeping my relationship with God strong and healthy. The physical demands of playing, the pressure to perform at a high level, the travel, and the separation from family made walking closely with God a challenge. You may not be a professional athlete, but I'm sure you have pressures that make your walk with God a challenge too. It's a problem that virtually every Christian faces because the secular world is so set against us.

That's why I'm thankful for a book like *Every Day Is Game Day*. It offers all believers a daily opportunity to spend some time with God, thinking through biblical truths and reflecting on what they mean for us as we try to keep the faith. Virtually every situation you can face in life is covered in these 365 devotions. What's even better is that they are fun as well as deeply spiritual and motivating. Pat and Mark have packed this book with sports history, trivia, and some of the greatest anecdotes you'll ever read. I suspect you'll find it very easy to stick with your daily devotions when you discover how fun and interesting they are.

I urge you to give some time to this book every day because, for Christians, every day really is game day. You'll be amazed at how often one of these devotions hits you smack in the middle of your circumstances. That's how real and relevant they are. You might even think Pat and Mark have been spying on you! I assure you, they haven't. They just have a knack for connecting God's Word with real life.

Enjoy the journey!

Allan Houston,

Two-time NBA All-Star and Olympic gold medal winner

EVERY DAY IS GAME DAY

CAL RIPKEN JR. put up a lot of great numbers during his twenty-one-year career: 431 home runs, 1,695 RBIs, and a very respectable .276 lifetime batting average. But the only number most people think of when they hear his name is 2,632: the number of consecutive games he played between 1982 and 1998.

Imagine Cal taking the field on May 20, 1982. He was a second-year big leaguer, hoping only to play well enough to earn a chance to play again the next day. If you'd told him that he wouldn't be getting another day off for over a decade and a half, he most certainly would have pegged you for a nutcase. But that's what happened.

Or did it?

It certainly isn't our intention to diminish Cal's tremendous accomplishment, but the truth is that he had over three thousand days off during those record-setting years because, in the sporting world, every day is *not* game day. Even if you stay healthy and answer the bell for every contest, you'll still have off days, travel days, practice days, and of course, the off-season.

Many parallels can be drawn between the sporting life and the Christian life. The Bible contains a surprising number of sports metaphors. But this is one striking difference: in the life of faith, there's no such thing as a day off. Every day, from the moment you open your eyes in the morning until you fall asleep at night, the game is on. Even if you're hurt and don't feel like playing, the game is *still* on. Satan never rests, and you mustn't either, if you want to be a winner when the final out is made.

That's why we're so glad this book found its way into your hands. We're glad to have you join us on what we hope will be an entertaining yet challenging journey toward a deeper, more meaningful relationship with Christ. And if you learn something along the way that makes you a better competitor in your chosen sport, well, that'll be icing on the cake.

Reflect: Hebrews 3:13 says, "You must warn each other every day, while it is still 'today,' so that none of you will be deceived by sin and hardened against God." This scripture is a good example of how the Bible emphasizes the everyday aspect of the Christian life. Be honest. Do you take days off in your walk with the Lord? Have you been known to set your faith aside for a while so you can enjoy some questionable activity? What makes you think this is acceptable to God?

OUTSIDE THE LINES

DON'T LET THE movie-star looks fool you. Danica Patrick is a fierce competitor who silenced all her critics when she became the first woman to win an IndyCar race. But if you read your sports page on the morning of December 10, 2008, you probably saw that she was ticketed for driving nineteen miles over the speed limit in her hometown of Scottsdale, Arizona. The article also noted that, about a year before, she was ticketed for exceeding the speed limit by seventeen miles an hour and ordered to attend traffic school.

Talk about a weird situation.

Danica Patrick belongs in traffic school like John Grisham belongs in a remedial English class. She belongs in traffic school like Oprah Winfrey belongs in a welfare line. But there Danica was, studying the same "rules of the road" handbook that a pimply faced teenager pores over as he's counting down the hours and minutes until his sixteenth birthday.

Athletes learn at an early age to respect authority and play by the rules. It's one of the great benefits of involvement in athletics. But a disappointing number of them leave that respect and self-discipline behind when they step off the floor, the field, or the track. We doubt that any of them would claim to be above the law, but that's often how they act. It's why hardly a week goes by that we don't hear about an athlete getting into some kind of trouble. Sometimes, as in Ms. Patrick's case, that brush with the law is relatively harmless. But we can all recall incidents that were anything *but* harmless.

NO MATTER HOW GOOD YOU ARE INSIDE THE LINES, IT'S WHAT YOU DO OUTSIDE THE LINES THAT WILL MAKE YOU OR BREAK YOU.

As a Christian athlete who understands that every day is game day, one of your biggest challenges is to translate the disciplines you develop on the field into real life. No matter how good you are *inside* the lines, it's what you do *outside* the lines that will make you or break you.

Reflect: "Oh, that my actions would consistently reflect your decrees! Then I will not be ashamed when I compare my life with your commands" (Ps. 119:5–6). Have you been known to turn your faith on and off, depending on whether you're in the spotlight? Do you relax your standards when you think no one is looking? If so, which person is the real you? More importantly, which person do you think God sees as the real you?

GETTING SCHOOLED

EVERY TEAM AND EVERY player has a bad day now and then. No matter how good you are, sooner or later you're going to get schooled by an opponent. We call it a blowout. When it happens, conventional wisdom says you should just forget about it and move on. Turn the page. Let it go.

Pat Summitt couldn't have agreed less.

She coached the University of Tennessee Lady Vols basketball team to 1,098 wins, 16 SEC titles, 18 Final Fours, and 8 NCAA championships. If anybody ever knew what it takes to win, she did.

In 1988, her team was clobbered 97–78 by the Lady Longhorns from the University of Texas, one of the most lopsided losses in her coaching career. Coach Summitt didn't just call it "one of those nights" and tell her players to forget it and move on. Instead she had the score painted in big orange letters on the training room wall. She also had T-shirts made with the score printed on the front and required her players to wear them during practice.[1] She was determined that her team would remember that awful night, learn something from it, and find motivation in it.

As a Christian, you're going to have bad days too; days when you'll fall far short of your own standards, not to mention God's. You certainly don't want to convert them into baggage that you'll end up dragging around for the rest of your life. God gives us grace so we can live free from the sins of the past.

On the other hand, you *do* want to learn from your mistakes. Toward that end, we encourage you not to dismiss your blunders too quickly or cavalierly. A crushing defeat is a treasure trove of valuable lessons. If you have the patience to dig through them, you'll no doubt find something that will make you a tougher opponent the next time around.

Reflect: "Don't keep looking at my sins. Remove the stain of my guilt. Create in me a clean heart, O God. Renew a loyal spirit within me" (Ps. 51:9–10). As you read these words, notice how David used the painful memory of his affair with Bathsheba as a springboard to greater faithfulness. Can you think of a time when you got schooled by Satan? What did you learn from that experience that has made you a better Christian?

YOUR ULTIMATE DESTINATION

I (PAT) KNEW WHAT I wanted to do with my life when I was seven years old. My dad took me to my first Major League Baseball game. We sat in the upper deck on the third base side for a Sunday doubleheader between the Philadelphia A's and the Cleveland Indians. From that day on, I was determined to be a big-league ballplayer. And I got pretty close. The Phillies gave me the opportunity to play in their minor league system for two years.

I still remember when Bob Carpenter, the owner of the Phillies, sent me off to Miami as a minor league catcher. He told me to keep my eyes open both on and off the field. That was the first inkling I had that the organization was looking at me as a possible executive and not just a player. Now, all these years later, I see that my ultimate destination was never going to be catching fastballs and sliders, but catching fastballs and sliders was a stepping stone to my ultimate destination.

Right now you might have dreams and plans that you're committed to. That's great, but don't be surprised if your dreams and plans turn out to be mere stepping stones to something you could never imagine. Something far greater than what you had planned for yourself. God is full of surprises. He took a shepherd (Moses) and turned him into a head of state. He took a fisherman (Peter) and turned him into arguably the greatest preacher in history. He took a lawyer (Saul of Tarsus) and turned him into the world's greatest church planter and evangelist. All of these people thought they had already reached their ultimate destination, but they still had a way to go.

What does God have in mind for you? Only he knows. My advice is for you to be open to whatever it is … to follow him wherever he leads. Speaking from experience, I will tell you he knows best!

Reflect: Proverbs 16:9 says, "We can make our plans, but the Lord determines our steps." Why is it important to make plans and set goals in life? What might be some indicators that God is trying to lead you in a different direction? How can you be committed to your plans without being stubborn toward God's will?

WHEN YOUR A GAME ISN'T GOOD ENOUGH

ON SEPTEMBER 9, 1965, Bob Hendley, a journeyman pitcher for the last-place Chicago Cubs, took the mound against the Los Angeles Dodgers and pitched the game of his life. He mowed the Dodger hitters down for nine innings, giving up one scratch hit in the fifth. Unfortunately for him, his opponent that night was Sandy Koufax, arguably the greatest lefthander of all time. That night Koufax pitched the game of *his* life—a perfect game—and beat Bob Hendley, 1–0.

As an athlete, you've probably had an experience like this. You brought your A game, but your opponent brought his A-*plus* game and left you shaking your head at what might have been.

When this happens, it might help you to know that God also knows the disappointment of giving his best and still finishing second. The first time it happened was at the beginning of time, when he gave Adam and Eve the very best of everything he had to offer and still finished second … to a snake, no less! Sadly, he's still giving his very best and still finishing second to that same ole snake in a lot of people's lives.

Surely, if God isn't able to escape disappointment, there's no reason for us to think we'll be able to. On this side of eternity, we will often see our best efforts wasted, our plans go awry, and our hopes and dreams wash away like sandcastles at high tide.

That's why our focus must be on Christ and not on the things of this world. Yes, we live in the world, and we compete for worldly trophies, but no man-made trophy can meet the deepest needs of your heart. The next time you see a championship team celebrating, remember that many of those players will be going home to all kinds of personal problems that no trophy can fix.

Speaking of Jesus, Romans 10:11 says, "Whoever believes in him will not be put to shame." (NASB) Remember that verse and smile the next time you play the game of your life and still finish second.

Reflect: "So do not throw away this confident trust in the Lord. Remember the great reward it brings you!" (Heb. 10:35). Think of some recent disappointment you experienced. Did you handle it well? If not, what do you need to change about your thinking and your behavior the next time you find yourself in a similar situation?

DON'T STEAL IF YOU AREN'T FAST

THE 1926 WORLD SERIES was a dandy between two now-iconic franchises, the Cardinals and the Yankees. Hall of Famers were all over the field for both teams, with neither team showing an advantage. They were tied after six games.

In game seven, something crazy happened.

Jesse Haines, a knuckleballer who started the game for the Cardinals, had a 3–2 lead when manager Rogers Hornsby brought in Grover Cleveland Alexander, a move that defies the imagination. Yes, he was a great pitcher, but he was aging and had pitched a complete game the day before. Such a thing would never happen in today's game. But Cleveland came in and retired the first two hitters, and that's when things got crazy.

None other than Babe Ruth came up and walked. That brought the winning run to the plate in the person of clean-up hitter Bob Meusel, with Lou Gehrig on deck. The fans were on their feet; the tension was palpable. Everything was on the line. One swing could give the Yankees the championship.

That's when Babe Ruth, one of the slowest runners in the history of baseball, tried to steal second. He was thrown out. Game over. Cards win.

I can only imagine how stricken the Yankees and their fans were. "What is he doing? He's the *last* guy who should be trying to steal!"

The lesson here is painfully simple: Do what you're good at and don't do what you're not good at. Not the most graceful sentence in the world, but the point is clear enough. A good many failures happen because people are trying to live beyond their giftedness. You'll be much happier and more successful if you just stick with what you do well.

And the people around you will be happier too.

Reflect: 1 Peter 4:10 says, "God has given each of you a gift from his great variety of spiritual gifts. Use them well to serve one another." Have you ever tried to work outside your giftedness? What was the result? What are some of your gifts? Can you name specific ways you use them, not just to make money but to serve your fellow man?

POISE

WHEN THE 2009 NFL season began, nobody expected much from the Atlanta Falcons. Michael Vick, once considered the heart and soul of the franchise, was in prison on dogfighting charges, a new coach was at the helm, and a rookie quarterback named Matt Ryan was being asked to step in and play immediately. Even though Ryan was the third overall pick in the 2008 draft, there wasn't a sports pundit in America that thought the Falcons would be anything but terrible because, well, everybody knows rookie quarterbacks are supposed to wear baseball caps and carry clipboards.

But a funny thing happened on the way to the NFC South cellar: The Falcons finished 11–5 and made the playoffs.

Their new coach, Mike Smith, connected with his players, and the running game was better than expected, but everyone agrees that the number one reason why the Falcons prospered was Matt Ryan. He didn't just have ability; he had poise. His composure under pressure earned him the nickname "Matty Ice" in high school (because he had ice water in his veins) and made him an immediate force to be reckoned with in the NFL.

Poise is a great attribute for a Christian to have too. Why? Because not even the NFL can produce the kind of pressure that everyday life does. Avoiding a safety blitz is nothing compared to dealing with divorce, cancer, financial ruin, or the death of a child.

Sadly, many people ruin their lives in life's pressure-packed moments: an angry husband slugs his wife; a harried executive has one drink too many before slipping behind the wheel of his car; a lonely secretary gives in to her boss's sexual advances.

Just as athletes are judged by their performance under pressure, so the tale of your Christian life will ultimately be told not by how you handled yourself when things were going well, but how you handled yourself when life was coming with the blitz.

Reflect: "We are pressed on every side by troubles, but we are not crushed. We are perplexed but not driven to despair. We are hunted down but never abandoned by God. We get knocked down, but we are not destroyed" (2 Cor. 4:8–10). In these verses, Paul gives a vivid description of the poised Christian. Can you honestly say that you live this way? If not, what needs to change?

AVOIDING THE HARD HITS

WARRICK DUNN QUIETLY became one of the most proficient running backs in NFL history. By the end of the 2009 season, he had piled up 10,967 yards on the ground, ranking him nineteenth on the all-time NFL rusher's list when he retired. Not bad for a guy that no one thought would be big enough to play pro football. Listed at five feet nine and 187 pounds, he looked like a little boy alongside defensive linemen that were ten inches taller and over one hundred pounds heavier. That he played twelve years without a serious injury is amazing.

There are three factors that combined to keep him healthy. One was his conditioning; he always kept himself in great shape. Second was his elusive running style; he made it hard for defensive players to lay a good lick on him. But the third reason may be the most important: he was smart enough to avoid the unnecessary hard hit.

Warrick explained it this way: "Because of my size, I run for my life on the field. I've done it for so long and am so used to it that it comes naturally to me to protect myself. I've learned to live for another down, live for another play. I don't need to get every yard on every play. I can get the extra yard and get hurt and never play again, or I can get up and go back to the huddle and make something happen on the next play."[2]

In life, as in football, it's important to avoid the hard hits. You won't always be able to, of course, but many times you *will* be able to, simply by practicing good judgment. For example, being able to identify the people you shouldn't hang out with, the places you shouldn't go, and the things you shouldn't put in your body can spare you a lot of pain.

DON'T GIVE THE ENEMY OF YOUR SOUL A FREE SHOT AT YOU. IF YOU DO, HE'LL BE MORE THAN HAPPY TO TAKE IT.

We've known countless people, from "average Joe" church members to world-famous athletes, who've endured very hard hits that could have been easily avoided. Don't be dumb. Don't give the enemy of your soul a free shot at you. If you do, he'll be more than happy to take it.

Reflect: Proverbs 4:5–8 says, "Acquire wisdom! Acquire understanding! Do not forget nor turn away from the words of my mouth." Have you taken a lot of hard hits in your life? If so, do you feel that some of them could have been avoided with a little better decision-making? What tendencies in your thinking or behavior need to be corrected so that you take fewer hard hits in the future?

REINVENTING YOURSELF

ON MAY 7, 1957, a promising twenty-three-year-old lefthander by the name of Herb Score was on the mound for the Cleveland Indians as they faced the New York Yankees. When Yankee shortstop Gil McDougald stepped into the batter's box, the assembled fans had no idea they were about to see a swing that would change the course of the young hurler's career. McDougald ripped a line drive that hit Score in the face. It dropped him like a well-aimed bullet and left him bloodied and motionless on the mound.

Many thought Herb Score would never pitch again, but he did. He came back the next season and thrilled everyone with a three-hit, thirteen-strikeout performance. But that performance turned out to be fool's gold. His career ended quietly just three years later because he couldn't get anybody out.

But that wasn't the end of Herb Score's baseball career. He became a broadcaster for the Indians in 1964. He held that job for thirty-three years and was inducted into the Broadcasting Hall of Fame in 1998.

Ironically, his last broadcast was the seventh game of the 1997 World Series, which ended with his beloved Indians blowing a ninth-inning lead and losing the championship to the Florida Marlins.

You will often hear Herb Score referred to as a tragic figure, but we disagree. We see him as a guy who suffered a tough break but didn't let it ruin him. He could easily have turned bitter and given up on life. Many people who've seen their dreams disappear do just that. But he chose to reinvent himself, to let go of what he could no longer do and concentrate on what he could.

Someday your dream may vanish from before your very eyes through no fault of your own. You might suffer a debilitating injury, get laid off from your dream job, or watch your business go belly-up in a bad economy. If it happens, refuse to cry about what you can't do, and concentrate on what you can. Reinvent yourself!

Reflect: "Hope deferred makes the heart sick, but a dream fulfilled is a tree of life" (Prov. 13:12). How's your dream coming along? Is it limping and wheezing? Is it on life support? If so, is it time to find another dream? How could you reinvent yourself?

INTEGRITY

MICHAEL PHELPS, A swimmer who ended his career with twenty-eight overall medals, twenty-three of which were gold, had no equal in the water. Out of the water, his life was more of a struggle. In 2004, he was arrested for driving under the influence of alcohol, a charge to which he pleaded guilty. In 2009, he was photographed using a bong, which is a device used to smoke marijuana. Some speculated that the photograph was a fake, but Phelps admitted that he was indeed the guy in the picture and apologized for using bad judgment.

In a social media culture, where anybody with a cell phone can take a snapshot or a video and plaster it all over the internet, you'll often hear people talk about the importance of behaving. "You never know when someone might be standing nearby with a camera," they say. Athletes and show business people are particularly vulner-

THIS IS THE ESSENCE OF INTEGRITY: DOING THE RIGHT THING JUST BECAUSE IT'S THE RIGHT THING.

able in our celebrity-obsessed culture. Our position is that the presence or absence of a camera should have no bearing on how you behave. You should behave not because you're afraid you'll get busted but simply because it's the right thing to do.

This is the essence of integrity: doing the right thing just because it's the right thing. Few virtues will have a greater impact on the quality of your life. If you prove that you are the same person in every situation and that you're always going to do what you believe is right, people will trust you, and that trust will be the proverbial wind beneath your wings. It will make your spouse adore you, your children respect you, and your employer want to promote you.

Yes, integrity will sometimes put you in awkward situations. That's inevitable when the people around you don't live to the same standard. But never will you regret doing the right thing. And you certainly won't have to explain any embarrassing pictures.

Reflect: "Joyful are people of integrity, who follow the instructions of the LORD" (Ps. 119:1). Would the people who know you the best say unequivocally that you are a person of integrity? If you're not absolutely sure, think about why. What have you done (or not done) to cause them to have reservations about you?

CLASSROOMS

MANY PEOPLE KNOW that I (Pat) have nineteen children, fourteen of which are adopted. People ask me what that's like. I tell them that the experience has helped me understand why some species of animals eat their young. Seriously, it has been an incredible experience.

One thing I did was get all of my children involved in sports. The minute they got off the plane from South Korea, the Philippines, Romania, or Brazil, I got them plugged in. We had enough ball gloves, bats, soccer balls, and basketballs to open a sporting goods store. Yes, it was a tremendous commitment of time and money, but I truly believe it was one of the most important things I did for them. Why? Because of the life lessons they learned. Sports teach you self-discipline. They teach you teamwork. They teach you to respect authority and follow instructions. They teach you that every day isn't going to be a good day, but that you can come back and make tomorrow a better day.

There are people who disparage sports. There is even the common stereotype that we call the "dumb jock." But I am convinced that a soccer field, baseball diamond, basketball court, or any other field of competition can be just as much of a classroom as the science lab at school. Most people who have played sports have at least one coach that they remember fondly and credit with helping to shape their character. So let's hear it for the soccer moms and volunteer coaches and umpires and officials and countless others who make it possible for our kids to have an experience that will benefit them for the rest of their lives.

Always remember that the whole world is a classroom.

Reflect: Matthew 13:55 says, with reference to Jesus, "He's just the carpenter's son …" Picture a young Jesus helping his dad in his carpentry shop. What life lessons do you think he picked up there? Name some lessons you've learned outside the traditional classroom setting. What nontraditional classrooms are you frequenting today, and what are you learning?

UNDERDOG THEOLOGY

SOLOMON SAID, "THE strongest warrior doesn't always win the battle" (Eccles. 9:11). Nowhere is this more vividly demonstrated than in the world of sports. Boxing in particular has given us example after example.

Like Sonny Liston, the heavyweight champ who was known for his toughness and raw punching power. A young Muhammad Ali climbed into the ring with him as a 7–1 underdog in 1964. Not only did Ali beat him, but he did it in a way that left spectators stunned. Incredibly light on his feet, Ali often left his hands down by his sides, dancing, dodging, and ducking the lumbering Liston's flailing punches. And the victory wasn't a fluke, which is what a lot of boxing fans thought, for Ali beat him in the rematch as well as in a shocking first-round knockout.

And then there was Marvin Hagler, he of the sinister glare and chiseled physique. Marvelous Marvin Hagler he was called, bouncing on his toes, slamming his fists together, looking to all the world like a human buzz saw. Until he climbed into the ring with Sugar Ray Leonard, another Ali-like, light-as-a-feather, cat-quick ballet dancer in boxing trunks. One sportswriter commented that Hagler looked so slow fighting Leonard that he might have been wearing snowshoes.

Apparently, Goliath's demise at the hands of young David wasn't as surprising as those who witnessed it first thought. It was, in fact, only one of countless such scenarios that have played out over the centuries, which means that underdogs always have hope. Far too many people in this world give up before they even try, because the odds appear to be stacked against them. Or because they've seen others they admire fail at the same endeavor. Or because someone who is a complete stranger to optimism is in their ear telling them they're wasting their time.

We say never be afraid to step into the ring. Pay no attention to the oddsmakers or the naysayers. Come out swinging with everything you've got. You might lose. But you just might be the next in a long line of underdogs to shock the world.

Reflect: Mark 10:31 says, "But many who are the greatest now will be least important then, and those who seem least important now will be the greatest then." Can you think of a time when you felt hopeless only to find yourself experiencing victory? What factors do you think turned the tide in your favor? If you've never experienced this kind of surprising victory, is it because you've been too timid to step into the ring? Where does that timidity come from, and what can you do to change it?

"KILL THE UMPIRE!"

IN 1888 ERNEST THAYER wrote a poem that is beloved to this day by baseball fans everywhere. "Casey at the Bat" tells the story of the Mudville nine, down 4–2 in the last inning when mighty Casey steps to the plate with two men on. One swing from our hero's bat will win the game. Of course, Casey strikes out, but it's what happens before he strikes out that is of interest here. Casey takes the first and second pitches for strikes, prompting the fans to scream, "Kill him! Kill the umpire!"

What you may not know is that in those days, umpires were abused in ways that would be unthinkable today. If players or fans didn't agree with a call, they not only screamed curses but threw things at the umpires, such as balls, bats, food, and even shoes. Sometimes the umpires were attacked by mobs after the game. To top it off, they got little, if any, support from the team owners because everyone believed it would be bad for business to restrain people.

While such antics are not allowed today, there have been many professional athletes and coaches in the modern era that have become at least as famous for their tirades against officials as for their performance. Billy Martin, John McEnroe, Rasheed Wallace, and Bobby Knight would certainly be some of the first inductees if anyone ever establishes a Poor Sport's Hall of Fame.

What is your attitude toward the officials in your sport? If you are one to be constantly barking and complaining, how do you think that behavior impacts your Christian witness? There is a school of thought that allows a person to lose his temper in the heat of battle. Invariably, the hometown announcer will try to bail out the misbehaving player or coach by remarking what a competitor he is. He'll be called "fiery" or "intense" rather than "childish" or "immature," even though he may be more the latter than the former.

We would not want to drain any athlete or coach of his or her competitive spirit. Certainly, there is a time when judgment calls should be challenged because officials are not perfect. But as a Christian, there is a line that shouldn't be crossed. Cursing or in any way denigrating an official is wrong.

Reflect: "Godly people find life; evil people find death" (Prov. 11:19). Have you ever gotten into a heated argument with an official? Have you ever been ejected from competition? Have you ever been told by a coach that you need to just shut up and play? If you answered yes to these questions, what specifically can you do to get your anger and your mouth under control?

IT'S NOT THE CLUBS

HAVE YOU EVER NOTICED how golfers love to blame their equipment?

I (Mark) once had a guy walk into my office carrying thirteen putters. He laid them on my desk and asked if I saw anything in the pile I might be interested in trying. He said that if I did, I could have it because he needed to get rid of some putters. When I asked how he ended up with thirteen putters, he said he had a habit of buying a new one whenever he got into a bad putting slump. I said, "Wouldn't it have been cheaper just to take a putting lesson?"

But I guess we shouldn't be surprised by this. Pick up any golf magazine, and you'll see ad after ad promoting the latest and greatest in golf club technology. As I write this, I'm looking at the latest issue of *Golf Digest*. One ad promises, "More accuracy, more forgiveness, fewer expletives." Another ad has a hot new driver saying, "Hello, fairway, nice to own you."

Puh-lease! Could we just stop with this nonsense? If you're slicing or duck-hooking balls into the woods or if you're knocking ten-foot putts twenty feet past the hole, it's not the clubs; it's your stroke!

Sadly, some Christians sound a lot like golfers when they talk about their spiritual hooks and slices. Recently, I counseled a man who got caught cheating with his best friend's wife. He admitted that what he did was wrong, but in the same breath began talking about how *she* came onto *him*, as if that somehow made him a victim.

One of the signs of spiritual maturity is your willingness to *completely* own your mistakes. I like to call this a "no buts confession," meaning that you never do what the man I just mentioned did. You never say, "I cheated, *but* she came on to me." Instead you say, "I cheated, period." That's the only kind of confession God honors.

Besides, the "but" never fools anybody. The other members of your foursome know it's not your club that stinks; it's your swing. Just like God knows that the mug shot of the person who made you sin can be found on your driver's license. You're way ahead if you just go ahead and admit it.

Reflect: "Finally, I confessed all my sins to you and stopped trying to hide my guilt. I said to myself, 'I will confess my rebellion to the LORD.' And you forgave me! All my guilt is gone" (Ps. 32:5). Are you an excuse maker by nature? Can you think of a time when an excuse might have gotten you off the hook, but you chose to confess anyway and take the heat? Why do you think people respect a stand-up guy (or girl) more than a buck passer?

THE SHELF LIFE OF GLORY

THOUGH THE DEFINITION of a mile has changed across the centuries and from country to country, men have always been obsessed with running it and timing themselves. For many years it was believed that a sub-four-minute mile was impossible. But in the nineteenth century, timepieces became more sophisticated and made it possible to record fractions of seconds. This seemed to pour fuel on man's burning passion to break through that theoretical barrier.

Finally, it happened.

On May 6, 1954, Roger Bannister recorded a time of 3:59.4. After trying for centuries, man had finally done the impossible. The world celebrated, and Roger Bannister became a celebrity. It's a shame the record only stood for forty-six days. Imagine being the first person in history to accomplish something and only getting to bask in the glory for a month and a half.

But this is the nature of glory. It just doesn't have much of a shelf life. Quick …

Who won the 1997 NBA title?

Who was the American League MVP in 2002?

Who won the British Open in 2004?

All of these things were front-page news when they happened. Every media outlet in the country was covering them. But now, unless your favorite player or team happened to win, you don't even remember.

Glory fades, and it fades quickly, which means you need to be striving for something more substantial and more lasting. Athletes tend to dream of earthly

GLORY FADES, AND IT FADES QUICKLY, WHICH MEANS YOU NEED TO BE STRIVING FOR SOMETHING MORE SUBSTANTIAL AND MORE LASTING.

trophies and championships. How many times have you heard a player say that winning a ring was his ultimate goal? But that kind of glory, as thrilling as it is, is still perishable. To paraphrase Jesus, what does it profit a man if he wins a handful of rings but loses his soul?

Reflect: "And this world is fading away, along with everything that people crave. But anyone who does what pleases God will live forever" (1 John 2:17). Can you think of a great accomplishment of yours—either athletic or otherwise—that is now a long-faded memory? Right now, are you investing your time and energy in things that are going to last or things that are going to fade?

THE FOSBURY FLOP

THERE AREN'T MANY athletic competitions where the participants are required to move predominantly backward. Other than swimming (backstroke) and rowing, athletes are accustomed to moving mostly forward, retreating only when the circumstances of the game require it.

Realizing this helps you appreciate Dick Fosbury, a high jumper who believed that the standard method of getting over the bar could be improved upon. Running forward and "scissor kicking" seemed limiting, so he pioneered a technique that involved jumping backward over the bar. People laughed and dubbed his new method the "Fosbury Flop." But they didn't laugh long. When Fosbury "flopped" his way to the gold medal in the 1968 Olympics, suddenly everyone was running out and practicing his move. Today, the Fosbury Flop is the standard approach to the high jump.

One of the most important truths you can learn in life is that you don't have to do things the way everybody else does, either in sports or in the Christian life. We hate to say it, but many older Christians are set in their ways. They have very firm (and sometimes narrow) ideas about what a Christian ought to look like, and they will try to impose those ideas on everyone else. Obviously, there are core values—biblical essentials—that must never be compromised. But beyond that, we believe there is great freedom in Christ and that when people try to press you into a mold of their own design, it will stifle your spiritual growth. In the Bible, Jesus stands as the ultimate example of a guy who refused to be shaped by the expectations of people.

Our advice is for you to be faithful to the core truths of Scripture but to express your faith in ways that make sense for *you*, not some critic or know-it-all who would like to turn you into a religious clone.

Reflect: 1 Corinthians 12:5–6 says, "There are different kinds of service, but we serve the same Lord. God works in different ways, but it is the same God who does the work in all of us."

Is there someone in your life—perhaps a parent, friend, or teacher—who thinks you're out of step with what's normal? What can you point to in your life that indicates you are still grounded in the core truths of Scripture?

THE CLOCK IS ALWAYS TICKING

THERE'S NO BASEBALL PLAYER more famous than Babe Ruth. With his spindly legs and potbelly, he wasn't the most impressive physical specimen. And his stats, while impressive, have been surpassed by a few players. Nevertheless, the Babe, aka "The Sultan of Swat," is the ultimate baseball icon.

In 1927, Babe posted numbers that would be a nice career for some players. He ended the season with a .356 batting average, 60 home runs, and 164 RBIs. He was at the absolute peak of his career, the most feared slugger in the game by far.

But even then the clock was ticking.

You see, even the most mind-boggling physical abilities erode over time. Even as the Babe was soaking up all the accolades, the clock was ticking on his career. It was only a matter of time before he would officially be a has-been.

That day came on June 2, 1935, when he announced his retirement. Now wearing a Boston Braves uniform, Babe had become a rather pitiful sight, flailing helplessly at pitches he used to crush. His .181 batting average told him the cold, hard truth. Time had won yet another victory.

Right now, you may be a weekend warrior, a hot prospect, or an established superstar. You may have a wicked curveball or a silky-smooth jump shot or a world-class time in the one-hundred-yard dash. Just remember: it won't last. The clock is always ticking.

This means two things.

First, you need to enjoy your abilities while you have them. Squeeze every single drop of pleasure out of them. Never forget that the things you're doing now will someday be your memories.

Second, plan for the future. Think about what you want to do when the sport you love kicks you to the curb, lay out a strategy for getting there, and stick with it. If you need motivation, just stop and listen. The sound will always be there: *Tick ... tick ... tick...*

Reflect: "Don't let the excitement of youth cause you to forget your Creator. Honor him in your youth before you grow old and say, 'Life is not pleasant anymore.'" (Eccles. 12:1)

Have you noticed any deterioration in your physical skills? If so, how does that make you feel? Do you think the end of your athletic life will be hard to face? Do you have another passion in life that might fill that void?

IT'S ABOUT POTENTIAL, NOT WINS

YOU'VE HEARD PEOPLE SAY, "Winning is all that matters." And it's true; there is a sigh of relief that comes when you win that is perhaps the greatest feeling in sports. But is winning really all that matters? What if you win but play horribly? What if you win but only because your opponent turned in a horrendous performance? Is that something to feel good about?

Eddie Arcaro is perhaps the greatest jockey ever to sit astride a horse. In the 1950s he rode a horse named Nashua, which won twenty-two races before retiring as only the second horse to amass over $1 million in earnings. People noticed, however, that Mr. Arcaro rarely had anything good to say about Nashua. When the horse's trainer asked him why he continually spoke harshly about the horse when all it did was win, Arcaro said, "Because he ought to be fifteen lengths better than he is."[3]

What about you?

Should you be better than you are? Can you honestly say you're reaching your potential, or are you just doing what it takes to get by?

It's been said that when we reach the end of our lives and look back, it won't be the things we did that trouble us the most; it will be the things we didn't do. It will be the effort we didn't put out and the time we didn't put in. It will be those times when we settled and coasted and contented ourselves with just getting the job done instead of giving it our best.

Jesus talked about the importance of going the second mile (Matthew 5:41). The first mile was the required mile. It didn't make a man special in any way; it just kept him from getting into trouble with the Roman authorities. It was the second mile that set him apart, that made him a great witness for Christ.

Today that second mile, that extra effort, that push to do more than just get by is still one of the greatest secrets of success. It may not get you a win every time, but it will always put you at the level of your potential, which is all anyone can ever ask.

Reflect: "Give your complete attention to these matters. Throw yourself into your tasks so that everyone will see your progress" (1 Tim. 4:15). Are there responsibilities you have that don't excite you? That feel like drudgery? Do you sometimes just go through the motions? What are some blessings you might be missing out on as a result? Would going the second mile in these areas really cost you that much in terms of time and effort?

DO WHAT YOU CAN

WE ARE NOT proponents of that silly philosophy that says you can do anything if you put your mind to it. What nonsense! If you weigh three hundred pounds, you are not going to make it as a jockey, no matter how committed you are to the idea. If you have poor reflexes and very little hand-eye coordination, you'll get killed if you try to become a boxer. Perhaps you remember when Michael Jordan tried to become a baseball player. He failed miserably, not because of a lack of desire but because of a lack of ability.

Our advice is for you to do what you can, as much as you can, as well as you can.

Like Tom Dempsey.

He was born with two birth defects: a deformed right hand and a right foot that was merely a stub. Yet he was also blessed with a big, strong body. At six feet two and 255 pounds, his size screamed "Football!" but his birth defects seemed to answer, "No way!"

So Tom did what he could, as much as he could, as well as he could.

He decided to kick footballs instead of catching them or throwing them.

And oh, did he kick footballs!

In just his second season with the New Orleans Saints, Tom lined up for an unthinkable sixty-three-yard attempt. His team was down one point to the Detroit Lions with just two seconds on the clock. Lions fans and players were feeling very good about their chances of winning, but those smiles turned to stares of disbelief when the ball sailed between the uprights.

Don't listen to people who tell you that you can do anything you want. You can't. But you can do more than you think, and that's the key! Your challenge in sports and in life is to identify those things God has gifted you to do, figure out which one ignites your passion, and then pursue it with every ounce of strength you have. Someday perhaps *you'll* leave people staring in disbelief.

Reflect: "In his grace, God has given us different gifts for doing certain things well" (Rom. 12:6). Can you think of a dream you had to abandon because it became apparent that you didn't have the necessary ability? Can you name something you're currently doing that fits your skill set perfectly? Do you have an ability that you have never tried to do anything with? If so, what's stopping you?

IT *CAN* HAPPEN TO YOU

LEN BIAS WAS ONE of the greatest college basketball players the country has ever seen. He was so good that in 1986 the Boston Celtics used their number two overall draft pick to reel him into their organization. That very night Len went out to celebrate with some friends and died from an overdose of cocaine. He was only twenty-two years old.

When the news broke, a high school boy named Alonzo Mourning happened to be washing cars at a Pontiac dealership in Hampton Roads, Virginia. Here's how he described the moment:

> We had the radio on right there in the wash area. The news came on, and it was announced that Len Bias had died. I dropped the bucket and scrub brush I was carrying in shock … his death really scared me. It made me scared off any kind of drugs. I sat there and thought, *If drugs could take down a guy like that, if drugs could end Len Bias' life, then they could*

take me down too. That's why I was never around anybody who did that stuff. [4]

Alonzo showed maturity far beyond his years when he concluded that he, too, could become a victim of the drug culture if he allowed himself to dabble in it. So many athletes tell themselves that they're strong and self-disciplined enough to have some fun and yet keep things under control. They have an "It can't happen to me" mentality.

But it can. It can happen to anyone in a heartbeat.

This is because cocaine is no respecter of persons; it is an equal opportunity killer. When it attacked Len Bias' system and put a stranglehold on his heart, all the honors and accolades he had won meant nothing. He could have been a Skid Row bum for all it cared.

Don't be foolish enough to think it can't happen to you.

It can.

Reflect: "If you think you are standing strong, be careful not to fall" (1 Cor. 10:12). Are you playing with fire right now? Are you fooling around with something dangerous? If so, what makes you think you won't get burned?

BE YOURSELF

WHEN I (PAT) was the general manager of the Philadelphia 76ers, we drafted Charles Barkley. Today Sir Charles is a member of the Naismith Memorial Basketball Hall of Fame, a worthy honor for someone who was an eleven-time All-Star and a league MVP. But back then Charles had yet to play his first NBA game when we sat down for a chat. Keep in mind, Charles has always been a bit pudgy. He didn't get the nickname "the Round Mound of Rebound" for nothing. So I said to him, "Charles, you're going to have to get in shape." To which he replied, "Mr. Williams, round *is* a shape."

That's what we love about Charles Barkley. Of all the people I've ever known, he is as determined as anyone to be himself. Once when someone brought up the subject of baldness, he said, "Why do bald guys always wear beards? When I started to go bald, I took it like a man."[5] That's Charles.

Too few people nowadays are committed to simply being themselves. We feel the pressure of expectations. We try to impress people.

We see people who are popular and try to be like them. We suffer from inferiority and try to pretend we're different than we really are. It all adds up to a disingenuous presentation of ourselves to the world. The problem is that, sooner or later, we are always exposed as frauds. Perhaps you've had the experience of discovering that someone you were feeling drawn to was not who he or she seemed to be. If so, you know how disappointing that is.

Let me encourage you to just be you. For one thing, God made you and wired you and gave you your personality. I'm sure it disappoints him when you disregard all of that and try to be someone else. Being yourself will also enrich your life with healthier relationships that are built on honesty and not gamesmanship. Always remember, your highest potential will be found in the real you, not in some fake version of you.

Reflect: In Galatians 1:10, the apostle Paul said, "If pleasing people were my goal, I would not be Christ's servant." What are some of the characteristics of a people pleaser? How does pleasing people keep you from being yourself? Can you think of some things you are currently doing because you want to be popular or accepted and not because they're really a reflection of who you are?

RAZOR-THIN MARGINS

WHAT'S THE DIFFERENCE between winning and losing?

Ask Rick Mears.

He was one of auto racing's rising stars and driving the fastest car in the time trials when he slipped behind the wheel for the Indy 500 on May 30, 1982. With just five laps to go, he was in second place, just 4.6 seconds back, but making a bid for the lead at a speed of 199 miles per hour. Up ahead, Gordon Johncock knew he was in trouble. His left rear tire had overheated, causing it to push out in the turns. He could see Mears pouring it on from behind.

But Mears eventually ran out of track and finished second by a razor-thin margin of 0.16 seconds, or slightly more than one car length.

In life, as in sports, the difference between success and failure can be razor thin. For example, marriages are not always nuked by adultery or alcoholism or abuse. Sometimes they're eroded by a simple lack of communication. I (Mark) have counseled unhappy couples that were literally one honest conversation away from a healthy marriage. They felt like their marriage was in deep trouble, but after sitting down and opening up, they realized that they were actually very, very close to the happiness they sought. One or two adjustments put them right where they wanted to be.

If you're not having the kind of success in life you always dreamed of, don't just assume that you need to make sweeping, wholesale changes. It could be that you're doing a lot of things right, and one or two small adjustments could synergize your efforts and catapult you to a whole new level of success. Your challenge is to find that razor-thin margin and fill it in. Maybe it's an attitude problem or a time-management issue. Maybe you're hanging out with the wrong people. If you can find the problem and change it, you could suddenly find yourself on the fast track to dream fulfillment.

Reflect: Proverbs 24:33–34 says, "A little extra sleep, a little more slumber, a little folding of the hands to rest—then poverty will pounce on you like a bandit; scarcity will attack you like an armed robber." How are you tracking with regard to your hopes and dreams? If you seem to be falling short, think about the advice you've received from your parents, employers, supervisors, coaches, and teammates. Is there a common thread running through it? If so, you could be looking at the one problem you need to fix.

YOUR BREAD AND BUTTER

WHAT'S YOUR BREAD AND BUTTER?

Muhammad Ali's bread and butter was his extraordinary quickness.

Kareem Abdul-Jabbar's bread and butter was an unblockable hook shot.

Nolan Ryan's bread and butter was an overpowering fastball.

Your bread and butter is that one thing that sets you apart from the crowd ... that one gift or ability that makes you special. We have a tendency to assume that only the greatest athletes in any sport have a bread-and-butter ability, but that's not true. Thousands, if not millions of athletes possess truly special gifts but have never sharpened or developed them.

When I (Mark) coached baseball, I had a thirteen-year-old pitcher who seemed to have greatness written all over him. Often at that age there is one kid who is bigger than all his peers and dominates the league for that reason. But that wasn't the case with this boy. He was average size, but he had a beautiful delivery and an eye-popping fastball. He struck out almost every batter he faced and rarely gave up a hit. It's a long way from Babe Ruth League to the majors, but everyone who saw this kid throw agreed that he was a phenom.

I encouraged his father to get his son some professional coaching so that he could continue to develop his enormous ability, but the man was extraordinarily controlling and didn't want anyone messing with his son. Many times over the years I have wondered whatever became of that boy. Somewhere he may be sitting at a desk, stuck in a dead-end job with a big-league arm hanging from his shoulder.

Has God given you a bread-and-butter caliber gift? Maybe it has nothing to do with sports. Maybe your knack is for music or mathematics or business. Whatever it is, we encourage you to develop it. Don't let yourself wake up someday and wonder what might have been.

Reflect: "Using a dull ax requires great strength, so sharpen the blade." (Eccles. 10:10) What is your greatest natural ability? Have you gone out of your way to develop it further, or have you just used it as is? If you haven't developed it, what has held you back? How might your life have changed if you "sharpened your blade"?

BOBBY'S EMBARRASSMENT

QUICK ... DO YOU KNOW what the biggest sporting event of 1973 was?

No, it wasn't the Super Bowl or the World Series or the Masters or any of the other mega-events that we sports fans usually obsess over. It was a tennis match. But it didn't happen at Wimbledon or the US Open. No, this one occurred on September 20 at the Houston Astrodome. It was televised by ABC and was called by Howard Cosell and Frank Gifford. More than thirty thousand people watched in person, with another forty million parked in front of their television sets.

The match was between Billie Jean King and Bobby Riggs and was promoted as the ultimate Battle of the Sexes. The event was Bobby's brainchild, his effort to show the superiority of the male athlete. At fifty-five, he intended to embarrass his twenty-nine-year-old opponent (who happened to be the reigning Wimbledon champion) with his arsenal of trick shots. But a funny thing happened on the way to superiority: Bobby Riggs got a big dose of humility. He was run ragged by a far superior player and suffered an embarrassing 6-4, 6-3, 6-3 defeat.

This is not a devotion about gender equality. We believe both male and female athletes ought to be the best they can be, period. Rather, our concern is with the kind of ego that goes out of its way to try to make somebody else look bad. It is our view that anyone who does this will end up looking worse and will likely set him or herself up for a dose of humility.

In Scripture, Absalom is a good example of an angry son who set out to make his father, King David, look bad. You can read his story in 2 Samuel, chapters 13–17, and see how it all blew up in his face. Not only did he embarrass and humiliate himself, but he died as a direct result of his shenanigans!

If you have a rival or an adversary, forget about trying to show your superiority. Besides, if you have to knock someone else down so you can step up, does your so-called superiority even count? Just apply yourself to being the best you can be.

Reflect: Psalms 18:27 says, "You rescue the humble, but you humiliate the proud." Have there been moments when your desire to show your superiority clouded your judgment? If so, what do you think is lacking in your own character that causes you to want to diminish other people? Would you be happier if you simply wished your competition well and applied all of your energies to your own performance?

PRACTICE DOESN'T MAKE PERFECT

BUZZ "SHOT DOCTOR" BRAMAN probably knows more about how to shoot a basketball than any living human. And he doesn't just know about it; he can do it. Once he gave a shooting demonstration at Villanova University, shooting 250 three-pointers from nineteen feet nine inches. He made 246, including the first 92 in a row. If this seems almost impossible, consider that he shot 300 three-pointers a day for six months to prepare for the demonstration. But even that didn't ensure his success because, as Braman is quick to point out, practice doesn't make perfect; *perfect* practice makes perfect.[6] In other words, you could shoot a thousand free throws a day, and you still might not become a great shooter if your technique is flawed.

We see a parallel to the Christian life. There are a lot of ways a believer can "practice" to strengthen his or her faith for the challenges of everyday life. Going to church, praying, and studying the Bible are a few examples of things we do to prepare for those moments when we must face our adversary (Satan) on the battlefield. But *just* going to church, praying, or reading the Bible isn't going to cut it. These things have to be done the right way.

Go to church, but go to the *right* church with the *right* attitude. Millions of people sit in church pews every week that are basically just putting in time and walking away empty.

JUST GOING TO CHURCH, PRAYING, OR READING THE BIBLE ISN'T GOING TO CUT IT. THESE THINGS HAVE TO BE DONE THE RIGHT WAY.

Pray, but pray with the right spirit and in harmony with God's Word. You can beg God for something over and over again, but if he's already said in his Word that it isn't his will, you're wasting your time.

Read your Bible, but read it with an open mind and a teachable heart. If you just use the Bible to try to prove your preconceived notions, you're going to get no benefit from it whatsoever.

Remember, practice doesn't make perfect; *perfect* practice makes perfect. Work hard and smart behind the scenes, and you'll be victorious when it really counts.

Reflect: "But when you pray, go away by yourself, shut the door behind you, and pray to your Father in private. Then your Father, who sees everything, will reward you." (Matt. 6:6) As an athlete, do you like to practice? Do you work as hard in practice as you do in a game? As a believer, do you spend time preparing for spiritual conflict? How seriously do you take your church attendance, prayer life, and Bible study? Which of these needs the most improvement? What do you need to do to make that improvement happen?

CHEMISTRY

THE WORD "ICON" is thrown around too casually. Lots of athletes, while truly great, are not true icons of their sport. Mia Hamm is one that is. She is a two-time Olympic gold medalist and a two-time FIFA Women's World Cup champion. She played soccer for almost twenty years (1987–2004). She is not just seen as a great player but also a great leader.

Mia, like so many well-decorated athletes, understands the concept of teamwork and how important it is to leave your self-interest in the locker room. In her 1999 book, she wrote: "Selflessness is a key ingredient for a winning team. Everyone has to play her role, embrace it, and excel at it. Selfish people, those who are only concerned about how many goals they score, how many minutes they play, or who is playing with them, are liabilities."[7]

This explains the age-old mystery of how a team with many good players can be lousy. We've all seen that squad that is loaded with talent but fails to live up to expectations. Players and fans alike will grumble and blame the coach or the front office. But more often than not, it's a simple matter of the players being too focused on their own stats and not making the sacrifices that are required to win consistently.

When people talk about the chemistry of a team, this is what they're referring to. Good chemistry is not achieved just because everybody gets along well together. Good chemistry is achieved when every player is willing to sacrifice his or her personal glory without hesitation or complaint for the overall good.

If you're a part of a team that doesn't seem to be meeting expectations, whether it's a sports team, a business, or a church, it's easy to tell yourself that some new plan or program will fix things. Maybe it will, and maybe it won't. You'd probably be better off evaluating the chemistry of your team before you launch some radical change in your system. If people's attitudes are the problem, you can make all the structural changes you want, and nothing will get any better.

Reflect: "As iron sharpens iron, so a friend sharpens a friend" (Prov. 27:17). Think about the teams you are a part of: sports, school, business, etc. In each case, can you name a specific way that you help sharpen your teammates? Can you name some teammates that have helped sharpen you? Name a personal sacrifice you've made for the good of your team.

PLAYING HURT

IT WAS GAME ONE of the 1988 World Series. The Oakland A's had a one-run lead on the Los Angeles Dodgers with two out in the bottom of the ninth. Dennis Eckersley, the A's brilliant closer, who had piled up forty-five saves during the regular season, had retired the first two hitters. When pinch hitter Mike Davis drew a walk, it was the pitcher's turn to bat, so manager Tommy Lasorda called on Kirk Gibson to hit.

The key here is that Gibson was so badly injured he could barely walk. In fact, he had spent almost the entire game in the training room. When he hobbled to the plate, A's fans were thrilled, and Dodger fans were worried. It appeared to be a mismatch. Eckersley clearly had the upper hand, but Gibson managed to work the count to 3–2.

The next pitch went over the wall and down in history as one of the most memorable home runs of all time. Rarely do you see an MLB highlight reel that doesn't show Gibson limping around the bases and pumping his fist, with the venerable Jack Buck screaming, "I don't believe what I just saw!"

It isn't just in sports that you are sometimes called upon to play hurt. In life, too, there are times when you are needed but don't feel like getting involved. Maybe your feelings have been hurt by a lack of consideration or, even worse, rude treatment. Because of our high-profile occupations, we both know the sting of criticism and how tempting it can be to take one's ball and go home.

But playing hurt is a sign of maturity and class. Let's face it; anybody can pout. Only a very special person will be able to find the strength of character to set tender feelings aside and go ahead and serve the greater good. When you can do that—and do it with a smile—you are well on your way to becoming a great Christian.

Reflect: 2 Corinthians 4:8–9 says, "We are pressed on every side by troubles, but we are not crushed. We are perplexed but not driven to despair. We are hunted down but never abandoned by God. We get knocked down but we are not destroyed." Are your feelings hurt right now? If so, how have you been responding to the person (or persons) who hurt you? If you choose to withdraw and pout, who are you really hurting?

GET WITH THE PROGRAM

FEW FANS WOULD argue that John Wooden is the greatest college basketball coach of all time. He was the gentlest of souls but the strongest of leaders. He knew what he was shooting for and refused to compromise.

One day Bill Walton showed up at practice after a ten-day layoff with a beard, in direct violation of Coach Wooden's team rule that no player would sport facial hair. As the team was getting loose, Wooden walked over and asked him if he had forgotten something. Walton said, "Coach, if you mean the beard, I think I should be allowed to wear it. It's my right."

Coach Wooden said, "Do you believe that strongly?"

"Yes, I do," Walton replied.

Without raising his voice, Wooden said, "Bill, I have great respect for people who stand up for things in which they believe. I really do. The team is going to miss you."

Walton immediately went to the locker room and shaved off his beard.[8]

There will be times in life when you will be faced with rules you don't like. Expectations will be placed on you that feel oppressive. You may feel that your style is being cramped and your ability diminished. Your first inclination will be to push back and see what kind of response you get. If the person in charge waffles, you may see an opportunity to strong-arm your way to a more comfortable situation.

Our advice is for you to think twice before bucking the system. Rules, even the ones you hate, are put in place for a reason, and the reason isn't always obvious. For example, Coach Wooden's facial hair rule really wasn't about facial hair; it was about team unity. When Bill Walton shaved, he was choosing team over self, which was the whole point to start with.

We're not saying there aren't bad rules in this world that need to be challenged. But by and large, life will go much better for you if you get with the program and stick with the program.

Reflect: "Remind the believers to submit to the government and its officers. They should be obedient, always ready to do what is good" (Titus 3:1). Do you feel stifled by a rule? If so, think about the *real* purpose of the rule. Is it something you agree with? What repercussions might occur if you decided to ignore it? Would the damage you might do to your reputation be worth the freedom you would gain?

NEGATING THE GOOD

IN 1964 THE US surgeon general filed a landmark report that deemed cigarettes bad for your health. At that point, many baseball players started switching to chewing tobacco and snuff, believing that they were safe alternatives. We now know they're not safe, yet many players continue to chew in spite of the risk.

Doesn't it seem odd that people who otherwise take such good care of their bodies would do something so obviously harmful? How much of their healthy eating and working out is canceled out by their steady nicotine consumption? Probably quite a bit, since one tin of smokeless tobacco contains as much nicotine as sixty cigarettes.

We need to be careful that we don't make a similar mistake in our spiritual lives. As believers, we generally do a lot of good. We may be generous with our money, helpful to friends in need, and involved in ministry at church. But with one thoughtless habit, we can undo a lot of that good.

Years ago, I (Mark) played on a church basketball team with a man who was a dynamic leader in the church. I didn't know him well because I was new to the congregation, but it was clear to me that he was the guy everyone looked up to. I'd heard nothing but great things and, to be honest, was a little in awe. You can imagine, then, how shocked I was the first time I heard him utter a profanity on the court.

I would never be so judgmental as to condemn someone for letting a bad word slip. I suppose heaven would be a pretty lonely place if only people who have never said a bad word were going to be allowed in. At the same time, I never quite looked at that fellow the same way again, especially after I heard him curse a second time. Somehow his image didn't fit the reality of what I was seeing. Or rather, hearing.

It must be heartbreaking to the Lord when his children do good and then turn right around and wipe it out with unbecoming behavior.

Reflect: "We live in such a way that no one will stumble because of us, and no one will find fault with our ministry" (2 Cor. 6:3). What's your worst habit? (Be honest!) What impact do you believe it has on your witness for Christ? How hard have you tried to break it? If you've tried and failed to break it, what can you do differently that might help you be successful this time?

WEARING THE GOAT HORNS

SAY BILL BUCKNER'S NAME, and Mets fans will break out in giggles while Red Sox fans burst into tears. The guy was an outstanding major-league player. He lasted twenty-two seasons, several of which were spent hobbling on a gimpy ankle. Yet even playing through severe pain, he still managed to pile up 2,517 hits and over 1,200 RBIs. Even so, the one designation he will most be remembered for is E3.

The ground ball was one that most Little Leaguers could have handled, or at least knocked down. But somehow it got through Buckner's legs and rolled into right field. On May 15 or June 15 or August 15, the error would have barely garnered a mention on the evening sportscast. But this was October 15, and it gave the Mets game six of the 1986 World Series. Bill Buckner wore the goat horns from that day on.

There may come a time when your mistake is judged to be the reason for some colossal failure. This could happen in your marriage or in your business, among other places. Here are a couple of things to keep in mind.

First, colossal failures are rarely, if ever, the result of one mistake. Baseball historians agree that while Bill Buckner's error came at an inopportune time, it followed some lousy pitching and a managerial blunder by John McNamara. Implosions are almost never the fault of one person.

Second, heaven will be full of people who wore goat horns on earth. Hebrews 11 makes it clear that some of the biggest bunglers in history will be walking the streets of gold. In fact, our guess is that just before you pass through the proverbial pearly gates into heaven, if you'll look to the side, you'll see a huge mound of used goat horns … horns that were happily discarded by God's people as their final farewell to a cruel world.

Reflect: Revelation 21:4 says, "He will wipe every tear from their eyes, and there will be no more death or sorrow or crying or pain. All these things are gone forever." Have you ever made a mistake that caused people great suffering? How were you treated? Were you able to forgive yourself? If not, what could you do that might finally enable you to move beyond the guilt and pain?

AT THE MERCY OF OTHERS?

KEITH MCDONALD HAD an incredible career in Major League Baseball. On July 4, 2000, he stepped to the plate for the St. Louis Cardinals and popped a home run in his first big league at bat. Two days later, he stepped to the plate again and popped another home run in his second big league at bat, becoming only the second player in major-league history to homer in his first two at bats. As good starts go, his was epic. And he wasn't done. Keith McDonald put up some of the greatest stats in baseball history, including a .333 lifetime average and more home runs per at bat than any player in history who played in multiple seasons.

You're wondering why he isn't a household name, aren't you?

It's because, while he was on the Cardinals' roster for parts of two seasons, he batted only nine times.

We said he had an incredible career. We didn't say he had a long one.

Imagine a player batting nine times, hitting three home runs, driving in five, and never getting another at bat. Ever. Doesn't make sense, does it? But for whatever reason, the Cardinals' brass, including manager Tony La Russa, only allowed him to play in eight games.

This is a good reminder to all of us that sometimes we seem to find ourselves at the mercy of others.

The manager who makes out the lineup card.

The publisher who reads your book proposal.

The employer who scans your resume.

The jury that hears your case.

The officer who pulls you over.

At such times it's important to remember that no one—no manager, publisher, employer, jury, officer, or anyone else—will ever be able to hinder God's plan for you. If God wants you to go from point A to point B, you will get there no matter how many people stand against you. And if he doesn't want you to go from point A to point B, you won't get there no matter how many people stand in your favor.

You, of course, can hinder God's plan for you. You can quit. You can refuse to follow his leading. But no other person on this earth can stop God's plan for your life from unfolding.

Reflect: Acts of the Apostles 17:26 says, "From one man he created all the nations throughout the whole earth. He decided beforehand when they should rise and fall, and he determined their boundaries." If God determines who rises and falls and sets our boundaries as this verse says, does it still matter if we set goals and try to achieve them? Why or why not? Can you think of a time in your own life when God seemed to overrule the people in authority over you?

THE IMPORTANCE OF A STRATEGY

ALICE COOPER IS TWO PEOPLE. Not because he was born Vincent Furnier but is known to the world by his famous stage name. That would make him one person with two names. He has often said he is two people: the Godfather of Shock Rock and a normal dude who plays golf every chance he gets. People who only know him as a rock star in scary costumes and face paint would never be able to picture him wearing a trendy polo shirt and a sun visor while knocking a little white ball around the grounds of an exclusive country club.

What's interesting is the reason why he took up golf.

It was to save his life.

He'd been an alcoholic. One that, by his own admission, drank all day long. To his credit, he gave it up and got sober. But he quickly found that if he wasn't going to drink all day, he was going to have to find something else to do. Idle hands are the devil's playground, and Alice Cooper knew that just sitting around the house was a recipe for failure. So he bought some clubs and ended up playing thirty-six holes a day that first year, mostly as a strategy for staying sober.

Many people fail in their endeavors because they don't have a strategy. They have a stated goal. They have an idea of what their life would be like if they could reach that goal. They might even have the willingness to work hard in pursuit of the goal. But they don't have a plan that takes into account the challenges and obstacles they'll face along the way. Zig Ziglar always said that people fail not because they plan to fail but because they fail to plan.

Do you dream of living a life that's different from the one you live now? Maybe you'd love to give up your boring job and pursue your passion. Maybe you'd like to go back and get that college degree you pooh-poohed when you graduated from high school. Or maybe, like Alice Cooper, you dream of conquering a demon that hounds your every step.

Whatever your dream is, you can be sure it won't happen easily, and it won't happen without a strategy. So sit down, clear away all distractions, and start thinking about what it's going to take to get you where you want to go. Write it down, hang it up in places where you'll see it often, and go for it.

Reflect: "But don't begin until you count the cost. For who would begin construction of a building without first calculating the cost to see if there is enough money to finish it?" (Luke 14:28). Why do you think so many people haphazardly chase their goals instead of laying out a detailed strategy? If you have a goal or a dream right now, could you clearly articulate your strategy for reaching it? If you have a strategy that doesn't seem to be working, how could you modify it to make it more effective?

TONGUE-TIED

PAT SUMMERALL, THE LEGENDARY sports broadcaster, told an interesting story about Reggie White. Reggie played defensive end in the NFL for fifteen years during the 80s and 90s and was a thirteen-time All-Pro selection. He was also an outspoken Christian, a fact that earned him the nickname "the Minister of Defense."

One day Reggie's Green Bay Packers were playing the Dallas Cowboys. Reggie was lined up against a Dallas rookie. The ball was snapped; Reggie put an All-Pro move on the youngster and sacked Troy Aikman. As they were walking back to the huddle, the rookie blasted Reggie with a string of curse words. On the next play, Reggie hit him with another move and slammed Troy Aikman to the turf again. This time, on his way back to the huddle, Reggie said, "Rookie, Jesus is coming soon, and you're not ready."

Your speech says a lot about you.

We don't know if this young rookie claimed to be a Christian or not, but we've known countless athletes who *did* claim to be Christians yet somehow believed that any cursing they did on the field of competition didn't count against their witness. "I got caught up in the moment," they'll say, shrugging as if their meltdown was no big deal. One big-league manager who has spoken openly about his faith, when questioned about his use of the f-word that was caught by field microphones, merely chuckled and said, "My mom would probably wash my mouth out with soap if she were here." No apology. No remorse. Just a joke.

That's not good enough.

It's in the heat of the moment that your Christian witness is put to the test. If your beliefs and values aren't strong enough to exert themselves when the pressure is on, what good are they? Anybody can be a Christian when everything is calm and peaceful and circumstances are falling in your favor. Ask yourself if your witness for Christ is tied up and being held captive by your tongue.

Reflect: "And I tell you this: you must give an account on judgment day for every idle word you speak. The words you say will either acquit you or condemn you." (Matt. 12:36–37) Why do you think the tongue is so hard to tame? Do you have a tendency to take on a different personality and lower your spiritual standards when you're in a pressure-packed situation? What are some practical measures you could take to bolster your self-discipline in stressful moments so that your witness won't be tarnished?

LEGAL VS. WISE

CRAIG MACTAVISH WAS a center for the St. Louis Blues of the National Hockey League. His retirement in 1997 marked the end of a very dangerous era in the sport, for he was the last NHL player to legally play without a helmet. The rule requiring helmets had been established in 1979, but that was one year after MacTavish entered the league, which meant that he was allowed to decide for himself whether to wear one. It's surprising enough that he decided not to, considering that hockey pucks routinely fly through the air at more than 100 miles per hour. It's even more surprising that MacTavish played almost twenty years in the league without a serious injury.

Mr. MacTavish's decision to go helmetless brings up an interesting question that all serious Christians should think about: Just because something is legal, does that mean it's wise?

Take marijuana, for example. Before long, it will be legal everywhere. Does that mean it would be wise for you to become a pot smoker?

Or think about alcohol. A lot of twenty-year-olds talk about becoming "legal" on their twenty-first birthday, promising to go out to a bar and drink or even get drunk to celebrate the occasion.

In our culture there's also a differentiation between legal porn and illegal (child) porn. Would it be wise for you to get involved with either kind?

When trying to decide if you should do something, don't ask, "Is it legal?" Ask, "Is it wise?" Legal just means you won't get arrested or kicked out of the competition. It doesn't mean your life won't get wrecked. The world is full of people who facilitated their own demise without ever breaking a law or violating a rule.

Reflect: Proverbs 4:6 says, "Don't turn your back on wisdom, for she will protect you. Love her, and she will guard you." Can you name something you did that was legal but turned out to be a terrible choice? Did you weigh the wisdom of that choice before you acted? If so, what did you misjudge or fail to take into consideration? What are some questions you could ask of any future choice as you try to determine if it's wise or foolish?

HAVE MORE FUN

AT THE END OF the last century, there were dozens of lists published that recognized the best and the worst of just about every industry over the previous one hundred years. *Sporting News* got into the act by coming up with their list of the most powerful sports figures of the twentieth century. One name on that list was a surprise to everyone. It was an individual who never played, coached, scouted, or owned a team. It was the San Diego Chicken.

Ted Giannoulas first put on a chicken suit as a part of a radio promotion in 1974. A short time later, the same radio station had him appear at a San Diego Padres game. Because of his wildly entertaining antics, he became a fixture at Padres games, eventually performing at over 2,500 of them. The Chicken was such a popular character that other teams started creating their own mascots. Team owners realized that even on nights when the home team was taking it on the chin, fans could still have fun watching a goofy character pulling shenanigans in the stands.

For the record, we love mascots! Some sports purists pooh-pooh them, but aren't sports supposed to be about having fun? What's wrong with a colorful character traipsing around making people smile and giggle? It's our view that there should be more fun and laughter in the world, not less.

What's the "fun quotient" in your life?

Have you given up fishing or playing golf or taking vacations because you have so much to do? When was the last time you took a day off work to go do something fun? How long has it been since you laughed so hard your stomach hurt? Far too many people are so absorbed in work and school and family obligations that they rarely have any fun.

Our recommendation is that you make having fun a priority in your life. Not *the* priority, but *a* priority. You'll no doubt be a lot happier, as will the people in your world (spouse, kids, classmates, coworkers) who currently see you as a big stick in the mud.

Reflect: 1 Timothy 6:17 says, "Teach those who are rich in this world not to be proud and not to trust in their money, which is so unreliable. Their trust should be in God, who richly gives us all we need for our enjoyment." This verse says that God gives us everything to enjoy. Do you think some Christians have missed this point and believe that being spiritual means being super serious all the time? Where do you think such a notion comes from? Can you name some wholesome activities you engage in just for fun? If not, what can you do to change that?

SLOW LEARNERS

WHEN MAJOR LEAGUE BASEBALL started back in the 1800s, no one thought of using batting helmets. Even when a player named Ray Chapman died after being hit in the head in 1920, there was no big push for players to wear protective headgear. It wasn't until 1939 that a Negro league player by the name of Willie Wells wore a miner's helmet during a game because he was tired of being hit in the head. He is credited with introducing the batting helmet to baseball, even though batting helmets as we know them weren't used in the Majors until 1952.

What took so long?

We could ask the same question about seat belts. Only a moron would argue that seat belts don't save lives, but it wasn't until 1984 that the first seat belt law was passed in New York. Before that, seat belt use was optional, which means a lot of people didn't wear them and were maimed or killed unnecessarily in vehicle crashes.

Life is a learning process. It begins at birth and, hopefully, continues throughout our lives. The key is to be a quick learner. Far too many people come to important life realizations the

THE KEY TO BEING A FAST LEARNER IS TO QUESTION EVERY SITUATION YOU GET YOURSELF INTO, ESPECIALLY THE BAD ONES.

way baseball came to batting helmets or the way state governments came to seat belts: after all kinds of damage has already been done.

The key to being a fast learner is to question every situation you get yourself into, especially the bad ones.

How did I end up here?

Is there anything I could have done to prevent this?

Should I have handled the situation differently?

What can I take away from this that will help me in the future?

These can be very uncomfortable questions, which is why so many people don't ask them. But they just might save your life. Or at least keep it from turning into a mess.

Reflect: Proverbs 26:11 says, "As a dog returns to its vomit, so a fool repeats his foolishness." Is there one mistake in particular that you have made multiple times? Why do you think you keep making it? What needs to change in your life so that you don't make that mistake again?

WHEN YOU FEEL DISRESPECTED

HAVE YOU EVER felt that you didn't get the attention or respect you deserved for a job well done? If so, you will be able to relate to Ivan Lendl, winner of the 1986 US Open.

If you think that winning the US Open would put you on the cover of *Sports Illustrated* with a glowing headline, you're half right. Lendl was on the magazine's cover but was given a gut-punch headline: "The Champion That Nobody Cares About." The article talked about how boring Lendl was and even suggested that he could empty a room faster than the smell of smoke. Perhaps part of Lendl's problem was that the media would have preferred to see the volatile and often profane John McEnroe win. A McEnroe victory would have kept the trophy in the hands of an American and given them more interesting quotes for their stories.

We don't know if Ivan Lendl saw or even knew about that article. Probably he did. And if he did, it surely stung. It's painful to give a task your all, perform magnificently, and then be shown no respect.

I (Mark) remember when my father set an all-time sales record for the company he worked for. He had pushed himself hard to exceed the high-water mark of every previous salesperson in the company's history. When I noticed that he seemed to be down in the dumps, I asked him what was wrong. He said, "When the owner saw my numbers, he didn't even say thank you. He just said, 'So how are you going to top that next month?'"

Such times are when we need to remember that a job well done is its own reward. If people recognize your work and show you respect, fine. If they don't, you still know what you did. You know how hard you worked. You know what an important contribution you made to the greater good.

Oh, and by the way, so does God.

If you're going to care about what somebody thinks, let it be the person whose opinion really matters.

Reflect: Galatians 1:10 says, "Obviously, I'm not trying to win the approval of people, but of God. If pleasing people were my goal, I would not be Christ's servant." Why do you think most people care so much about what others think? Have you ever done something because you were hoping for recognition and praise? Why do you think such a move disappoints God? Do you need to show more appreciation to the people in your world who do great work?

TEMPER, TEMPER

TOMMY BOLT WAS a good golfer. He won fifteen PGA tournaments, including the 1958 US Open. But almost everyone agrees that he could have been better. Some have said he could have been the greatest player in history if only he could have controlled his temper. Tommy was a legendary club thrower, earning him some telling nicknames, including "Thunder Bolt" and "Terrible Tommy." And the PGA took notice. It established a rule which says that any player who throws a club during competition will receive a two-stroke penalty. If you're wondering who the first player was to break the rule and be assessed the penalty, it was, of course, Tommy Bolt.

Rarely is anything gained by flying off the handle. A tantrum almost never changes anything. It erodes morale, destroys concentration, and diminishes you in the eyes of others. It also keeps people at arm's length by discouraging honest conversation. People choose not to tell you things you may need to know because they don't want to set you off. Worst of all, angry outbursts often become habit forming.

When tantrum throwers see people scurrying to appease them, they know they've found a tool they can reach for again and again, which can easily lead to an increase in frequency and an escalation of intensity. Flying words can lead to flying objects, which can lead to flying fists, which can lead to flying bullets.

Almost everybody knows someone with a short fuse: a teammate, a coworker, a neighbor, a family member. The important question is this: Is there someone close to you who sees *you* as that person with the hot temper? If there's one, there are probably many.

If so, you may not realize the damage you're doing to yourself and others. Maybe you feel that your outbursts are justified. In rare cases one might be, but probably not. In all likelihood, you are simply diminishing the quality of your life and relationships in ways that may be irreparable if you don't change.

It's time to get a grip.

Reflect: "Human anger does not produce the righteousness God desires" (James 1:20). When was the last time you lost your temper? (If you can't remember, good for you!) If you *can* remember, what exactly did you accomplish that would honor God? Did you end up having to apologize later? What steps can you take to get yourself under control?

INTEGRITY

DANNY ALMONTE SKYROCKETED to fame when he became the first kid in over forty years to pitch a no-hitter in the Little League World Series. He was mentioned on every sportscast in the country. When Randy Johnson and Ken Griffey Jr. heard that they were his big-league heroes, they called to congratulate him. Even Mayor Rudy Giuliani got into the act by giving the entire team the key to New York City.

But Danny's fame soon turned to infamy.

A couple of his team's rivals hired private investigators to check into his background because there were persistent rumors that Danny was older than he claimed. Finally, *Sports Illustrated* tracked down a birth certificate which was authenticated by the Dominican Republic. It showed that Danny was born exactly two years earlier than he said he was, making him fourteen instead of twelve and rendering him ineligible for Little League competition. Today, there is no record of him or his team ever having played in the Little League World Series because all of their statistics and accomplishments were removed.

In just about every area of life there is a way to cheat. In school, in sports, in business, and even in relationships there are rules that can be broken. And sometimes it's really tempting, especially if you see other people doing it and gaining an advantage. It's the old "if you can't beat 'em, join 'em" impulse. But people who cheat often discover that it's not worth it. Even if you don't get caught, you have to live with the knowledge that you didn't really earn what you got; you stole it. And if you do get caught, you subject yourself to public humiliation. We say it's better to lose and know you gave it your best shot than to cheat and win.

Reflect: "Honesty guides good people; dishonesty destroys treacherous people" (Prov. 11:3). Have you ever been cheated out of something that should have been yours? If so, did that experience make you hate cheating or see it as a possible way to get what you want? Do you think there's a difference between bending rules and breaking them? If so, where would you draw the line?

"UH-OH!" OR "OH BOY!"?

WHEN STAN MUSIAL stepped out of the dugout and onto the on-deck circle, opposing pitchers and managers groaned. "Uh-oh. Here comes that man again!" they said, which is how Musial got the nickname, "Stan the Man."

On the other hand, when all-time saves leader, Mariano Rivera, trotted in from the bullpen with the Yankees up by a run in the ninth, Yankees fans everywhere thought, "Oh boy! We've got this!"

"Uh-oh!" and "Oh boy!"

Two opposite exclamations, one full of trepidation, the other full of hope. One a brow wrinkler, the other a smile producer. One a spirit crusher, the other a spirit lifter.

Here's a good question for you to chew on: When people see you coming, are they more likely to say "Uh-oh!" or "Oh boy!"? Does your arrival on the scene produce grins or groans?

I (Mark) am writing this book with a guy that everybody loves to see coming. Pat Williams has a gift for encouraging and motivating people unlike any I've ever seen. Every time we get together, I find myself wanting to climb a mountain or run through a wall! And I've noticed that this amazing quality comes from two things.

First, Pat never complains. I don't mean he seldom complains, I mean he *never* complains. I've known Pat for almost twenty years, and I've never known him to complain about anything, even when he was battling cancer for all he was worth.

Also, Pat is what I call an "upward trajectory" guy. I was with him one day when someone approached him and congratulated him on his retirement. He said, "I'm not retired; I'm refired!" That kind of energy is contagious. Every time I'm in his presence, I find myself wanting to step up my game.

So what do people think when they see you coming?

"Uh-oh!" or "Oh boy!"?

Reflect: Philippians 4:8 says, "And now, dear brothers and sisters, one final thing. Fix your thoughts on what is true, and honorable, and right, and pure, and lovely, and admirable. Think about things that are excellent and worthy of praise." Make a list of the qualities you most admire in people, and ask yourself how many of them you possess. (You may need to ask a trusted friend to help you with this.) Pick one or two of those qualities you don't have, and think about what it would take for you to develop them.

SETTING RECORDS

MOST WORLD RECORDS in track and field are broken by the tiniest of margins. But on October 18, 1968, one was completely obliterated by a margin so great it was thought the record might never be broken. Bob Beamon executed a long jump of 29 feet, 2¼ inches. To appreciate this, you must understand that no one had ever jumped 28 feet before. In fact, the existing world record at the time was just over 27 feet, meaning that Beamon exceeded it by almost two whole feet. The accomplishment was so mind-boggling at the time that many sports commentators referred to it as the greatest athletic achievement of all time.

Greater than DiMaggio's fifty-six-game hitting streak.

Greater than Maris's sixty-one home runs.

Greater than Wilt the Stilt's one-hundred-point game.

Today, as we write these words, the world record for the long jump is 29 feet, 4¼ inches, exactly 2 inches farther than Bob Beamon's record. Mike Powell set the new mark in 1991. We have no doubt that one of these days, an athlete will fly through the air and land just a little bit beyond Powell's record.

The world obsesses over records, and there's nothing wrong with that. It's fun. But in everyday life, the focus should not be on living up to the world's potential but living up to yours. If you don't make straight As or outsell everyone else on the team or build the biggest church in town, it's OK as long as you have given your best to the effort.

Here's something to think about: In Scripture, God never commands success. He never challenges us to be better than anyone else. He never even hints that we will be judged by the records we set or the trophies or championship banners we earn. He does say that whatever we do will be good enough if we give it our best and do it all for his glory.

Reflect: Colossians 3:23 says, "Work willingly at whatever you do, as though you were working for the Lord rather than for people." Do you feel jealous when you see someone outperforming you? Do you feel pressure to try to do more? What are some ways you can evaluate your work to make sure you really are doing your best?

GAMERS

PETER GAMMONS PROVIDED the following list of top ten reasons why baseball players missed games:

1. Rickey Henderson: sidelined with frostbite after leaving an ice pack on his foot.

2. Kevin Mitchell: missed a week with a pulled rib cage muscle after vomiting.

3. Dave Nilsson: sidelined with a strain of malaria after getting a mosquito bite.

4. John Smiley: slammed a car door on his hand.

5. Bob Ojeda: missed a start when stung by a bee.

6. Dennis Martinez: strained his shoulder tossing a suitcase on an equipment truck.

7. Jack Clark: stressed out because of a $10 million debt including eighteen luxury cars.

8. Dwight Gooden: hit by a golf club swung in the clubhouse by Vince Coleman.

9. Pascual Pérez: couldn't find his exit on the Atlanta beltway.

10. Chris Brown: missed a game with a strained eyelid after sleeping on it wrong.[9]

Some of these reasons probably made you chuckle. Some may have caused you to roll your eyes. (We hope you didn't strain your eyelid!)

There are always legitimate reasons to miss work. Stuff happens. But if you're a member of a team, you always want to be known as a "gamer"— a person who shows up ready to do your job when others might not. We believe that in a world where statistics are scrutinized and analyzed ad nauseam, the gamer is underappreciated. That person who may not earn the most accolades or put up the biggest numbers but can always be counted on to be present and ready to give his or her best shot is invaluable to any team, if for no other reason than to be a reminder to all the other team members of what true commitment looks like.

Reflect: "Never be lazy, but work hard and serve the Lord enthusiastically" (Rom. 12:11). Have you ever called in sick when you weren't really sick? Have you ever made excuses to get out of some task simply because you were too lazy to do it? How do you think the person who got stuck doing your job felt? How successful would your company, church, or school be if everyone on your team had *your* work ethic?

REMINDERS

RULON GARDNER DID something most people weren't sure was possible. A Greco-Roman wrestler, he defeated Russia's Aleksandr Karelin for the 2000 Olympic gold medal. The victory raised eyebrows because Karelin hadn't lost in international competition in thirteen years.

But that's not why we bring up Mr. Gardner.

We wanted you to know about something else that happened to him two years after his Olympic victory. He had a snowmobile accident and suffered terrible frostbite, resulting in the amputation of one of his toes. We aren't sure what most people do with amputated limbs and appendages, but Rulon decided to keep his toe. When he speaks, he talks about the toe and what a great reminder it is that his snowmobile accident could have turned out a lot worse.

Hanging onto a severed toe might seem a little odd to some people, but we can all agree that reminders are important.

A wedding ring reminds us of promises made to our spouses.

A flashing engine light reminds us that it's time to get the car serviced.

A phone message reminds us of a doctor's appointment the following day.

The Lord's Supper reminds us of the atoning sacrifice of our Lord.

And why do we need reminders? Because we're forgetful! I (Mark) once served a church that had a day care center. Believe it or not, there were parents that actually forgot to pick up their children at the end of the day. Once a couple drove forty-five miles to a college basketball game, and only after arriving at the game did they realize they had forgotten to pick up their son!

OFTEN THE DIFFERENCE BETWEEN AN UNHAPPY PERSON AND A HAPPY PERSON IS MEMORY. THE UNHAPPY PERSON FORGETS HOW BLESSED HE IS, AND THE HAPPY PERSON DOESN'T.

Often the difference between an unhappy person and a happy person is memory. The unhappy person forgets how blessed he is, and the happy person doesn't.

Reflect: 1 Chronicles 16:12 says, "Remember the wonders he has performed, his miracles, and the rulings he has given …" Have you ever forgotten something important that turned out to be especially embarrassing? Do you have a keepsake that reminds you of some important moment in your life? What are some ways you can be more intentional about remembering important moments and blessings in your life?

JUST A LITTLE BIT OFF

I (MARK) HAVE PLAYED golf since I was thirteen years old. I've hit a few good shots, lots of bad shots, and a few crazy shots. I'll never forget the time my brother and I were involved in a tight match. I walked up on the tee box and addressed the ball, carefully positioning my feet and hands, silently reminding myself to keep my head down and my left arm straight. With absolute concentration, I drew the club back slowly and cut loose with a mighty swing. The ball was absolutely crushed but considerably off line. It hit a tree, ricocheted back over my head, rolled into a rest shelter, and came to a stop underneath a water fountain. I probably couldn't have repeated that feat if I had tried a million more times.

But that shot wasn't as crazy as one Hale Irwin made in the 1973 Sea Pines Heritage Classic. His ball hit a woman in the chest and stuck in her bra. After serious consideration, he decided to take a drop and incur a two-stroke penalty. Much to the woman's relief.

If you've ever played golf, you know that there's an infinitesimal difference between a great shot and a horrible shot. The same is often true in life. The difference between a happy person and a sad person … the difference between a successful person and a failure … the difference between a free man and a prison inmate often boils down to a single choice. We make a terrible mistake when we think that disaster is always the result of many bad choices. There are millions of broken and hurting people in this world who can point to one day, one moment, one choice that ruined their lives.

If you're facing an important choice right now, be very careful.

Reflect: Proverbs 3:5–6 says, "Trust in the Lord with all your heart; do not depend on your own understanding. Seek his will in all you do, and he will show you which path to take." Can you think of an instance where a single poor choice brought you an extraordinary amount of misery? Looking back, what did you fail to see or consider when you made your choice? How did that experience change your decision-making? Why is human understanding often unreliable?

WHY?

ON AUGUST 7, 2002, Clint Hurdle, formerly manager of the Pittsburgh Pirates, and his wife, Karla, welcomed a baby daughter, Madison Reilly, into the world. Of course they were happy, but something seemed off. After three weeks in the neonatal unit, little Maddie was diagnosed with Prader-Willi Syndrome, a rare genetic disorder that can severely affect a child's physical development and behavior.

Clint told me (Pat) that as he and Karla were wrestling with this diagnosis and wondering why, they received the following clipping written from the point of view of God, which helped to bring them peace:

> I know what you are thinking. You need a sign. What better one could I give than to make this little one whole and new? I could do it; but I will not. I am the Lord and not a conjuror. I gave this mite a gift I denied to all of you ... eternal innocence. To you she looks imperfect, but to me she is flawless, like the bud that dies unopened or the fledgling that falls from the nest to be devoured by ants.

She will never offend me, as all of you have done. She will never pervert or destroy the work of my Father's hands. She is necessary to you. She will evoke the kindness that will keep you human. Her infirmity will prompt you to have gratitude for your own good fortune. She will remind you every day that I Am who I Am, that my ways are not yours, and that the smallest dust mote whirled in darkest space does not fall out of my hand. I have chosen you; you have not chosen me. This little one is my sign to you. Treasure her!

Almost everyone eventually comes to a "why" moment. Something painful happens that makes no sense, especially when you think about a loving God in the heavens who is supposed to be watching out for you. But pain is often the pathway to unspeakable joy. Some of God's greatest gifts arrive with an excruciating jolt but end up blessing us in ways we could never have imagined.

Reflect: Isaiah 55:8 says, "'My thoughts are nothing like your thoughts,' says the Lord. 'And my ways are far beyond anything you could imagine.'" Think about a time when your life journey turned in a very unwelcome direction. Did it cause a rift between you and God? Looking back, can you see some good that has come from the experience? What have you learned about God and yourself as a result of this experience?

LITTLE THINGS

THE PGA TOUR Qualifying Tournament, known to golf fans as "Q-School," is the way a lot of golfers earn their way onto the PGA Tour ... or earn their way *back* onto the Tour, since a lot of Q-School competitors are actually older players who have lost their Tour card.

The Q-School amounts to a series of competitions that whittles over a thousand players with high hopes down to thirty. The competition is fierce, and the margin for error is slim. Even a lot of veteran golf stars say that the Q-School is the most intense pressure you'll ever feel on a golf course.

So consider one Jaxon Brigman. In 2000, he shot 65 on the last day of Q-School to earn a PGA Tour card by a single stroke. He was ecstatic. Until he learned a few minutes later that his partner accidentally wrote down "66" on the scorecard. Jaxon didn't notice the mistake, turned in the card, and was immediately disqualified.

It's pretty easy to get the big things in life right because they are, well, big things. Noticeable things. Obvious things. It's the little things that often slip by us unnoticed and end up undermining our success.

Take, for example, the typical married couple. They remember to go to work, pay the bills, feed the kids, and fix the plumbing. But do they talk? Do they really know what's going on in each other's hearts and minds? Most marriages end not because of adultery or abuse but because the husband and wife slowly drift apart.

Think about your witness as a Christian. You may go to church, serve on a committee or two, and place generous gifts in the offering plate. But do you also remember to pray? Do you spend a little time in the Word every day?

Our encouragement to you is to always double-check the little things because those little things are way bigger than you think.

Just ask Jaxon Brigman.

Reflect: Matthew 25:21 says, "The master was full of praise. 'Well done, my good and faithful servant. You have been faithful in handling this small amount, so now I will give you many more responsibilities. Let's celebrate together!'" How do you prioritize your responsibilities? If you've never done so, make a list of the significant things you do in order of their importance. Then flip the list upside down. Could it be that the upside-down list is more accurate than the right-side-up list?

NOBODY'S PERFECT

QUICK ... NAME THE GREATEST pitcher of all time.

Did you name Sandy Koufax, Bob Gibson, Cy Young, or Alan Francis?

Right now, your eyes are scrunched up and you're thinking, *Alan Francis? Who in the world is Alan Francis?*

He is, hands down, the greatest pitcher of all time. Horseshoe pitcher, that is. He's won the World Horseshoe Championship 25 times, throws 90 percent ringers, and once threw sixty-four ringers in a row. He's been called the most dominant athlete in any sport in the country. When opponents find out they're going to be matched against him, their hearts sink. How do you beat a guy who throws 90 percent ringers?

We'll leave it to the horseshoe experts to answer that question. We'll simply point out that as impressive as Mr. Francis's ringer percentage is, he's not perfect. He still misses one out of ten. That's not exactly a wide-open window of opportunity for his opponents, but it is a flicker of hope.

The truth is, nobody's perfect. Nobody does it right 100 percent of the time. This may not be the most comforting thought in the world when a surgeon is about to cut open your body, but it is a very comforting thought when you find yourself sitting in the dusty debris of a very bad choice. If Abraham could tell a lie, and King David could have an affair, and the apostle Peter could deny that he knew Jesus, it's safe to say that *anybody* can mess up. The important thing is what you do after you realize you've sinned.

If you're a Christian, the Bible gives two clear instructions: confess (1 John 1:8–9) and repent (Acts 3:19). In other words, plead guilty and commit to doing better in the future. There may still be some lingering consequences related to your sin, but at least you can know you are right with God.

Reflect: David said, "Create in me a clean heart, O God. Renew a loyal spirit within me" (Ps. 51:10). Is creating a clean heart in you something God does by himself, or is it something he does in partnership with you? What might your responsibilities be? Do you think God initiates this cleansing or takes his cue from you?

WHAT PASSION LOOKS LIKE

AS WE WRITE these words, it is the morning after the St. Louis Blues won their first Stanley Cup in the fifty-two-year history of the franchise. Their storied season was remarkable for many reasons, including the fact that they had the worst record in the entire NHL in early January. The players and coaches deserve a ton of credit for turning things around and bringing home the championship.

But maybe the fans deserve even more credit.

If you happened to be watching the seventh and deciding game of the championship series on television, you saw something incredible. While the Blues were slugging it out with the Bruins in Boston, Blues fans were back in St. Louis showing the world what passion looks like. The Blues' home arena, the Enterprise Center, was packed with people watching the game on the big screen. And almost unbelievably, a few blocks away, Busch Stadium held over eighteen thousand more Blues fans who were also watching on the big screen … in a driving rainstorm! No one was seeking cover. They would rather have gotten soaked than miss a single second of the game.

Sports fans are known for being crazy. And why not? The word "fan" is short for fanatic. And yes, sometimes they carry the craziness a little too far. But we need sports fans because they remind us what passion looks like. Passion is that thing that takes you where others will not go. Yes, it could be sitting in a driving rainstorm to watch a hockey game. But it might also be pushing yourself against long odds to get that degree, or to work those extra hours, or to keep trying long after others have given up and gone home. Passion is what makes you look crazy to people who don't have it.

This world tends to be very good to people who have passion. So don't just do something with your life; do something you're passionate about.

Reflect: Colossians 3:23 says, "Whatever you do, do your work heartily …" What kind of images does that word "heartily" conjure up in your mind? Can you name something you do heartily? If not, is there something you're not doing that you long to do? How can you make room for it in your life?

WHERE IS YOUR "CAN'T LINE"?

WHEN PEOPLE SAY, "You can do anything if you put your mind to it," they are lying. Or else they are incredibly naive. Every person has a "can't line," a line beyond which he or she cannot go. If you put enough weight on the bar, even the strongest weightlifter in the world won't be able to lift it.

IN OTHER WORDS, NONE OF US CAN DO ANYTHING WE WANT, BUT WE CAN ALL DO MORE THAN WE THINK.

But here's what we want you to understand: The "can't line" for most people is not where they think it is. It's much, much farther down the road. In other words, none of us can do anything we want, but we can all do more than we think.

Jim Abbott is a great example. He was born without a right hand. Even as a newborn, family and friends looked at him and sighed. *Poor kid. He might play some sports, but he'll never be very good.* But Jim's "can't line" was not where people thought it was. He learned to play baseball and was good at it. Good enough to make it to the majors. But even then he still hadn't reached his "can't line." He not only made it to the Majors, but he excelled, even pitching a no-hitter against the Cleveland Indians in 1993.

Here's a critical question: Have you set up camp short of your "can't line"?

We believe the world is full of people who could do more than they're doing, who could be more than they are. Sometimes we listen too much to others who try to define and confine us. Sometimes we lack confidence. Sometimes we quit trying to go any farther because we meet a little resistance. Sometimes it takes surprisingly little resistance to stop us.

If there's a dream that you've given up on because you concluded it was beyond your "can't line," we encourage you to revisit it. Your "can't line" probably isn't where you think it is. It may well be far from where you think it is.

Reflect: Paul said, "I can do all things through Christ who strengthens me" (Phil. 4:13). Do you think Paul was saying that he could *literally* do all things? If not, what was he saying? In what ways does Christ affect the location of your "can't line"?

STAND YOUR GROUND

JACQUES PLANTE IS one of the greatest hockey players ever to lace up a pair of skates. His career as a goalie lasted from 1947 to 1975, which is incredible all by itself. During his tenure with Montreal, the Canadiens won the Stanley Cup six times, including five in a row. In 2017 he was named one of the one hundred greatest NHL players in history.

But perhaps his greatest contribution to the sport had nothing to do with his on-ice performance. In 1959, Jacques gave his coach an ultimatum: either he would be allowed to wear a mask, or he wouldn't play. He'd had two broken cheekbones, his nose smashed four times, and a fractured skull. Enough was enough.

Interestingly, his coach didn't want him to wear a mask. No one had ever worn a mask before, and it was thought that a mask would diminish a player's performance. But Jacques stood his ground, and the coach gave in. Every hockey goalie playing today should be thankful for Jacques Plante's willingness to stand firm on a matter of critical importance.

All of us will eventually come to that moment when someone will try to get us to back down from what we believe. And sometimes backing down is OK if the issue at hand is not of great importance. But if it is, we need to find the courage to stand firm. Sometimes people say, "But I don't want to seem selfish." Jacques Plante is our reminder that the stand you take in your own self-interest could benefit other people coming behind you.

If you are a student of history, you know that just about every great advancement or innovation to benefit mankind came from someone who dug his heels firmly into the dirt and said, "This is not acceptable anymore. Something needs to change."

Reflect: 1 Corinthians 15:58 says, "So, my dear brothers and sisters, be strong and immovable." Can you think of a blessing you enjoy today because someone before you dared to take a stand? Is there something in your world that's been bothering you that you feel needs to change? What's keeping you from taking a stand and fighting for that change?

PERSONAL CONNECTIONS

THE UNITED STATES Football League started in 1983 with twelve teams in Los Angeles; New Jersey; Tampa Bay; Denver; Chicago; Arizona; Detroit; Boston; Birmingham; Oakland; Washington, DC; and Philadelphia. The idea was to provide fans with a high level of football after the NFL season ended. Most people rolled their eyes at the idea until Heisman Trophy–winner Herschel Walker skipped his senior year at the University of Georgia and signed a USFL contract. Suddenly people were looking at the league differently. If Herschel Walker believed in it, maybe it wasn't such a crazy idea after all.

But the league didn't make it. It folded after just three seasons. There weren't enough people in the seats, the TV ratings were anemic, and teams started losing money at an alarming rate. Naturally, the league's demise was analyzed and scrutinized. What went wrong? Why didn't an idea that seemed so good on paper work? One theory is that professional sports is very much about the relationships the fans have with the players. Yes, they love their teams, but they love their favorite players too. With very few exceptions, the USFL offered a cast of unknown players that the fans felt no connection to.

Relationships—personal connections—are so important. Think about how much more fun school was because you were surrounded by your friends. For a lot of people, it's a cast of pleasant coworkers that makes a job tolerable. Even at church, research shows that people are likely to stay or drift away depending on how quickly they make personal connections.

I (Pat) have spent my life making connections. Some people call it networking, but it's more than that. Your network is a list of contacts that enrich your business; connections are the friends that enrich your life. Trust me when I say that when you come down to the end of your life, it won't be your "contacts" that bring you joy; it will be your friends. It won't be the size of your Rolodex; it'll be the number of people who love you.

Reflect: At the very beginning of time, God said, "It is not good for the man to be alone" (Gen. 2:18). Can you think of a critical time in your life when a friend (or friends) came through for you in a big way? Right now, do you have more contacts or friends? Do you need to work harder at making connections with people around you?

CONFESSION

A MARATHON IS a grueling test of conditioning and commitment. I (Mark) am writing this book with a man who has run fifty-eight more marathons than I have. That's because Pat has run fifty-eight, and I have run none. Pat and I have a number of things in common. An affection for running marathons is not one of them.

Rosie Ruiz was not much of a marathon runner either. Everybody thought she was when she won the women's division of the Boston Marathon in 1980 in record time. But it turned out that she cheated, and I don't mean she bent the rules to her advantage. I mean she took a truckload of dynamite and blew the rules from here to kingdom come. She actually skipped the first twenty-five miles of the race! You're probably wondering why she attempted such an outrageous and unlikely-to-succeed scam. Well nobody knows, because Rosie has never admitted any wrongdoing and actually kept her medal.

Can you imagine her pulling out that medal at a dinner party and showing her friends? "Hey, everybody, here's the medal I got when they thought I won the Boston Marathon." No, I can't imagine it either. I suspect Rosie keeps that medal tucked away out of sight.

I happen to think that Rosie Ruiz's biggest mistake was not cheating in the Boston Marathon but refusing to admit that she cheated. It's one thing to make a bad choice—or in her case, a horrendous choice—but living in denial of it means you can never be free. Your bad choice will own you and define you, medal or no medal. You will essentially be living in a prison with invisible walls.

The good news is that those invisible prison walls can be torn down in an instant with an honest confession. The key word is "honest." You don't just say what you think people want to hear. You don't just say what you have to say to get back in someone's good graces. Rather, you tell the truth—the painful, ugly truth—about what you did.

Reflect: Proverbs 28:13 says, "Whoever conceals their sins does not prosper, but the one who confesses and renounces them finds mercy." Do you find it hard to admit your mistakes? Is there a bad decision in your past that you've never owned up to? How might your life improve if you did?

CONCENTRATION

IF YOU'VE EVER been to a college or pro basketball game, you've seen fans do some pretty crazy things behind the basket in an attempt to distract a player from the other team who is shooting free throws. They yell and scream and wave their arms, and that's just for starters. I (Mark) once attended a game at the University of Alabama where the student section chanted "Rogaine, Rogaine, Rogaine ..." in an effort to rattle an opposing player who was going prematurely bald. On another occasion, I saw the Antlers, the notorious student group at the University of Missouri, unfurl life-size pictures of women in bikinis as opponents stepped to the free throw line.

These things happen because everybody knows how important concentration is. Throwing a basketball through a hoop from fifteen feet with no one guarding you is not that difficult. Lots of people can make 90 percent or more of such shots. But game pressure and a little distraction behind the hoop can throw you off.

Free throw shooting isn't the only thing that requires concentration. So does marriage. So does parenting. So do spiritual disciplines like prayer and Bible study. These things, like free throw shooting, are not that difficult in themselves, but if you're distracted, you can easily fail.

One way to sharpen your concentration is to resist the temptation to multitask. Multitasking is often seen as a virtue. People brag about their ability to do two or three things at once. But there's a good chance that if you're doing two or three things at once, you're not doing your best at any of them. You may be getting by, but just getting by should never be the goal. We need to deliver our best for our families, our friends, and especially for God.

Reflect: Proverbs 4:25 says, "Look straight ahead, and fix your eyes on what lies before you." Can you name some areas of your life that need more of your attention? Do you have habits or hobbies or petty distractions that take your attention away from more important things? How are you doing with the spiritual disciplines of prayer and Bible study?

WATCH YOUR MOUTH

ALLEN IVERSON WAS great on a basketball court. In front of a microphone, well, let's just say he wasn't so great. In 2002, just after his team, the Philadelphia 76ers, was eliminated from the playoffs, he was asked about some comments his coach made about him missing practices or not working hard in practice. He said:

> I know it's important; I honestly do. But we're talking about practice. We're talking about practice, man. [Laughter from the media] We're talking about practice. We're talking about practice. We're not talking about the game; we're talking about practice.[10]

Coaches at every level, from elementary school to the pros, teach their players that the work they put in during practice will have a huge impact on their success during the games. If there were a Ten Commandments of Athletic Success, "Take practice seriously" would no doubt make the list. Allen Iverson blew that whole concept to pieces in just thirty seconds and earned the scorn of millions of coaches and athletes in the process.

Sometimes it's just better to keep your mouth shut. The pages of history are filled with people who embarrassed themselves by saying something dumb, inappropriate, inaccurate, or hateful.

Here's a suggestion: Don't be one of those people who always takes the bait. You don't have to answer every question you're asked. You don't have to give an opinion on everything that happens. People will try to provoke a comment or a response, especially if the topic is controversial. Understand that, even if you have strong feelings on the subject, words in this generation are scrutinized and analyzed and twisted like never before. Don't be that person who always wishes he'd kept his mouth shut after it's too late.

Reflect: Psalms 141:3 says, "Set a guard, O Lord, over my mouth; keep watch over the door of my lips." Have you ever been shamed or embarrassed because of something you said? If so, what was it that caused you to speak up? Anger? Impulsiveness? A desire to be noticed? What does this verse suggest as one way to keep from getting into trouble with your mouth?

SETBACKS

JOHN UELSES IS a pole vaulter who once had a nightmarish experience.

The year was 1962. He was at the Millrose Games in Madison Square Garden. He wasn't a favorite to win. In fact, he garnered very little attention prior to his shocking performance. What made it shocking is that he went over the sixteen-foot mark with a fifteen-foot pole, which no one thought was possible. His secret was that he used a fiberglass pole instead of the normal bamboo. The pole bent almost double and launched him not only over the bar but also one-quarter of an inch over the world record.

So right about now you're wondering what was so nightmarish about that experience. It's the fact that an overzealous photographer rushed in to get some close-up shots and accidentally made contact with the upright, causing the crossbar to fall before officials could certify the record. Imagine! An athlete works his entire life to try to break one record one time, then when it happens, he hears, "Oops! Sorry! Want to try again?"

Thankfully the nightmare only lasted twenty-four hours, because the very next day, Mr. Uelses went over the bar again, even higher this time ... and no one bumped the upright!

SETBACKS ARE A FACT OF LIFE. THE QUESTION IS NOT WHETHER YOU WILL HAVE THEM, BUT WHAT YOU WILL DO WHEN THEY COME.

This story reminds me (Mark) of the time I wrote twelve chapters of a novel and then deleted them by accident. One little ole keystroke was all it took to send hours and hours of work into cyber oblivion. It felt like a gut punch. So what did I do? I sat down and wrote those twelve chapters again, only better the second time. I ended up actually being glad I was forced to start over.

Setbacks are a fact of life. The question is not whether you will have them, but what you will do when they come. It's OK if you give yourself a moment to grieve. (I certainly did when I realized what I had done.) But no more than a moment. It's important to knuckle down and get back to work. If you did it once, you can do it again.

Reflect: Philippians 3:13–14 says, "Forgetting the past and looking forward to what lies ahead, I press on ..." What's the worst setback you ever suffered? How long did it take you to let it go and move forward? What are some ways a setback can actually help you?

NITPICKERS AND GRACE GIVERS

WANT TO SEE a sports list that will surprise you? Look at these names and see if you can figure out what the category is:

1. Jim Kaat

2. Gaylord Perry

3. Steve Carlton

4. Bert Blyleven

5. Warren Spahn

6. Frank Tanana

7. Don Sutton

8. Phil Niekro

9. Ferguson Jenkins

10. Robin Roberts

Those are some great pitchers, right? Several Hall of Famers in there. Have you figured out what list they are a part of? They are the major-league pitchers who have given up the most career home runs. The reason only good pitchers are on this list is because you have to play a long time to give up hundreds of home runs, and only good pitchers get to play a long time.

So what does this teach us? That you can always find something to criticize in even the best people. It's your choice whether you focus on the good or the bad. You'll be much happier if you give people grace for their weak moments and focus on the good in them.

Reflect: Jesus said to Levi the tax collector, "Follow me" (Luke 5:27). There was a lot to criticize in Levi, but Jesus saw good in him. Do you look for the good in people? Would you describe yourself as a grace giver or a nitpicker? What weaknesses in your own life do you hope people are willing to forgive?

DRAG

HAVE YOU EVER WONDERED why golf balls have dimples? Neither of us is an expert in aerodynamics, but it's our understanding that way, way back in the early days of golf, players noticed that scarred or scuffed balls seemed to perform better. Further experimentation confirmed the notion that a smooth ball wouldn't fly as far as a ball with depressions in its surface. We'll let people a whole lot smarter than us explain it, but the bottom line is that drag keeps balls from flying higher and farther, and dimples help eliminate drag.

Drag keeps people from soaring higher and farther too.

Stress can be a drag on anybody's life. So can anger and unresolved guilt and discouragement. There are millions of people who have all the talent and intelligence they need to soar successfully through life but flounder instead because something is weighing them down.

Job spoke for millions of people then and now when he said, "If my misery could be weighed and my troubles be put on the scales, they would outweigh all the sands of the sea" (Job 6:2–3).

We've noticed that a lot of people spend all their time trying to eliminate what's dragging them down. They get counseling, read self-help books, lose weight, buy a new wardrobe, dump their old, tiresome friends, get some cool, new friends, etc. And even then they often end up wondering why they can't seem to soar. More often than not, the problem is that they have forgotten to include Jesus in the process. He is the greatest burden lifter of all time. He said, "Come to me, all of you who are weary and carry heavy burdens, and I will give you rest" (Matt 11:28). Any plan to eliminate drag from your life that doesn't include a deeper commitment to Christ is a flawed plan that is destined to fail.

Reflect: Psalms 55:22 says, "Give your burdens to the Lord, and he will take care of you." When you find yourself feeling burdened, what is your first impulse: to work harder or stop working and go to your knees? Why do you think so many people try to carry their burdens alone? Can you name a burden that you need to give to the Lord right now?

EVOLUTION

WHEN THE GAME of basketball was invented, it looked quite a bit different than it does now. Not only did they shoot at wooden peach baskets instead of iron rims with nets but dribbling was illegal. The ball was to be moved around the court only by passing. Players could run here or there, but as soon as the ball was passed to them, they had to stop and either shoot or look for someone else to pass to.

Then players had the bright idea of passing the ball to themselves. By throwing it and then running and grabbing it, they could change their position on the court. From there they started running with the ball while batting it up in the air so that they wouldn't actually have possession. The final step in the evolution of ball movement was dribbling, which many people, including the game's administrators, were against because they said it was too hard and very few players would be able to do it.

Go to a college or pro game today and watch the point guards warm up. They will be dribbling two balls, one with each hand, behind their backs, through their legs, and crisscrossing them from side to side while laughing and having a conversation with a teammate!

Just as sports evolve, so do technologies, customs, cultural expectations, relationships, churches, and a hundred other things. The trick for us as Christians is to identify which changes are unhealthy for our faith and which ones aren't. In recent years, attitudes and behaviors that were once taboo have become widely accepted. As a result, worldliness has seeped into the church as countless Christians have lowered their standards.

It's a challenge to stay true to your convictions when practically everyone around you is becoming more secular and less spiritual. The Bible calls this "standing firm," and it just might be the number one challenge that Christians face in this generation.

Reflect: "Be on guard. Stand firm in the faith. Be courageous. Be strong" (1 Cor. 16:13). Name some faith-related matters that have evolved in your lifetime. Do you find it harder to remain faithful to the Lord than you once did? In what ways do your efforts to stand firm bring ridicule or persecution into your life?

THAT JOYNER GIRL

EAST ST. LOUIS is one of the most depressed communities in America. It was no different in the 1960s when a teenage couple, Alfred Joyner Jr. and his wife, Mary, had a baby girl. That little girl lived like most kids in East St. Louis, wearing clothes until they wore out and shoes until they fell off of her feet. During the winters, she huddled with family members in the kitchen because the stove was the only source of heat in the house.

Few people look at such a home and think, "Greatness will come from this place." We tend to judge by appearances and forget that countless great people in history started out in humble circumstances. Such was the case with Mr. and Mrs. Joyner's little girl, Jackie. She grew up to become Jackie Joyner-Kersee, just about everybody's pick for the greatest female athlete of all time. In the Olympics in 1984, 1988, 1992, and 1998, she wowed the world with her performances in the heptathlon and the long jump. What's even better is that Jackie is a tremendous human being, giving back to her community and touching countless lives with enormous generosity and personal acts of service.

Don't ever make the mistake of thinking that humble circumstances early in life will hinder a person's success. People turn out the way they do, not because of what's going on around them but because of what's going on inside them.

Right now, if your circumstances are less than ideal, there's a good chance that you, like most people, are focused on them and feeling disadvantaged and probably complaining. If so, you're giving those circumstances way too much credit. They can't stop you if you've got a dream and the heart to succeed. We encourage you to throw those circumstances into the furnace of your heart and let them burn, becoming fuel for the pursuit of your aspirations.

Reflect: Romans 5:3–4 says, "We can rejoice, too, when we run into problems and trials, for we know that they help us develop endurance. And endurance develops strength of character, and character strengthens our confident hope of salvation." How have you responded to difficult circumstances in your life? Have you allowed them to shape your life or fuel your dreams?

OLDIES BUT GOODIES

FORTY-PLUS-YEAR-OLD Major League Baseball players are not unheard of, but you can usually count them on one hand every season. And they're generally not superstars at that point. Often they're role players, sometimes earning a spot on the roster because of their experience and ability to mentor the younger players.

OK, you can take everything we just said and throw it out the window when talking about Nolan Ryan. None of it applies to him. The Ryan Express just seemed to get better with age, as evidenced by the fact that he threw two no-hitters after the age of forty. Most forty-year-old pitchers are situational relievers or spot starters who hope to somehow get through four or five innings. Nolan Ryan was a threat to toss a no-no every time out.

Sometimes it might seem like a young person's world, and in many ways it is. But older people have tremendous contributions to make. If you're reading this book and you're a senior, what does the trajectory of your life look like? Is it still moving upward? Do you still have plans for things you want to do? Not just a bucket list of places to visit, but actual accomplishments that you want to add to your body of work? Are you still involved in your church, volunteering, making your presence felt in the ministry? Are you refusing to let the aches and pains (we know you have them) get you down, but pushing through them and continuing to be productive?

Far too many people don't just retire from their jobs; they retire from all their volunteer and service responsibilities as well. One of the most common comments you hear from older people who are still in good health is, "I've done my share; it's somebody else's turn."

Please don't be that person.

Reflect: 2 Corinthians 4:16 says, "Though our bodies are dying, our spirits are being renewed every day." If you're under thirty, can you name an older person who is an inspiration to you and explain why? If you're over sixty, what are some ways you can work smarter to allow for your age but still keep your production level up?

THE PUNCH

MOST SPORTS FIGHTS outside of hockey don't amount to much. There's generally a lot of pushing and shoving and trash talking, and that's about it. Guys who make millions of dollars don't want to risk injury, and who can blame them? But on December 9, 1977, there was a melee in a basketball game between the Los Angeles Lakers and Houston Rockets. Lakers forward Kermit Washington threw a punch at the Rockets' Rudy Tomjanovich, who didn't see it coming, and almost killed him. He had a broken skull, jaw, and nose. It's been called the most devastating punch in sports history. Washington was fined $10,000 and suspended for sixty days.

MORE THAN ANYTHING, FORGIVENESS IS A GIFT THE OFFENDED GIVES HIMSELF (OR HERSELF). IT'S THE GIFT OF FREEDOM.

You might think that these two men would never want anything to do with each other again, and they certainly never did become bosom buddies. But they did talk, and Rudy Tomjanovich gave Kermit Washington his forgiveness.

Most people think forgiveness is a gift the offended gives to the offender. And it can be. But more than anything, forgiveness is a gift the offended gives himself (or herself). It's the gift of freedom. When you forgive, you get to lay down the burden of having to carry the offense around with you, reliving it, scheming ways to get even, and worst of all, feeling sorry for yourself. Forgiveness allows you to close out that chapter of your life and move on. It allows you to be happy again.

You might say, "But you don't realize how deeply I was hurt!" We figure that if Rudy Tomjanovich could be almost killed and find a way to forgive his assailant, you can too. Or if Rudy's example is not enough to sway your thinking, consider Jesus, who forgave the guys who were driving nails into his hands and feet. Yes, you *can* forgive.

Reflect: Ephesians 4:32 says, "Be kind to each other, tenderhearted, forgiving one another, just as God through Christ has forgiven you." Are you carrying resentment toward someone right now? How long have you been lugging it around? Are you honest enough to admit what nursing that hurt has cost you? What's keeping you from granting forgiveness?

SIDEKICKS

IT'S A FUNNY THING about sports superstars: they often have at least one other great player alongside them.

Ruth had Gehrig.

Chamberlain had West.

Magic had Kareem.

Jordan had Pippen.

Montana had Rice.

You get the idea. A capable sidekick can make you better. We see this in the Bible too.

Moses had Joshua.

Joshua had Caleb.

Peter had John.

Paul had Silas.

The question is, who do you have?

It's dangerous to make your way through life without a close friend to walk beside you. Samson tried. He was the ultimate loner.

Nowhere in Scripture are we told that he had a friend. And his life was a wreck. There was no one to encourage him to do the right thing or hold him accountable for his actions. This is undoubtedly one of the reasons why he squandered such potential.

If you don't have a sidekick, maybe it's time to start looking for one.

Reflect: Ecclesiastes 4:12 says, "A person standing alone can be attacked and defeated, but two can stand back-to-back and conquer." Can you think of a time in your life when you played the role of the sidekick and helped a friend do the right thing? Do you have a believing friend that you trust completely and are comfortable confiding in? If not, what has kept you from developing that kind of relationship?

PERSPECTIVE

THERE IS ONE member of this writing team that is an expert on baldness, and it's not Pat Williams. Pat knows all about building pro sports franchises and drafting and signing superstars. I (Mark) know about going bald. I started doing it when I was in my twenties. I've gotten more sunburns, bought more hats, and heard more bald jokes than most people would in two lifetimes. And I'm not bitter, though I do feel a little secret pleasure when I see some guy getting his picture taken outdoors with his hair blowing all over the place.

Paul Azinger, a terrific PGA golfer, started going bald when he was thirty-three. But it wasn't genetics; it was lymphoma. He'd been suffering with pain in his shoulder for years. There had been tests before, but finally a bone scan and MRI showed the cancer. Surgery, chemo, and radiation took a terrible toll on his body. A pro athlete in peak condition, his weight dropped from 178 to 158. He lost his hair. He suffered from terrible nausea. But he came through it with the help of his wife, Toni, and his faith.

Paul has reflected on that part of his life's journey: "What I've learned from this is that I am not bulletproof. I'm as vulnerable as the next guy, and now I'm grateful for every blessing I have."[11]

Nothing changes your perspective like suffering. Suddenly, things that once seemed important, like having a nice head of hair, are not important at all. And things that once seemed trivial, like being able to get out of bed, become huge blessings. It's not hard to understand why people who have been through a lot of bad stuff are so impressive.

Reflect: James 1:2 says, "When troubles come your way, consider it an opportunity for great joy." What's the worst thing you've suffered in your life so far? How has that experience changed your thinking? Do you feel you're a better person for having gone through that experience?

TRAINING

JEAN DRISCOLL'S ARRIVAL in this world was a gut check for her parents. Doctors informed them that she had spina bifida and would probably never walk. Her life would be filled with hardship, and she would be dependent on them for much of what most people can easily do for themselves. But Jean, while being born with a devastating birth defect, was also born with the heart of a lion. Today, she is one of the most decorated athletes in the world, winning countless championships, medals, and awards, including eight Boston Marathons, all from her wheelchair. She was elected to the US Olympic Hall of Fame in 2012.

One of the secrets to Jean's success was her conditioning. When she was competing, she worked out two to three hours per day, six days per week, year-round. She logged countless hours on the track in her wheelchair, often tallying 130 miles per week. There may have been other athletes with similar talent, but no one outworked her. Her entire body was packed with power.

Life is a lot like sports in that what you do behind the scenes when no one is looking determines how things turn out. When you read your Bible and pray behind closed doors, it's like an athlete pumping iron or running sprints. In the moment, you can't see the benefit. But sooner or later, when life decides to try to smack you around, you'll find reserves of strength you didn't know you had.

If you read the Gospels, you'll see that Jesus often went off by himself to pray. This frustrated some of his followers who thought he should have been more accessible. But Jesus understood what Jean Driscoll and every great champion understands: it's what you do quietly behind the scenes that makes you successful when the lights come on.

Reflect: 1 Timothy 4:7–8 says, "Train yourself to be godly. 'Physical training is good, but training for godliness is much better.'" How would you describe your spiritual training regimen? If you're hanging your head and kicking the dirt with your toe, ask yourself why that question is embarrassing to you. What are some things you could do to better prepare yourself for the challenges of the Christian life?

AN IMPORTANT QUESTION TO ASK

WHAT WOULD YOU do if you went to a baseball game and caught a foul ball? No doubt you would yell and scream and high five your friends and take a selfie and post it on social media and take the ball home and put it on your mantel. If you did those things, you would have Robert Cotter to thank for not going to jail.

Robert Cotter was eleven years old in 1922 when he went to a Philadelphia Phillies game and caught a foul ball. It was common in those days for fans to give the balls back, but that day Robert Cotter decided he wanted to take the ball home and kept it. For that, he was taken into custody and spent the night in jail.

The next day, a judge concluded that he was only following his natural impulses and ordered him to be set free. Suddenly baseball teams had to ask a question: Is our policy to arrest fans who keep foul balls a good one? They decided it wasn't and chose instead to buy more baseballs and let the fans keep the ones they catch.

If you run a school or a business or a church, you no doubt have policies in place. How often do you review them? Could it be that some of your policies are outdated or counterproductive to what you're trying to accomplish? Even in your personal life, you probably have a certain way you're accustomed to doing things. Could it be that your practices are holding you back or creating hurdles for your loved ones?

It's always important to look at how you're living your life and ask, "Is there a better way? Do I need to change?"

Reflect: Proverbs 18:15 says, "Intelligent people are always ready to learn." Are you a creature of habit? How do you handle new ideas? Think about some of the common practices of your business or church or personal life. How long has it been since anything changed? If it's been a while, what could you do to freshen things up?

IT SEEMED LIKE SUCH A GOOD IDEA

THE NFL'S ATLANTA FALCONS were an expansion franchise in 1966. Naturally, they wanted to have an opening-game ceremony that would send chills up and down the fans' backs. "Why not have the team led onto the field by a real, honest-to-goodness falcon?" somebody said. "Great idea!" somebody else said. And so, before you could say "What could possibly go wrong?" the search was on for a falcon.

Opening day arrived. The majestic bird was to be released, whereupon it would fly out over the field, make a couple of laps over the spectators, and then assume its perch to watch over the home team as it engaged the opposition. Unfortunately, the falcon had a mind of its own. It flew out over the field and soared straight out of the stadium, never to be seen again. The facetious among us might say that the bird was actually pretty smart and had no interest in watching a team that would eventually lose its first nine games.

Ever had a good idea that turned out not to be so good?

When I (Mark) first moved to Florida, my family was enthralled with the gorgeous weather. It was early winter, a time when we would have been shivering up north, so seventy-five-degree temperatures were like a little slice of heaven. One day, someone in our family (no one ever admitted it) opened the glass sliding door to our patio to let some of that luscious fresh air in. The fresh air came in, all right. So did a rattlesnake.

"It seemed like a good idea at the time" is one of the most common laments known to man. The good news is that even failed ideas help educate us. Smart people are smart not because they never fail; they're smart because they've failed enough to learn what does and doesn't work.

Reflect: Proverbs 16:25 says, "There is a path before each person that seems right …" Can you think of a seemingly great idea you had that didn't work out? In retrospect, what went wrong? Has that experience made you reluctant to keep coming up with new ideas? Can you name something you learned from that failed idea that has helped you?

DEFINING SUCCESS

TOM LEHMAN WAS trying to make it as a pro golfer in 1989 and sinking fast. Down to his last few hundred dollars, he decided to enter a tournament in South Africa, seeing it as a last-gasp attempt to salvage his career. If he didn't do well, he would be done. But he did do well. He won $30,000, which breathed a little life into his sagging hopes and kept him going.

Fast-forward to 1995.

Lehman is now an outstanding pro. In fact, he is playing in the final group at the US Open. He doesn't win, but everyone suddenly sees him as a player to be reckoned with.

Fast-forward to 1998.

Tom Lehman is now in his fourth consecutive year of being ahead or tied for the lead on the final day of the US Open. But for the fourth consecutive year, he doesn't win.

"Good golfer, but can't win the big one." People were saying it with a shake of the head, as if describing the death of the family pet. "Yup, it's too bad about old Tom. How sad."

But wait.

Since when is a guy who plays in the final group at the US Open multiple times someone to be pitied? Aren't there millions of golfers who would love to be able to do that? And that's before you even consider the fact that Tom Lehman won 5 PGA tournaments and millions of dollars during the decade of the 1990s. We *know* there are millions of golfers who would love to do *that*!

Sometimes our definition of success is far too narrow. We get it into our heads that anything short of perfection, anything short of the ultimate prize, is failure. As a result, we walk around feeling disappointed when we should be praising God for our blessings.

Do you need to redefine success for your life? Are you doing better than some of your critics seem to think? Are you doing better than you've allowed yourself to believe?

Reflect: Micah 6:8 says, "This is what he requires of you: to do what is right, to love mercy, and to walk humbly with your God." Based on this verse, what constitutes success in this life? Are career success and life success related? Can you have one without the other? Where do you think most people who misdefine success go wrong?

THE RIGHT THING TO DO

EUGENIO MONTI WAS the leader of the Italian bobsled team in the 1964 Winter Olympics in Innsbruck, Austria. His team was a heavy favorite to take home the gold medal, but the Austrians and Canadians were also good and expected to contend. Surprisingly, the Canadians set an Olympic record on their first run and held a commanding lead. Unfortunately, they also damaged an axle and would be disqualified if they couldn't get it fixed before their next scheduled heat.

In one of the greatest acts of sportsmanship in history, Eugenio Monti called upon his Italian mechanics to help the Canadians fix their sled. Fifteen minutes before the heat, they had the sled upside down and were working frantically to get it ready to go. They did, and the Canadians went on to win the gold. The Italians took home the bronze.

As you might expect, Eugenio Monti was vilified in the Italian press. But it didn't bother him. His contention was that the Canadians didn't win because he had his mechanics help them; they won because they were the best bobsled team.

As we go through life, certain questions need to be asked on a regular basis. One of those is, "What's the right thing to do?" Too many people are constantly thinking about what's the most advantageous thing to do, or the most profitable thing to do, or the most popular thing to do. This, of course, is why our world is so messed up.

Doing the right thing above all else not only helps make our world a better place but also enables you to sleep better at night. And while some people might be mad at you for not taking advantage, most people are going to love and respect you.

By the way, Eugenio did eventually win his gold medal four years later at Grenoble, which dispels the myth that nice guys finish last.

Reflect: In Matthew 7:12, Jesus said, "Do to others whatever you would like them to do to you." Have you ever been the recipient of a kind and benevolent act that you never would have expected? Have you ever given one? Have you ever been in a situation where you didn't know what the right thing to do was? How did you make your decision?

FINDING PEACE

PISTOL PETE MARAVICH was one of the greatest basketball players of all time. He compiled the kind of stats that look like they belong on a video game, including a ridiculous 44.2 points per game for his entire college career. Keep in mind this was before the three-point shot. Some have studied his games and say that if there had been a three-point line in his day, he would have averaged fifty-seven points per game.

Unfortunately, injuries forced the Pistol to retire early. Aimless and drifting, he began looking for a way to fill the void in his life which, unknown to a lot of people, he'd been experiencing for a long time. Sadly, he looked in all the wrong places: astrology, drugs, mysticism, Eastern religions, and alcohol. Of those years, he said, "Nothing satisfied me. The money didn't. Success didn't. The popularity didn't. The fame didn't. The adulation didn't. There was such an emptiness in my life."[12]

In 1982, he finally found what he was looking for in Christ. Those who knew him speak of how different he was from that point on. By all accounts,

PEACE IS NOT WHERE MOST PEOPLE THINK IT IS.

the next six years leading up to his untimely death of a heart attack were the happiest of his life.

Peace is not where most people think it is. Most people think it is to be found in worldly success or a nice, fat income or the applause of adoring fans. Ironically, most people discover that those things actually make you feel emptier and more troubled because of the disappointment factor. You think they're the answer and then are crushed when you discover they're not. Which, of course, often leads to desperation and even more poor choices, which lead to even more disappointment.

Sadly, most people never find Jesus and never find peace. It is a narrow road, after all. If you have found him, you are very blessed. No matter what else in your life has gone wrong, the one thing that truly matters has gone right.

Reflect: In John 16:33, Jesus said, "I have told you all this so that you may have peace in me." Assuming you have found peace in Christ, who was instrumental in helping you? Have you expressed your gratitude? What are you doing to help others find him?

MONKEY BUSINESS

TIM FLOCK WAS a 1950s-era NASCAR driver who liked attention and was looking for a way to get more of it. The best way would be to win more races, of course. But if that's not happening, an alternative would be to have a monkey ride along with you. Sounds crazy, right? But it happened. Flock acquired a rhesus monkey named Jocko from a pet store and immediately dubbed him "Jocko Flocko." He had a little helmet, goggles, and racing suit made for Jocko and installed a seat on the passenger side of his race car that was high enough to allow Jocko to look out the window and enjoy the ride.

The two teamed up for nine races before disaster struck. For some reason, Jocko went ballistic during a race and attacked his master. Imagine driving one hundred miles an hour and having a crazed monkey shrieking and scratching your face! At the next pit stop, Flock kicked Jocko out of the car, thus ending the monkey's racing career.

In life, we don't travel alone. People make the journey with us. Family members, classmates, coworkers, friends, and colleagues will be in our company at different stages. Sooner or later, one of those people is going to pull a Jocko Flocko and make him or herself a hindrance. Yes, we believe in forgiveness. Yes, we want to be tolerant and flexible. But there comes a time when the troublemaker must be asked to get out of the car.

Ending a relationship is never easy, which is probably why so many people carry on toxic relationships for years or even decades. But the pain of ending a relationship is usually a drop in the bucket compared to the suffering involved in carrying a dysfunctional relationship for years.

Reflect: Jesus said, "And if your hand—even your stronger hand—causes you to sin, cut it off and throw it away" (Matt. 5:30). Is there someone in your life right now who is a source of unpleasantness … someone who diminishes the quality of your life and steals your joy? Have you thought about ending that relationship? If so, what keeps you from doing it? How will you know when it's time?

ENDURANCE

THERE'S NO BUSINESS like shoe business. For many years now, companies like Nike and Reebok have been competing tooth and nail to see who can sell the most sneakers. Sleek styles, crazy colors, celebrity endorsements, and space-age technologies are combined in an effort to make runners, athletes, and ordinary people shell out insane amounts of money. And by "insane," we mean as much as $1,200 or more per pair as of this writing.

But are sneakers as important as we are led to believe? Jesus walked all over Judea without a Nike swoosh on his footwear, and not once did he complain (that we know of). And an Ethiopian runner by the name of Abebe Bikila set a world record in the marathon during the 1960 Olympics, running over the cobblestoned streets of Rome … barefoot!

Actually, the answer is yes. Even considering Abebe Bikila's incredible feat (or feet, if you will), every runner knows that footwear matters. When you run, your feet absorb about three times your body weight every time they hit the ground. That's a brutal pounding by any measurement. If you don't have the right shoes, you're headed for trouble.

The Bible says that life is a race. And this race is supposed to be run with endurance (Heb. 12:1). Endurance requires good conditioning and getting rid of encumbrances. But the Bible gives another somewhat surprising reminder to anyone wanting to run with endurance. It's simply not to try to run too fast. Run, yes, but don't get ahead of God: "But those who wait on the Lord will find new strength. They will fly high on wings like eagles. They will run and not grow weary …" (Isa. 40:31). Only in the life of faith does running slower increase your chances of being a winner.

Reflect: Ecclesiastes 9:11 says, "The fastest runner doesn't always win the race." Have you ever known a Christian who seemed like a "fast" runner, always ahead of the pack, doing more than everyone else? Do you pride yourself on being such an exemplary Christian? What are the dangers that threaten to waylay those speedy believers?

LITTLE THINGS

JOHN WOODEN WAS the greatest coach of all time in any sport. Almost no one disputes that. So one day I (Pat) asked him to pinpoint one secret of success in his life. I realize that's a bit like asking Shakespeare to share just one of his countless brilliant stanzas, but I was curious to see what he would say. And his answer was, "A lot of little things done well." Coach Wooden believed that little, seemingly insignificant things done well would eventually add up to a competitive advantage.

Which is one reason why he had so many rules about socks and shoes and hair. Those hair rules used to drive his players crazy. They thought he was an old fogy from the sticks. But they eventually learned that he had a reason for every rule. Keith Erickson, who played for Coach Wooden, said that one time in an NBA game, he ran his fingers through his long hair, which got them all sweaty. Seconds later someone passed him the ball, and it slipped right through his hands because of the moisture. Right then and there it dawned on him: *This is why Coach Wooden always made us wear short hair!*

The world is full of underachievers, people who have talent, sometimes by the truckload, but never seem to live up to their potential. Often the problem is that they rely on their talent to get them through and don't focus on details. Sooner or later they come up against an opponent with similar talent who *does* pay attention to details, and that's when they lose.

And it's not just true in athletics. Have you ever walked into a restaurant that offered great food but terrible service? Have you ever walked into a store that offered nice products but was cluttered and dirty? Have you ever visited a church that offered a nice sermon but seemed disorganized and unfriendly? It's the little things that make you or break you in the end.

Reflect: Jesus said in Luke 16:10, "If you are faithful in little things, you will be faithful in large ones." Do you sometimes wonder why you work so hard and don't see more success? Do you sometimes wonder why your marriage isn't better, considering how much you love your spouse? Could it be that there are little things in your life that need attention?

DON'T CHANGE EVERYTHING

LEGENDARY ANNOUNCER PAT SUMMERALL tells a wonderful story from the 2002–2003 NFL season. That year Pat called ten games for the Cowboys, who had a dismal season. After one especially poor performance, the Cowboys' owner, Jerry Jones, was completely frustrated. He handed Pat a legal pad and asked him to write down every mistake he felt Jerry had made with the team and what he needed to do to correct the situation.

Pat said, "Jerry, if I do that, you will never speak to me again."

But Jerry insisted, so Pat wrote three words on the pad: "Hire Bill Parcells."

Jerry Jones did, and the next year the Cowboys were in the Playoffs.

Complex, seemingly gigantic problems sometimes have simple answers. Jerry Jones was expecting Pat Summerall to fill a legal pad with suggestions for how to fix his team. All it took was three words.

The same is true in life. Many people who are struggling assume that they are miles and miles from a better life when they are, in fact, only one good decision away. An attitude adjustment, a change of routine, a restructuring of one's priorities, a narrowing of focus … any of these things applied at just the right moment can have a dramatic impact on the flow of a person's life.

If your life is a mess, our encouragement to you is not to overreact. "Blow it all up and start over" is a common phrase you hear. Don't do it! There's a very good chance that one or two thoughtful choices will make the difference you're looking for. The key is to figure out which ones. You might need to do what Jerry Jones did … ask a trusted friend for his or her opinion. But be prepared … you're probably going to hear something that will hurt just a little. That's OK. A little emotional sting will be worth it if you can turn things around.

Reflect: 2 Corinthians 5:17 says, "Anyone who belongs to Christ is a new person. The old life is gone; a new life has begun." Understanding that Christ is the one who gives *new* life, what is our responsibility when that new life goes off the rails and needs repair? If your life is in need of repair, what one key change do you feel would make a difference? What's keeping you from making it?

IF YOU CAN'T BEAT 'EM, BITE 'EM

ON JUNE 28, 1997, Evander Holyfield and Mike Tyson fought at the MGM Grand Garden Arena in Las Vegas. It was a rematch that, at the time, set a world revenue record of $100 million. Even though Holyfield won the first fight, Tyson entered the fight as the favorite to win.

That fight will forever be remembered as the one where Tyson bit off a portion of Holyfield's ear. We don't mean he bit him and left tooth marks; we mean part of the ear was completely gone. In fact, a hotel employee found it in the ring after the fight and returned it to Holyfield's team. Eight stitches were needed to close up the wound.

So why did Mike chomp down on Evander's ear in the third round? In a word, frustration. He felt that he'd been intentionally headbutted in the second round without Holyfield being penalized. But it was a costly overreaction, as Tyson was fined $3 million and given an eighteen-month boxing ban.

Costly overreactions are commonplace for frustrated people because frustration usually comes from a sense that there is an injustice being perpetrated that isn't being addressed. The pressure builds and builds until they feel like they have to do something themselves. By then, anger has become part of the equation, and you have the perfect setup for a very bad choice to be made. An unending parade of mistreated husbands and wives, disgruntled employees, angry customers, head-butted boxers, and other frustrated people have created mountains of misery. Everything from verbal abuse to workplace violence can be traced back to frustration.

The good news is that Mike Tyson and Evander Holyfield are good friends today, having made up several years ago. But not all overreactions have such happy endings. The next time you feel frustrated, be very careful. You're on dangerous ground.

Reflect: Proverbs 25:28 says, "A person without self-control is like a city with broken-down walls." What is one of your biggest sources of frustration? Have you ever overreacted when frustrated? Have you apologized for the hurt you may have caused? What can you do to stay more under control in the future?

IT DON'T MEAN A THING IF YOU AIN'T GOT THAT RING?

THERE IS A notion floating around that an athlete's career is not validated until he wins a championship. You can be an outstanding player, but you can't be one of the all-time greats until you get at least one ring. For anyone who believes that, we have two words:

Ted. Williams.

If those two words aren't enough, here are two more:

Ty. Cobb.

If you need more words, we have plenty in reserve. The pages of history are filled with the stories of incredible athletes who never got champagne poured on them after a championship game. A guy like Patrick Ewing, for example, was selected as one of the top fifty NBA players of all time but never won a ring. And what about Dan Marino? The guy threw for 61,361 yards and 420 touchdowns but never won a ring.

This whole line of messed-up thinking rears its ugly head in our everyday lives from time to time as well. For example, Preacher A is considered a great pastor because his congregation grew to mega-church status, while Preacher B is given nowhere near that kind of respect because he preaches in a small country church. Or Parent A is revered as amazing because both of his children became missionaries, while Parent B is given nowhere near that kind of respect because his kids didn't go to college and work hourly wage jobs.

We are convinced that God does not evaluate people this way. Man looks at the outward appearance, the things you can see and measure, like awards and trophies and rings. But God knows there's a lot more to it than that. He looks at the heart, where the true story of a person's life is told.

Reflect: Proverbs 4:23 says, "Guard your heart above all else, for it determines the course of your life." Do you sometimes feel inferior to peers who have accomplished more than you in terms of worldly success? What's more important to you: the respect of men or the approval of God? Are you trying too hard to gain worldly status?

TOOLS

IN BASEBALL, THERE are five tools a player can have. Leo Durocher is credited with saying it first, but they've always been there on display in every game ever played. The five tools are running, throwing, catching, hitting for average, and hitting for power. You don't always find all of these tools in one player. In fact, you seldom do. Five-tool players are extremely rare. But good teams will have all of these tools represented on their roster, and a good manager will blend them together to produce good results.

Here's something that might surprise you. Being a five-tool player doesn't guarantee that you'll be any good. It's not our intent to disparage anyone by naming names, but the history of baseball is filled with players who were "can't miss" prospects because they possessed all five tools but never were any good. "There's nothing he can't do!" the scouts say, and that may be true. But often there are things a talented player *won't* do. Things like staying in shape, working on their craft, clearing away distractions, etc.

It's the same in life. There's always that person who is loaded with talent but never amounts to anything … the student who has all kinds of brains but won't study … the pastor who has an amazing gift for oratory but rips his sermons off the internet … the writer who is an amazing wordsmith but doesn't discipline himself to sit down and write. You can probably think of someone right now who has tremendous potential but has never come close to reaching it.

THE NUMBER ONE TOOL A PERSON CAN HAVE IS PASSION.

All of this leads us to say that the number one tool a person can have is passion. Some people call it "want to." None of the other tools you possess will amount to much until you truly *want* to be great and are willing to do what it takes.

Reflect: 1 Corinthians 9:24 says, "Run to win!" Think about the talents you've been given. Make a list. Are there some you aren't using? Are you skating through life without really pushing yourself to be the best you can be? What would it take for you to dig deeper and get more out of the gifts you've been given?

BRAIN FREEZE

SPORT IS NOT just about physical ability; it also takes brains. Now and then, a player's brain freezes up and creates an embarrassing moment, or worse, loses a game. Sometimes even a championship. Just ask Chris Webber.

It was right at the end of the 1993 NCAA National Championship basketball game. Michigan, Webber's team, was down to North Carolina by two with eleven seconds left. During the previous time-out, Michigan's coach had reminded his players that they were out of time-outs. To call a time-out would incur a technical foul and almost certainly cost them the game.

So North Carolina shot a free throw and missed. Michigan rebounded the ball, but Webber got trapped in the corner. His options were to try to throw the ball out of bounds off an opponent's leg and retain possession or attempt a desperation jump pass toward the other end of the court. Not high-percentage plays, mind you, but at least there would have been hope. Instead he did the one thing he absolutely could not do … he called time-out.

Bye-bye, national championship.

There's no adult alive who hasn't had a brain freeze. When one happens, someone invariably asks you what you were thinking, as if you were working through all your options and just decided to go with the stupidest one you could think of. "Yes, I knew I had better options, but I just felt it was a good idea to choose the one that would make me look like an idiot."

Here's a suggestion. When someone close to you suffers a brain freeze, show some compassion. If possible, give them a hug, laugh it off, and move on. It's called grace. Sooner or later, you're going to need some too.

Reflect: Jesus said, "Do unto others whatever you would like them to do to you." (Matthew 7:12) Have you ever been laughed at or ridiculed or vilified because you did something really dumb? How did those reactions affect your ability to move on? Is there someone in your life right now who needs some grace? What are some ways you could give them some?

THE MYSTERY OF THE FIVE-DOLLAR T-SHIRT

IT HAPPENS AT ALMOST every major sporting event. At some point during a stoppage in play, a squad of extraordinarily attractive young men and women who are all decked out in the home team's colors come charging onto the floor or the field to send T-shirts flying into the crowd. And they do this using a variety of techniques, including three-person slingshots, hand-held cannons, T-shirt machine guns, and of course simply throwing them. The T-shirts themselves are wadded up swatches of cotton bearing the team's logo alongside the name of whatever sponsor helped pay for them. As for quality, they typically last through a handful of washings and then move on to a second career as a dust cloth.

But boy, do people love those T-shirts. As soon as the squad trots out the T-shirt bazooka, people start yelling and screaming and waving their arms. You'd think they were preparing to shoot one hundred–

dollar bills into the crowd. Sometimes people risk life and limb, diving over seats and friends to get their hands on a shirt they might never even want to wear once they get a close-up look at it. People have been so severely injured scrambling for shirts they've ended up in the hospital.

So what's the deal? Why do people go so crazy over practically worthless T-shirts?

There can only be one answer: people get caught up in the moment.

Music is blasting, people are yelling and screaming while the T-shirt brigade eggs them on. The T-shirt itself is held up like some mystical treasure for everyone to see before it's launched into the boiling sea of screaming fans. People wouldn't give a hoot about that shirt any other time, but in that moment there's nothing they want more.

Be very careful when you make important choices. Are you thinking clearly, or are you just caught up in the moment? Have you inflated the value of a worthless item simply because there's excitement in the air? Often, when people come to their senses after a bad decision, they wonder what they were thinking. The answer sometimes is that they weren't. They were just caught up in the moment.

Reflect: Proverbs 14:15 says, "The prudent carefully consider their steps." Have you ever gotten caught up in the moment and done something you regretted? Have you ever made an impulse buy and then had buyer's remorse? What is it about people that makes us so susceptible to this kind of mistake? What can we do to guard against this mistake?

DO THE MATH

RUBÉN RIVERA WAS an outfielder for the New York Yankees. He was making $1 million, which certainly seems like it would be enough to pay the rent and buy groceries. But for some reason that defies common sense, Mr. Rivera stole a bat and glove from Derek Jeter's locker and sold them to a sports memorabilia dealer for $2,500. He got them back and returned them the next day, confessing his sin, but by then the damage was already done. His teammates voted unanimously to kick him off the team. The Yankees negotiated a $200,000 buyout of Rivera's contract, and he was gone.

So now, let's do the math.

$1 million (Rivera's contract).

Minus $1 million (Contract voided).

Plus $200,000 (Negotiated settlement).

Equals a net loss for Rubén Rivera of $800,000 (not to mention his job and reputation), all because he tried to make an extra $2,500. When the dust cleared, he must have felt like a complete idiot.

Have you ever done the math on some of your choices?

I (Mark) once asked a smoker how much he spent per month on cigarettes, and he said, "I don't want to know. I know it would make me sick." I also know a man who had an affair. It broke up his marriage and caused him to have to pay a huge sum in alimony and child support. And I remember a guy who lost his cool and cursed out his boss. Bye-bye, $50,000-a-year job.

There are many ways to measure a decision. We're not suggesting that money is the most important factor in any situation. But sometimes doing the math will show you the truth in a little different way. The Bible calls this "counting the cost" and suggests you do it *before* you make the decision, not after the damage is already done.

Reflect: Luke 14:28 says, "Which of you, wishing to build a tower, does not first sit down and count the cost …" Think of a personal struggle (such as a bad habit) that you might have. Have you ever counted the cost of it in terms of money, wasted time, or harm to your relationships or reputation? If not, why? Are you afraid of what you might learn?

WIFE TOTING

WE'VE COVERED QUITE a few different sports in this book. Here's one neither of us has participated in: wife carrying. Every year the Sunday River Resort in western Maine sponsors the competition, which is based on a nineteenth-century Finnish legend about an outlaw who required all of his recruits to pass a grueling physical fitness test that included stealing a woman and carrying her a long distance over difficult terrain. Somebody got the bright idea of turning it into a sport, only without the stealing-a-woman part. Contestants are allowed to use their own wives.

If you've seen pictures of this competition, you know that the men do not cradle their wives in their arms the way a groom might carry his bride over a threshold. A common method of competing is for the wife to be upside down, clinging to her husband's back with her legs around his neck and her arms around his waist. Her cheek is pressed against his lower back.

Sounds weird, but the key is weight distribution and leaving the husband's hands free for climbing and balance.

Weight distribution is a key factor in life as well. Burdens will always be a part of our lives in this fallen world. Stuff happens, and we have to deal with it. Yes, we can cast our cares on Jesus, but even then he doesn't give us a free ride. He expects us to manage our challenges and responsibilities wisely. It's part of living out our faith.

So here are two quick suggestions for carrying weight effectively. First, get adequate rest. Even God rested on the seventh day. And second, stay balanced. Don't let one problem or responsibility take over your life. Picture a man carrying two buckets of water, one on each end of a long pole balanced on his shoulders. As long as the buckets are the same weight, he's fine. But if one is significantly heavier than the other, he's in trouble.

God gives us strength, but we still need to be smart about how we deal with life's burdens.

Reflect: Ephesians 5:15 says, "So be careful how you live." How often do you take stock of your burdens and responsibilities to make sure you're not carrying too much? Do you feel guilty when you think about quitting something in order to lighten your load? How many things are you doing not because you have the time or energy but because someone has guilted you into it?

HUMANISM? NO, THANKS

SINCE WE DID a weird sport yesterday, let's make it two in a row: competitive eating.

Joey Chestnut is the Babe Ruth of competitive speed-eating. And no, he doesn't weigh 400 pounds. He's six feet one and goes about 230. His titles on the Major League Eating circuit are almost endless, but his claim to fame is the Nathan's Hot Dog Eating Contest. He's won the crazy thing every year except one since 2007. In 2018, he wolfed down a record seventy-four hot dogs and buns in twelve minutes.

If you're thinking that competitive eating sounds like it could be dangerous, you're right. Contestants have to practice, just like competitors in any other sport. Some have eaten as many as sixty hot dogs at a sitting three times a week to stay in shape for the competition. Others have developed methods of stretching their stomachs that include drinking a gallon of water at a time. Those who have studied

GIVE MAN A BLESSING, AND HE'LL FIND A WAY TO PERVERT IT.

the sport confirm that competitive eaters can develop gastric ruptures, chemical imbalances, and eating disorders, not to mention the harm that comes from such a large volume of junk food. Critics of the sport have called speed-eating dozens of hot dogs and buns self-abuse. It's just like man to take something good and figure out a way to make it dangerous and unhealthy. We've done it with so many things.

Work? Check.

Sex? Check.

Technology? Check.

Food? Check.

Religion? Check.

Give man a blessing, and he'll find a way to pervert it.

This is one reason why we are not humanists. Humanism suggests that humans are this world's greatest hope, that we need to just trust people to solve this world's problems. Really? Humans, who are constantly thinking of new ways to *cause* problems, are this world's greatest hope?

No thanks. We'll continue to put our faith in God.

Reflect: Psalms 108:12 says, "Oh, please help us against our enemies, for all human help is useless." Why do you think so many people continue to promote humanism in spite of the overwhelming failures of man? In what ways can humanism victimize people? In what ways can humanism creep into our thinking unnoticed?

THE IMPORTANCE OF CONTEXT

ON DECEMBER 20, 1980, something happened in an NFL game that had never happened before and hasn't happened since. NBC broadcast the game between the New York Jets and Miami Dolphins without announcers. Don Ohlmeyer, the legendary NBC executive, decided to do it in an effort to increase the ratings of a game that had no real significance, since neither team had qualified for the playoffs. The game's ratings were higher than they otherwise would have been, but the idea was ditched and never tried again for one main reason: viewers had a hard time putting what they were seeing into context.

Imagine not having an announcer to tell you that the star running back is on the bench because he turned his ankle. You'd be screaming at the coach for not putting him in, not realizing he *can't* put him in. People saw with their eyes what was happening, but they couldn't understand why it was happening without context.

Context is important in day-to-day life too. For example, when someone you know—a coworker, for example—behaves in a way that seems off-putting, you can take offense and form a judgment about that person. But how would that judgment change if you knew the person's backstory? Suddenly that off-putting behavior might make perfect sense and make you feel sympathetic instead of irritated.

When the Bible talks about not judging people, it's not just because judging is God's purview and not ours. It's not just because a judging spirit lacks love. And it's not just because we are usually guilty of the very sins we condemn. It's also because we never—*never*—have enough information to make the proper judgments. We lack context.

Remember that the next time someone does something that rubs you the wrong way.

Reflect: James 1:19 says, "Be slow to get angry." Do you have a tendency to judge people's character from their actions without knowing their backstory? Have you ever had someone draw the wrong conclusion about you because they didn't understand the context of your words or behavior? Why do you think people are so quick to judge others?

YOU HAD HELP

IT WAS DURING the 1956 World Series that the New York Yankees' Don Larsen pitched the only perfect game in Series history, against the Brooklyn Dodgers. There were 64,519 fans in attendance who surely were not expecting such a feat, especially since Larsen had been knocked out in the second inning of game two.

Obviously, Larsen had great stuff that day. Opposing players even said that his stuff got better as the game went along. But he also had some help. There were three fielding gems in the game, one coming off the bat of none other than Jackie Robinson. He hit a hot shot at Andy Carey, who deflected the ball to Gil McDougald, who picked it up and fired to first in time to nip Robinson by a hair. Another line shot was hit into deep left center and looked like extra bases for sure, but a speedy young Mickey Mantle flew across the outfield grass and snagged it at the last possible second. The third close call was in the eighth inning, when another smash was hit to Carey. It bounced off of his glove up into the air, but he was able to grab it on its way down before it hit the ground.

It's taking nothing away from Larsen to say that he had some help.

So did we. So do you. So does everybody who accomplishes anything significant in life. From the person who changed your diapers to your teachers in school to the person who hired you and gave you an opportunity, the list of people who contributed to your success in large ways and small would have no end. Some of them you wouldn't even know about.

Even if you've accomplished great things in your life … even if people praise you for what you've done, be humble. You didn't do it alone.

Reflect: Proverbs 18:12 says, "Haughtiness goes before destruction; humility precedes honor." What do you consider to be your greatest accomplishment in life? Who else had a hand in it in some way? In your opinion, what are the marks of a genuinely humble person?

FACING THE MUSIC

THE TWO OF US planned this book in Sam Snead's restaurant in Orlando, so it seems only fitting that we share a Sam Snead story with you.

Slammin' Sam was a terrific golfer, as everyone knows. What most people today don't know (because it happened so long ago) was that he lost the 1939 US Open in one of the most epic meltdowns of all time. With two holes to play, he needed only a couple of pars to tie the all-time Open record, which seemed like it would be enough to secure the championship.

He bogeyed the first of those two holes because he hit his approach shot over the green and chipped back short, missing a five-foot putt. Still, he was in good shape. He just needed to pull it together and play the last hole well. But he didn't. In a comedy of errors that was completely uncharacteristic of such a great player, Snead carded the dreaded "snowman." That would be an eight, for those of you who are not familiar with golf lingo.

After the round, Snead headed to his hotel room with his head hung in embarrassment. But his friend, Johnny Bulla, dragged him out of his room and made him go to a restaurant to eat dinner. His reasoning was that when you really mess up, it's best not to hide but to face it right away. And yes, the press was unmerciful. One writer said that from then on, totally blowing a golf hole would be known as "Sneading" the hole. Ouch!

But at least Sam Snead faced it like a man instead of running and hiding.

"I just want to be alone" is what a lot of people say when they are ashamed or embarrassed. But avoiding people doesn't change what happened and likely won't change people's reactions when you finally do face them. Often, it's better to face the music right away. Get it over with. The longer you hide out and lick your wounds, the harder it will be.

Reflect: Speaking of Adam and Eve, Genesis 3:8 says, "So they hid from the Lord God among the trees." Think of an embarrassing or shameful moment in your life. Did you hide afterward? If so, did you gain some benefit from that decision, or did it just delay the inevitable? What are the advantages of facing the music right away?

FIRST, DO NO HARM ... TO YOURSELF

TY COBB IS ONE of the most ill-tempered, difficult-to-get-along-with characters in the history of sports. His blowups and tirades are legendary. Some people even thought of him as psychotic.

Near the end of his life, he was living in an eighteen-room mansion in California. One day a sportswriter stopped by to interview him and found the entire house in darkness, except for a few candles that allowed him to move through the house without bumping into furniture or walls. When he was asked why he was living in the dark, he said, "I'm suing the Pacific Gas and Electric Company for overcharging me on the service. Those rinky-dinks tacked an extra sixteen dollars on my bill. Bunch of crooks. When I wouldn't pay, they cut off my utilities. OK—I'll see them in court."[13]

The interesting thing about this incident is that Cobb didn't live in darkness for a few days or a week; he lived in darkness for months. He cooked on a Coleman camping stove and took freezing cold showers. He had no working refrigerator, stove, or television. He was so stubborn that he chose to live in hardship rather than to pay an extra sixteen dollars.

As strange as this seems, we've seen countless people put themselves through all sorts of discomfort and hardship simply out of stubbornness. The most common example would be the person who refuses to try to patch up a once-valued relationship because of some perceived offense. With shoulders squared and heels dug in, the person refuses to budge … and in the process costs him or herself a wonderful blessing.

If you're angry, fine. Maybe you have a right to be. But think carefully about your response. Don't be so stubborn that you compound your misery by hurting yourself even more.

Reflect: Proverbs 19:11 says, "Sensible people control their temper; they earn respect by overlooking wrongs." Can you think of a time when your anger and stubbornness caused you to suffer? What finally enabled you to come to your senses? What are some indicators that a person is overreacting to an offense?

DOING IT ALL

THERE'S A PITHY QUIP in sports: "He does it all. Why, I wouldn't be surprised to hear that he sells tickets before the game!"

It actually happened during the first World Series in 1903. Cy Young, one of the greatest pitchers of all time, was in his late thirties, already established as the greatest pitcher of his era. He would eventually win 511 games, the most ever, and have an annual pitching award named after him. What most people don't know is that he could hit, too, compiling a .341 batting average that season. Yes, he could do it all.

So that year, to more easily accommodate the large number of fans who wanted to attend the Series, Boston set up some extra ticket booths. The problem was that they had more ticket booths than they had ticket sellers, so they put out the word in the clubhouse that the first players to arrive should come down to the ticket office and help out. Cy Young was one of the first to arrive. You can imagine the surprise on people's faces when they walked up to buy a ticket and found their team's superstar handling the transactions.

You'll find very few people today who are willing to step even one inch outside of their job description to help out. Or if they do, they want to be paid extra for it. "Not my job," or "Not my problem," they'll say. And they may be right. But people who take this attitude seldom excel in their careers or in life. Doing only what you're required to do is a one-way ticket to mediocrity. You'll almost never find a highly successful person who isn't willing to do whatever he can to help the team succeed … even if it's not his job.

Reflect: Philippians 2:4 says, "Don't look out only for your own interests, but take an interest in others too." Can you think of a time when you couldn't get help because you happened to find yourself just outside someone's job description? Have you ever taken a step back from a job that needed doing because it wasn't in your job description? What are some of the long-term dangers of this attitude both for individuals and society?

EVERYBODY HURTS

IN JUNE OF 2000, Julius Erving—known to most of the world as Dr. J.—called me (Pat) and told me that his son Cory was missing. He was nineteen and had gotten into his car to drive to the store to pick up some bread for a Memorial Day cookout. The Ervings were about ready to go public with the situation and asked me to serve as the family spokesperson.

Cory had led a troubled life but was doing much better. He was enrolled in college and had a job. It was hard for anybody to imagine that he had simply run away. The family put up a $25,000 reward for any information, and Julius appeared on *Larry King Live* to spread awareness. When a caller asked how Julius and his wife were holding up, he shared that their faith was sustaining them and that the parable of the Prodigal Son was especially helpful. He said that when his son returned home, they intended to have a great feast, just like in the famous Bible story.

On July 6, the sheriff's deputies found Cory's car submerged in a retention pond with Cory's body inside. He'd lost his life in a terrible accident.

The family went ahead with their plans to have a great feast with their family and friends to celebrate their son's return. It wasn't the kind of return they were hoping for, of course. But their faith remained strong. They were at least thankful to have closure.

I think about Julius and the thrills and accomplishments that have filled his life, and I am reminded everybody hurts. Even the famous, the rich, the seemingly invincible star that everyone adores will shed tears in moments of private pain. You may not see it, but it happens. And if it hasn't happened yet, it will.

Be nice. Everybody hurts.

> *Reflect:* Galatians 6:2 says, "Share each other's burdens, and in this way obey the law of Christ." Think of times when you have suffered. Was there a person who added to your suffering by being cold or judgmental? Was there a person who lightened your load by being kind and compassionate? Is there some hurting person in your world right now who needs a touch of kindness from you?

YOU'RE BEING FOLLOWED

AL CAPONE WAS a notorious crime boss during the time of prohibition. The gangster, who was also known as "Scarface," had a seven-year run as the founder and leader of the most powerful crime organization in Chicago. Bootlegging, prostitution, gambling, loan-sharking, and even murder were woven into the fabric of Capone's life. So much so that it's hard to imagine him doing anything normal.

Occasionally, however, he would take time out from his nefarious duties and head for the golf course. One day, his caddie was toting his bag and getting tired. The fatigue caused him to be a little lacka-daisical, which caused him to drop Mr. Capone's golf bag onto the ground a little harder than usual. The jolt caused a pistol that Capone had hidden in the bag to go off. The bullet tore through the bag and ended up in Capone's leg.

No word on whether the caddie was fitted with a pair of concrete shoes.

We like this story because it illustrates an important truth: you can't get away from who you are. Al Capone was a gangster, and his "gangsterhood" followed him to the golf course. Even when he tried to get away from it all, he ended up getting shot in the leg.

IT'S THE SIMPLE REALITY THAT WHO YOU ARE FOLLOWS YOU AROUND.

It's true of all of us. Who you are follows you around. You probably know people who always seem to be in trouble. It's like trouble follows them wherever they go. The opposite is true too. Some people just seem to find blessings wherever they go. The Bible calls this "reaping what you sow." It's the simple reality that who you are follows you around.

So an important question to ask is, who are you? If your life isn't what you always dreamed of, answer that question, and you just might begin to understand why.

Reflect: Galatians 6:7 says, "You will always harvest what you plant." Think about how your life is going. Does it seem like trouble follows you? If so, what is it about your lifestyle that seems to serve as a magnet for trouble? If you don't know, perhaps a trusted friend or mentor could help you answer that question.

BE CAREFUL

ON APRIL 30, 1993, Monica Seles was playing in a tennis tournament in Germany. She was the number one ranked player in the world at the age of nineteen, having already won her eighth Grand Slam title. It is no exaggeration to say that she was possibly on her way to becoming the greatest female tennis player of all time. But that day the unthinkable happened.

During Monica's match against Magdalena Maleeva, a deranged fan came out of the stands and stabbed her in the back with a boning knife. The cut was between her shoulder blades and was less than an inch deep, which means it wasn't life-threatening. But it was terrifying and psychologically damaging, as it would be for anyone. It was two years before Monica was able to return to competition. She only won one more Grand Slam title.

The assailant, Günter Parche, was obsessed with Steffi Graf and was angry that Monica had moved past Graf in the world rankings. He was charged but only spent six months in pretrial detention.

An incident like this is a stark reminder that there are dangerously unbalanced people in the world. School, church, and nightclub shootings, as well as many workplace violence incidents should impress upon us all the importance of safety. We need to practice it and teach it to our children.

We are old enough to remember when, other than locking doors, very few safety precautions were taken. People were seldom aware of their surroundings or keeping their eyes open for trouble. In today's world, that's a prescription for disaster.

Reflect: Jesus said, "Look, I am sending you out as sheep among wolves. So be as shrewd as snakes and harmless as doves" (Matt. 10:16). What do you think Jesus meant when he said that we should be as shrewd as snakes? How have your routines changed in this age of growing violence? Are there additional measures you should take?

THE HEIDI BOWL

THERE ARE SOME great bowl games. The Rose, the Peach, the Fiesta, the Citrus, the Gator, the Cotton, and on and on and on. As of this writing, there are forty competitive bowl games. That number can change from year to year. We'd like to tell you about the most unpopular bowl game ever played. (Actually, it wasn't really a bowl game; it was just dubbed "The Heidi Bowl" for the following reasons.)

It was 1968. The Oakland Raiders were playing the New York Jets on NBC. In an improbable turn of events, the Raiders scored two touchdowns in a nine-second span to overtake the Jets and win. The problem is that the TV audience didn't see it because the guy who made such decisions for the network, a man named Dick Cline, decided to switch over to their regularly scheduled programming with one minute and five seconds left in the game. That regularly scheduled programming was the movie *Heidi*.

To say there was an outcry would be an understatement. If people could have gotten their hands on Mr. Cline, they probably would have strangled him. But here's what nobody knew until later: network executives were trying desperately to call Dick Cline and tell him to stay with the game ... but the lines were busy.

How many bad situations have been created throughout history because of a breakdown in communication? Sometimes, as in this case, the breakdown can't be helped. But most of the time, the problem is simply a lack of diligence. We don't tell people what they need to know, or we don't tell them in a timely manner.

Our recommendation for anyone who's part of a family or who works with people is to overcommunicate. Tell people what they need to know. Then remind them. Then remind them again. Don't take anything for granted. If you do this, you will experience fewer failures or embarrassing moments.

Reflect: Proverbs 15:23 says, "It is wonderful to say the right thing at the right time." Have you experienced any embarrassing moments or failures because of poor communication? Do you need to become a better communicator? Would it help you at work? At home? What are some ways you could accomplish this?

TEAMWORK AT ITS FINEST

THE TOUR DE FRANCE is a bicycle race held every year in July. About twenty teams of nine cyclists compete over a distance that would be about like riding from New York to Arizona. In terms of the physical demands on the riders, they are basically doing the equivalent of running a marathon every day for three weeks. It is one of the most grueling of all sporting events.

One thing we find compelling about the race is how the teams work together. Every team has one elite rider and eight supporting riders who are there simply to make his job easier. They could, for example, grab drinks from the team's support car or maneuver to clear a strategic spot in the pack for the elite rider to slip into. Most often, one of the support riders will ride just ahead of the elite rider, creating an air pocket that enables him to conserve his energy for that moment when he chooses to burst out of the pack and improve his position.

Most teams in any sport have superstars and role players, so the concept isn't new. But we like how, in the Tour de France, there's a complete absence of ego among the supporting cast. In many major sports, the role players often complain that they aren't getting more playing time, feeling that they should be given a chance to become stars too. In the Tour de France, more so than any other sport, the support riders only have one goal: to help their team win.

It is our view that countless families, churches, businesses, and organizations would be healthier and more productive if there were more people who were willing to say, "I don't need to be the star; I just want to help." If you find yourself in a supporting role in the home or at work, our challenge to you is to embrace it wholeheartedly. Otherwise, you are hurting the team more than helping it.

Reflect: Proverbs 27:17 says, "As iron sharpens iron, so a friend sharpens a friend." Can you name something you do that would be impossible without the support of others? Can you name something you do that is essential to the success of others? What are some of the unique blessings of serving in a supporting role?

APRIL 2

FADING GLORY

IN THE LATE 1970s and early 1980s, I (Pat) was the general manager of the Philadelphia 76ers. My job was to assemble a team, coaches and players, that could go out and win a championship. Of course, every other general manager in the league was doing the same thing. And there are lots of good players and coaches to choose from, so finding just the right combination was a challenge. I remember thinking that if I could just win an NBA championship ring, I'd be riding on a cloud for the rest of my life.

Well, it happened. In 1983, the Sixers team I helped assemble swept the Los Angeles Lakers to win the NBA championship. And yes, it was truly thrilling—for a while. But eventually the thrill of victory wore off. I have a championship ring, but I never wear it. I put it in a drawer a long time ago and haven't looked at it in years.

It's funny how things happen to us and, in the moment, they seem world-shaking. But two things cause them to diminish more quickly than we expect. First, the world moves on. People might celebrate your accomplishment for a while, but a day later or a week later, most people have forgotten what happened and are looking ahead to the next big thing. Second, life has a way of reminding you that you're not as hot as you thought you were. Trouble, failure, sickness ... it comes to champions just like it comes to everyone else, reminding you that you don't walk on water, never did, and never will.

This is why we need Jesus. He offers that which doesn't fade, no matter how much time passes or how many struggles we face.

Reflect: The apostle Paul said, "Everything else is worthless when compared with the infinite value of knowing Christ Jesus my Lord" (Phil. 3:8). What do you consider to be your greatest accomplishment in life? Does it excite you as much as it once did? What is your greatest source of joy at this point?

NOT SO FAST

SOME SAY BROOKS ROBINSON was the greatest third baseman Major League Baseball has ever seen. His hands were soft and, though he was a slow runner, his reflexes were cat quick. And he could hit, too, as indicated by his 264 career home runs. Brooks won the American League MVP award in 1964 and the World Series MVP award in 1970.

Brooks loves to tell the story of his first big-league game and its aftermath. He went two for four in that first game and drove in a crucial run. To say he was feeling pretty cocky afterward would be an understatement. He was eighteen years old and thought the game was no match for his talent. Then, starting in the next game, he went eighteen consecutive at bats without a hit, a streak that included ten strikeouts. He later said, "Being humbled like that was just about the best thing that could happen to me. There's nothing worse than a ballplayer with a swelled head."[14]

We'd like to add that there's also nothing worse than a salesman with a swelled head. Or a teacher with a swelled head. Or a preacher with a swelled head. Or ... well, you get the idea. People with swelled heads are annoying, obviously. But they're also a detriment to whatever organization they're a part of for one primary reason: people who think they're already great have no incentive to work hard and keep improving. That zero for eighteen slump that Brooks Robinson had was life saying to him, "Not so fast there, young man. You don't have this game mastered just yet."

Even though they hurt and are embarrassing, thank God for those experiences that keep you from getting a swelled head.

Reflect: James 4:10 says, "Humble yourselves before the Lord, and he will lift you up in honor." Have you ever had an embarrassing experience that humbled you? At the time, did it occur to you that God might be behind it, that he was trying to teach you something? What are some of the identifying marks of a truly humble person?

YOU STILL HAVE TO SWING THE BAT

BACK IN THE 1980s, when Whitey Herzog was the manager of the St. Louis Cardinals, I (Mark) was privileged to sit in his office at Busch Stadium and have a brief conversation. The day before, the Cardinals' catcher, Darrell Porter, had struck out three consecutive times without swinging the bat once. He simply stood there and watched strike after strike go by. Whitey was still worked up about it and gave this account of his conversation with Darrell after the game:

Whitey said, "Darrell, what are you doing standing there taking all those pitches? You struck out three times!"

Darrell, in his typical laidback manner, responded, "Whitey, I'm a man of faith. I believe everything is in God's hands. If God wants me to hit, I'll hit. If God wants me to strike out, I'll strike out."

Whitey, rolling his eyes, said "Darrell, son, the Lord is a good guy and all that, but he can't help you if you don't swing the bat."

Whitey Herzog will never be accused of being a great theologian, but he nailed that one dead center. God is willing and able to work in our lives, but he expects us to do our part. When the Israelites came to the edge of the Promised Land, God said, "Let's go. I'll help you conquer those Canaanite tribes." He did *not* say, "You all just sit right here, and I'll go clear out the land and let you know when I'm finished."

As you live your life, understand that God wants to partner with you and work through you. He will bless you and help you in amazing ways, but only if you're willing to step up to the plate and swing the bat.

Reflect: James 2:26 says, "Just as the body is dead without breath, so also faith is dead without good works." Why do you think some Christians minimize the importance of their own efforts? Do you believe God is impressed by the kind of faith that leaves everything up to him? Is there some area of your life where you need to put out more effort?

LUCK

FAR TOO MANY people analyze their successes and failures through the lens of a kind of vague belief in some sort of cosmic force that tilts matters to our favor in some cases and against us in others. When a friend has something good happen to him, a person will say, "Oh, you're so lucky!" Or if something bad happens: "What a stroke of bad luck!" If a person returns from a fishing trip, people will say, "Did you have any luck?" And if a person has a string of bad things happen, then people start thinking he might be jinxed or completely devoid of luck. To hear some people talk, we're all just beneficiaries or victims of this weird cosmic force, and nothing we do can stop it from blessing us or cursing us.

However, we like Don Shula's thought on the matter. Don is the legendary Super Bowl–winning coach of the Miami Dolphins and the coach of the only team in NFL history to have a perfect season, which, of course, compels some people to say that he and his team were lucky. Coach Shula said, "Sure, luck means a lot in football. And not having a good quarterback is bad luck."[15]

To pick up on Coach Shula's point, we have noticed that people who work really hard tend to be lucky in their careers. People who make wise financial decisions tend to be lucky in their finances. People who are devoted to their spouses tend to be lucky in marriage. Just like football teams with great quarterbacks tend to be lucky in football.

It's strange how that works. Almost leads one to believe that there really isn't any such thing as luck, that our lives tend to turn one way or the other based in large part on our actions and attitudes.

Reflect: Galatians 6:7 says, "You will always harvest what you plant." Do you have a good luck charm? A lucky hat? A lucky shirt? A rabbit's foot in your pocket? As you reflect on your life, do you see no rhyme or reason for the things that have happened to you, or do you feel that you've basically reaped what you've sown?

HANG IN THERE

JOHN DALY WAS well stocked with golf talent. Maybe as much as anyone. He could hit the ball a mile off the tee, had a nice short game, and could roll balls into the cup from all over the green. His two major championships attest to his raw ability. Sadly, his mental game was as bad as his physical game was good. He lacked self-discipline in his personal life, as evidenced by his four marriages and struggles with tobacco and alcohol, so it's no surprise that he lacked discipline on the course too. If he was having a bad day, he might completely melt down and do something crazy, like teeing off with a putter or putting with a driver. If things really got bad, he might intentionally break a rule and quit in the middle of the round, leaving his playing partner to finish the round by himself. One thing his fans and critics will agree on is that John Daly was never boring.

John Daly is a good example of how a person's reputation is mostly shaped by how he handles his bad days. When John Daly's name comes up, rarely will somebody say, "Oh wow, that guy could really putt!" Rather, most people say, "Oh wow, that guy was a head case!" For whatever reason, people tend to remember our struggles and embarrassing moments as much or more than they remember our successes.

Which leads us to offer this word of advice: Hang in there on your bad days. Don't give up. Don't get crazy and do something stupid. Don't cheapen yourself by cursing or blaming others. And above all, don't make excuses. Instead stay calm. Hang in there. Keep your head together. Weather the storm, and come back to try again another day with your dignity intact.

People won't remember that you had a bad day, but they will remember if you lose your head and act like a fool.

Reflect: Proverbs 29:11 says, "Fools vent their anger, but the wise quietly hold it back." Have you been known to lose your cool on a bad day? If you said no, would your spouse or children or closest friends agree? What are some of the dangers of overreacting to a bad situation?

TOMATO CANS

SOME WOULD SAY you have to be a little off in the head to be a boxer. You really have to be off in the head to be a paid stiff. That's what Bruce "The Mouse" Strauss was. A tomato can, as they say. A guy who gets to fight because he's almost certain to lose. Young fighters on their way up need victories, so they schedule fights against the likes of The Mouse, who, by the way, was knocked out on every continent except one: Antarctica.

So one night The Mouse was knocked out in the second bout of a nine-bout card. When he woke up, he overheard the promoter saying that a heavyweight who was supposed to fight in the evening's main event hadn't shown up. Seeing a chance to make some extra money, The Mouse left and came back in different clothes, volunteering to fill in for the AWOL heavyweight. Naturally, he was recognized and told to get lost, but he claimed to be his own twin brother, and the promoter, who was desperate, allowed him to fight. He was, predictably, knocked out for the second time that night.

The Mouse reminds us of people we've known who seem to not mind getting beat up. And we're not talking about boxers. We're talking about people who subject themselves to consistent mistreatment, whether it's at home at the hands of an abusive family member or at work at the hands of an unreasonable boss. It's true that hardship is a part of life, and no one should turn tail and run just because of a little conflict. But when someone is clearly beating you up, it's time to make some changes. God expects you to be patient and long-suffering, even forgiving. But he doesn't ask you to be a punching bag.

GOD EXPECTS YOU TO BE PATIENT AND LONG-SUFFERING, EVEN FORGIVING. BUT HE DOESN'T ASK YOU TO BE A PUNCHING BAG.

Reflect: Ecclesiastes 3:5 says, "There is a time to embrace, and a time to turn away." Are you currently suffering consistent mistreatment that shows no sign of stopping? If so, what can you do to stop it? Why haven't you done something already?

BE NICE

FROM THE 1950S to the 1990s, Howard Cosell was involved in sports broadcasting. He was highly intelligent and as articulate as any broadcaster who ever lived. His most famous gig, Monday Night Football, turned him into a household name. In fact, *TV Guide* named him the All-Time Best Sportscaster in its issue celebrating the first forty years of television. His signature call came anytime a player broke into the clear and was racing for the end zone: "He ... could ... go ... all ... the way!"

But Howard Cosell was not a nice man, and he freely admitted it and seemed proud of it. Very few people encountered him without getting cursed at or yelled at or demeaned in some way. Broadcaster Marv Albert tells the story of the time early in his career when he called Howard Cosell and asked for some career advice. Cosell said, "I don't care about you. I get calls like this all the time. Guys like you are a dime a dozen." Then he hung up.[16]

You meet people like this from time to time. Often, as was the case with Howard Cosell, they are highly intelligent, exceptionally gifted, and in a position of authority or power. If they weren't, they'd never be able to get away with being so rude. Imagine a bottom-rung-of-the-ladder employee walking around insulting everyone in the workplace. He'd be gone in a flash! But that guy who is the meal ticket for the organization can get away with a lot.

We encourage you to be nice to people. It's not as if being nice is hard. To smile and greet people warmly and put up with a few idiosyncrasies requires so little time and energy, but it makes a huge difference in the atmosphere of your home or workplace. It will also make a big difference in your legacy.

Reflect: Ephesians 4:32 says, "Be kind to one another." Do you find yourself apologizing a lot for saying hurtful things? Do you find that people seem to walk on eggshells around you or avoid you when something upsets you? What needs to change in your heart so that you can become a kinder person?

NOTHING IS EASY

A COMMON STATEMENT that is made about great athletes is that they make what they do look easy. A batter steps into the box to start the game and hits the very first pitch into the upper deck for a home run. Wow, that was easy. A wide receiver streaks down the sideline and catches a sixty-yard bomb perfectly in stride and hauls it into the end zone. Just like taking candy from a baby.

But is it really?

Jim Fregosi was a major-league shortstop and manager. One day when he was playing shortstop, he booted a ground ball that led to the winning run scoring and a loss for his team. The next day in the paper, a sportswriter made the comment that the game would have been won if Fregosi hadn't booted an easy ground ball. Livid, Fregosi approached the writer at his next opportunity and said with considerable heat (and we're paraphrasing here) that in the big leagues, there's no such thing as an easy ground ball.

We agree with Jim. Even what appears to be the simplest, most routine endeavors can become more difficult depending on the situation. There's this little thing called "pressure" that can up the ante considerably. You also have to factor in all kinds of other variables, such as how the person feels at that moment … his health, his emotional state, his recent success or lack thereof. Our view is that even things that look easy often aren't, so don't belittle people for making mistakes. Show them grace and give them encouragement. There will no doubt come a day when *you'll* be the one who just blew it.

Reflect: Proverbs 10:32 says, "The lips of the godly speak helpful words." Do you have a talent that demands a lot from you but that people think looks easy? How do you react when they don't seem to appreciate the difficulty of your work? Can you think of a benefit of doing something so well that it looks easy?

EVERYBODY NEEDS A COACH

COACHING IS AN essential part of the fabric of sports. Coaches are like players in the sense that there are great ones, decent ones, and bad ones. If you land a great one, you've got a real treasure.

Good coaching involves several things. The ability to motivate players, x's and o's, and game planning are among the most important. Not every coach is good at all of these. That's why there are assistant coaches. Many a head coach will tell you that without his assistants, he wouldn't have a prayer of being successful. This is especially true in football, where there are so many different units: offense, defense, special teams, etc.

One of the ways coaches are evaluated is player development. In other words, do players get better under their tutelage? They should, for that's the whole point of coaching … helping players, and ultimately teams, reach their full potential.

We feel it's important to have a coach in life. Not someone with a whistle and a clipboard who follows you around and makes you run laps if you mess up, but someone who can help you reach your potential. Your coach could be a close friend who believes in you, a mentor that you look up to, a pastor, teacher, or even a relative. The possibilities are many.

We would like to suggest that you let God coach you too. Of course, he is much more than a coach, but through his Word, the Bible, he speaks to every situation you could ever face in life. He offers wisdom, instruction, correction, encouragement, motivation … everything you need to be able to reach your potential. And the good news? He won't yell and scream at you and make you run laps if you mess up!

Reflect: 1 Timothy 4:8 says, "Physical training is good, but training for godliness is much better, promising benefits in this life and in the life to come." Can you name a coach—athletic or otherwise—that had a profound impact on you? What was it about that person that you appreciated most? To what degree are you allowing God to coach you through his word?

OCTOBER 1, 1961

ON THE ABOVE DATE, I (Mark) was six years old, too young to understand or appreciate what was happening in the Bronx as Roger Maris hit his sixty-first home run, breaking Babe Ruth's thirty-four-year-old record. I've since read a lot about that historic chase for the record and find myself wishing I could have enjoyed it with an adult's understanding of what was really happening. It was a time when America was breathless, hanging on every pitch.

Roger Maris was a nice guy, by all accounts. He was quiet and humble, well liked. But it didn't matter; a lot of people were rooting against him. I mean, we're talking about Babe Ruth's record. You just don't mess with the Babe, especially in New York.

And Maris felt the heat. Teammates talk about how he began losing his hair. He was twenty-seven years old, but his hair was falling out of his head. His doctor told him it was stress and that it would grow back. People also talked about how sullen he seemed, but it wasn't because he was ill tempered; it was because he didn't like the spotlight, didn't like being followed everywhere and having microphones shoved in his face.

Times of stress come to us all. Sometimes, as was the case with Maris, there's nothing you can do to remove the cause of the stress. You can only press on and hang in there until the situation resolves itself. Hanging in there is a lot easier when you're walking with God. His word can offer insights and encouragement, and his Spirit can give you the strength you need to keep plowing forward. As a pastor for forty-seven years, I have actually been amazed at what some people have been able to endure because of their faith.

Reflect: The apostle Paul said, "I can do everything through Christ, who gives me strength" (Phil. 4:13). Is there stress in your life right now? If so, what is the source? Is it something you have control over? What can you do to make the situation better? Are you drawing strength from your relationship with God, or has your situation pulled you away from him?

REPUTATION

DAVE WINFIELD WAS an extraordinary athlete, so extraordinary that when he came out of the University of Minnesota, he was drafted by four professional teams in three different sports. He was even drafted by the Minnesota Vikings even though he never played college football, a true testament to how big and strong and athletic he was. But he ended up being a baseball player and spent several years with the Yankees.

During those Yankee years, he sued George Steinbrenner for refusing to pay the $300,000 a year to his foundation that was stipulated in his contract. Steinbrenner, in his anger, retaliated by paying a shady character named Howie Spira $40,000 to uncover some dirt on Winfield. When the plot against Winfield became public, the Commissioner of Baseball suspended Steinbrenner from being involved in the Yankees operations for two years. What we like is that Steinbrenner and his paid flunky weren't able to find anything that would sully Dave Winfield's reputation.

We've heard it said that everybody has a skeleton or two in a closet. We disagree. Yes, everybody makes mistakes, and we surely all have things in our past that are cringeworthy, that we regret, or that we would be embarrassed to have made known. But that's life! The key to building a good reputation is not to keep yourself from ever making a mistake but to keep yourself from compromising your values.

We think it's ironic that Mr. Steinbrenner, in trying to dig up some dirt on someone else, threw a shovelful of dirt on his own reputation. There's a kind of poetic justice in that, and a reminder to us all to watch our own p's and q's and not stick our noses into other people's business.

Reflect: Proverbs 22:1 says, "Choose a good reputation over great riches; being held in high esteem is better than silver or gold." Do you think building a good reputation is more about what you do or what you don't do? If someone hired an individual to dig up dirt on you, how successful would he be? What might be some ways you could improve your reputation if it is a bit soiled?

PASSION CHASING

IT'S ALREADY BEEN mentioned in this book that I (Pat) have run fifty-eight marathons. I'll never forget the time my wife, Ruth, and I were in Manhattan preparing to run in the New York City Marathon. While we were there, we walked into a Barnes & Noble bookstore where we had a chance to meet syndicated columnist George Will. When we told him that we were in town to run in the marathon, he said, "Why?"

The question made me think. Why *was* I there? Why *was* I going to put myself through such a physical test? The only answer I could come up with was that I didn't know. Somehow it was uncontrollable, like I was being drawn to it by some invisible magnetic force. Call it an urge or a passion, whatever you want. It's that mysterious pull that reels you in like a fish on the end of a line.

This is why we tell our children to do what they love … to find something that offers an attraction they are unable to resist. It is in this passionate pursuit that they will find their greatest happiness.

Unfortunately, a lot of people never chase their passion. They settle for something else simply because it's safer or easier or the opportunity is more readily available. It reminds me of that old saying that is so very true: When you come to the end of your life, it won't be the things you did that will trouble you the most; it will be the things you didn't do.

Get out there and do that thing that is pulling at you. Give it a shot. Even if it doesn't work out, you won't have to live with the regret that comes from knowing you never even tried.

Reflect: 2 Chronicles 15:7 says, "But as for you, be strong and courageous, for your work will be rewarded." Do you have a passion? Are you chasing it? If not, why? Think of some things you need to do in order to put your passion on the front burner of your life.

SOMETHING PEOPLE NEVER FORGET

JIM HICKMAN PLAYED thirteen seasons in the big leagues with the Mets, Dodgers, Cubs, and Cardinals. In what has to be a rarity, all four of his managers ended up in the Hall of Fame: Casey Stengel, Leo Durocher, Red Schoendienst, and Walter Alston.

Jim Hickman was a good player, but one season he had a miserable year. In just ninety-eight at bats, he hit .163. You'd think that would be a year he'd want to forget, but actually one of his favorite memories comes from that season. On two separate occasions, Walter Alston took him into his office and thanked him for having a great attitude, for working hard in practice, and for always encouraging his teammates. After all these years, Jim still remembers and cherishes those conversations.

It's true of all of us … we remember people who are kind and encouraging to us when we're going through a hard time. Often people will shy away from someone who's going through a difficult time, because they don't know how to help or even what to say. Many struggling people talk about how their friends seem to disappear when times get hard. It's where the term "fair-weather friends" comes from. Most people don't mean to become fair-weather friends; it just happens.

Here's a suggestion that might help you avoid becoming a fair-weather friend to someone in your life who is struggling. Don't think you have to explain their struggles or offer answers for what will solve their problems. Most of the time, they don't really even want that. They just want to know somebody cares. If you just stay available and offer kind, encouraging words, they will never forget you.

Reflect: Proverbs 18:24 says, "A real friend sticks closer than a brother." Have you ever had friends disappear when you were going through hard times? Have you ever hesitated to reach out to a struggling friend because you didn't know what to say? Is there someone you know right now who is struggling … someone you should reach out to?

WHEN MONEY MAKES YOU A FOOL

IT'S TAX DAY! We know you're thrilled about this. There's nothing better than forking over a huge chunk of your income to the government, knowing that the government has turned wasting money into an art form and that they are, even now, plotting to raise your taxes again. So to help you celebrate this wonderful day, we offer a couple of money-related stories.

First, good ole Mike Tyson. You may remember that he was married to the actress Robin Givens. One Christmas he was puzzled about what to get her. He finally settled on a bathtub. You might be nodding your approval, thinking, "That's a nice, unique gift." Would you change your tune if you knew the bathtub cost $2 million? It did. And apparently Robin wasn't enthralled with the gift either, judging by how quickly the marriage ended.

And then there was boxer Floyd Mayweather. He was notorious for throwing money around, but surely one of his most extravagant purchases was a $50,000 iPod case studded with diamonds. Then, wouldn't you know it … a new iPod came out (which Floyd just had to have) that didn't fit the old case, rendering it obsolete. He might have sold it on eBay, but who can afford that kind of money for an iPod case?

It's easy to make fun of people who do such ridiculous things with their money. But we wonder if the only thing keeping a lot of us from being that dumb is simply the fact that we don't have that kind of money. If someone were to examine your financial choices, would they gain respect for you or lose it? We advise you to be very careful when and if money starts flowing more freely into your life. It can turn you into a fool if you're not careful.

Reflect: Proverbs 23:5 says, "In the blink of an eye wealth disappears, for it will sprout wings and fly away like an eagle." What's the most extravagant purchase you ever made? Did you have buyer's remorse afterward? What are some factors it's wise to consider when making an expensive purchase?

THROW AWAY THE COOKIE CUTTER

PHIL JACKSON WAS a great NBA coach. People say, "Well of course he was. Look at how many great players he had, and maybe the greatest of them all ... Michael Jordan." Actually, handling that kind of elite talent is not easy, because along with the talent, you also get the egos. But Jackson knew what he was doing.

One thing that made him great was that he spent one-on-one time with all of his players. This was not easy for a couple of reasons. One was simply time. An NBA coach is a busy man who works long hours. Another reason is that Phil was so very different from a lot of his players. He was a couple of generations older than his rookies and from a far different background and upbringing. It would have been so much easier just to talk basketball with the guys and let that be it. But no, Phil was determined to treat his players as individuals and really get to know them.

We think it's remarkable that, at Christmastime, Phil would buy his players a book that he thought might help them grow as men. But he didn't just buy fifteen copies of the same book and pass it out. He bought each player a unique book that was chosen just for him.

Phil Jackson threw away the cookie cutter in his relationships with people. We recommend that you do the same, especially if you have the kind of life or job where you deal with a number of different people. That staff you work with at your church, that crew you work with on the job site, those customers who wander in and out of your place of business, they are unique individuals. You give them an amazing gift when you treat them as such.

And here's something else: You give yourself an amazing gift too. Among those people you get to know on a deeper level, you will find amazing friends who will enrich your life.

Reflect: Romans 12:5 says, "We all belong to each other." Have you ever felt that people you've been acquainted with for a long time didn't really know you? Have you ever made a wonderful discovery about someone you thought you knew? Are there people in your life you need to get to know better?

TONGUE TALK

SADLY, IT'S HARD to be a sports fan without hearing some cursing. Your intrepid authors once attended a Cardinals game in St. Louis and sat right by the dugout. (This was in the days before instant replay.) When a close play at the plate went against the Cardinals, Tony La Russa came flying out of the dugout spewing some of the vilest four-letter words you can imagine with astonishing enthusiasm. The umpire was not impressed, but most of the fans were cheering and egging Tony on.

Even Christian coaches who speak openly about their faith have been known to curse. Jeff Duke coached for Bobby Bowden for three years and said that he heard him curse three times, though each time he used a word that by most people's standards would be considered mild.

> WE'RE NOT HERE TO JUDGE, BUT IT IS OUR CONVICTION THAT PARTICIPATION IN SPORTS PRESENTS CHRISTIANS WITH A UNIQUE OPPORTUNITY TO LET THEIR LIGHTS SHINE.

We're not here to judge, but it is our conviction that participation in sports presents Christians with a unique opportunity to let their lights shine. Fans have come to expect tantrums and cursing. And why shouldn't they? Over the years we've seen epic meltdowns that have resulted in everything from dirt kicked on umpires to watercoolers destroyed to chairs thrown across basketball courts. It's when such things *don't* happen in the heat of battle that the world is shown a better way.

Tony Dungy is an example of a coach who understood the opportunity he had to let his light shine. In a sport (NFL football) that might produce more profanity per play than any other, players say they never heard him curse. Players such as the colorful and sometimes profane Warren Sapp still talk about Tony's self-discipline and how it won their respect.

Christians are called to be different, to live by a higher standard. It's OK to be frustrated, but we encourage you to watch your mouth.

Reflect: Ephesians 4:29 says, "Don't use foul or abusive language." Why do you think sports is so associated with foul language? Some have said that cursing in the heat of competition doesn't really count. Do you agree or disagree? How would you rate your own self-control?

OOPS!

THE YEAR WAS 1969; the American Football League had just merged with the National Football League, and commissioner Pete Rozelle had an idea. Since football was growing in popularity, why not do something really outside the box, like having a weekly game played sometime other than on Sunday afternoon. Like, say, maybe Monday night?

Rozelle approached CBS with the idea, thinking they would jump at the opportunity. They declined because they didn't want to bump their Monday night prime time hit, *The Doris Day Show*. So Rozelle turned to NBC and found them reluctant to buy in as well. After all, their Monday night hit was *Laugh-In*. Everyone loved *Laugh-In*! NBC did reconsider, however, when Rozelle threatened to take *Monday Night Football* to the Hughes Network. Looking back, CBS executives must have kicked themselves. *MNF* turned into one of the most popular and longest-running programs in history.

Is there a decision in your life that haunts you? Did you once take a pass on an opportunity that would have dramatically changed your life? Does it make you cringe every time you think about it? Allow us to offer two suggestions on how you can make peace with that decision.

First, cut yourself some slack. All decisions would be easy if you could foresee the future, but you can't. Brilliant people make countless decisions every day that will prove to be unfortunate. Remember, Decca Records executives rejected the Beatles in favor of Brian Poole and the Tremeloes.

And second, keep moving forward. CBS may not have gotten *MNF*, but the network has done better than OK over the years. Just because you made a bad decision yesterday doesn't mean you can't make a good one today.

Reflect: Philippians 3:13–14 says, "Forgetting the past and looking forward to what lies ahead, I press on ..." What process do you work through when you're faced with a big decision? When a decision you make doesn't turn out well, how do you process it? Do you believe unfortunate decisions can actually work to your benefit?

IF MAMA ISN'T HAPPY, THEN NOBODY'S HAPPY

YOU'VE HEARD THE saying a thousand times. Maybe said it that many times. We're not sure when it originated, but it might have been after a light heavyweight boxing match back in 1989.

The boxer's name was Tony Wilson. He was fighting a spirited fellow named Steve McCarthy, who had him on the ropes. McCarthy had knocked him down in the third round and was looking to finish him off. With Wilson on the ropes taking a beating, the unthinkable happened. Tony Wilson's sixty-two-year-old mother climbed into the ring and started beating Steve McCarthy over the head with her shoe. She opened a gash in McCarthy's head that would require four stitches to close and, in a decision that adds new meaning to the word "controversial," Wilson was named the winner on a technical knockout.

As you might guess, a near-riot ensued. Wilson's mother had to be hustled out of the room by a security guard. When the dust settled, the commissioners of the sport ordered a rematch, but it never happened.

This bizarre incident serves as a reminder to us all that, no matter how much you might want to step into a situation and get involved, it's often best to stay out of it. Parents, for example, make a terrible mistake when they try to fight their kids' battles (with some exceptions, of course). Kids need to learn to stand on their own two feet. And they need to learn that life, to a great extent, is about learning to cope with failure.

As a parent, you won't always be around to fix things for your kids. The last thing you want to do is shelter and protect them so much that they become weak and helpless.

Reflect: James 3:2 says, "Indeed, we all make many mistakes." Have you ever had someone (a parent, perhaps?) step into your business to try to help you, only to end up doing more harm than good? Why do you think it's important to struggle on your own, even if you fail from time to time?

CLICHÉS

PERHAPS THE WORST thing about any professional sporting event is the postgame interview. A reporter sticks a microphone in the face of a player who's just coming off of an adrenaline rush and asks him or her the very same question he asked the day before, and the day before that, and the day before that. So naturally, the player gives the very same response that yesterday's player gave, and the one before that, and the one before that.

Baseball: "I just tried to see the ball and hit it."

Basketball: "My teammates got me the ball."

Football: "It was a hard-hitting game."

Duh, duh, and duh.

The sporting world is not the only place you run into clichés. Hang around Christians very long, and you'll hear them too.

"Let go and let God."

"You can't out-give God."

"When God closes a door, he opens a window."

"Let's do life together."

"God must've needed an angel." (When someone dies.)

Sometimes I don't blame unbelievers for rolling their eyes when Christians speak. So many of our favorite sayings are as stale as month-old bread. We encourage you to disdain clichés. Don't try to sound spiritual. Just be real. Speak from your heart. You'll have a much stronger witness if you do.

Reflect: Jesus said in Matthew 12:36, "You must give an account on judgment day for every idle word you speak." In your opinion, what makes a word "idle"? Clichés may seem harmless, but are they really? What could be some of the negative results of using a lot of religious clichés?

BETTER LATE THAN NEVER

IN SPORTS, WE are obsessed with speed. We cheer for those who run or pedal or ski or sled or drive the fastest. But we have a story for you about someone who was slow—really slow—and deserves a standing ovation. His name was Shizo Kanakuri, and he just happens to have the slowest Olympic marathon time in history. He crossed the finish line after 54 years, 8 months, 6 days, 8 hours, 32 minutes, and 20.379 seconds.

This is not a joke.

Shizo started his marathon in 1912 and finished it in 1966. You see, in 1912 he got sick and passed out. A local family took care of him, but by the time he was feeling better, the race was over, so he took a train home. Olympic officials never knew what happened to him and listed him as a missing person.

In 1966, it was discovered that he was still alive, so he was contacted and asked if he wanted to finish the race. At the age of seventy-five, he went back to Stockholm and finished. Thus he was able to say that between the start and the finish of his race, he got married and had six children and ten grandchildren. Better late than never, right?

Better late than never is a concept we believe in and strongly recommend.

Apologizing to someone you offended? Better late than never.

Going after your dream? Better late than never.

Getting that diploma? Better late than never.

Overcoming that bad habit? Better late than never.

Getting serious about your marriage? Better late than never.

It's better if you can do the right thing in the moment. Timeliness is good. But it's never too late to do the right thing.

Reflect: 2 Corinthians 8:11 says, "Now you should finish what you started." Can you name something worthwhile that's unfinished in your life? What kept you from finishing? What's keeping you from going back and trying again?

ANTISOCIAL MEDIA

SOME HAVE QUESTIONED whether the rise of social media has triggered the decline of Western civilization. It's impossible to count the social media disasters that have embarrassed and shamed people, and new ones are happening every day. And it's not just because of individuals being dumb, though that's part of it. Even well-intentioned companies and organizations have ended up red faced.

In 2014, the New York Mets launched a social media campaign using the hashtag #IAmAMetsFanBecause. They expected to get all kinds of heartwarming tweets about the origins of people's love for the Mets. Instead, Mets haters—in particular, Yankees fans—saw an opportunity. They started chiming in with denigrating comments, such as, "I am a Mets fan because it is marginally less painful than smashing your hand with a hammer." (That's one of the milder, printable examples.)

We admit there is some humor in this debacle. Fans of competing franchises will always troll each other. It is a cautionary tale, however.

Things can go wrong quickly and easily in the world of social media because there are millions of people who have their noses in their phones all day long, just looking for someone to pounce on. And sometimes it's not just innocent fun. Even a comment with no ill intent behind it can be blasted as racist or bigoted or misogynistic. With the definition of what's politically correct (PC) constantly changing, it's almost impossible to stay out of the way of the PC mob.

Here are two suggestions:

One, don't let social media take over your life. Use it sparingly.

Two, stay above the fray. Nothing good can come from you being a part of the daily social media food fight. If you want to try to change the world, there are a thousand better ways to do it.

Reflect: James 3:17 says, "But the wisdom from above is first of all pure. It is also peace loving ..." How much time do you spend on social media each day? If it's a lot, why do you think you're so attached to it? Can you think of some ways social media might be diminishing you? Have you ever considered taking a social media sabbatical? What could be the benefits if you did?

THE RAZOR'S EDGE

BICYCLE RACERS ARE some of the fittest athletes around. Finding a half ounce of body fat on one of them is like finding a palm tree at the North Pole. And racers are always looking for ways to increase their times. One way they can do it is by shaving their legs.

Wind tunnel experiments have proven that a racer with shaved legs has a competitive advantage over a racer with unshaved legs. You wouldn't think those tiny hairs would make a difference, but they do. But it's not just an aerodynamics issue. Hairy-legged riders are much more apt to develop infected sores if they fall and scrape their skin. And a trip to the masseuse will be much simpler if all those little hairs don't get tangled and knotted during a postrace rubdown. Who would have imagined that a razor and some shaving cream would give an athlete such advantages?

It's also true in spiritual endeavors that small disciplines can make a positive difference. One reason we're writing this devotional book is because we know that just a few minutes of positive reflection and prayer on a key thought and a verse of Scripture can make a big difference in your life. There are 168 hours in a week. If you spend just 10 minutes a day reading, reflecting, and praying, you would still have 166 hours and 50 minutes left. Such a discipline would be hardly a drop in the bucket, but those 70 minutes could someday be what makes the difference between a good and bad decision. Just having your head and heart right at a key moment could save you untold heartache.

The difference between success and failure is often smaller than we think. That small discipline that seems so insignificant could be what saves your life.

Reflect: 1 Corinthians 9:25 says, "All athletes are disciplined in their training. They do it to win a prize that will fade away, but we do it for an eternal prize." Can you name some things you routinely do that fall into the category of personal discipline? Are there things you've tried to work into your routine without success? What changes could you make that would help you find success?

MEET YOU AT THE FIRST TEE

HAVE YOU EVER wondered how many golf balls are lost every year? I (Mark) googled it, and the answer was 300 million. That's 300 million bad golf shots a year, shanking, slicing, hooking, and rolling balls into forests and ditches and bodies of water. I'd estimate that at least a thousand of those are mine.

Don't you wonder why people continue to play a sport they're terrible at? Millions of people every day trudge to the golf course dragging a heavy set of clubs, knowing full well they are going to spend hours hacking and chopping and throwing chunks of sod and splashes of sand into the air, only to finish frustrated and disappointed with their final score more often than not. And to think that they even pay for this privilege! Why would any sane person do this?

The answer is we love the company.

With very few exceptions, recreational golf is a game we play with our friends. We might hit balls on the range and practice our putting and talk about bettering our scores, but the truth is, we weekend hackers know we're never going to be much better than we are. We might hope for that epic round or memorable shot, but for the most part, we play because we enjoy the camaraderie.

All the way back at the beginning of time, God said that it wasn't good for man to be alone. That means he built the need for fellowship into our DNA. Nobody was thinking about golf at the time, but golf and a million other activities have sprung out of our love of being with friends and enjoying time together. So whatever you do that connects you with your friends, cherish it and thank God for it. It's something he made you for. He smiles at your fun friend times, even if you are driving a ball right into the water.

Reflect: In Genesis 2:18 God said, "It is not good for the man to be alone." Do you ever feel lonely? If so, how often? If you feel that you could use some more friends, what are some steps you could take to find some? Are there any old friends you need to reconnect with?

WHAT'S WRONG WITH THIS PICTURE?

ROCKY **IS ONE OF** the classic sports movies of all time, written by and starring Sylvester Stallone. The picture was made for about $1 million and earned $225 million at box offices around the world. Not bad.

Mr. Stallone has talked about trying to fill the part of Clubber Lang. He thought it would be cool to have "Smokin' Joe" Frazier in the film and figured he would make a good Clubber. So he invited Joe to a sparring session. He thought they could move around the ring together and get a feel for what it would be like to film the scenes. Stallone thought he'd just dodge a few punches and that would be that.

Wrong.

Smokin' Joe started landing bombs to Stallone's head and ribs. He said that one overhand right felt like a piano had landed on his head. In that moment, as he saw stars, Stallone decided that Smokin'

Joe would get a small cameo, and the Clubber Lang part would go to Mr. T.

Sometimes we have what we think is a good idea, but then when we put the pieces in place, it doesn't work like we thought it would. Unfortunately, some people continue to plow forward in denial, thinking that somehow, some way, things will work out. Like the girl who sees alarming character traits in the guy she's dating but marries him anyway. Or the guy who feels uneasy about the job he's being offered but takes it anyway.

LIFE HAS A WAY OF SENDING SIGNALS.

It's a mark of wisdom to walk away from something enticing because you're getting a bad feeling. Life has a way of sending signals. The difference between a good life and a troubled life often boils down to whether you heed those signals.

Reflect: Proverbs 4:8 says, "If you prize wisdom, she will make you great. Embrace her, and she will honor you." Have you ever charged into a bad situation because you didn't heed warning signs? What made you think everything would be OK? What did you learn about yourself through that experience?

ROLE MODELING

MANY PEOPLE, ESPECIALLY young people, look up to athletes. It's nice when those athletes understand this and do their best to set a good example.

One such athlete is Carli Lloyd. She's just about as good a soccer player as there is, a four-time Olympian and two-time gold medal winner. She scored the gold medal–winning goals in the finals of both the 2008 and 2012 Summer Olympics. Here's something she wrote that we love:

> I've been approached by *ESPN The Magazine* to pose in the body issue. *Dancing with the Stars* has reached out to me, and so has *Maxim* magazine for a photo shoot that I'm pretty sure would have had more to do with skin than soccer. Thanks, but no thanks. A number of prominent athletes— soccer players among them—have been featured in the *Sports Illustrated* swimsuit issue and other publications. It is not a decision I am judging in any way. To each her own. I'm sure

they feel proud of their bodies and see no reason not to show them off. It's just not for me. I want to be a role model, not a runway model. I want to be known for the body of work of my career. If that makes me old fashioned or out of step with the times, so be it.[17]

We wish more people were "old fashioned" and "out of step with the times." In a world where traditional values are getting harder and harder to find, it's refreshing to find someone of influence who is so well grounded. We especially like how Carli doesn't judge others but is simply determined to be true to what she believes. That is the essence of good character.

Reflect: Romans 12:2 says, "Don't copy the behavior and customs of this world …" Have you ever been called "old fashioned" or "out of touch"? Can you point to sacrifices you have made or opportunities you have declined because you were concerned about your witness? How do you determine what is acceptable and unacceptable for you to do?

THE GOLDEN BEAR'S SECRET

PEOPLE IN THIS generation think of Tiger Woods when someone brings up the subject of great golfers. People of our generation think of Jack Nicklaus, known as The Golden Bear. Jack was Tiger before Tiger was Tiger, and if you judge by the number of majors won, Jack still holds the edge.

Naturally, everybody wants to know the secrets of the world's great performers in any field of endeavor, especially golfers because there are so many weekend hackers who'd like to knock a couple of strokes off their handicaps. So what is a trick or a technique Jack might share? He doesn't have one. Not even one. He has said many times that he is all about the fundamentals. In other words, he believes all golfers should do the very same things: line up properly, hold the club properly, have good balance, etc. Great golf doesn't come from gimmicks or tricks; it comes from doing basic things well and repeating them over and over again.

The same can be said of the life of faith. Many believers are always looking for some kind of gimmick to help them be more faithful. Remember the "What Would Jesus Do?" bracelet from a few years ago? They were selling like hotcakes, the perfect aid to living the Christian life. But now they're long gone, relics of a bygone era. Apparently, wearing them didn't suddenly make people more spiritual after all.

The Christian life is lived best by people who focus on the fundamentals: faith, Bible study, prayer, service, giving. There's nothing fancy or glamorous in any of it. In fact, these things can be hard. But a million trends and gimmicks and bestsellers and catchy slogans have come and gone while these things remain.

Take it from The Golden Bear ... greatness comes from doing basic things well and repeating them over and over and over again.

Reflect: Micah 6:8 says, "This is what he requires of you: to do what is right, to love mercy, and to walk humbly with your God." What gimmicks or passing fads have you tried during your Christian walk? How long did you stick with them? Do you excel at the fundamentals listed above, or do you need to step up your game?

WORDS SPEAK LOUDER THAN ACTIONS

WE KNOW YOU'VE heard it the other way around: Actions speak louder than words.

But sometimes it's the opposite. Sometimes people can roll along giving every appearance of good sense and self-control, then something happens, and they lose it. What comes out of their mouths reveals what their previous conduct never did.

Take Bryan Price, for example. He was managing the Cincinnati Reds in 2015. The Reds had just lost their fourth game in a row. It was only April, so there was no reason to panic. But someone in the Cincinnati media had reported that catcher Devin Mesoraco was not with the team in St. Louis, which Bryan felt gave the Cardinals an advantage. To say he voiced his displeasure would be an understatement. He went on an epic rant that included seventy-seven f-bombs. As meltdowns go, it was the stuff of legend.

I (Mark) have had many instances over the years where, as a pastor, I encountered people who seemed perfectly godly and sweet spirited and poised, only to later observe them in a stressful or frustrating moment and be shocked at what came out of their mouths. Think Dr. Jekyll and Mr. Hyde. When such things happen, my eyes pop open and I think, "Who are you? You're not the person I thought I knew!" It's a case of the person's words speaking louder than his or her actions.

Our challenge to you is to remember that when something bad happens, something that ticks you off big time, your duty to put forth a Christian witness isn't suddenly suspended. God would never say, "Oh go ahead and let 'er rip. I'll put my fingers in my ears." Rather, that's the moment when the depth of your character and commitment is revealed.

> *Reflect:* James 3:10 says, "And so blessing and cursing come pouring out of the same mouth. Surely, my brothers and sisters, this is not right!" Have you ever melted down and lost control of your mouth? Did you apologize to the people who heard you? To God? What do you think that incident said about you? Have you taken any measures to keep it from happening again?

PRESSURE

THERE'S PRESSURE IN professional athletics. Part of it comes from the competitive spirit of the athletes. They want to win. Even if they weren't getting paid a dime, the great ones would still have that drive. But there's also the money and the fact that some younger, very talented, and much less expensive athlete has his eye on the old veteran's job. You can bet that every grizzled veteran remembers when he or she was just getting started and trying to earn a spot on the team, one that likely belonged to some older player who was trying to hang on.

So what's the secret to handling pressure?

Let's face it. Some people are just good at it. Jack Nicklaus, for example, seemed unflappable. And who would question that Michael Jordan was born for the big moments? But we like what Goose Gossage, a former big-league relief pitcher said. He often came in with the game on the line where one bad pitch could ruin everything. He said, "Every time I come into a game, I think of my home in the

Rockies, and that relaxes me. And I tell myself the worst thing that could happen is that I'd be home fishing there tomorrow."[18]

Beautiful!

One way to cope with pressure is to stop and think about what is the worst thing that could happen. Pressure gets a stranglehold on us when we allow ourselves to believe that failure would be catastrophic. But often it isn't catastrophic at all. It might be disappointing. It might be frustrating or maybe even a little embarrassing. But most of the time we go right on with our lives and don't look back.

Goose had it right. Don't blow things out of proportion. Failure isn't the end of the world. When the worst-case scenario is that you get to go fishing, you can relax and enjoy the moment.

Reflect: Jesus said in Luke 12:25, "Can all your worries add a single moment to your life?" Based on your experience, how well do you perform under pressure? Have there been opportunities you have turned down because you felt intense pressure? What are some reasons why failure is often thought to be worse than it actually is?

A WORD TO LIVE BY

DABO SWINNEY IS the NCAA football national championship-winning coach of the Clemson Tigers and a devout Christian. Two things are often said about Coach Swinney: the man can coach, and the man can talk. To say he has the gift of gab would be like calling the Grand Canyon a little hole in the ground.

At the same time, Dabo understands that when it comes to leading young men, there can be too many words in play. That's why, every year, he picks one word to be his team's theme throughout the season. Not a sentence or a quip ... just a word. And often it's a small word. A simple word.

One year he chose the word "love." Not a very macho, tough-sounding word, but one that he felt communicated an essential priority. "Guys, we gotta love what we do: love the grind, love each other, love your school. Be passionate."[19] The young men bought in and won the national championship over a formidable Alabama squad, 35–31.

We would never suggest that a single word drummed into the head of those players was the reason Clemson won, but it surely didn't hurt. There must have been many moments during the year—moments of fatigue and frustration and discouragement—when those young men stopped to think about how much they loved their teammates and the game they were privileged to play and then sucked it up and dove back into the work.

In a world where words flow in torrents and threaten to bury us, often it's a single, well-chosen word that clarifies things and brings us back to the center.

Reflect: In Matthew 12:37 Jesus said, "The words you say will either acquit you or condemn you." If you had to pick one word to describe your life to this point, what would it be? If you had to pick one word to describe the life you dream of, what would it be? If you had to pick one word to describe what it would take to get there, what would it be?

SAND TRAP SENSE

SAND TRAPS WERE CONCEIVED in the pit of hell to bring misery to the human race. No one who has ever played a round of golf would disagree with this. Sand traps have probably spurred more curse words than anything else in sports. Millions of good rounds have died a violent, hacking death in a bunker.

This is why every newfangled sand wedge that comes along is a big hit. Just shape it a little different, give it a name like "Master Blaster," and make an infomercial that shows some dude using it to lob balls to within a foot of the cup, and you'll make big bucks.

Here's a question though: What if, instead of spending so much time and energy and money on learning how to get out of a trap, a person channeled that time and energy and money into learning how to *stay* out of a trap? Ever hear the old saying, "An ounce of prevention is worth a pound of cure"? OK, maybe you couldn't *always* avoid traps, but what if you could cut your trap shots in half or more? Wouldn't that also be a way to lessen the sand's influence on your game?

There's something to be said for simply making fewer mistakes.

Take the person who comes dragging in to work with a hangover. He's disheveled, complaining about his headache, and

LEARNING HOW TO DEAL WITH BAD SITUATIONS IS FINE. LEARNING HOW TO HAVE FEWER OF THEM IS BETTER.

cursing the day he was born. He tells his office mate that he overdid it the night before, that he hates it when that happens. His office mate says, "Yeah, I used to do that too, but I learned my lesson and stopped."

Learning how to deal with bad situations is fine.

Learning how to have fewer of them is better.

Reflect: Colossians 3:5 says, "So put to death the sinful, earthly things lurking within you." Do you have a sin or weakness that has troubled you for years? What have you done to try to overcome it? Have you found that it's easier to cope with it than it is to eliminate it?

WARREN'S WIERSBE'S GREAT ADVICE

WARREN WIERSBE DIED on this date in 2019. It was a sad day for me (Pat) because of the influence he had on my life. It was way back in 1973, when I was the general manager (GM) of the Chicago Bulls, that I started attending Moody Church where Mr. Wiersbe was the pastor. I sat under his teaching for three years, which was a great blessing, and got to know him personally.

My career had taken off like a rocket. I was thirty-two years old and already the GM of an NBA team, but suddenly I was having struggles. A series of difficulties had come into my life, enough to cause me to question God. I remember thinking, "I'm your boy, Lord. What's going on here?"

Confused, I sat down to speak with Pastor Wiersbe. He listened attentively as I told him about the difficult things I was going through. I fully expected him to sympathize with me and try to encourage me. Instead, he leaned forward and said in a serious voice. "Pat, don't waste these sufferings." Then he added, "Sufferings help us become better people. We're all just well-fed housedogs if everything is peachy all the time."

It's one of the most important things anyone has ever said to me. I needed to hear it, especially since I had some even tougher things in my future: divorce, cancer, and the death of a child.

So I offer that same advice to you. Don't waste your sufferings by sitting around whining and complaining. Learn from them. Let them strengthen you and prepare you to be a help to others.

Reflect: James 1:2 says, "When troubles of any kind come your way, consider it an opportunity for great joy." Are you a whiner or complainer? Why do you think so many people are? Why is whining and complaining so damaging?

YOU GOTTA START SOMEWHERE

JOE BUCK IS ONE of the most recognized sportscasters around. He is the son of Hall of Fame broadcaster Jack Buck, who started announcing for the St. Louis Cardinals in 1954. On April 25, 1987, Joe was sitting in the booth while his dad and Mike Shannon called a Cardinals game against the Mets. He wasn't even paying attention to the game. He was brooding about the girl who'd just decided she didn't want to go to his high school prom with him. Suddenly his dad said, "Well, now, to take us through the fifth inning is my son, the birthday boy, Joe Buck."[20] Then he and Mike Shannon got up and walked out of the booth.

This is the broadcasting equivalent of a novice swimmer being picked up and thrown into the deep end of the pool. Joe says that, fortunately, it was a 1-2-3 inning and only lasted a few minutes. But it was a start. And maybe it was best that he didn't know what his dad was going to do. He didn't have a chance to get nervous or run away and hide.

The hardest thing about many endeavors is getting started, taking that first step. There are a few folks around who love to dive right into things, but most people are hesitant, timid, or nervous at the beginning of a new endeavor. The important thing is not how you feel about starting, but that you start. It's OK if you feel nervous. It's OK to *want* to run and hide, as long as you don't. Always remember that the first step is the hardest. They always get easier from there.

Reflect: Psalms 121:8 says, "The Lord keeps watch over you as you come and go, both now and forever." Is there something you've always wanted to do that you've been afraid to try? What has held you back from starting that journey? What do you need to do to clear the way so you can start?

DISHING OUT ASSISTS

MY ASSOCIATION WITH the Orlando Magic brought many wonderful people and experiences into my life (Pat). And that's before I begin to even think about the actual games. Among the most memorable games was one that was played against the Denver Nuggets on December 30, 1990, in Orlando. Our point guard at the time was Scott Skiles, a player we drafted the year before in the expansion draft. That night, everything came together in a way that rarely happens, and Scott dished out thirty assists, which was, and still is, an NBA record. An interesting sidebar is that Scott got thirteen of those assists in the fourth quarter alone. Most NBA guards would love to have thirteen assists in an entire game. As you might guess, with the ball moving around like that and our guys knocking down shots, we won the game 155–116.

The assist is a respected stat in basketball. It speaks to the self-lessness of a player, of his willingness to feed his teammates the ball and help the team excel. Assists are important in life too. Just about everywhere we go, we encounter people who could use some help. From the elderly person who needs to get to a doctor appointment but feels overwhelmed by the traffic, to the neighbor who just watched a storm drop a large tree limb on his porch, life offers us countless opportunities to lend a helping hand.

There are two secrets to being a good assist person.

One, live every day with your eyes open. Needs are all around, but you have to see them.

And two, never let yourself get too busy to reach out and help. Very rarely—perhaps never—will anything you're doing be more important than stopping to help someone in need.

Reflect: In Matthew 23:11, Jesus said, "The greatest among you must be a servant." What do you think of when you hear the word "servant"? Think of someone you know who epitomizes the idea of helping others. Are you like that? If not, what changes would you have to make to become like that?

YOUR WORST MOMENT

IMAGINE BEING A world-class athlete. Imagine being so good at something that only a few people in the world could even compete with you. And then imagine yourself being forever remembered for the worst moment you ever had in competition. Wouldn't that be awful?

It actually happened to Vinko Bogataj.

He was the skier who went flying head over heels off the ski ramp every week as ABC's *Wide World of Sports* came on the air. He was twenty-two years old at the time and competing for Yugoslavia in the 1970 Ski Flying World Championships in West Germany. ABC decided to use the tape of his horrifying run to mesh with Jim McKay's "agony of defeat" line, and suddenly our boy Vinko was permanently engraved on the minds of sports fans everywhere.

Lots of people are remembered for their worst moments. Politicians, celebrities, athletes, even pastors. They're good at what they do, but one unfortunate moment—usually one that could have been avoided—ends up haunting them forever. It isn't fair, you say? We agree! But whoever said this world was fair?

Our advice is for you to be intentional about eliminating those moments from your life. Yes, you're going to make mistakes … everyone does. Mistakes make you human. We're talking about those especially foolish choices that brand you forever. They can happen in a moment and change the way people think about you forever.

Here are three suggestions that will help you avoid one of those "agony of defeat" moments:

Choose your friends carefully.

Keep a clear head at all times.

Run at the first sign of trouble.

Reflect: The apostle Paul said to Timothy, "Run from anything that stimulates youthful lusts" (2 Tim. 2:22). Spiritually speaking, do you have an "agony of defeat" moment in your past? Can you put your finger on the primary cause of it? What do you believe is the main reason why people end up crashing?

THE $4.6 MILLION TITHE

KURT WARNER CAME out of nowhere to become one of the best quarterbacks in football. When he led the St. Louis Rams to the Super Bowl championship, he got his big contract. And by big, we mean $46 million. Because Kurt is open about his faith, it was inevitable that he would be asked by a reporter if he was going to tithe his salary to the Lord's work. (The word "tithe" means "tenth," so tithing would be giving one tenth of your income to the Lord. In this case, $4.6 million per year.)

Kurt admits that he hadn't thought about it. He'd been tithing since his Arena Football days, so it was ingrained in his behavior. But that was before he was making eight figures. Suddenly, he had to ask himself if he was *really* going to give $4.6 million to the Lord. He thought about the things that much money would buy.

Many people have had such thoughts. Tithing seems easy when the amount is paltry, but when you start adding zeroes, all of a sudden you get a lump in your throat. Satan starts whispering in your ear.

Images start flashing through your head of what you could do with that money. But then, hopefully, another thought elbows its way into your mind: God has blessed you. Those extra zeroes are from him. The last thing you want to do is fail to honor him with his blessings.

It's easy to pray and tell God you're thankful for what he's given you. That's probably the easiest prayer there is to pray. It's what you give back to him that proves how thankful you really are.

Reflect: James 1:17 says, "Whatever is good and perfect is a gift coming down to us from God our Father." Do you find that it's easy to tithe or difficult? If it's difficult, why do you think that is? What are some adjustments you need to make in your thinking to make it easier?

FACTS VS. TRUTH

MOST GOLFERS ARE NOT PGA Tour material. They hack and chop their way around a golf course, hitting a few good shots and rolling in the occasional long putt. They have fun with their friends and shrug off their shanks and hooks and slices.

If you're such a golfer, we have a course we want to tell you about. It's a short course. It has no water hazards on the entire course. That's right: none. It also has very few sand traps and only one fairway bunker. Best of all, you can roll the ball onto every green from the front. You're salivating, aren't you? You're thinking, "Now there's a course I could play!"

Actually, everything we've said about the course is true, but it's one of the toughest courses in America. It's called The Olympic Club, and it's in San Francisco. It's hosted the US Open three times, and each time it crushed a golf giant, namely Ben Hogan, Arnold Palmer, and Tom Watson. Each had the championship in his grasp down the stretch, only to have that short, water-free, sparsely bunkered little golf course rise up and defeat them. No wonder sports columnist Jim Murray called it "a 6,700-yard haunted house."[21]

Here's something to remember: Facts don't tell the whole story. Based on facts alone, the Olympic Club should be an easy course. The truth is, it's a hard course. So facts are true, but they don't always tell you the truth. Why is this important? Because people are often more (or less) than what the facts of their lives would lead you to believe. You look at what they've done or where they've been, and you draw certain conclusions. But those conclusions can be wrong.

The point is, get to know people. Don't just draw conclusions based on what you know (or have heard) about them. As you get to know them, you may be pleased or you may be disappointed, but at least your conclusions will be true.

Reflect: Philippians 4:8 says, "Fix your thoughts on what is true." Have you ever had an impression of someone that turned out to be inaccurate? Have you ever been misjudged by someone who knew some facts about you but not the truth? Why do you think people tend to draw conclusions about each other so quickly?

THE SYSTEM MATTERS

WHEN LEW ALCINDOR, known to us as Kareem Abdul-Jabbar, was playing at UCLA, the Bruins were practically unbeatable. Their record was an unthinkable 88–2, and they brought home three consecutive national championships. Even the two games they lost, one to the University of Houston and one to rival USC, were games that had unusual circumstances attached to them. They were, quite possibly, the best college basketball team in history.

You can imagine what sportswriters were saying when Lew Alcindor graduated. Story after story was written about the end of a dynasty. No one could conceive of a future for the team that would in any way resemble what they'd just been through. *Prepare yourselves, Bruins fans. It was a good run, but you can kiss this kind of success goodbye!* But what do you know … along came a young man named Bill Walton and a nifty little eighty-eight-game winning streak.

Nobody questions the greatness of players like Kareem or Bill Walton or many others that played on those Bruins teams. But it eventually became obvious that it was Coach Wooden's system that kept cranking out all those championships. It was everything from the assistants he hired to the players they recruited to the rules he instituted. It was the way they practiced and the disciplinary action he took if someone didn't get with the program. Lots of coaches knew the x's and o's and had good players, but few had the system to produce such machine-like efficiency.

HOW THINGS ARE DONE IS ULTIMATELY MORE IMPORTANT THAN WHO IS DOING THEM.

Here's some good advice: Build a good system, and success will come. If you do things the right way and build a healthy culture, good things will happen. This is not just true in sports, but in business, school, church, marriage, and family life. How things are done is ultimately more important than who is doing them.

Reflect: Galatians 6:9 says, "So let's not get tired of doing what is good. At just the right time, we will reap a harvest of blessing if we don't give up." How would you describe the "system" you have established in your personal life? Is it well thought out? Is it consistent? Is it goal oriented? Does it produce positive results? If you answered no to any of these questions, what needs to change?

THRILLS

EVERY YEAR IN PAMPLONA, Spain, people run with the bulls. Or maybe *from* the bulls would be more accurate. It's part of the San Fermín Festival, a celebration that includes music, food, parades, and bullfights. In the beginning, the running of the bulls was simply a way to move the animals from the corral to the bullfighting arena. Over time, daredevils saw the running as a chance to have a thrill, so more and more of them lined up to be chased by the rampaging beasts through the narrow street. Every year there are injuries that range from mild to serious. Many have been gored, and more than a few have died, yet every year people can't wait to make themselves a target. Some travel from all over the world.

It's amazing what people will do in search of a thrill.

We've all seen that crazy motorcyclist flying down the highway at least twenty miles an hour over the speed limit, weaving in and out of traffic ... and not wearing a helmet! Or how about the perfectly intelligent and highly successful married man sneaking around with a woman who is not his wife? Or the college student at the frat party who takes one of those mysterious little pills that are being passed around in the dark?

There's nothing wrong with wanting to experience some thrills. On some level, we all want to have our breath taken away, whether it's at a nail-biting sporting event or on a roller coaster at the local theme park or in a darkened theater staring at some hair-raising drama unfolding on a fifty-foot screen. God must be a lover of thrills, too, because he's sure given his people a lot of them down through the centuries. Remember that Red Sea thing?

We encourage you to live a thrilling life. Go places and do things that might seem a little crazy to some. But don't be dumb about it. Don't break the law. Don't invite disaster. Don't mess with drugs or alcohol. Don't pointlessly endanger yourself. The point is to have a thrill, not a funeral.

Reflect: 1 Timothy 6:17 says, "God richly gives us all we need for our enjoyment." Do you think some people are too reserved and don't enjoy enough experiences in God's creation? What about you? What's the biggest thrill you've had? Is there a thrill you haven't had but would like to?

YOU JUST NEVER KNOW

IN 1949, CHARLIE NICKLAUS injured his ankle and needed surgery. As it was healing, the doctor told him to move it as much as he could. He said that walking on soft ground would be just the kind of exercise it needed. Charlie decided that golf would be a way to exercise the foot and have a little fun, too, so he took his son, Jack, and headed for the course.

Charlie quickly discovered that he could only play a hole or two at a time without resting his tender ankle. While he rested, young Jack, with his cut-down set of clubs, chipped and putted around the green. Neither of them saw those trips to the course as the tip of an iceberg, but they were. They were the first steps in what would become an epic journey to the very top of the golfing world for little Jack, who would one day become the great Golden Bear.

Struggles often produce positive results that couldn't possibly have been anticipated. If an injured ankle could trigger the development of the world's greatest golfer, what might a car accident trigger? Or a storm? Or a job loss? Or a house fire? Or an illness?

You just never know.

Which is why no one should ever panic when unfortunate circumstances arise. If there's one thing we know, it's that the pages of history are filled with beautiful things that grew out of difficult circumstances. Even our Savior, Jesus, was born to an unwed mother at a time when such happenings were considered scandalous. And thirty-three years later, his death on the cross looked like the tragedy to end all tragedies. Yet it made our redemption possible.

You just never know.

Reflect: Job 11:7 asks a question: "Can you solve the mysteries of God?" Can you think of a difficulty in your life that produced a positive though unexpected outcome? If so, did that experience change the way you look at troubles? What conclusions can you draw about God when you see his ability to bring good out of bad?

FAMILY

WILMA RUDOLPH IS one of the great names of track and field. In 1956 she won a bronze medal at the Melbourne Olympics as part of the team that ran the 4x100-meter relay. In 1960, she won gold medals in the 100-meter, the 200 meters, and the 4x100 relay. What makes this so astounding is that Wilma, the twentieth of twenty-two children, suffered from polio, double pneumonia, and scarlet fever as a child. At a time when many children died of polio, the disease rendered her left leg useless, necessitating the use of a brace at the age of six.

How did she get from being a sickly child in a leg brace to the gold medal ceremony at the Olympics? Naturally, a lot of personal determination and hard work was involved. But her family played a huge role too. They got her the medical treatment she needed, massaged her leg every day, encouraged her, challenged her to get on her feet and be active, and made sure she got into college at Tennessee State University.

This is how life is supposed to work.

We're not dropped into this world all alone in the middle of nowhere. We're born to a mother and, hopefully, into a family. Ideally, that family becomes a support system that helps us grow and develop and reach our potential. Obviously, not everyone is so blessed. We live in a fallen world, which means that some will not know the benefits of a healthy family life.

If you had/have a great family, thank God.

If you didn't/don't, we suggest that you make your own. Find someone—a child, perhaps—that doesn't have a family, and lend your friendship, support, and encouragement. Perhaps become a Big Brother or Big Sister. Just because you don't share DNA doesn't mean you can't share love.

Reflect: In Matthew 10:42, Jesus said, "And if you give even a cup of cold water to one of the least of my followers, you will surely be rewarded." Can you think of some ways your life is better because of the love and support of your family? Is there someone among your acquaintances that needs a family? What could you do to be a blessing to that person?

FINISHING SECOND

THE MINNESOTA VIKINGS are a great NFL franchise. Let there be no mistake about that. Since the merger of the AFL and NFL, they have made the playoffs twenty-seven times, which is third best in the league. They've had great players like Fran Tarkenton and great coaches like Bud Grant. They've even had great nicknames, like a defensive line that was called the Purple People Eaters. And they've made it to the Super Bowl four times.

The problem is, they've never won it.

They could have. Several times they were plenty good enough. In fact, in 1998 they went 15–1. Everybody thought they were going to roll right over their opponents and win the big one. But footballs bounce in crazy ways and, for whatever reason, the Vikings have never been able to get over the hump. Some people say they're jinxed. We don't believe that. We simply believe that life is often weird and unpredictable.

Sometimes, in spite of our passion and hard work, we never quite get over the hump. Some other team wins the championship. Some other candidate gets the job. Some other employee gets the promotion. Some other guy gets the girl. It's enough to make you want to scream.

We say ... go ahead and scream if you want. Let out that frustration. But when you're done screaming, stop and realize that it's what you do that defines you, not what you don't do. So you didn't win the big one ... so what? The Vikings remind us that you can earn a lot of respect just by winning a lot of smaller ones. And remember, haven't is not the same as won't. Maybe you *will* win the big one before it's all over.

Reflect: James 1:12 says, "God blesses those who patiently endure ..." Do you have an unfulfilled dream ... something you've worked hard for but never achieved? Can you put your finger on a reason why it has eluded you? What are some things you *have* accomplished that are worthwhile and respectable?

WHY ARE YOU LISTENING TO HIM/HER?

CAL RIPKEN TELLS a great story from 1984. He was on a hot streak, lashing base hits all over the field and building a nice hitting streak. One day, when the Orioles were playing the Angels, Ruppert Jones hit a double and ended up on second base. Cal walked over from his shortstop position, and Ruppert said, "Cal, you look good with your hands away from your body. You're red-hot at the plate these days. Keep swinging it."[22]

That statement about his hands being away from his body got into Cal's head. He hadn't thought about it and suddenly wondered if that's why he was hitting the ball so well. So the next time he went to bat, he concentrated on keeping his hands away from his body. As you can probably guess, he made an out and went into a slump. After that, he wondered if Ruppert Jones said that on purpose, actually *trying* to get inside his head. A good question for Cal to have asked himself was, "Why am I listening to Ruppert Jones?" He wasn't on Cal's team and wasn't Cal's coach. Plus, he and his team stood to benefit if Cal cooled off.

All of us make this mistake at times. We listen to the wrong people. And not only do we listen to them but we give their words much more weight than they deserve.

One day a pastor was approached by a church member. The member said, "You're doing better with your preaching." When the church member walked away, the pastor felt uneasy. *Was that a compliment? Or was it her way of telling me that my preaching hasn't been very good in the past?* The longer the preacher thought about it, the more her comment troubled him.

When you choose to listen to someone and give his/her words weight, you make yourself vulnerable. Make sure you choose wisely.

> **WHEN YOU CHOOSE TO LISTEN TO SOMEONE AND GIVE HIS/HER WORDS WEIGHT, YOU MAKE YOURSELF VULNERABLE. MAKE SURE YOU CHOOSE WISELY.**

> *Reflect:* Proverbs 4:7 says, "Whatever else you do, develop good judgment." Have you ever gotten into trouble by listening to the wrong person? What are some things a person should consider when deciding who he is going to listen to? Is there someone in your life right now that you need to stop listening to?

FIX IT

JIM THORPE DIED in 1953. For this reason, very few people, if any, alive today saw him compete. But the fact that the Associated Press named him the greatest athlete of the twentieth century gives you some idea of his greatness. We marvel at two sports athletes, but Jim Thorpe was an Olympic gold medal winner in addition to playing professional football, baseball, *and* basketball. Come to think of it, he might be the greatest athlete of *any* century.

At the 1912 Olympic games, he won gold medals in the pentathlon and decathlon. But only a few weeks later, he was disqualified because it was learned he had been paid to play baseball. The governing body that oversaw amateur athletics said that accepting money in any sport made you a professional in every sport.

Dumb rule, right?

Yes, and everybody thought so. Fans protested, but to no avail … until 1983. Finally, after over seventy years, the International Olympic

Committee acknowledged the injustice of the decision and reinstated Jim Thorpe's victories and returned the medals to his family.

In almost every area of life, there are dumb rules and bad decisions that result in injustices. You can protest, of course, and maybe the perpetrators of that injustice will make it right. But what if you're the one who made the decision? Our encouragement to you is to always keep an open mind after you've made a judgment call. Maybe it seemed right in the moment, but further information or keener insight reveals that it wasn't. When that happens, swallow your pride and fix it.

And don't wait seventy years.

Reflect: Jesus said in Matthew 5:23–24, "If you are presenting a sacrifice at the altar in the Temple and you suddenly remember that someone has something against you, leave your sacrifice there at the altar. Go and be reconciled to that person." Have you ever been the victim of an unjust decision? How did you respond? Why do you think some people have a hard time admitting they are wrong? Do you?

BLINDERS

ALEX RODRIGUEZ WAS a great baseball talent. He was also a liar and a cheater. His use of performance-enhancing drugs (PEDs), as well as attempts to hide the fact and obstruct Baseball's investigation into the matter, tarnished what would have been an epic career. When he hit his 660th home run, Red Sox fans weren't about to give him a grudgingly respectful cheer the way they might've for Mariano Rivera or Derek Jeter. Oh no, they greeted him with catcalls and boos and all sorts of signs and T-shirts, calling him "A-Fraud" or "A-Roid."

What makes this interesting is that one of the Red Sox's great sluggers was also a cheater and a repeat offender to boot. Manny Ramirez tested positive twice and retired in disgrace after a third violation. But if you talk to a Red Sox fan about Manny, he'll likely chuckle about Manny's slip-ups and talk about "Manny being Manny." Even the Red Sox hero David Ortiz, otherwise known as Big Papi, was linked to PEDs, though in a much more clouded way. Yet A-Rod was treated like the Great Satan while the other players were wildly cheered.

In sports, you see this kind of thing a lot. People wear blinders when it comes to their favorite teams and players. What's dangerous is when we wear blinders in life. Parents will sometimes blind themselves to the faults of their kids. Many individuals will criticize actions in others that they themselves are guilty of; like Christians will skewer preachers or other church leaders for not being holy enough, even as they dabble in their own sinful habits.

It's the old double standard.

We encourage you to take your blinders off. Don't ever criticize someone else until you've spent a lot of time looking in the mirror.

Reflect: Lamentations 3:40 says, "Let us test and examine our ways." Have you ever been the victim of a criticism that was rooted in a double standard? Why do you think people are often so blind to their own weaknesses and mistakes? What is the best way to handle a criticism that comes from someone who is just as guilty as you?

TROPHIES

(MARK) WE HAVE ALREADY established in this book that my writing partner, Pat, has an NBA championship ring. If I had to pick *my* most memorable trophy, it would be a toss-up between a long-ball hitting contest at a Little League picnic or the longest drive competition I won at a minister's golf tournament, where my ball hit the cart path and bounced an extra forty yards. (The trophy included a gift card for free barbecue, so I took it.)

Nowadays, kids don't need to win anything to get something to sit on their bedroom dresser because our culture has embraced a little thing called the "participation trophy." You don't have to do anything but show up, and you walk away with the hardware. Proponents say that we are wounding our kids, making them feel left out or second rate if we don't do this. Others counter that we are warping our kids by failing to teach them that there are winners and losers in life, and it's best to try to be a winner.

You can make up your own mind how you feel about this issue. What you do need to realize is that, in God's eyes, there are definite winners and losers in life, and only the winners get a trophy. James 1:12 says, "God blesses those who patiently endure testing and temptation. Afterward, they will receive the crown of life that God has promised to those who love him."

On Judgment Day, God is not going to ask everyone to line up and pass by to pick up their trophy as they waltz through the pearly gates. I fear that a lot of people are going to be stunned by this. I sense that many people see God as an old softy who'll end up letting everybody into heaven when all is said and done.

Sadly, a lot of people make God into what they want him to be rather than letting him be who he is.

Reflect: 1 Corinthians 9:24 says, "Don't you realize that in a race everyone runs, but only one person gets the prize? So run to win!" What assumptions, if any, have you made about Judgment Day? Do you believe God chooses who goes to heaven or that people choose for themselves? Why should God award you the crown of life?

THE VALUE OF A STRUGGLE

THERE IS SOMETHING really counterintuitive about professional sports managers and coaches. It's the fact that the worst players tend to make the best managers and the best players tend to make the worst managers. Consider the following major-league managers:

Sparky Anderson, who won 2,194 games as a manager and three World Series titles, was a career .218 hitter with 34 total RBI.

Tony La Russa, winner of 2,728 games and three World Series titles, was a career .199 hitter and had a whopping 7 total RBI.

Bruce Bochy, the outstanding long-time manager of the San Francisco Giants, is approaching 2,000 wins as we write these words and has three World Series titles. Yet he was a .239 career hitter with 93 total RBI.

We could go on, but you get the idea.

One school of thought is that bad players make good coaches because they understand how hard the game is. To make it as far as they did as players, they had to work harder at their craft and study the nuances of the game. At the time, it felt like a monumental struggle, but they were being groomed and prepared for a different kind of success without realizing it.

The same thing can happen in life. People who fight through life's struggles often become uniquely qualified to help others. They have an empathy and a perspective on difficult situations that often escapes people who haven't walked that road.

Which means, dear reader, that if you are going through a struggle, God may be preparing you for ministry. You probably don't feel like it right now, but it could be. You may emerge from your struggle with all the tools necessary to save someone's life.

Wouldn't that be something?

Reflect: Revelation 2:10 says, "Do not be afraid of what you are about to suffer." What's the worst struggle you've been through? What important lessons did you learn about life or yourself? Have you been able to share some of that wisdom with others who were going through similar struggles? What might be some things you need to beware of before you "coach" someone else?

UNDERDOGS AND UPSETS

"MY TEAM'S NOT in it, so I'll just root for the underdog." How many times have you heard that? How many times have you *said* that? There's something woven into the human spirit that makes us want to root for the player or team that seems to have the least chance of winning.

Perhaps one reason we like underdogs and upsets is because there is (in most of us, at least) a sense that the little guy almost always takes it on the chin in this world. We like seeing the script flipped once in a while.

A second reason we like underdogs and upsets is because they stick with us, sometimes forever, providing thrilling memories and conversational fodder. For example, the words "Miracle on Ice" give millions of people a tingle up and down their spines.

But perhaps the biggest reason we like underdogs and upsets is probably because every time an underdog knocks off a favorite, we're reminded that crazy things happen in this world and we, too, might someday experience something wonderful and unexpected.

As Christian men and sports fans, we know—and we want to remind you—that there are no underdogs among God's people. Oh, it looks like there are. Christians always seem to be persecuted and oppressed and disadvantaged in some way. In terms of sheer numbers, we are always outnumbered and often outvoted. But no person who stands with God is ever at a disadvantage.

Think about Moses standing before the pharaoh.

David standing before Goliath.

Daniel standing before the lions.

Jesus standing before Pilate.

We stand with the same God they did, which means we are no more underdogs than they were. We should never let the world intimidate us.

Reflect: Psalms 46:1 says, "God is our refuge and strength, always ready to help in times of trouble." Have you ever felt like an underdog as a Christian? In what ways? Have you seen God bring you safely through situations that seemed overwhelming in the moment? In difficult times, what are some ways you can remind yourself of God's power and faithfulness?

FISHERS OF MEN

SHAW GRIGSBY IS A pretty good bass fisherman, judging from the fact that he's been a pro for thirty-five years and has won well over $2 million in various fishing tournaments. He also has a TV show, *One More Cast with Shaw Grigsby*, that has been on the air for twenty years and is one of the most popular fishing shows ever produced.

When Shaw takes his boat out, he's well equipped. He's been known to carry sixteen tackle boxes with over $10,000 worth of lures. But Shaw is quick to make sure everybody understands that it's not the lure that catches the fish; it's the fisherman. The greatest lure in the world can be thrown into the water, but if the guy holding the rod doesn't do his job right, there will be no fish caught.

The same principle applies to Christians as we strive to be "fishers of men." We have the Gospel, which is exactly what every person needs. It offers help, hope, encouragement, correction, instruction, insight, and the Plan of Salvation. No matter what a person is going through, the Word of God will meet the need.

Unfortunately, a lot of Christians negate the power of the Gospel with their conduct. With our lousy attitudes and bad behavior, we are like fishermen beating the water with our poles, yelling and screaming, scaring the fish and driving them to the other side of the lake. Lots of people who truly need Jesus are turned off not by the Gospel but by the people who are telling them about it.

This, of course, is a tragedy of epic proportions. The Gospel will do its work if we can just manage not to mess things up.

Reflect: In Matthew 4:19 Jesus said, "Come, follow me, and I will show you how to fish for people." Before you came to faith, did you find that Christians encouraged or discouraged your search for truth? What are some ways Christians unknowingly drive unbelievers away from Christ? How diligent have you been when it comes to being a "fisher of men"?

SAM AND TIGER

WHEN SAM SNEAD was seventy years old, he played two holes of golf with a six-year-old boy named Tiger Woods. Sam talked about what a nice swing the kid had and how he hit the ball better than a lot of people two or three times his age. No one knew at the time that Tiger would develop into one of the greatest golfers in history, but if they had, you can bet there would have been media present, snapping pictures of Sam and Tiger. Imagine how historically significant those pictures would have eventually become. Kind of like Babe Ruth having his picture taken with a young Mickey Mantle.

There are great athletes in every generation. Maybe because of improvements in diet, conditioning, and equipment, today's players in most sports would defeat those of some generations ago. But those old timers, from Sam Snead to Ted Williams to Bill Russell, were no less great. They met the challenge in front of them with the tools they had to work with and excelled.

Likewise, there are great Christians in every generation. The young family that walks into church on Sunday morning today may have no idea that fifty or seventy-five or one hundred years ago, dedicated believers were making extreme sacrifices that allowed that church to exist. When that family settles into a pew and listens to a sharp young preacher offer some powerful teaching, they may have no idea that that preacher was educated in a Bible college that was started by the sacrifices of faithful Christians several generations ago.

It is good for us to have an appreciation of people who have gone before us, from the prophets and apostles of ancient times to the more recent believers whose sacrifices and hard work now bless us in countless ways. Now it's our turn to leave a legacy for those who will come after us.

Reflect: Psalms 145:4 says, "Let each generation tell its children of your mighty acts; let them proclaim your power." Can you name some spiritual blessings you now enjoy because of the faithfulness of people in prior generations? What kind of spiritual legacy are you leaving? Name a sacrifice you're making now that will be a blessing to someone someday.

A DARK CONFESSION

I (MARK) HAVE A confession to make. I hope you don't think less of me after reading it. It's that I root against people and teams I don't like. I know, I know … I shouldn't be a hater. I should adopt a "live and let live" policy and just be happy for all the winners. But I can't do it. In fact, there are times when I think I find as much joy in the losses of the teams I don't like than in the wins of the teams I do.

As a die-hard Mizzou Tigers fan, I find profound joy in a Kansas Jayhawks loss. As a lifelong St. Louis Cardinals fan, I feel a little tingle when I see the Cubs go down in defeat. And please understand, Jayhawks and Cubs fans, it's nothing personal. OK, it is personal. What I mean is, I do realize there are fine people on your teams. Perhaps even godly people. It's just … well, the rivalry. The history. The toe-to-toe, knock-down, drag-out battles we've been through. (And I know you feel the same way about my teams!)

I honestly believe it's OK to root against athletes and teams as long as we don't wish them any real harm. Rivalries are part of what make sports so much fun. However, that can't be said of our dealings with people in everyday life. Taking joy in the troubles of others is a terrible thing.

In the New Testament, we are told to love our neighbor. The word in the original language is "agape," and it means to desire the best for someone. You don't have to like them. You don't have to be bosom buddies. You don't have to hang out with them. But you do have to want what's best for them. That can be hard, especially when they've taken pleasure in making your life miserable. But it's one of those important things that distinguish believers from the rest of the world.

Reflect: In Luke 6:27 Jesus said, "Love your enemies; do good to those who hate you." Have you ever taken satisfaction in the pain of someone you didn't like? Did you eventually repent of that sin? What thoughts or ideas do you draw on when you face the challenge of loving someone who has not been good to you?

ALMOST

ON APRIL 15, 1983, Jerry Hairston Sr. of the Chicago White Sox came to the plate as a pinch hitter in the ninth inning of a game against the Detroit Tigers. There were two outs, and the Sox were down 4–0. You might assume the fans were streaming toward the exits.

They weren't.

The reason is because Milt Wilcox, the Tigers' pitcher, had retired twenty-six batters in a row. One more, and he would have a perfect game.

So Hairston dug into the box, knowing the game was probably a lost cause, but bearing down like never before. He didn't want his at bat to be shown on every sportscast in the country as the Tigers players celebrated a perfect game.

He got a base hit up the middle.

What a tough outcome for Milt Wilcox, who was phenomenal that night. Imagine how he must've felt. It can be incredibly painful when you come oh-so close to accomplishing your dream only to fall a tiny bit short.

Has it happened to you?

Maybe you were a finalist for your dream job, but the company chose the other candidate. Maybe you ran for office but lost by a handful of votes. Maybe you started a business but couldn't quite make enough money to survive.

Bitterness and regret often encumber people who have these experiences. A much better attitude is to learn what you can and, if you so choose, try again. Or take what you have learned and channel it into a new endeavor. The pages of history are filled with stories about people who had to try multiple times to finally see their dreams come true.

Reflect: 2 Chronicles 15:7 says, "Be strong and courageous, for your work will be rewarded." Have you ever experienced a disappointment where you felt like your work *wasn't* rewarded? What did you learn from that experience? How did you benefit from those lessons as you moved forward?

DON'T MESS WITH YOUR HAPPINESS

COACHES AND MANAGERS move around a lot. And not always because they fail. Many Hall of Fame coaches and managers have worn various teams' colors. And there can be as many reasons for this as there are coaches and managers. Family concerns, health concerns, the desire for a new challenge, and limited success are just a few of the reasons why a coach might relocate.

Jim Valvano was the fiery, charismatic coach of the North Carolina State Wolfpack who died tragically from cancer at the age of forty-seven. In one of the most thrilling finishes in NCAA tournament history, his NC State squad won the 1983 national championship. This, of course, made him a hot commodity. At one point, the New Jersey Nets interviewed him and offered him their coaching job. Jim agreed to the deal but one week later called them and backed out. When he was asked why, he said, "I'm really happy where I am, and I don't want to mess with it."[23]

There are lots and lots of people who have messed with their happiness to their deep regret. Leaving a job you love for a few more dollars somewhere else is one way it happens. Exchanging flirtations with someone you are not married to is another. And then, of course, there is the simple failure to maintain and nurture the things in your life that bring you happiness.

As Americans, we are guaranteed the right to pursue happiness, but no one can guarantee that we will find it. If you *have* found it, whatever you do, don't mess with it. Enjoy and cherish it!

Reflect: Proverbs 10:28 says, "The hopes of the godly result in happiness." Are you happy? If not, why do you think that is? Have you been happy in the past? If so, what changed? If you *are* happy, are you currently dabbling in something that could endanger your happiness?

PRAISE, PLEASE

THE LATE DICK ENBERG was a legend in the broadcast booth. His signature "Oh my!" punctuated some of the most exciting moments in sports over the last fifty years. But he was rarely satisfied with his work. He was extremely hard on himself, and after years of reflection, he felt that he knew why.

He told a story about when he was a boy. His father, a farmer, rarely attended his sporting events, but one night he went to one of Dick's high school basketball games. Dick happened to have the best game of his life, scoring twenty-three points. When he got home, he hoped his father would compliment him on his performance, but he didn't mention it. So Dick told him that he scored twenty-three points. His father said, "Yes, but how many did your man score? I believe it was twenty-six."

That's when Dick broke down in tears and said, "You're never going to say anything nice about me, are you?" To which his father replied, "The day you think you're so good you can't improve, you'll only have one way to go, and that's down."

Years later, Dick said he knew that what his father said was true, but it wasn't what he needed at that moment. He needed encouragement, a pat on the back, a compliment on a job well done, especially from his father. Maybe if he'd gotten it then and on other occasions, he wouldn't have grown up being so hard on himself.

It's not just kids who need praise; we all do. Be generous with it. Make it a point to always find something good to say. The whole world echoes with words of criticism. Make it a point to be different.

Reflect: 1 Thessalonians 5:11 says, "Encourage each other, and build each other up." How much praise and encouragement did you get as a child? How do you feel that has affected you as an adult? Do you give praise freely? Is there someone close to you who needs to hear something encouraging from you?

FAIRNESS

GERALD FORD DIED in 2006 at the age of ninety-three. He's most remembered for being the only person to serve as both vice president and president without being elected to either office. He's also remembered for being clumsy. In fact, Chevy Chase owes his fame and fortune to the skits he did on *Saturday Night Live* portraying Mr. Ford as a bumbling klutz. Many think it's a miracle that Mr. Chase never broke his back doing all those pratfalls.

But the portrayal couldn't have been more unfair.

Gerald Ford was about as far from a klutz as you could get. He won three letters playing center on the University of Michigan football team. In 1932 and 1933, his teams won back-to-back national championships while going undefeated both years. And don't get the idea that he was a benchwarmer who spent all his time hauling water and equipment. He was voted the team's Most Valuable Player in 1934 and turned down offers from two NFL teams when he graduated. Still, he'll always be remembered as a guy who deserved a round of applause if he managed to still be standing upright when he reached the bottom of the stairs exiting Air Force One.

Jesus was also portrayed unfairly. In fact, the mockery Chevy Chase made of Gerald Ford paled in comparison to the smear campaign the Jewish leaders ran against our Lord. Matthew 26:59 says, "The leading priests and the entire high council were trying to find witnesses who would lie about Jesus so they could put him to death."

The next time someone treats you unfairly, remember what Jesus went through and smile ... for two reasons. First, because he was willing to endure that for you. And second, because you have the opportunity to share in his suffering. 1 Peter 4:13 says, "Be very glad because these trials will make you partners with Christ in his suffering, and afterward you will have the wonderful joy of seeing his glory when it is revealed to all the world."

Reflect: Psalms 7:11 says, "God is an honest Judge." Have you ever been judged or portrayed unfairly? How did you react? Have there been times when you have intentionally misrepresented yourself to gain an advantage? Why is it always best to portray yourself accurately to others?

A RARE COMMODITY

STEVEN BARTMAN MEANT no harm. He simply did what any lifelong baseball fan would have done. When he saw a foul ball coming his way, he reached out and tried to catch it. Only afterward did he realize that he might have prevented the Chicago Cubs' left fielder, Moises Alou, from making the grab and securing a valuable out in the sixth inning of the 2003 National League Championship Series.

The umpire ruled (and replays verified) that the ball was outside the field of play and that Mr. Bartman did nothing wrong. Nevertheless, he instantly became an object of scorn. Beer was thrown on him. Curses were hurled at him. Threats were made. To avoid a riot, police draped a jacket over his head and led him to safety. In less than twenty-four hours, his name, address, and phone number, along with the names and addresses of his family members, were listed on the internet. As a precaution, his family was given round-the-clock police protection, and Steven himself went into hiding. And to top it all off, he became the butt of countless jokes, especially from Jay Leno and David Letterman.

When something like this happens, we are reminded of what a rare commodity grace is. We are also reminded of why the world needs Christians. We are the conduit through which the love and grace of God can flow into a hateful world.

At least we're supposed to be.

We hate to say it, but sometimes we can be just as harsh and judgmental as those who've never given Jesus a second thought. Just let somebody step out of line, and we immediately go on the attack, like sharks catching the scent of blood in the water.

We ought to be ashamed.

Those of us who've had the hangman's noose removed from around our necks ought to be the last ones to put it on someone else.

Reflect: Ephesians 4:32 says, "Be kind to each other, tenderhearted, forgiving each other, just as Christ in God forgave you." How critical are you of other people's mistakes? Do you find that you easily get caught up in the feeding frenzy when others around you are attacking someone? Have you ever spoken up in a sinner's defense when others were on the attack?

MAY 27

THE BEAUTY OF GOOD TIMING

IN 2004, I (PAT) had lunch with Gene Conley. Gene was unique for a couple of reasons. One, he was six feet eight, and two, he played both Major League Baseball and NBA basketball. He told me the following story:

> It was 1959, and I had just joined the Phillies. We were playing the Cardinals in a doubleheader. I was down in the bullpen when my manager, Eddie Sawyer, called down and said, "Get Conley ready." I jumped up and started to throw, excited because it would be my first appearance and because it was a close game.
>
> When I came in, it was the bottom of the ninth, two out and two on. And who should be coming to the plate but The Man himself, Stan Musial. That day the baseball gods smiled on me. I struck him out to end the game. As I walked off the field, Eddie Sawyer was standing on the dugout steps. He

shook my hand and said, "Thanks, Gene. I really appreciate what you did."

Gene told me that it's hard for him to tell that story without getting emotional, even though it happened forty-five years ago. I thought to myself, "Why would that story be so emotional?" Then I realized that such is the power of a kind word spoken at just the right moment. I don't know what was going on in Gene's life at that time, but he must have really needed that handshake and those words of appreciation.

Words that seem insignificant to you can mean the world to someone else. So always try to offer a word of support or encouragement. The person may still remember it a half century later.

Reflect: Proverbs 15:23 says, "Everyone enjoys a fitting reply; it is wonderful to say the right thing at the right time." Can you think of a time when someone said just what you needed to hear just when you needed to hear it? Why is it best not to try to guess when people need to hear a kind word? Can you think of someone you know who is going through a hard time and might need to hear a word of kindness or encouragement?

PIVOTAL MOMENTS

IN 1935, WILLIAM WRIGLEY, the owner of the Chicago Cubs, was approached by Charles Graham, the owner of the San Francisco Seals of the Pacific Coast League. Graham told Wrigley that he had a good young ballplayer he'd be willing to sell for $25,000. Wrigley was hesitant because the ballplayer in question had suffered an injury the year before. Understanding his reluctance, Graham offered to let Wrigley have the player on a trial basis. If he performed well, Wrigley could pay the $25,000. If he didn't, Wrigley could return the player, and it wouldn't cost him a cent. It was a no-lose proposition, but William Wrigley still refused.

Of course, you're wondering who that ballplayer was.

His name was Joe DiMaggio.

We all come to pivotal moments when we have to seize or pass on opportunities. Sometimes, like in the case just mentioned, the choice is a no-brainer. But most of the time, there's risk involved. We wouldn't insult your intelligence by telling you that we know the secret of always making the right choice. We can look back over our lives and see quite a few missed opportunities.

But we do know this: God intends for his people to be opportunity seizers. The Bible is loaded with the accounts of courageous people stepping out on faith and claiming great blessings and victories. And don't forget: an angry God banished his people to a forty-year trek through an unfriendly wilderness because they refused to seize an opportunity that he put right in front of them.

GOD INTENDS FOR HIS PEOPLE TO BE OPPORTUNITY SEIZERS.

Are we saying that you should be greedily groping at every opportunity that comes along? Absolutely not! That's a good way to get into deep trouble!

But we do believe that as you grow stronger in your faith, you'll begin to recognize opportunities that you once would have missed. And you'll be able to better discern which opportunities God would want you to seize.

Reflect: Proverbs 10:5 says, "A wise youth harvests in the summer, but one who sleeps during harvest is a disgrace." Have you ever passed on a great opportunity and ended up kicking yourself later? If so, what held you back? Do you think it's better to take more risks, even if some of them turn out bad … or fewer risks, even if you miss some great opportunities?

UNWANTED DELAYS

DURING THE 1907 Boston Marathon, a passing train divided the field. The ten frontrunners had already crossed the tracks, but the rest of the participants had to stop and wait a minute and fifteen seconds for the train to pass before they could continue.

Among those who had to wait was Bob Fowler. He was an experienced marathoner who understood the importance of running slowly during the first half of the race and saving energy for the second half, which is mostly uphill. You can imagine the horror he must have felt when he saw the train coming and knew he wouldn't be able to beat it. As he stood there helplessly, he not only lost seventy-five precious seconds to the front-runners, but many of the runners that were behind him were able to catch up!

When the train finally passed, Bob Fowler took off and pushed himself to the limit of his ability and endurance. He turned in an actual running time that would have won most Boston Marathons, but the unanticipated delay gave the victory to a man named Tom Longboat.

If you're a person who lives with the pedal to the metal (and who isn't these days?), having to unexpectedly slam on the brakes no doubt drives you crazy. But it's always helpful to remember that for every Bob Fowler, there's a Tom Longboat. For every person who is hurt by a delay, there's another person who is helped.

Not long ago, I (Mark) got a phone call just as I was in a hurry to leave the house. The call lasted a couple of minutes, and then I was on my way. Not far from my house, I came upon an accident that had just happened. I couldn't help wondering if that two-minute phone call kept me from being in that accident.

The next time you encounter a delay, relax.

It might be God's way of protecting you.

Reflect: Lamentations 3:9 says, "He has blocked my way with a high stone wall; he has made my road crooked." What is generally your response to unexpected delays? Do you know of any situations where an unexpected delay worked to your benefit? Have you ever thought that delays might be God's way of slowing you down? What are some ways you could maximize the time you spend waiting?

LIGHTEN UP

PHIL MICKELSON MAY NOT be the best golfer in the world right now, but many people would say he's number one when it comes to being likable. He's a humble, soft-spoken family man who often seems embarrassed by the applause of the crowd.

Phil's short game coach, Dave Pelz, tells about something that happened just before the 2004 Masters:

> About a month before the Masters, we were having a casual conversation when I mentioned to Phil that I thought he looked too serious on Sundays. "When you are at the top of your game, you're smiling and laughing," I said. "When you play with your friends, you are almost unbeatable—because you are enjoying yourself. That allows your mind and body to perform at the top of your game. If you try to be too serious, it's like tying one hand behind your back. Phil, you need to lighten up on Sundays."

At first, Phil looked at me like I was crazy. But then he thought about it. And I think he realized that all of his best final rounds occurred when he was having fun—not when he was being too serious.[24]

Oh, and by the way, Phil won the 2004 Masters.

Isn't it true that we're always more effective when we decide to lighten up and enjoy ourselves? Aren't you a better boss when you decide to lighten up? (We'll bet your employees would say so!) Aren't you a better spouse when you decide to lighten up? (We'll bet your spouse would say so!) Aren't you a better parent when you decide to lighten up? (We'll bet your kids would say so!)

Imagine how much brighter life could be for you and the people in your world if you decided to put a smile on your face and enjoy yourself every day.

Reflect: Proverbs 13:9 says, "The life of the godly is full of light and joy." In general, do you believe you are viewed as an easy-going person or a "high strung" person? Do you find that there's tension in many of your relationships? How long has it been since you shared a hearty laugh or acted silly with your colleagues or family members?

DON SHULA'S SURPRISE

AN OFTEN-TOLD STORY about Don Shula is one of our favorites. Don, the highly successful head coach of the Miami Dolphins, was on vacation with his wife and children in Maine. They decided to go to a movie, and when they walked into the theater, the twelve people who were already there stood and applauded.

Of course, Don was used to being recognized around Miami, but being recognized in Maine surprised him. But he nodded and acknowledged the applause and reflected on the power of network television. People in Maine obviously watched Dolphins games and appreciated his coaching ability.

When Don and his family took their seats, a moviegoer sitting nearby leaned over and said, "We don't know who you guys are, but we're all glad you came because the theater owner told us a little while ago that he had to have fifteen people in attendance in order to show the movie."

Life has a way of keeping us humble.

I (Mark) remember the time I went to a concert at Disney's Epcot featuring a very famous singer. I'm talking about a woman who's sold millions of records. Apparently, she was running late because they were just finishing the sound check when my wife, Marilyn, and I walked in and sat down in our seats. We were thrilled to get to see something that audiences rarely get to see. But suddenly, we gasped. Our eyes popped open and we looked at each other, speechless. We were indeed seeing something audiences rarely get to see … the singer's pants were ripped wide open in the back. She had no idea, but the few early-arriving fans in the seats were all snickering.

We suggest that you make it a point to stay humble. If you don't, life will find a way to humble you.

Reflect: Jesus said in Luke 14:11, "For those who exalt themselves will be humbled, and those who humble themselves will be exalted." What are some of the ways pride can have a detrimental effect on your life? Have you ever had an embarrassing moment that humbled you? What are some of the thoughts you rely on to keep you humble?

MARCH MADNESS

THE NCAA BASKETBALL tournament is one of the most popular sporting events of the year. Dozens of teams from all over the country are in it, which creates widespread interest, and every year there are astonishing upsets. Some years, a whole slew of Goliaths come crashing to earth. Which is why almost every office in the country has a tournament pool, and after the first weekend, we're all bemoaning the sorry condition of our brackets.

Logic would suggest that the NCAA tournament would hurt the NBA, that it would take eyeballs away from the NBA as the NBA season builds toward the playoffs. However, the NBA actually loves the NCAA tournament because it showcases the NBA's future stars. People fall in love with standout college players and then feel compelled to follow their careers right into the NBA. It also creates huge interest in the NBA draft, so much so that the draft has become a highly rated television event in itself.

Sometimes truth can be very counterintuitive. In other words, sometimes situations, as in the case just mentioned, that seem to make so much sense at a glance really don't if you look more closely. This is why we need to think things through and not make snap decisions based on first impressions.

The job that pays you the most money may not be the best one for you.

The girl (or guy) that is the best looking may not be the best one for you.

The church that is the biggest and flashiest may not be the best one for you.

We encourage you not to live by first impressions or appearances or impulses, especially when it comes to major life choices. Make sure you do your homework. There are always more relevant facts than meet the eye. You'll make much better decisions and live a much happier life if you do.

Reflect: Proverbs 4:6 says, "Don't turn your back on wisdom, for she will protect you. Love her, and she will guard you." Have you ever made an impulsive decision based on a good first impression and regretted it? What was the critical fact you missed by not taking a closer look? How has that experience changed the way you make decisions?

WATCH YOUR P'S AND Q'S

THE DATE WAS July 4, 1976. It was our bicentennial. America was in a festive mood, and baseball games were part of the celebration. Players were excited about all the celebratory activities surrounding the games and played with great enthusiasm. At least one got a little too excited. His name was Tim McCarver. He would eventually become a Hall of Famer, but not because of what happened on that particular day.

Tim was playing for the Phillies in a game against the Pittsburgh Pirates. With the Phillies trailing 1–0, he came up with the bases loaded, desperately wanting to deliver a big blow. He did. A towering fly ball to the right sailed over the fence for a grand slam home run. Naturally, Tim watched the ball as he ran to first base, and when he saw it disappear over the fence, he clapped his hands and gave a shout. That's when he noticed that he had passed his teammate, Garry Maddox, who was on first but had gone back to the bag to tag up. By rule, Tim was called out, and the play went down as a three-run single.

It was an embarrassing moment that never would have happened if Tim had been paying attention.

We've noticed that countless bad situations arise in people's lives simply because they don't pay attention. One of the most common complaints of wives in unhappy marriages is that their husbands don't pay attention to them. One of the most common reasons kids get into trouble is because their parents aren't engaged in their lives.

We live in a culture where it's easy to be distracted from what's important. Social media is just one of many things that competes for our attention. Often, God gets very little of our attention while we spend hours each day on our phones.

If your life is messy, ask yourself if there's something or someone you need to be paying more attention to. We're guessing the answer is yes.

Reflect: Philippians 1:27 says, "Above all, you must live as citizens of heaven, conducting yourselves in a manner worthy of the Good News about Christ." How easily distracted are you? How much discretionary time do you spend on your phone or computer each day? Is there someone or something you need to be paying more attention to?

ARNIE'S EMBARRASSMENT

ARNOLD PALMER WAS one of those people no one ever says a bad word about. He wasn't perfect, but you couldn't prove it by the testimonials of the people who knew him. They offered one glowing story after another. However, Arnie spoke of his own weaknesses and poor choices, like this personal confession I (Pat) heard him share about his smoking:

> If I had known what cigarettes were doing to me, regardless of what other people were saying about my smoking, I would have quit sooner than I did. I quit smoking on the golf course thirty years ago completely. Jack used to smoke. Lee Trevino too. When I see some of the old clips and see how silly I looked with that thing hanging out of my mouth, I could just cringe. My father tried to convince me of that when I was younger, but I thought I knew more than he did. Fortunately, I began to feel what those things were doing to

me. I can run now at seventy better than I could forty years ago when I was puffing on cigarettes.

Sadly, we often don't realize how dumb we're being in the moment we're actually being dumb. It's true of smokers. It's also true of adulterers. How many people come out of an affair saying, "I can't believe how stupid I was?" It's also true of people who fall for get-rich-quick schemes. The next time someone tries to tell you you're being dumb, take him (or her) seriously. In all likelihood, that person is seeing what you aren't able to in that moment. By heeding the warning, you just might be able to correct your foolish behavior before it has a chance to ruin your life.

Reflect: Psalms 38:5 says, "My wounds fester and stink because of my foolish sins." Has anyone ever tried to tell you that you were being foolish? Did you accept or reject their opinion? What are some ways you can check yourself to make sure you haven't slipped into some foolish habit?

UNCOMMON COURTESY

NEWSPAPER COLUMNIST BOB GREENE took his son to a small pitch-and-putt golf course in Chicago to knock some balls around. Afterward they went to the snack bar for a drink. Only two other people were in the place, and one of them was the legendary Cub Ernie Banks. Bob's son saw him first and was thrilled at the possibility of asking for an autograph.

With encouragement from his dad, he grabbed a napkin, borrowed a pen, and walked hesitantly over to Ernie's table. Bob stayed put and couldn't hear what was said, but he saw that when his son spoke, Ernie got up and left. "Oh no! This is bad," Bob thought.

Looking out the window, he saw Ernie walk to his car, but he didn't get in and drive away. He opened the trunk, pulled out some things, and started back inside. He brought Bob's son a baseball, which he autographed, and an 8x10 photo that he also signed. Then he talked to the boy as if he was the only person on earth.

Here's the part we love: This was not unusual for Ernie Banks. He carried balls and pictures in his trunk just so he would be able to give young baseball fans such memorable moments.

You've heard the term "common courtesy." It refers to ordinary acts of courtesy that everyone expects and no one thinks much about. Uncommon courtesy is when someone goes far beyond what's expected simply because they choose to and stand to gain nothing. Like Ernie Banks with young Mr. Greene.

People say this world needs more common courtesy. Let this be our call for more uncommon courtesy. Planned, strategized, and executed as often as possible. More than just little baseball fans need it.

Reflect: Galatians 5:22 says, "The Holy Spirit produces this kind of fruit in our lives … kindness." Can you think of a time when someone was uncommonly kind to you? Why do you think more people don't practice this kind of kindness? How could you strategize to be uncommonly kind to the people you meet?

A BATTING PRACTICE BALL FINDS A HOME

MIKE HERMAN FROM Illinois was on a lifelong quest to get a baseball at a major-league game. Catching a foul ball, a home run ball, or even having a player toss him one during batting practice would have been fine. He just wanted a ball.

One day he was watching batting practice at Busch Stadium in St. Louis and found himself standing beside a five-year-old boy who was also trying to get a ball. The little guy was tiny and spoke with a slight speech impediment. His chances of getting a ball were practically nil, which made Mike want to help him get one. It became his mission, so much so that he made up his mind that if he, Mike, managed to get a ball, he would give it to the little guy.

You can probably guess what happened.

After twenty-eight years of trying to get a ball, within five minutes of deciding he would give the ball to the little boy if he got one, Mike Herman got his first ball … and promptly gave it away to the little boy.

Later, Mike reflected on the experience and wondered how many times God waits to give us something until we are willing to give it away.

How tightly do you cling to things? Do you see your possessions as yours and nobody else's? Perhaps this is why God hasn't given you more than he has. We don't claim to know why God does all the things he does, but it seems like Mike Herman might've been onto something: When God sees we're ready to be generous, he knows he can give to us, and good things will come of it.

WHEN GOD SEES WE'RE READY TO BE GENEROUS, HE KNOWS HE CAN GIVE TO US, AND GOOD THINGS WILL COME OF IT.

Reflect: 1 Timothy 6:18 says, "Tell them to use their money to do good. They should be rich in good works and generous to those in need, always being ready to share." Have you ever given something away that was very precious to you? Was it a painful or a blessed experience? What made you do it? Do you tithe? If not, why?

CATCHING THE *REALLY* BIG ONE

FISHING IS PERHAPS the most relaxing of all sports. What's better than taking your cooler and some snacks out to the old fishin' hole on a pretty day? But fishing is not without its dangers, as every true fisherman knows.

One of the biggest dangers arises when your lure gets caught on a log or some unseen underwater impediment. You're cranking your lure when suddenly it slams to a stop. For half a second, you think a bass has hit your lure, but quickly you realize it's just snagged on something. This is the moment at which countless fishermen have chosen the dumbest option available to them: tugging as hard as they can on the line. Often the lure dislodges and, due to the spring in the rod and the line, comes flying back at the fisherman at a hundred miles an hour. If the fisherman is lucky, the lure and the hooks fly on by, missing him completely. If he's not so lucky, they embed themselves in his skin, making him or her the catch of the day.

(Mark) As one who has "caught myself" this way more than once, I have learned that a violent response is seldom the best way to solve a problem. It's far better to pause, think, and choose an option that stands less of a chance of landing you in the hospital. Cutting the line and sacrificing a lure is far better than having a treble hook embedded in your cheek. And having a reasonable conversation or making a compromise is far better than shouting or coming to blows.

This is not a call for pacifism. Sometimes you have to fight. But far too many people go for the violent response first and end up suffering unnecessarily.

Reflect: Psalms 16:8 says, "I know the Lord is always with me. I will not be shaken." Have you ever lost your temper and made a tense situation worse? Do you ever feel tempted to blow up at someone in order to intimidate them and take control of the situation? What do you think God would prefer you to do in such a circumstance?

THERE'S NO SUCH THING AS A "GIMME"

RAY WATSON KNEW HIS son had a talent for golf. Even before he was ten years old, he was learning how to cut and draw the ball. By the time he was a teenager, he was playing with adults and winning many of the one-dollar wagers they put on their games. At the age of fourteen, he won the Kansas City Men's Match Play Championship against a man twice his age. He was well on his way to becoming the great Tom Watson.

One interesting story comes from when Tom was fourteen and playing against his dad in the Walloon Lake Country Club Championship in Northern Michigan. They came to the hole that could decide the match. Ray had holed out, and Tom had a three-footer to halve the hole and continue the match to the next hole. Normally, the golfer in Ray's position would concede the putt because it was so short, but Ray didn't. He offered his son no "gimme" and made him putt it. Tom missed the putt and lost the match to his father.

Some criticized Ray, suggesting that he was harder on his son than he would have been on any other player. But Tom took a different view. He said he knew that his father was teaching him that he would have to earn what he got in life. Tom learned his lesson well. He went on to "earn" championships in seventy professional tournaments, including nine majors.

"Gimmes" are fine in a gentleman's game like golf, but in real life, don't expect them. Real success comes to people who knuckle down and work hard and give their best. People who look for shortcuts and handouts and free passes will never know the best of what life has to offer.

Reflect: Psalms 90:17 says, "And may the Lord our God show us his approval and make our efforts successful." Have you ever been the recipient of a "gimme": something important that you didn't have to work for? How do you feel when other people get things for free that you had to earn? What do you think are the benefits of having to earn everything you get?

EMBRACING THE NEW

IT WAS 1976 when the International Olympic Committee introduced ice dancing as a sport. Not everyone was keen on the idea. There was no ball in play. There was no scoreboard ringing up points. Fans could understand when a ball went through a hoop or a runner crossed the plate or a puck landed in a net, but watching dancers on skates required a discerning eye that most fans simply didn't have.

It wasn't until 1984, at the Sarajevo games, that ice dancing exploded in popularity, and it was because of Great Britain's Jayne Torvill and Christopher Dean. They performed a program to Ravel's *Boléro* to such exquisite perfection that judges and spectators alike were in awe. Even without a ball or a scoreboard, people suddenly saw a display of grace, quickness, and skill that couldn't be denied. Today, ice dancing is well respected as an athletically difficult and demanding sport.

Throughout our lives we will encounter new ideas that will be difficult for us to embrace. This is especially true when beloved traditions are involved. Churches, for example, can face backlash from members when they try to introduce a new way of doing things. Educators can face a backlash from students and parents when a new way of working math problems is introduced.

We encourage you to remember that every idea was once a new idea. Yes, even that old beloved tradition that so warms your heart. Once upon a time, somebody somewhere was saying, "But we've never done it that way before!"

Be open minded. Loyal to the Scriptures, yes, but open minded. Remember: if it wasn't for new ideas and methods, you'd be going out every day to hunt for your next meal with a club.

Reflect: In Isaiah 43:19 God said, "I am about to do something new. See, I have already begun!" Can you think of a new idea or methodology that you had trouble embracing? Do you feel there should be a balance between the old and new or that the new should always take precedence? Do you believe that new is always better? Why?

T-BALL TRUTH TELLER

THE YEAR WAS 1989. The sport, T-ball.

Nine-year-old Tanner Munsey of Wellington, Florida, scooped up a grounder and attempted to tag a passing runner. He missed, but the umpire, Laura Benson, called the runner out. Troubled by what he knew was an injustice, Tanner approached the umpire and admitted he didn't tag the runner. The ump, also concerned about the injustice, reversed the call and gave the runner the base.

Jump ahead two weeks.

Same team, same umpire.

Tanner Munsey scooped up a grounder and attempted to tag a passing runner. The umpire called the runner safe but could tell that Tanner was troubled by the call. She asked Tanner if he tagged the runner, and when Tanner said yes, she reversed herself again and called the runner out. Naturally, the opposing coach was upset, but Ms. Benson said that she had found young Tanner to be completely honest previously, so she trusted him and would give him the call.

This story illustrates an important truth about honesty. It builds trust and goodwill like almost nothing else. When you prove yourself to be a truth teller, even when the truth works against you, it makes an impression that people don't forget. Truth tellers are often fast-tracked for promotions in businesses and organizations because executives know how important it is to surround themselves with people they can trust.

I (Pat) heard Warren Buffett say, "I look for three things in hiring people. The first is personal integrity, the second is intelligence, and the third is a high energy level. But if you don't have the first, the second two don't matter."

And here's the best fact of all: Honesty is a choice, not a talent, which means anybody can do it. No matter what your skill set is, all of the advantages honesty offers can be yours.

Reflect: Proverbs 12:22 says, "The Lord detests lying lips, but he delights in those who tell the truth." Have you ever told the truth even when you knew it would hurt your cause in some way? Did that decision eventually benefit you, and if so, in what way? Why do you think so many people lie, even though truth telling so often benefits us more than a lie ever could?

NINE PIRATES

SEPTEMBER 1, 1971, was a history-making day in Major League Baseball. Danny Murtaugh, manager of the Pittsburgh Pirates, made out the following lineup to go against the Phillies and pitcher Woody Fryman: Rennie Stennett, second base. Gene Clines, center field. Roberto Clemente, right field. Willie Stargell, left field. Manny Sanguillén, catcher. Dave Cash, third base. Al Oliver, first base. Jackie Hernández, shortstop. Dock Ellis, pitcher.

Nobody noticed anything unusual about the lineup at first, but eventually it was discovered that Danny Murtaugh had made out the first lineup in major-league history that was comprised entirely of nonwhite players.

Suddenly, reporters and historians were asking questions. Was it some kind of statement? What did the players think? Was Mr. Murtaugh pressured to do it? We love Danny Murtaugh's response. He said he didn't give a thought to the races of the men he put on the field … he was just putting Pirates out there.

We live in a time when accusations of racism are hurled with startling ease and almost no thought. It's become the go-to accusation when you really want to hurt somebody. The tragedy is that when everything becomes racist, we lose sight of what *true* racism is, which allows it to slip under the radar and go unchecked. Politicians are often the worst, hurling accusations of racism merely to try to score political cheap points.

We long for a world where people think like Danny Murtaugh did back in 1971, where people are seen as people and their color doesn't even cross one's mind. Won't you help build that world?

Reflect: Galatians 3:28 says, "There is no longer Jew or Gentile, slave or free, male and female. For you are all one in Christ Jesus." Have you ever been the victim of racism? How did you process that experience emotionally? What can people who aren't racists do to tamp down the racist poison that is boiling in our culture?

HOW THE BABE GOT HIS 3 (AND GEHRIG GOT HIS 4)

THERE ARE SO many things we see when we go to a sporting event that we take for granted … like names and numbers on uniforms. It was back in the early 1900s that the New York Yankees started putting numbers on their uniforms. However, the numbers made little difference because they were very small. In 1929, someone in their organization suggested enlarging the numbers so the new fans they were attracting would be able to identify the players. They eventually decided to make the numbers bigger for the fans' sake, and how they did it explains the numbers we now have ingrained in our minds. They numbered the players consecutively, starting with the leadoff man and continuing on through the batting order to the bench players. This is why Babe Ruth's iconic number was 3 and Lou Gehrig's was 4.

Interestingly, it took almost thirty more years for the rest of the teams to put numbers on their uniforms, and all because of a concern that still troubles a lot of people today: money. Teams thought that if they put numbers on the players' uniforms, they wouldn't sell as many scorecards.

Financial considerations dictate so much of what we do. This can be a good thing, of course. Jesus said that we should count the cost of things. But some things are more valuable than money, like the human soul, for instance. What are souls worth to God? So much that he gave his only Son to die on a cross to save them.

Every week when you sit in church and the offering plate goes by, you make a judgment call about the worth of human souls. Are they worth more than that cute top you saw at the mall? Are they worth more than that new Titleist driver you saw at the pro shop? No one is saying you shouldn't be able to buy some things you like and enjoy. But your giving to God is always going to be a reflection of your values.

Reflect: 1 Corinthians 6:20 says, "God bought you with a high price." When was the last time you made a truly sacrificial gift to help save souls? Has your giving to the Lord increased the longer you have been a Christian? How do you decide how much to spend on yourself and how much to give to God?

BLOWING OFF STEAM

I (MARK) HAVE BEEN a pastor for forty-seven years. If I had to pick a sport that was most like being a pastor, I would pick golf. Why? Because golfers and pastors have one gigantic thing in common: we both must keep a lid on our emotions when we are on the job.

Football players can go tackle or block somebody to blow off steam. Basketball players can rattle the rim with a two-handed slam. Hockey players can drop their gloves and duke it out. Baseball players can take vicious hacks at the baseball and, failing to hit it, turn their attention to a more stationary target like the dugout water cooler. But golfers play a "gentleman's game" and are expected to maintain control even at the most frustrating moments. Miss a four-foot putt on the eighteenth hole to lose the US Open? You're expected to calmly walk over and shake the champion's hand and congratulate him. And smile!

Preachers, likewise, simply cannot give vent to their emotions in public, no matter how they might be disrespected or mistreated. If you do, you are judged to be "unspiritual" or "unfit to lead." I can't count the number of times when I have been so angry or frustrated I couldn't see straight but had to keep it bottled up because people were watching.

It's during those times that I find myself being so thankful for the Holy Spirit. One of the fruits of the Spirit is self-control. I have walked away from situations before where I couldn't believe I didn't blow my top. "How did I *not* just throw a screaming fit?" I ask myself. And then I realize that I just experienced the Spirit's work in my life.

SOME PEOPLE ARE AMAZED BY WHAT THE SPIRIT ENABLES THEM TO DO. I AM OFTEN AMAZED BY WHAT THE SPIRIT KEEPS ME FROM DOING.

Some people are amazed by what the Spirit enables them to do. I am often amazed by what the Spirit keeps me from doing.

Reflect: Galatians 5:22 says, "The Holy Spirit produces this kind of fruit in our lives … self-control." Have you ever completely melted down in public? How did you feel afterward? What kind of damage did you do? What steps did you take to keep it from happening again? Why do so many Christians fail to manifest the fruit of the Spirit?

UPSIDE-DOWN THINKING

THE 1950s WERE good to the Oklahoma Sooners football team. The soft-spoken Bud Wilkinson came along and took the program to heights rarely seen. In seventeen years, the Sooners won three national championships and fourteen conference titles and put together four perfect seasons, including an unbeaten streak of forty-seven games. Overall, Wilkinson's coaching record at OU was 145–29–4. With numbers like that, it's no surprise that the football team became the first thing people across the country thought about when someone mentioned the university.

One day the university president, Dr. George L. Cross, was asked about the school's academic goals. He said, "We're trying to build a university our football team can be proud of."[25] The comment was meant to be a joke, but it does remind us of how sometimes our thinking can get turned upside down.

When a father gets the notion that excelling at work is more important than excelling as a husband or father, his thinking has been turned upside down.

When a student gets the notion that skipping classes is OK as long as he can still pass the course, his thinking has been turned upside down.

When a politician gets the notion that hanging onto power is more important than serving his constituents, his thinking has been turned upside down.

When a church gets the notion that filling the seats is more important than making disciples, its thinking has been turned upside down.

We don't have to tell you that there's a lot of upside-down thinking going on in the world right now. Have you taken inventory of your thoughts and motivations lately?

Reflect: In Matthew 6:33 Jesus said, "Seek the Kingdom of God above all else ..." How much thought do you give to your priorities? Has anyone (your spouse, for example) ever suggested that your thinking might be upside down? What systems do you have in place to make sure your priorities don't get out of order?

PICK GOOD ASSOCIATES

VINCE LOMBARDI AND TOM LANDRY are two of the greatest coaches in NFL history. Did you know there was a time when they coached on the same team at the same time? It was back in the 1950s. Jim Lee Howell, who was the head coach of the New York Giants, hired Lombardi to coach his offense and Landry to coach his defense.

Kyle Rote, a Giants player, told about walking down the hallway at training camp. He passed by one room and saw Vince Lombardi working with the offense. He passed by the next room and saw Tom Landry working with the defense. Then he passed by the third room and saw Jim Lee Howell sitting back with his feet up on his desk, reading a newspaper. Howell used to jokingly say that with assistant coaches like Lombardi and Landry, all he had to do was keep the footballs aired up and enforce curfew.

The value of good associates can't be overstated. But what is a good associate? Is it someone who agrees with everything you say or someone who respectfully challenges your thinking? Is it the person who makes the fewest mistakes, or the person with the most creative ideas, some of which you know will flop? Is it the person with the most talent or the person with the most passion?

You don't always get to pick your associates, but if ever you do, we have two suggestions. First, consider the person's heart. God chose young David over his brothers not because of his resume but because of his heart. And second, consider the person's happiness. Discontented, unhappy, sour-faced, complaining people will not help you, no matter how talented they are.

Reflect: Proverbs 13:20 says, "Walk with the wise and become wise; associate with fools and get in trouble." Have you ever been stuck with a bad associate? What were some of the ways he/she made your life more difficult? Based on that experience, what are some of the qualities that you feel make a good associate?

FOOT FEATURE

IF YOU'RE LIKE MOST sports fans, you have some sports equipment around your house: golf clubs, tennis rackets, an old ball glove, a fishing rod or two. Maybe you've never thought about it, but some of your most important sports equipment is attached to your body, just below your ankles. Yes, we're talking about your feet.

Notorious for smelling bad and never once thought beautiful enough to put on the cover of a fashion magazine, your feet are nonetheless amazing, an intricately formed collection of 26 bones, 33 joints, and 112 ligaments. They balance you, propel you, guide you, stop you, and launch you into the air. And they serve as shock absorbers. If you run one mile, your heels will slam onto the pavement 1,500 times, absorbing multiple times your body weight with each landing. (No wonder sneakers are such big business!) A testament to the beating the sportsman's feet take is the fact that over 600,000 people a year make a trip to the emergency room because of foot injuries related to some sort of sporting activity.

As Christians, we do not believe that we are descended from tadpoles. We believe we are created by the God of the universe. Every day when we put on our shoes, we should be reminded of the genius of our Creator. And when we get a little older (like your intrepid authors), and aches and pains start to visit us more frequently, we should be reminded that God has an answer for that too. We'll get new bodies in heaven (2 Corinthians 5:1–3).

Put us down as a couple of guys who are looking forward to that.

Reflect: Psalms 139:14 says, "Thank you for making me so wonderfully complex! Your workmanship is marvelous—how well I know it." Do you have any physical disabilities? If so, how have you learned to compensate with other parts of your body? What is your most notable athletic ability? When was the last time you thanked God for it?

ACT TWO

GREAT SHOWS, WHICH we both enjoy, usually unfold over two acts. The first act sets up the story and creates tension; the second act resolves that tension. Lives often unfold the same way. A great example would be Bob Uecker.

Bob was signed as a catcher in 1956 and played nine seasons with three different teams. Obviously, anybody who plays nine seasons in the big leagues is not terrible. However, Bob's career batting average was a measly .200, and when asked how he caught a knuckleball, he often said that he waited until it stopped rolling and picked it up.

Bob's second act started in 1971, when he was hired to broadcast games for the Milwaukee Brewers. He did a fine job as a play-by-play man, but where he really won the fans over was with his wit. He presented himself as a lovable loser who was an awful baseball player. He was so funny that he ended up making dozens of appearances on *The Tonight Show* and even starred in his own sitcom, *Mr. Belvedere*, on ABC. He was inducted into the Radio Hall of Fame in 2001 and had a jersey retired by the Brewers in 2005.

Stories like this should be a great inspiration to you if you're in the first act of your life and it isn't going very well. They are a reminder that things can change for the better. You don't always have to do what you're currently doing. You can create a second act. You can chart a new course and perhaps find greater happiness and fulfillment than you ever dreamed would be possible.

We encourage you to think big and, by all means, outside the box. If you've got a long-suppressed dream or passion, let that be where you start.

Reflect: Psalms 37:4 says, "Take delight in the Lord, and he will give you your heart's desires." Which act of your life are you in right now? Are you satisfied with how things are going? If not, what do you think the problem is? What would it take for you to create a second act that might be better?

THE SNOWFLAKE GENERATION

THERE IS A term recently coined that describes people who are so fragile emotionally that just about everything upsets or offends them. They're constantly pleading for safe spaces where no one is allowed to say or do anything that might hurt their feelings. Such people are called "snowflakes" because, well, what's more fragile than a snowflake?

In our view, the snowflakes of the world need to acquaint themselves with Jack Youngblood. He played defensive end for the Los Angeles Rams, and on December 30, 1979, broke his leg in a playoff game against the Dallas Cowboys. We don't mean he strained a ligament or twisted his knee. The man actually snapped his fibula like a dry stick. Then he made one of the most courageous (and perhaps foolhardy) decisions we've ever heard of: he ordered the training staff to tape up his leg so he could go back into the game. He did and then accomplished one of the most mind-blowing feats in sports history. He somehow got around offensive tackle Rayfield Wright and chased down Roger Staubach for a sack.

We don't recommend playing sports on a broken leg, but we have to admit that reflecting on Jack Youngblood's grit and courage is refreshing in this generation that seems to have lost its backbone. Christians in particular are going to have to toughen up and show some courage as our culture becomes more and more secular and progressive. If we don't, our light will be dimmed. Not extinguished, because God will always have his remnant. But the Church will not have the influence it otherwise would.

Please don't be a snowflake. Don't curl up in the fetal position if someone challenges your faith. Stand tall and firm, knowing you have the Spirit and strength of the living God within you.

Reflect: 2 Timothy 1:7 says, "For God has not given us a spirit of fear and timidity, but of power, love, and self-discipline." Have you ever been attacked, ridiculed, or persecuted because of your faith? How did you react? Would you react any differently today? What are some reasons why a Christian should never be a snowflake?

CLOSED DOORS AND OPEN WINDOWS

KEN VENTURI IS A member of the World Golf Hall of Fame. He played on the PGA Tour from 1956 to 1967 and won fourteen tournaments, including five majors. When his playing career was done, he became a golf analyst for CBS, a job he held for thirty-five years. As impressive as the tournament wins are, we are most impressed with Ken's broadcasting career because, as a boy, he had a terrible problem with stammering.

Ken often said that his struggles with stammering were the reason why he took up golf. He was an outstanding baseball player and might've had a pro career, but baseball is a team sport that requires interaction with other people. Golf is an individual sport that requires little interaction with other people. Ken, who was teased unmercifully as a child, often felt uncomfortable around people and opted for the sport that would allow him to be by himself most of the time.

Ken was forced to retire from competitive golf due to carpal tunnel syndrome. The numbness in his fingers made it impossible for him to hold a golf club properly. But by the time that happened, he had overcome his stammering problem. When he was offered the color commentary job on the CBS golf telecasts, he took it, hoping that he would be an inspiration to other children who had trouble speaking.

Ken Venturi's story reminds us of that old saying, "When God closes a door, he opens a window." This saying is not in the Bible, and we are not holding it up as an example of great theology, but there are many times when it does seem to be true. That's why we encourage you not to mourn the closures in your life. It could be that God is merely clearing the way for a new thing he wants to do through you.

Reflect: Isaiah 43:18–19 says, "But forget all that—it is nothing compared to what I am about to do. For I am about to do something new." Have you experienced an unexpected transition in your life or career? Did you sense the hand of God at work at the time? As you reflect on the change, how do you feel it has impacted your faith and relationship with God?

TOMMY LASORDA, NICKNAMER

TOMMY LASORDA, LONG-TIME manager of the Los Angeles Dodgers, is one of the most colorful characters in major-league history. Orel Hershiser tells about the time, shortly after he joined the team, that Tommy gave him the nickname "Bulldog." Orel was young, thin, wore glasses, and was mild mannered … about as far in appearance and demeanor from a bulldog as you could get. That's why he hated the nickname. He felt it was given to try to make him *seem* tough when he knew he already *was* tough, in spite of his baby-faced appearance.

But as time went by, Orel saw that Tommy Lasorda gave lots of players nicknames. He began to realize that giving a player a nickname was Tommy's way of letting that player know he believed in him. It was essentially Tommy saying, "You belong here." Interestingly, the nickname Tommy gave Orel proved to be perfectly appropriate, for Orel was one of the toughest competitors in the league in the 80s and 90s, winning 204 games over seventeen seasons.

Tommy Lasorda understood how important it was for his players to know he believed in them. He knew that knowledge just might be the thing that would give the player an extra boost of confidence in a critical moment. In any sport, when you find players who are willing to run through a wall for their coach, it's because they don't want to let that coach down … they want to live up to the confidence that coach has placed in them.

THERE'S SOMETHING EMPOWERING ABOUT KNOWING SOMEONE BELIEVES IN YOU.

We encourage you, as a parent, teacher, employer, coach, or supervisor to adopt a similar approach with the people you're attempting to lead. Don't let them wonder if they have your confidence. Make sure they know you believe in them. (And if you *don't* believe in them, then you need to ask yourself what they're doing on your team!)

There's something empowering about knowing someone believes in you.

Reflect: In 2 Corinthians 7:16, Paul said to the Corinthians, "I am very happy now because I have complete confidence in you." Have you ever had someone in authority over you express confidence in you? How did that make you feel? Did it affect the way you performed? Is there someone you have authority over now who would benefit from your show of confidence?

TURN DOWN THE VOLUME

WHEN TONY DUNGY became the head coach of the Tampa Bay Buccaneers, he met with his team and told them something they probably thought they'd never hear. He told them that he would not be yelling at them. He said that when he was mad, he would talk to them in a conversational voice. When he was really mad, he would whisper. Then he informed them that if they needed a coach to yell and curse at them in order to motivate them and help them perform their best, they would probably not be playing for the Buccaneers very long.

Unconventional in this era of high-octane coaches?

Yes.

But it worked, to say the least. Tony's winning percentage as a head coach was .668. He won a Super Bowl and is in the Ring of Honor of two franchises, the Bucs and the Colts.

One reason we love Tony Dungy is because his gentle, soft-spoken style is a reminder that you don't have to yell at people to get results. Most people believe that turning up the volume and tossing in a curse word now and then will let people know they mean business and get them scurrying to produce. And it might for a while.

The problem yellers eventually run into is demonstrated every day in Walmarts and supermarkets all around the country. You see mothers yelling at their kids, and what are the kids doing? Usually ignoring their mothers. Yelling generally suffers the same fate that nagging and complaining suffer … it gets tuned out. Maybe not right away, but eventually.

We encourage you to turn down the volume. The people in your life will appreciate being spoken to in a respectful way. And your message will likely get through more cleanly because it won't have to battle its way through that wall of emotion that yelling creates.

Reflect: Proverbs 15:1 says, "A gentle answer deflects anger, but harsh words make tempers flare." Have you ever been routinely yelled at by someone in authority over you? How did it make you feel? Are there times when you yell at people in your life? Could it be that you yell more often than you realize? Might your relationships be improved if you yelled less?

THE POWER OF A HUG

THE 1983 NCAA basketball championship produced one of the most cringe-worthy endings in the history of the event. The North Carolina Tarheels, with two future NBA Hall of Famers (Michael Jordan and James Worthy) were playing the Georgetown Hoyas. With seventeen seconds left in the game, Jordan hit a jumper that put the Tarheels up by a point. Georgetown guard Fred Brown then brought the ball up the court with a chance to win. The crowd was on its feet. All across America, fans were holding their breath.

Suddenly, in the heat of the moment, Fred released a pass ... to a Tarheel, James Worthy, ending what had been a spectacular game on one of the biggest bonehead plays in the history of the sport.

But we bring this up not to ridicule anyone. We bring it up because of what happened immediately after the game. As fans were taunting and ridiculing Fred Brown, his coach, John Thompson, walked over and hugged him. Later, Fred Brown talked about how much that hug meant to him. It let him know that the sun would come up tomorrow and everything would be fine. It wasn't the end of the world.

A hug is one of the most underrated ways to encourage people. We live in a hypersensitive world where touching needs to be done thoughtfully, but for most people, a hug is a welcome expression of affection. For some people, that hug you give might be the only expression of love that comes their way all week. You might never know it, but the hug you give might be the only thing that keeps some beleaguered person going.

Some people aren't huggers, and that's fine. If you are, be generous with them. A hug can be good medicine for someone's heart.

Reflect: Ecclesiastes 3:5 says, "There is a time to embrace …" Can you think of a time when a simple hug meant the world to you? Why do you think a hug has such power? Is there someone in your life right now that could use a hug?

BE ATYPICAL

NANCY MERKI IS NOT a household name in the world of sports, but she should be. In 1934, when she was eight years old, she contracted polio. In those days, a child with polio was destined to wear heavy leg braces and walk on crutches. Nancy took up swimming as a way to try to strengthen her leg muscles. Jack Cody, an experienced swim instructor, took her under his wing, and before long she began to show a real aptitude for the sport. Over the next several years, she would compete in a wide range of amateur competitions, winning many of them and even setting records. The pinnacle of her career came in 1948, when she made the United States Olympic team and made the finals of the women's 400-meter freestyle. In 1955, Nancy's amazing story was depicted on an episode of *Cavalcade of America*, which was an anthology TV series.

Nancy Merki did something that is very rare: she refused to accept the typical outcome of her circumstances. In those days, most children with polio did not attempt a sport. They typically resigned themselves to a life of inactivity and tried to find other ways to express themselves. Nancy's dreams were bigger than that.

We wish more people could see beyond the typical outcome of their circumstances. For example, when betrayal happens in a marriage, the typical outcome is divorce. But why does it have to be? When disappointment happens at church, the typical outcome is to drop out. But why does it have to be?

Why not be atypical?

Why not say to yourself, "Just because most people go down this road doesn't mean I have to. I'm going to be different."

This is when greatness surfaces in people. This is when special things happen. This is when the world is reminded that life offers amazing possibilities.

Reflect: Ephesians 3:20 says, "Now all glory to God, who is able, through his mighty power at work within us, to accomplish infinitely more than we might ask or think." Have you ever refused to accept a typical outcome to some difficulty in your life? What made you refuse? Is there a situation in your life right now that you need to rise above and conquer?

PREPARATION

SHANNON MILLER BECAME famous at the 1996 Olympics. In a balance beam performance that many saw as flawless, she won a gold medal and became the first American to win both an individual and a team gold medal in a fully attended Olympics. She is currently one of the most decorated United States Olympic gymnasts with a total of seven medals and a member of the United States Gymnastics Hall of Fame and the United States Olympic Hall of Fame.

When Shannon won her medals at the 1996 Olympics, people saw her performances. They did not see the countless hours she spent practicing. For a precious few minutes, she was in the spotlight; for 20,000 hours she was in the gym, grinding as hard as she could to perfect every move. She arrived at the gym every morning at eight and worked for about four hours. Then she returned to the gym at three in the afternoon to work for another four hours. And she did this six days a week while managing to stay in school and keep up with her classes.

Shannon's incredible work ethic and dynamic success remind us that we make or break our hopes and dreams far away from the spotlight.

The best students spend hours with their noses in their books and their class notes.

The best preachers spend hours in isolation, carefully crafting their sermons.

The best musicians spend years running scales and developing their technique.

The best researchers spend years honing and perfecting new medical treatments.

Sadly, there are still people who undervalue preparation. Things like study and practice and research are not glamorous. They bring no cheers from adoring crowds and often get to be tedious and hard. But preparation is where success evolves from a dream to a possibility, from a possibility to a probability, and from a probability to a reality.

Reflect: Proverbs 24:27 says, "Do your planning and prepare your fields before building your house." Have you ever failed at an endeavor because you weren't adequately prepared? How did that experience change you, if at all? Why do you think people lose patience with practice and preparation?

BE A KID AGAIN

I (MARK) WAS ONCE invited to attend a six year old's T-ball game. His mom and dad were good friends of ours, so I decided to go. It was one of the more joyous experiences I've had at a ballgame. I couldn't help smiling as the shortstop wore his glove as a hat, the right fielder picked dandelions in the outfield, and the left fielder spun around like a top for reasons only he understood. But the *tink* of metal bat on ball brought them to attention. Wherever the ball went, and it usually wasn't far, all eight fielders were in hot pursuit, often fighting over the ball while the batter traveled a circuitous route to first base. The way the parents cheered, you would have thought their kids were playing in the World Series.

I contrast that with the intensity I see in big leaguers. Yes, they're professionals. Yes, they're playing for their jobs. Yes, there's a lot of money on the line. They *should* take it seriously. But I sometimes get the feeling they're not having any fun. The expectations, the pressure, the challenge of playing a very difficult game can produce grimaces and angry outbursts, some of which are not fit for the ears of those little T-ballers.

When I see this, I begin to understand why Jesus talked about how adults need to be more like children. Not just in baseball, but in many areas of life, we lose our sense of wonder and enjoyment. Everything becomes super serious, almost a matter of life and death. We torture ourselves if things don't go perfectly.

How great would it be if we could all lighten up a little bit and learn to enjoy ourselves? Solomon said, "When people live to be very old, let them rejoice in every day of life" (Eccles. 11:8).

Reflect: Psalms 118:24 says, "This is the day the Lord has made. We will rejoice and be glad in it." Do you tend to take things very seriously and get frustrated when they don't go perfectly? Do you feel your super seriousness sometimes works against you? How? What are some things you could do that might help you chill out a little and enjoy life more?

WHAT THE WORLD NEEDS NOW

IT WAS OPENING day, 1996. The Cincinnati Reds were hosting the Montreal Expos. Just seven pitches into the game, home plate umpire John McSherry called time-out and walked toward the Reds' dugout. He motioned for the second base umpire to come in and replace him and then collapsed. He was rushed to a hospital where he was pronounced dead from cardiac arrest within the hour.

From his home in Cincinnati, an eight-year-old boy named Christopher Harris watched everything that happened. Like everyone else, he was saddened by John McSherry's death. But he also felt anger because, when it was announced that the game would be postponed, many of the fans booed. He felt sorry for the McSherry family having to hear those boos and wanted to let them know that some Reds' fans were in favor of postponing the game out of respect for the umpire's life.

The next day, at his suggestion, his third-grade class made sympathy cards to send to the McSherry family. The cards were so deeply appreciated that John McSherry's girlfriend, Marion Doyle, arranged for the whole class to attend a Reds game and get a VIP tour of Riverfront Stadium.

Life can be very cold and hard.

People can too.

We've seen restaurant customers berate a server because a steak was overcooked or an iced tea glass was empty. We've seen drivers honk and scream and make obscene gestures at drivers who weren't moving fast enough to suit them. We've heard supposedly loving Christians skewer their preacher because his sermon didn't adequately entertain them.

According to an old popular song, what the world needs now is love, sweet love. We couldn't agree more. Those of us who are Christians should be the most loving people of all. Let us take a lesson from young Christopher Harris.

Reflect: In John 13:35, Jesus said, "Your love for one another will prove to the world that you are my disciples." Why do you think Christians are often so insensitive and unloving? Is your first impulse in an aggravating situation to criticize rather than to show compassion? If so, what needs to change in your heart and mind to make you a more loving person?

AWKWARDNESS

WHEN UCLA WAS a college basketball powerhouse, in the days long before there was a shot clock, they played a game against Oregon, a team that was no match for them. UCLA jumped out to a 10–2 lead, which was no surprise. What *was* a surprise is that UCLA then held the ball to avoid running up the score. Further, Oregon allowed them to do it. This means that ten players were just standing on the court doing nothing for almost the entire game.

Legendary announcer Dick Enberg was calling the game and suddenly had nothing to call. No plays being run, no passes, no shots, no rebounds … nothing. Dick ran through some stats and other prepared materials but quickly ran dry. That's when he resorted to humming "Raindrops Keep Fallin' on My Head," which was a song from a movie that was popular at the time, *Butch Cassidy and the Sundance Kid*.

Sometimes what other people do can put you in an awkward situation. For Dick Enberg, it turned out to be something everyone could laugh about. But sometimes the awkwardness is no laughing matter.

I (Mark) remember the time I walked into a local hardware store. The owner said, "Aren't you the pastor at Poinciana Christian Church?" I said that I was. He said, "Well, one of your church members was just in here and cursed me out because he thought I overcharged him." I groaned inwardly and told the man how sorry I was that he had to endure that.

PART OF HAVING A GOOD CHRISTIAN WITNESS IS BEING SENSITIVE TO THE NEED OF THE MOMENT AND BEHAVING IN A WAY THAT IS APPROPRIATE.

We encourage you not to be that guy—or that girl—whose behavior makes life awkward for others. Don't embarrass your spouse in public. Don't use inappropriate words in front of children. Don't overreact when you have a disagreement in public. Don't be irreverent or flippant in a serious situation.

Part of having a good Christian witness is being sensitive to the need of the moment and behaving in a way that is appropriate.

Reflect: In Luke 6:31, Jesus said, "Do to others as you would like them to do to you." What's the most awkward situation you've ever been in because of someone else's choices? Have you ever said or done something inappropriate that you later regretted? If so, what are some ways you can train yourself to show better judgment in social situations?

A NICE DOSE OF HUMILITY

TOM LANDRY, THE LEGENDARY coach of the Dallas Cowboys, once took his wife to dinner at a famous Southern California restaurant. They invited Louis L'Amour and his wife, Kathy, to join them. Then, as an afterthought, they invited another couple that they knew, a man that happened to be a well-known newspaper publisher and his wife. The key to this story is that the newspaper publisher had never heard of Louis L'Amour, one of the most successful novelists in history. The conversation went down something like this:

Newspaper publisher: What do you do for a living?

Louis L'Amour: I write.

Newspaper publisher: What do you write?

Louis L'Amour: Western novels.

Newspaper publisher: Have you written very many?

Louis L'Amour: About seventy.

Newspaper publisher: Have they sold pretty well?

Louis L'Amour: Each one has sold over a million copies.

At this point, Tom Landry was grinning ear to ear, loving the stunned expression on the newspaperman's face. He was having dinner with a Mt. Rushmore–type of legend in the publishing business—the very industry he was a part of—and didn't even know it.

As for Louis L'Amour, we don't know if he needed a dose of humility, but he sure got one. We've found that God often puts us in situations that tug us in the direction of humility. They are little reminders that we aren't quite as big and important as we might think.

Reflect: Romans 12:16 says, "Don't be too proud to enjoy the company of ordinary people." Have you ever had a truly humbling experience? At the time, did you feel it was God's way of adjusting your view of yourself? What are some reasons why we all ought to stay humble?

EXECUTION

JOHN MCKAY WAS one of the elite football coaches of the 1970s. When he signed on to coach the expansion Tampa Bay Buccaneers, everyone knew it was going to be tough. At one point, when the Bucs had lost several games in a row, McKay was asked how he felt about his team's execution. He said, "I'm in favor of it."

Funny line, for sure. But the other kind of execution, the kind that has to do with the way one carries out his or her responsibilities, is an important concept in sports and in life.

Vince Lombardi's teams used to run the same plays over and over again. They didn't worry about trying to trick or surprise their opponent. They believed that if they did what they were supposed to do—in other words, if they executed properly—they would succeed on a majority of plays which would ultimately lead them to victory.

This is a concept that works in life too. We can never predict what life might throw at us, though we know some of it is going to be bad. The key to thriving through it all is simply to continue to execute those things that we know keep us close to God: stay in the Word, pray, worship, and keep the bond of fellowship with other Christians strong. Executing these things well will keep us balanced and centered, which is often the hardest thing to accomplish in bad times. We tend to get angry or discouraged or confused when trouble comes and can find ourselves chasing after spiritual fads, quick fixes, or even falling into discouragement.

The best advice we can give to someone who's being treated rudely by life is simply to continue to execute the basics.

Reflect: Psalms 119:109 says, "My life constantly hangs in the balance, but I will not stop obeying your instructions." When you experience hard times, does your spiritual fire tend to die down or increase? What's the hardest thing about continually executing the spiritual basics? Right now, are you executing them as well as you could be?

JUNE 29

BE CAREFUL

WE DOUBT THAT YOU'VE heard of Rollen Stewart, but at one time he was the most recognized person in sports. No, he wasn't an athlete or a coach; he was the guy in the rainbow wig who held up "John 3:16" signs at nationally televised sporting events. He said he had a vision and that God told him to do this.

Today, Rollen Stewart is serving three consecutive life sentences in California. Not for wearing a clown wig and waving a sign but for brandishing a firearm and barricading himself inside a hotel room near the Los Angeles airport. His demand? He wanted three hours of television time to espouse his views on all kinds of issues, including politics and the Second Coming of Christ.

We are not psychologists, but it seems pretty obvious that Rollin Stewart isn't quite right. Perhaps he never was. But we remember seeing him with those "John 3:16" signs back in the day and thinking, "That guy must really love Jesus." Imagine if the world had known what the future held for that man.

Which begs the question ... what's the difference between a person who tells the world about God's love and a lunatic brandishing a weapon? Sometimes not much, which is why we need to be careful who we look up to, who we listen to, and who we follow. There are wolves in sheep's clothing everywhere, people who will use the things of God to try to advance their own selfish agendas. They'll say all the right words and try to make you think they love Jesus. They are very dangerous.

Be careful.

Reflect: 1 John 4:1 says, "Do not believe everyone who claims to speak by the Spirit. You must test them to see if the spirit they have comes from God." Have you ever been taken in by a wolf in sheep's clothing? If so, what were the qualities that drew you? How did you learn the truth? How did the experience change you?

YOUR "NOT FARS"

SPORTS IS FULL OF "NOT FARS."

When a team finishes the season one game out of the playoffs, they are not far from a postseason bid and a run at a championship.

When a running back is stopped on the six-inch line on fourth down, he is not far from a touchdown.

When a late-inning reliever throws a two-out, three-two pitch an inch outside to walk in the tying run, he is not far from being a hero.

But "not far" is far enough. As the old saying goes, "An inch is as good as a mile." It doesn't matter if a pitch is an inch out of the strike zone or three feet; it counts the same.

Fortunately in sports, our misses are very much in the moment and can be rectified in the next game. The hitter who goes hitless today can come back tomorrow and get four hits. Athletes often can't wait for the next game so they can try to redeem themselves.

In life, it's not so simple.

A miss in life can be difficult, if not impossible to redeem. A father, for example, who didn't give his children enough time and attention when they were young may find that they have no interest in him years later when he finally decides he wants to be a good dad.

We urge you to examine your life with an eye toward removing your "not fars." Don't be one of those people who looks back years later and says, "If I'd only made one little change, things would be different now." Of all the painful realities we can face at the end of our lives, that's one of the saddest.

Reflect: In Mark 12:34, Jesus said to a leading Jewish teacher, "You are not far from the Kingdom of God." Do you currently have a painful "not far" on your record? If so, is it possible for you to go back and redeem it? Why do you think so many people don't notice their near misses until it's too late?

NUMBER ONE

PERHAPS MORE THAN any other area of our society except the stock market, sports is about numbers. If you're a real sports fan (and have a little age on you), you will know what the following numbers represent without us having to tell you:

56: Joe DiMaggio's hitting streak.

18: Jack Nicklaus's record for most majors won.

100: Wilt Chamberlain's record for most points scored in an NBA game.

.406: Ted Williams's average as the last player to hit .400.

2,632: Cal Ripken's consecutive games played streak.

The list could go on and on. Sports history is built on numbers ... streaks and records and percentages and averages. Every game comes with a box score, a compilation of the statistics that particular contest produced.

In the Christian life, only one number really matters, and that is the number one.

How many people's actions can you control?

How many people's faith are you responsible for?

How many chances do you get to live your life?

How many Gods are there?

How many perfect people have there been?

How many people have been qualified to die for our sins?

The answers to these questions are one, one, one, one, one, and one.

The next time you go to a sporting event and see someone holding up a giant foam finger indicating, "We're number one!" let it remind you of the personal nature of the Christian life. It's about you and your one and only Savior, Jesus Christ.

Reflect: Ephesians 4:5 says, "There is one Lord, one faith, and one baptism." What are some of the dangers of believing that you are responsible for other people's faith? Have you ever allowed "other gods" to take over the throne of your heart? If a total stranger were to examine your lifestyle, would he find any evidence that you have surrendered to an idol?

STEPHEN KING, A DIFFERENT KIND OF BASEBALL FAN

AUTHOR STEPHEN KING is a big baseball fan. He shows up at Fenway Park, especially when the Red Sox are in the postseason. And from what we've seen, he gets really good seats! Of course, that's to be expected when you've sold 350 million books. The only place they probably wouldn't let him sit is on the pitching rubber.

But there's something about Stephen King as a baseball fan that is a little different. When he goes to a game, he always takes a book along. Some people take a ball glove or a sign or a jacket; he takes a book. There is a famous photo of him at a game, reading a mystery novel.

We applaud him for this. We are a couple of guys who also take a book just about everywhere we go. I (Pat) used to take a book to every Magic game and read during time outs and at halftime. I (Mark) often read a few pages while sitting in line at the drive-thru or in the doctor's office waiting room.

I (Pat) have long said that if you read five books on any subject, you will become an expert on that subject. That is, you will know more about that subject than ninety-five percent of the people in the world. Think about that! This minute you can choose what field you want to be an expert in and, within a couple of months, be there.

If you're not a reader, we want to encourage you to become one. You can go anywhere and experience almost anything in the pages of a book. You can learn and grow and understand and see what you've never seen before. We encourage you to read whatever interests you, but always—*always*—to be a reader of the Bible. There's lots of great stuff in print, but none of it is more critical to your happiness and salvation than what God has given us in his Word.

Reflect: Again and again, Jesus said, "It is written …" What was the last book you read? Can you even remember? If you're not a reader, what keeps you from it? How hard have you tried to find a book that interests you? Would you be willing to challenge yourself to read a book in the next month? Also, what changes would you need to make to spend more time in the Word?

ROLE MODELS

CHARLES BARKLEY, THE NBA Hall of Famer, is someone I (Pat) have known for many years. Though he is older now and has calmed a bit, he has gotten into some situations away from the court that have not served his reputation well. One of those was when he threw a man through a plate glass window at an Orlando nightclub. (To be fair, Sir Charles was minding his own business when the idiot approached him and dumped an icy drink on him.)

Back in 1993, Charles did a controversial TV ad for Nike in which he said, "I am not a role model. I am not paid to be a role model. I am paid to wreak havoc on the basketball court." What's interesting is that Nike, the company that sponsored the ad, apparently felt that Charles was indeed an influencer of people, otherwise they wouldn't have hired him to represent their products!

Let's face it: we're all influencers. Maybe not on the scale of a celebrity like Charles Barkley, but unless you live alone in a cave in the middle of a wilderness, you rub shoulders with people. You have conversations, conduct transactions, work together, share rides, etc. And every time you do, you leave an impression, for better or worse. You lift people's spirits or lower them. You inspire people or inhibit them. Even people who don't know your name will walk away with an impression of you.

What we need to do is embrace the reality that we are influencers and be intentional about making the most of every opportunity. If you're looking for a way to make a significant contribution to your world, start here.

Reflect: In Matthew 5:16, Jesus said, "Let your good deeds shine out for all to see." Can you name a role model that had a profound impact on your life? In what way did that person help to shape you? How seriously do you take your influence? What are some ways you can be intentional about your influence?

THE BEST MONDAY EVER

IN 1976, DURING a game between the Chicago Cubs and Los Angeles Dodgers at Dodger Stadium, a couple of hooligans jumped onto the field carrying an American flag, some lighter fluid, and some matches. They knelt in the outfield, doused the flag with lighter fluid, and then tried to set it on fire. Fortunately, the wind blew out the flame on their first try. This gave Cubs outfielder Rick Monday time to run over and jerk the flag away from the vandals and carry it to safety. The reaction to this patriotic act was as memorable as the act itself. The scoreboard operator put up a message that said, "Rick Monday—you made a great play." And the crowd started singing "God Bless America."

Sadly, we live in a time where the symbols and institutions of our country are not respected the way they once were. Athletes on every level of competition are refusing to stand for the national anthem. The Pledge of Allegiance is being quietly removed from public schools. Soldiers and first responders are treated like bad guys. Supreme Court justices are vilified. And government officials are harassed in restaurants and on elevators.

On this Independence Day, we encourage you to reflect on the blessings of living in this great country. No, America is not perfect and certainly should not be worshiped. We are redeemed by the blood of Christ, not the flag. But only a fool would fail to understand how blessed we are to live in a free country where life, liberty, and the pursuit of happiness are ours to enjoy.

According to surveys, Monday is the least popular day of the week. But there is one Monday—Rick—who inspires nothing but love and respect in us. No matter what day of the week the Fourth of July falls on, may we all have a lot of Monday in us.

Reflect: Psalms 33:12 says, "Blessed is the nation whose God is the Lord." Why do you think patriotism is in decline in this generation? What are some things you love about America? What are some ways you as an individual can contribute to the strength of our nation?

THE POWER OF REPETITION

BIG-TIME ATHLETES, either at the college or pro level, do things that boggle the mind. Have you ever seen a major-league hitter take a ninety-eight mile-an-hour fastball inside that misses his thighs by one inch without even flinching? The average person would be diving onto the ground to get out of the way of such a pitch.

Have you ever seen an NBA guard go through his pregame warm-up by dribbling a basketball with each hand, crisscrossing them, going between his legs and behind his back without looking at his hands, yet always keeping both balls under perfect control? The average person would be flubbing after one or two bounces and chasing the balls all over the room.

Granted, these athletes have tremendous natural ability. But they were not born with the ability to do these things. They learned to do them and honed their skills to a razor's edge through repetition. That big-league hitter has seen hundreds of thousands of fastballs. That NBA guard has bounced a ball millions of times.

You want to get better at something? Do it over and over and over again.

You want to be a better Christian? Make the spiritual disciplines a part of your life and do them over and over and over again. We're talking about worship, prayer, Bible study, and service to Christ. Far too many people do these things haphazardly—whenever it's convenient or they happen to be in the mood—and then wonder why they struggle when life decides to antagonize them in some way.

PEOPLE BECOME GREAT CHRISTIANS THE SAME WAY THEY BECOME GREAT ATHLETES: THROUGH HONEST COMMITMENT AND TIRELESS REPETITION.

There's a reason why the Bible has so many sports metaphors about running with endurance and intense training. It's because people become great Christians the same way they become great athletes: through honest commitment and tireless repetition.

Reflect: 1 Corinthians 9:25 says, "All athletes are disciplined in their training. They do it to win a prize that will fade away, but we do it for an eternal prize." Is there a skill—athletic or otherwise—that you have gained through much repetition? Have you ever been that dedicated to the spiritual disciplines? How might your life change if you were?

RULES

RAISE YOUR HAND if you like rules.

Maybe your mind just flashed back to when you were a kid and your parents placed you under what you thought was an unreasonable curfew. Or maybe you remembered the time you got suspended at work for inadvertently violating company policy. Or maybe it was that time your homeowner's association fined you for hanging an unapproved flower pot on your porch.

Rules can be really irritating.

But sports is our reminder of how important rules are. Imagine a football game where players were not required to stay on their side of the line of scrimmage before the snap. Imagine a baseball game where even balls in the dirt or a foot over the batter's head were called a strike. Imagine a basketball game where players could travel or double dribble at will.

Rules seem confining at first glance, but it doesn't take much to remind us that without them, everything would fall apart. This is one of the great truths of Scripture. We have freedom in Christ, but it's freedom with protective boundaries. Like a wide receiver is free to run a pass pattern wherever he wants downfield as long as he stays inbounds. If he runs up into the seats, the game becomes a travesty.

Yes, rules can be overdone. They can be oppressive. The pages of history are filled with stories of heartless authoritarian figures who stifle freedom. But everyone who values law and order and a peaceful existence should be thankful for reasonable, common sense rules, which is exactly what God's rules are. From the Ten Commandments to Paul's instructions in the Pastoral Epistles, God's rules are all designed for our health and happiness. If you doubt this, just look at the people who ignore them.

Reflect: 2 Timothy 3:16 says, "All Scripture is inspired by God ... it corrects us when we are wrong and teaches us to do what is right." Do you ever feel that God's rules are oppressive? Can you think of a time when ignoring them got you into trouble? In what ways does strict obedience lead to greater freedom?

MAKE IT PERSONAL

WHEN I (MARK) WAS about ten years old, our Little League team went to St. Louis to see my beloved Cardinals play. We managed to get down by the dugout before the game, where some of the players would stop to sign autographs. Lou Brock was my hero, and I was praying that he would stop. He did, but I was so flustered with excitement I couldn't speak. So my brother, who knew how much I loved Lou, decided to speak up on my behalf to the future Hall of Famer. When I handed Lou my brand-new, suitable-for-signing baseball and a pen, my brother said, "This is my brother. You're his favorite player."

Maybe you've had a similar experience meeting a celebrity that you admired. I remember the first time I met my coauthor, Pat Williams. He'd read one of my books and graciously phoned and invited me to lunch. As I drove to the restaurant, I was more nervous than if I had been going to speak in front of ten thousand people. I'd read his books and knew of his work in the world of professional sports. I was in awe. Now, seventeen years later, I'm still in awe, but I'm not nervous anymore. Pat is a great friend.

In Scripture, emphasis is placed on having a personal relationship with Jesus. He isn't just someone we think about and talk about and read about. He is someone we meet personally, someone we know, someone we talk to, someone we turn to for fellowship in good times and help in hard times. It's a relationship, a partnership, a friendship, a sharing of daily life, always with the understanding that Jesus is the one who is Lord.

As a pastor, I have long felt that the big thing missing from a lot of people's faith experience is a truly personal relationship with Jesus. He should not just be someone we know about but someone we know.

Reflect: In John 14:21, Jesus said this about those who seek him in obedience: "I will love them and reveal myself to each of them." How personal is your relationship with Jesus? Do you know about him or really know him? Do you talk to him often, like you would a real friend? What are some things you could do that might make your relationship with Jesus even closer?

THE SIX-MILLION-DOLLAR MAN

IF YOU'RE OLD ENOUGH, you remember the TV series with Lee Majors. It ran from 1974–1978 and featured Majors as Colonel Steve Austin, a secret agent of the United States who was superhuman due to various bionic implants. We all used to hear the title of that show and think, "Six million dollars is a lot of money."

Seems kind of cheap now.

In 2019, Bryce Harper of the Washington Nationals became a 330-million-dollar man, and he doesn't even have any bionic implants! He's just an outfielder who, as of this writing, is hitting .256 and .277 for his career. Remember when you had to be exceptional to be considered a superstar? Remember when the big money was reserved for guys who were cinches for the Hall of Fame?

But today is not a day to lament professional sports salaries. Our concern is for the spiritual health of people. Our culture has become so thoroughly and completely materialistic that we feel compelled to put forth a reminder that money is one of the most dangerous commodities in the world, even in small amounts. Any man is a fool who believes that it's only millionaires who are destroyed by avarice.

Right now you might be considering ways to get your hands on some more money. If you can't hit a baseball five hundred feet, your plans might include overcharging customers for your services or fudging on your expense account or cheating on your taxes. And you may try to justify it by saying you're not being treated fairly, that this extra money is owed to you. Any thoughts along these lines are a signal that your soul is in grave danger.

Remember: you cannot serve two masters (Matthew 6:24). If you love money so much that you are willing to compromise your integrity in order to get more of it, then it has become your god.

Reflect: 1 Timothy 6:9 says, "People who long to be rich fall into temptation and are trapped by many foolish and harmful desires that plunge them into ruin and destruction." Have you ever done anything unethical to try to make a little extra money? If so, how did you rationalize it? Looking back, was it worth it? What do you think more about: money or God?

THE VALUE OF SCOUTING

A PART OF THE SPORTING world that is rarely thought about by the average fan is scouting. We see the players and coaches on the field doing what they're famous for, but we rarely stop to think about all the organizational employees who are constantly gathering information and filing reports that help the team on the field succeed.

Go to a Major League Baseball game between contending teams during a pennant race and you will see them, maybe as many as a dozen or more, sitting in a group behind home plate. They'll have notepads and stopwatches. They'll be looking for tendencies and weaknesses, anything that might give the team that employs them an advantage.

And they do come up with valuable information: a pitcher who is unusually slow to the plate or has trouble holding runners on. A hitter who is vulnerable to inside fastballs. An outfielder who has a weak arm. Many highly competitive games come down to a single play or even a single pitch. A good scout who goes before his team and gathers good information can make the difference.

God is our scout in the sense that he knows what lies before us; he knows what we're going to face. He knows our enemy better than anyone and knows exactly how that enemy is going to try to defeat us. And he's filed a scouting report … it's called the Bible. But it's more than a scouting report; it's an actual game plan. And it's guaranteed to work.

The problem is that people don't pay attention to it.

It's unthinkable for a contending sports team to ignore its scouting reports. To do so is to offer the opponent a tremendous advantage. To do so is to invite disaster. Yet many Christians live day after day, week after week, and never open the Scriptures.

Don't be one of them.

Reflect: Psalms 119:133 says, "Guide my steps by your word so I will not be overcome by evil." How much time each week do you spend in the word? What do you need to do in order to make more time for the Scriptures? When you do pick up the Bible, do you have a plan for how to read and digest it?

DON'T CALL IT PASSION

BASEBALL PLAYERS AND FANS are used to seeing balls thrown by pitchers fly over the center field fence, but usually there's contact with a bat first. On July 28, 2019, Trevor Bauer, a pitcher for the Cleveland Indians, threw a fastball from the pitcher's mound straight over the center field fence. He was having a rough outing, and his manager, Terry Francona, was walking toward the mound to take him out of the game. It's standard operating procedure for the pitcher who's being removed to hand the ball to his manager. Instead, Bauer whirled and threw it as hard and far as he could. Video of the incident shows his teammates walking toward the mound from their infield positions and ducking in shock as he launched the ball over their heads.

One sports commentator said, "You've got to love that kind of passion. He was upset that he didn't perform well for his team." His cohost said, "Nope. I don't buy it. There are standards of professional behavior, and he just acted like a big baby. So you had a bad day … it happens. Show some class."

We side with the latter view. Far too many people—even Christians—try to justify bad behavior by labeling it "passion." Strings of curse words, slammed doors, holes punched in walls, and thrown household objects have all been chalked up to overwrought passion. "I just get so upset" is not a legitimate excuse for a Christian. We, of all people, who have the Spirit of God within us, should be able to meet frustration and disappointment without embarrassing ourselves and tarnishing our witness.

Sadly, Trevor Bauer, who is a pretty good pitcher, will forever be known as the guy who lost his head and did something stupid. The video of his meltdown will be shown until the end of time. Not fair, perhaps, but he has no one to blame but himself.

Reflect: Ephesians 4:26 says, "Don't sin by letting anger control you." Have you ever had a meltdown and done something dumb? Did you first try to use the "I was upset" defense? How long did it take you to realize the depth of your mistake? What steps have you taken to ensure that such a moment never happens again?

YOUR OPPONENT IS ...

WHEN I (MARK) WAS a kid, my uncle taught me to play golf. He was a PGA club professional who had no kids of his own, so he took my brother and me under his wing and taught us the game. I remember the following conversation from my teenage years, before I went out to play in a junior tournament:

Uncle Carl: Who's your opponent?

Me: Kevin Anderson.

Uncle Carl: Wrong. Who's your opponent?

Me: (After pausing to think.) Oh, I get it. The golf course is my opponent.

Uncle Carl: Wrong again. Who's your opponent?

Me: (Completely confused.) Uh, I don't know.

Uncle Carl: You! *You* are your opponent. You have no control over anything except what *you* do. To be a winner, you have to master yourself.

I have since learned that this is true not just of golf but of just about everything we do in life. Most students flunk out of school not because the work is too hard for them, but because they fail to discipline themselves and get the work done. Most divorces happen not because marriage is too hard for the man and his wife, but because they don't discipline themselves to make the little sacrifices that make for a great marriage.

It's not other people's successes but our own failures that muddy up our lives. So let go of your desire to be better than someone else and just concentrate on being the best you possible.

Reflect: Romans 14:12 says, "Each of us will give a personal account to God." Have you ever had a rival—someone you felt you had to best in some way? How did that pressure impact your choices? What are some of the traps we can fall into if we start competing with people?

SELL IT!

(PAT) **WHEN RICH DEVOS** was the owner of the Orlando Magic, it was felt that one more piece was needed to make the team a strong contender. Horace Grant was on our radar, but let's face it: Orlando, as the second-smallest market in the NBA, had a hard time competing with the likes of LA, Boston, Philly, and New York.

Mr. DeVos sent a helicopter to Chicago to pick up Horace and his agent, Jimmy Sexton, and bring them to his home in Holland, Michigan. When the chopper landed in the DeVos' backyard, Horace got quite a surprise. This incredibly wealthy and important man was standing there barefoot, wearing shorts and a casual shirt. After a friendly, conversational lunch, Rich took Horace out on his boat for a more personal talk about life and what it might be like playing in Orlando. Six weeks later,

SELLING IS NOTHING MORE THAN HELPING PEOPLE UNDERSTAND WHAT THEY NEED TO KNOW TO MAKE AN INFORMED DECISION.

Horace signed with the Magic and became a perfectly fitting piece that propelled the team into the 1995 NBA Finals. Only they know what was said on that boat ride, but one thing is clear: Mr. DeVos sold Horace on the notion of playing with the Magic.

"Selling" is a dirty word to some people. It has connotations of pressure and dishonesty, which is unfortunate. Selling is nothing more than helping people understand what they need to know to make an informed decision. When you tell people about Jesus or your church or a small group that you'd like them to join, you're selling! Don't ever feel bad about that.

At the same time, understand that selling goes beyond words. The greatest sales pitch in the world is immediately undermined when what you say turns out not to be true. So be careful what you say. Always be honest. But if you've got something wonderful, sell it!

Reflect: Psalms 105:1 says, "Give thanks to the Lord and proclaim his greatness. Let the whole world know what he has done." How dedicated are you when it comes to telling others about Jesus? Do you feel timid or act apologetic when you talk about him? Why do you think talking about Jesus and the church is so hard for people?

WHAT IF?

THE SPORTING WORLD is full of what ifs.

What if the Immaculate Reception had fallen incomplete?

What if Babe Ruth had continued to pitch?

What if Chris Webber hadn't called time out?

What if Don Denkinger had gotten the call right in the 1985 World Series?

What if Grant Hill's pass to Christian Laettner had been a little off line?

What if Curt Flood hadn't refused to be traded?

What if the Blazers had selected Michael Jordan instead of Sam Bowie?

There's no end to the what ifs, and depending on what team you root for, you can feel very wistful or sad as you think back. The same is true with life.

What if you'd had different parents?

What if you'd never met your wife (or husband)?

What if you'd accepted job A instead of job B?

What if you'd chased your passion instead of settling for a safer job?

What ifs can make you crazy if you let them. The good news is that, as Christians, we don't have to worry about them because God has promised to cause all things to work together for our good if we love him and are called according to his purpose. Don't worry that you might have missed out on something great because of a twist of circumstance in your past. God blessing your reality is far better than some hypothetical scenario that never was.

Reflect: Romans 8:28 says, "God causes everything to work together for the good of those who love God and are called according to his purpose ..." Is there a what if in your past that you have wondered about? Why do you think people tend to think about what might have been? Why is it important to let go of the what ifs and live in the present?

AMBASSADORS

"HE'S A GREAT AMBASSADOR FOR THE GAME."

You've heard this statement made about many great athletes: Arnold Palmer for golf, Kurt Warner for the NFL, David Robinson for the NBA, Roberto Clemente for baseball. Notice that the people who get this label slapped on them are all high-character types. Those who have used PEDs or abused their spouses or gotten into fistfights in strip clubs will never be given this kind of respect. And it's important to note that none of the sporting world's so-called great ambassadors, including the ones listed above, were given that title willy-nilly. They all earned it over time by treating people well, serving their fellow man, and displaying impeccable character.

Great ambassadors are not just found in the sporting world.

That tottery, elderly couple who after sixty years is still holding hands and treating each other with love and affection are great ambassadors for marriage.

That tireless nurse who pours her heart into the care she gives her patients is a great ambassador for the medical profession.

That faithful Christian who puts forth a godly witness in good times and bad is a great ambassador for Christ.

Sadly, the loudmouths, troublemakers, cheaters, and criminals get most of the attention. A teacher who has sex with a student will get hours of news coverage while a passionate, dedicated teacher who goes far above and beyond the call of duty will be lucky to get a simple thank-you. But don't let that discourage you! Your light will shine brighter the darker the world gets. And the darker the world gets, the more people will be drawn to the light.

Reflect: 2 Corinthians 5:20 says, "So we are Christ's ambassadors; God is making his appeal through us." Think of someone that you consider to be a good ambassador for Christ. What is it about that person who brought him or her to mind? How many of those same qualities do you possess?

THE FILM ROOM

IN NO SPORT IS game film more important than it is in football. Because there are so many players spread over such a large area, and because the players are often jumbled up in a crowd, it's impossible to see everything that's happening in the moment. When a handoff to the halfback goes for an eighty-yard touchdown, a coach might scream, "Where was the defender? There was supposed to be a linebacker in that gap!" The next day in the film room, he will find out and share a teaching moment with the linebacker who should have been there but wasn't.

What if film sessions were a part of all of our lives?

What if, every morning, you got to see a film of your life from the day before? And what if the film was edited? What if all your good moments were cut out and just your bad moments were left in because, let's face it, you really only need help with your weaknesses, right? And what if a life coach watched the film with you, pointing out all your mistakes and challenging you to do better?

That would be fun, wouldn't it?

Of course not.

Thankfully, we can reap some of the same benefits of a daily film session without the humiliation. How? By doing what you're doing right now. By caring enough about your relationship with God to read and reflect on his truth and how it fits into your own life. One of the great secrets of maintaining vibrant spiritual health is to regularly withdraw from the field of competition for times of prayer and self-reflection. Jesus did it (Luke 5:16) and in so doing set a great example for us.

Reflect: Lamentations 3:40 says, "Let us test and examine our ways." What are some of the factors that make it hard to have a regular time of prayer, study, and self-reflection? What are some things that might make it easier? Are there tendencies to be guarded against when you find yourself in one of these times of personal reflection?

A GIFT YOU CAN ALWAYS GIVE

IN A RADIO INTERVIEW I (Pat) did with sportswriter Gordon Forbes, I was struck by what he said about a couple of NFL legends:

"On off days Bill Walsh would call up a player and tell him, 'I love you.' Now that's unheard of. Can you imagine Bill Belichick or Chuck Noll doing that? Bill just knew how to make people feel special. Whenever I was with him, he'd start asking me questions. It was always about you, not him. Pete Rozelle was the same way. He knew how to make writers from all levels feel special."

Have you ever stopped to think about how many people there are in this world who do not feel special and may never have felt special in their entire lives? From childhood, many people are abused or mistreated or even just ignored. Some people go years without ever hearing another human being say, "I care about you" or "I love you."

Understanding this can open up an entire world of possibilities for an individual who wants to be a difference maker. Every day as you go about your business, you're coming into contact with people who are starved for even a small expression of love. You won't know who they are necessarily. It might be the clerk at the grocery store or your server at a restaurant. By being kind, by showing interest in people, by complimenting them, you will be giving them a precious gift.

And it takes so little time and effort. Mostly, it just takes an awareness of the need and a giving spirit. Even with empty pockets, this is a gift you can always give.

Reflect: 1 John 4:11 says, "Dear friends, since God loved us that much, we surely ought to love each other." Have you ever had someone, perhaps a stranger, lift your spirit by being kind and thoughtful? How conscious are you of daily opportunities to make people feel special? What would it take for you to do even better in this area?

HOW I MADE HER CRY

PICKING UP ON the theme of Pat's devotion from yesterday, let me (Mark) share a story:

There is a Mexican restaurant in Kissimmee, Florida, that I love. A couple of years ago, I fell into the habit of stopping in there for lunch on my day off. I asked for a corner table by a window so I could read and do a little writing as I ate. Pretty soon, the staff knew me and treated me like royalty.

My server was a tiny Mexican woman who barely spoke English, but she always greeted me with a huge smile and did a magnificent job. She checked on me often, made sure I always had a fresh drink, and gave me extra mints when I left. She was such a sweetheart, but we didn't converse much because there was a language barrier that made us both hesitant.

When Christmas rolled around, I decided I was going to give her a big tip. She had waited on me many times throughout the year, always giving impeccable service with a smile, so I decided to show her how much I appreciated it. When she saw the amount I left on the table, her eyes got big, and she slapped her hand over her mouth and started crying. I don't mean her eyes watered; I mean she started a shoulder-shaking cry.

Then she told me in very broken English that she was a single mom with three kids and that money would make a huge difference for them. Then it was my turn to tear up.

Everywhere we go there are people—good people—who need a little kindness, a little reassurance that they are appreciated, a little reminder that they are special.

And here's a truth I already knew but that was reinforced by that experience. However blessed the person on the receiving end feels, the person on the giving end feels just as blessed or more.

Reflect: Acts of the Apostles 20:35 says, "It is more blessed to give than to receive." Think about your daily routine. Is there someone you often come into contact with that you sense could use a little positive reinforcement? Why not make that person your project? Go out of your way to show him or her your appreciation.

THE SILENT TREATMENT

ROOKIES IN ANY professional sport go through a lot of good-natured ribbing. In one recent game, a rookie hit his first major-league home run. His excitement was off the charts as he pumped his fist and ran around the bases with a huge smile on his face. Naturally, he was expecting to be mobbed by his teammates not just because it was his first big-league dinger, but because it was a game changer. But when he got to the dugout, not one of his teammates acknowledged him. No one moved to give him a high five. None of them even turned their heads to look at him. It was as if he was the batboy bringing a broken bat in from the field.

The camera followed the rookie into the dugout. Surprise was written all over his face. His ear-to-ear grin melted away and a look of befuddlement took its place. He took off his helmet and stood there, trying to process the lack of response from his teammates. Then suddenly, those same teammates exploded in laughter and mobbed him with hugs and high fives, and the rookie knew he'd been had.

Silence can be worrisome, as in the example just given. When someone should be talking to you but isn't, that's a sign that you're being pranked or something is wrong. But silence can also be one of the great blessings of life. We live in a loud, dissonant world. The constant noise that surrounds us can prevent us from thinking clearly or, more importantly, from listening to God. This is critical because God is not a shouter. He speaks clearly, but he does not try to compete with the noises of the world. He expects us to give him our attention and listen.

We urge you to give *yourself* the silent treatment. Shut out the cacophony that surrounds you so you can hear what's really important.

Reflect: Zechariah 2:13 says, "Be silent before the Lord." Do you have times of intentional silence built into your daily routine? Do you, like some people, find yourself constantly trying to fill the silences in your life with music or the television? If so, what do you think this says about you? What are the dangers of never having any quiet time?

HAPPY BIRTHDAY IN HEAVEN, DAD

(MARK) TODAY IS my dad's birthday, so today's thought is in tribute to him.

I was fifteen and playing in a junior Babe Ruth League baseball game. Dad was the head coach of our team and generally coached third base when we were batting. Our team was in the third base dugout.

That night we were playing our archrivals from the next town over. It was a battle for first place, and they had their outstanding curveball pitcher on the mound. We were behind 2–0 and didn't have a hit even though it was late in the game.

Somehow, some way, I managed to throw my bat out over the plate and catch one of those wicked curves, lining the ball perfectly over the second baseman's head into right center. To say I was thrilled was an understatement. I broke up the no-hitter and made it possible for the tying run to come to the plate.

Actually, that's not quite how it worked out.

I did indeed line the ball to right center, but as I jogged to first, basking in the glow of my accomplishment, the center fielder picked up the ball and fired to first, nipping me by a step. If I had been hustling, he wouldn't even have thrown the ball.

The worst part of that experience was having to run past my dad to get to the third base dugout. Fans for the other side were laughing uproariously at my bonehead play. My own teammates were watching in stunned silence, trying to decide whether or not to strangle me. But the worst part was feeling like I had let my dad down.

You are blessed if you have (or had) a father who was so good, so kind, so supportive that you never wanted to disappoint him. Doug Atteberry was that kind of man, and I am truly grateful to have been able to call him Dad.

Reflect: Ephesians 6:2 says, "Honor your father and mother." Think about your father (or father figure). What are some lessons he taught you that you value? If your father is still living, have you expressed your love and appreciation for all he's done for you? If your father failed in his responsibility, how can you process that and turn it into positive motivation for yourself?

BE YOU

THE WORLD OF SPORTS is fascinating for countless reasons. One is that sports demonstrate daily that there's more than one way to do something and be successful.

One team wins with good defense and a ball control offense, while another team wins simply by outscoring the opposition with a run-and-gun approach to offense.

One pitcher succeeds with one hundred mile-an-hour fastballs, while another succeeds by floating knuckleballs up to the plate at seventy-five miles an hour.

One quarterback stands in the pocket and chucks the ball downfield, while another escapes the pocket and scrambles for more yards than his running backs.

It's also true in business. Red Robin is a burger place that has an extensive menu in a classy, carpeted environment. Five Guys is a burger place that offers a bare concrete floor, block walls, and a very limited menu. But both are great!

And how about churches? One is big and modern and offers contemporary everything, while another is smaller, more low-key, and leans toward the traditional. Yet both are successful in leading people to Christ.

The point?

Be you.

Don't look at other people who are successful and think you have to do everything the way they do. If you do and end up trying to be something you're not, you will almost certainly fail. The most successful people in life, whether you're talking about business, relationships, or spirituality, are those who keep it real.

DON'T LOOK AT OTHER PEOPLE WHO ARE SUCCESSFUL AND THINK YOU HAVE TO DO EVERYTHING THE WAY THEY DO.

Reflect: 1 Corinthians 12:4 says, "There are different kinds of spiritual gifts, but the same Spirit is the source of them all." Have you ever tried to duplicate someone else's success by doing exactly what they did? How did your efforts turn out? Why do you think so many people are reluctant to think and act outside the box, even when their nature is pulling them in that direction?

DON'T LET GO OF THAT VINE!

JOHNNY WEISSMULLER WAS an Olympic swimmer who piled up victories like UPS piles up boxes. In the 1920s he won five Olympic gold medals and became the first person to break the one-minute barrier for the hundred-meter freestyle. If that's not enough, he also won fifty-two United States national championships and set more than fifty world records.

But swimming is not what he was most known for.

In 1932 he signed a contract with MGM to play the role of Tarzan in *Tarzan the Ape Man*, from the novel by Edgar Rice Burroughs. Weissmuller ended up making twelve Tarzan films during the 1930s and 40s. He is by far the most famous of all the actors to play Tarzan, partly because he produced the iconic Tarzan yell that just about everyone in the civilized world has heard at least once.

Once during an interview, Johnny was asked what the key was to playing Tarzan. The interviewer may have expected him to comment on the importance of his on-screen relationship with costar Maureen

O'Sullivan, or even the challenges of working with a chimpanzee. Instead he said that the key to playing Tarzan was to never let go of the vine.

Sometimes success boils down to one critical thing that cannot be compromised. For Christians, that one critical thing is humility. It's not the only important priority for Christians, but it is the one that determines whether God opposes you or favors you. James 4:6 says, "God opposes the proud but favors the humble."

Humility is mostly just remembering that God is the Lord and you are not. Cling to that knowledge the way Johnny Weissmuller clung to that vine, and you'll never go too far wrong.

Reflect: 1 Peter 5:6 says, "Humble yourselves under the mighty power of God, and at the right time, he will lift you up in honor." In your mind, what would the act of humbling yourself under the mighty power of God look like? What are some things that could make humbling yourself difficult? What might be some indicators that you are not as humble as you should be?

LEAVE A GREAT LEGACY

WHEN TONY DUNGY was the coach of the Tampa Bay Buccaneers, the team prayed before and after every game. When Tony was
let go as the Bucs' coach, Jon Gruden replaced him. On the day of
Gruden's first game as the Bucs' coach, he went through his pregame
speech, reviewing the game plan and making a few motivational
comments. Then he dismissed the players to head out onto the field.

But most of the players hesitated.

This was the point at which the team had its pregame prayer
when Tony was the coach, but Jon Gruden had no way of knowing
that. Warren Sapp quickly took control of the situation. He ordered
everyone to come back. "We're going to pray," he said. "We've been
doing this for six years, so somebody's got to step up and pray."[26]

What a beautiful example of leaving a godly legacy. Tony Dungy
was gone, but the fragrant aroma of his Christian witness, along with
the godly habits he had instilled in his team, remained. That is not
to say that every Buccaneer was a Christian or even wanted to pray.

But the influence of their former coach was still being strongly felt in that room.

We all leave something behind when we leave a place. The question is, what?

The good news is we get to choose. By being intentional about the things we say and do every day, the attitude we demonstrate toward others, and certainly by the integrity we demonstrate, we can ensure that the legacy we leave is a good one.

But you can't wait until it's time to leave to start thinking about your legacy. Legacies, both good and bad, are built over time. We urge you to start thinking about how you want to be remembered on day one. Then do everything in your power to make that legacy a reality.

Reflect: 2 Timothy 2:2 says, "You have heard me teach things that have been confirmed by many reliable witnesses. Now teach these truths to other trustworthy people ..." If you were to die soon, what kind of legacy would you leave? What do you think is the biggest thing people will remember about you? Is that what you want them to remember?

UNSCRIPTED

PERHAPS THE VERY BEST thing about sports is that they are unscripted. People spend billions of dollars a year to watch movies and television shows that are carefully laid out on a drawing board. The endings are predetermined to get the most favorable response from the largest audience. And don't we hate it when people throw out spoilers and reveal those predetermined endings?

But sports are different. No one knows how a game will turn out, even when one team seems obviously superior to another. It's called an upset when David picks off Goliath and, unless your team is Goliath, it's thrilling. Upsets are one of the main reasons why we love March Madness so much.

It's also thrilling to see unsung players turn into heroes, like the end-of-the-bench sub who is pressed into action because of the star player's injury and then goes on to score the winning points at crunch time. You've probably heard some incredulous sports announcer say,

"You can't make this stuff up!" Nowhere is that statement made more frequently than in the world of sports.

Sometimes it feels like life is unscripted, too, and in some ways it is. When you get up in the morning, you have no idea what the day is going to throw at you. But at the same time, you can write much of your own script by the choices you make. For example, God promises that people who accept Jesus as Lord and Savior will be saved. This means you can write salvation into the script of your life.

We urge you to be your own scriptwriter, to decide where you want your life to go and how you want it to end, and then live it accordingly.

Reflect: Joshua 24:15 says, "Choose today whom you will serve …" What choices have you made that will determine how the script of your life goes? Have you thought about the ending of your life and what you want it to look like? Why are so many people reluctant to think or talk about death?

DO WHAT YOU LOVE

(PAT) STEPHANIE FLAMINI was the women's basketball coach at Guilford College in Greensboro, North Carolina. She is also a trail-blazer, though when she first became a trailblazer, being a trailblazer was the farthest thing from her mind.

As an eight year old, Stephanie was the first female in the state of Pennsylvania to play boys' Little League baseball. Later, she became the first female to play boys' basketball. She'll be the first to tell you that it wasn't easy. She took a lot of abuse from boys who resented her for "intruding" on their sport and wanted to make sure she knew who was boss. There were also lots of reporters around, snapping pictures and asking for interviews. But Stephanie said to me, "I didn't realize I was paving the way for equality. I was just doing something I loved to do."

Doing what you love is important for three reasons.

First, when you do what you love, you have fun. Someone said, "If you do what you love, you'll never work a day in your life." That may be a bit of an overstatement, as even the things we love to do can be hard sometimes. But the basic idea is true.

Second, when you do what you love, difficulties are reduced to mere annoyances. The opposite is true when you're doing what you hate. Every little problem that comes up seems like a big, hairy deal because you're already unhappy.

Finally, when you do what you love, you do a better job. You work harder, pay closer attention to detail, and refuse to take shortcuts.

Want a happier life? Figure out what you love to do and go do it.

Reflect: Colossians 3:23 says, "Work willingly at whatever you do, as though you were working for the Lord rather than people." Do you have a passion that you have so far failed to pursue? Why have you not gone after it? In what ways might your life improve if you decided to do what you love?

OPINION POLLS

WHO WAS THE greatest pitcher of all time? Gibson? Koufax? Ryan? Cy Young?

Who was better: Jordan or LeBron? Or Kobe?

Who would win a head-to-head matchup in their primes: Nicklaus or Woods?

If you were starting a baseball team, would you rather have: Mays or Aaron?

If you were starting a basketball team, would you rather have: Bird or Magic?

If you were starting a football team, would you rather have: Manning or Brady?

Which uniform is better, the Yankees' pinstripes or the Cardinals' birds on the bat?

These questions and a thousand more would bring passionate responses. They are part of what's so fun about sports. Not only do we love to watch it but we love to talk about it. And yes, argue for our favorite players and preferences.

Jesus asked poll questions too. Once he asked his disciples, "Who do people say the Son of Man is?" (Matt. 16:13). Two verses later he made it more personal: "But who do you say I am?" We suspect the disciples liked the first question far better than the second. The first question only required them to give information, while the second required them to give their lives.

This question reverberates down through the centuries and lands in our laps. By including this question in his eternal word, Jesus is not just asking the Twelve; he's asking us. In fact, this is the single most important question any person will ever answer. Who is Jesus? The answer will determine not only the direction and quality of your life on earth but the fate of your soul in eternity.

Reflect: Matthew 16:16 says, "Simon Peter answered, 'You are the Messiah, the Son of the living God.'" Who is Jesus to you? What impact has he had on your life? If you have recently accepted him as your Lord and Savior, how has he changed you? What would you say to someone who's still undecided about Jesus?

EGG LAYING FOR CHRISTIANS

SPORTS ARE FULL OF CRUSHING MISTAKES:

A missed free throw that would have won the game.

A fumble on the one-yard-line when a touchdown would have won the game.

A wild pitch with the winning run on third base.

A duck-hooked tee shot on the first playoff hole.

In the case of professional sports, these mistakes are made by the best athletes in the world, men and women who are paid enormous sums of money *not* to make such mistakes. But they make them anyway.

But it's not just players. Sometimes entire teams fall apart. A football coach's worst nightmare is when his offense, defense, and special teams are all awful on the same day. Recently, a coach who had that very nightmare said in his postgame interview, "We really laid an egg today."

What do you do when you lay an egg? If you're an athlete, you head for the batting cage or the practice field or the driving range or the film room. In other words, you work hard and try to fix what went wrong. As a Christian, you take a different approach. You understand that no amount of practice or effort will fix your sinful nature, so you humble yourself before God, confess your sin, and ask for forgiveness.

Only in the Christian faith do you not try to fix what's wrong with you. In the Christian faith, you humble yourself before God and seek his grace.

Reflect: 1 John 1:9 says, "If we confess our sins to him, he is faithful and just to forgive us our sins and to cleanse us from all wickedness." When you lay an egg as a Christian, what is your first impulse? Do you hold out hope that somehow your sinful nature can be fixed? Do you think of God more as the judge of your soul or the lover of your soul?

CONDITIONAL VS. UNCONDITIONAL

PROFESSIONAL SPORTS IS A TOUGH BUSINESS.

For one thing, on a professional sports team, you are surrounded by the very best in the business ... the elite of the elite from all around the world, which means that unless you're utterly fantastic at what you do, you don't fit in. Chances are that's not the case when you go to work every day.

Also, pro athletes are expected to produce. With only a few roster spots and hundreds of athletes out there who would love to have your job, if you're not producing, you're cleaning out your locker and making room for the next player.

Finally, the fans get to boo you at will. Imagine if customers got to sit in the garage and boo and hurl insults at the car mechanics.

What it boils down to is that love in the sports world is very conditional. You are employed and paid and revered and celebrated, but only if you produce.

We are thankful that God's kingdom does not operate this way. When we come to the Lord, we are not free agents hoping to perform well enough to stick with the team. We are not looking over our shoulders, hoping we don't get cut from the roster when someone comes along that's more productive or that Jesus loves more.

God's love is unconditional.

Romans 5:8 says that God showed his great love for us by sending Christ to die for us while we were still sinners. That means God loves you in spite of your lousy performance, in spite of that bad habit you struggle with, in spite of your record as a repeat offender.

Go ahead. Breathe that sigh of relief.

Reflect: 1 Timothy 2:4 says that God "wants everyone to be saved and love the truth." Do you sometimes find it difficult to believe that God could love you? If so, where do you think such a feeling comes from? In what ways might the idea of unconditional love lead to a false sense of security?

WHEN COURAGE *REALLY* MATTERS

DODGERS GREAT DON DRYSDALE had pitched four consecutive shutouts and was trying for number five, the major-league record. Appropriately, the Dodgers were playing their hated rival, the San Francisco Giants. It was late in the game, and the shutout was intact, but Drysdale was in trouble. The bases were loaded, and the count was two balls and no strikes on the Giants' catcher, Dick Dietz. The next pitch hit Dietz on the arm, forcing in a run and ending the bid for the record.

Or did it?

Suddenly, umpire Harry Wendelstedt came flying out from behind home plate, waving his arms and screaming, "No! No! No!" He ruled that Dietz had leaned into the pitch and therefore would not be awarded first base, keeping the run from scoring and the shutout intact. A couple of innings later, Drysdale nailed down the shutout and tied the record, which he broke a few days later.

Wendelstedt knew when he made that call that the Giants would collectively throw a fit. The call is rare in baseball, so rare that probably no one would have argued if he'd given Dietz first base. As it was, the Giants rained down verbal abuse on Harry Wendelstedt for several minutes before the game could continue.

COURAGE MATTERS ALL THE TIME, BUT IT REALLY MATTERS WHEN YOU KNOW YOU'RE GOING TO GET POUNCED ON IF YOU DO THE RIGHT THING.

Courage matters all the time, but it *really* matters when you know you're going to get pounced on if you do the right thing. Far too many people in this world suddenly become deaf, dumb, and blind to avoid trouble. We urge you to follow Harry Wendelstedt's example and do the right thing even when you know an attack will be forthcoming.

Reflect: 1 Chronicles 28:20 says, "Don't be afraid or discouraged, for the Lord God, my God, is with you." Have you ever faced the wrath of some person or group because you did what you thought was right? Did that affect how you handled the same situation the next time? What are some of the dangers of not doing the right thing out of fear?

DON'T GET HUSTLED

RECENTLY WE RAN across Gary McCord's list of suggestions on how to avoid getting hustled on the golf course. Here are a few that make a lot of sense:

- Look and see if he has a 1 iron in his bag. Only really good players can hit those things.

- If he uses an old ball, watch out. Bad players don't have old balls because they lose them too quickly.

- See if he has calluses on his hands. If he does, that means he plays or practices a lot.

- Same thing if his right hand is more tanned than his left. He's spent a lot of time wearing a golf glove.

- Be very wary if he has a bad grip. Players with bad grips generally find a way to make them work.

God would probably approve of this list. He actually made one of his own. It's called the Bible. From Genesis to Revelation, through principles, commands, prophesies, and historical events, he teaches us how not to get hustled by the devil.

One of the great concerns we have is that so many believers nowadays are not plugged into the Scriptures in any kind of regular way. This is a shame, considering how accessible the Bible is. You can read it in old-fashioned book form, on your phone, tablet, or computer, and even listen to it whenever you want.

One thing we know for sure: Satan licks his chops and digs quickly into his bag of tricks when he meets someone who isn't prepared for his hustles.

Reflect: Psalms 119:104 says, "Your commandments give me understanding." Everyone sins, but have you ever had a moment when you felt you'd been hustled by Satan? How much time do you spend in the Bible each week? What changes would you have to make to give God's word more of your time and attention?

BENCHWARMERS

ON EVERY COLLEGE or pro basketball team, there are guys who never get off the bench. They come out and do the stretching and run the layup drills before the game, then retreat to the end of the bench where they proceed to cheer on their teammates throughout the game. During the timeouts they stand in the huddle but can often be seen gazing into the crowd rather than paying attention, because they know the only way they're getting into the game is if seven or eight teammates suddenly have to run off to the bathroom with food poisoning.

It takes a special person to be a benchwarmer at the college or pro level. Without question, that player was a star at the next level down and has probably never ridden the bench in his life. But now, instead of doing the thing he loves (playing), he's doing the thing he doesn't love (sitting). Yet if you watch most benchwarmers, you'll see that they are upbeat and encouraging to their teammates.

Two things to consider:

First, if they weren't upbeat and encouraging to their teammates, they would be sitting in the stands wearing street clothes. No coach is going to put up with a pouter.

Second, if they've been well coached and taught, they understand that even benchwarmers are valuable team members. Who are the starters going to practice against if not the benchwarmers? And many a benchwarmer has been pressed into service to save the day.

Do you sometimes feel like a benchwarmer in life? Like God has never given you anything real important to do? Chances are your work is more important than you realize. Even so, you can always support and encourage others that you perceive are doing great work. There are no insignificant Christians.

Reflect: Ecclesiastes 9:11 says, "The fastest runner doesn't always win the race." What has God called you to do in the Kingdom? Do you sometimes feel your work isn't very important? If so, think about some unseen ways God might use your service. Is it time for you to think about expanding your role in God's Kingdom?

DR. TIME

I (MARK) STILL REMEMBER the day I learned that Albert Pujols had agreed to sign with the Los Angeles Angels. As a lifelong Cardinals fan, as a guy who had watched in awe as Albert put up eleven of the finest seasons in MLB history, and as a guy who had as much trouble picturing Albert in another uniform as I did picturing Santa Claus in a Speedo, I could not conceive of Albert saying yes to another team's offer.

And then he did.

I'll be honest. I walked around in a funk for a few days. I think I went through the stages of grief. I know I felt angry at Albert for a while. How dare he deprive us, his longtime fans, of his artistry? What had the Angels fans ever done for him? Wasn't our love and adoration good enough? How dare he disrespect the iconic birds on the bat?

It all seems pretty silly now, but at the time it broke my heart.

Here are a couple of observations.

First, only things we care about have the ability to break our hearts. When the Cubs lose a player to free agency, I yawn. (Or cheer if it's a good player.)

And second, time is an amazing healer. You can talk about your surgeons and specialists and miracle drugs all you want; Dr. Time is the greatest healer of them all. Two years after Albert left, I was rooting for the Albert-less Cardinals in the World Series and not giving him a second thought.

It's good for us to remember this any time life circumstances rise up and break our hearts. What seems so devastating in the moment and in the immediate aftermath will likely fade to the point of oblivion or almost. So treat your pain with time. Not alcohol. Not drugs. Not reckless sexual behavior. Those things may dull your pain in the moment, but they will leave you with guilt and shame in addition to a broken heart.

Just be patient and let the good doctor do his work.

Reflect: Romans 12:12 says, "Be patient in trouble." Can you think of a time when you were devastated emotionally by something or someone? What role did time play in getting you through that trauma? What are some factors that make being patient so difficult when we're hurting?

LOOK WHAT I DID!

SPORT FISHING IS all about landing the big one. Bass fishermen in particular throw every plug with the hope of reeling in a monster. The problem is that when it happens to amateur fishermen, they generally want to have it mounted and hang it on a wall. A big ole bass hanging on the wall is a man's way of saying, "Look what I did!"

But professional fisherman recoil at a mounted bass. They say that a mounted bass doesn't send the message that you are a great fishermen; it sends the message that you are selfish. Taking a big bass out of a lake obviously kills the fish, but it also harms the lake. It means that huge fish will never spawn again, thus eliminating its big-fish DNA from being passed on to future generations. It also brings to an end an amazing life. Experts say that in order for a bass to become extremely large, it has to survive the equivalent of biblical plagues: predators, pollution, droughts, and countless fisherman who have tried to catch it.

A large bass should be photographed and measured. A fiberglass replica can even be made that will look like the real thing. But a large bass should never be killed just so the fisherman can brag.

The human ego can easily become inflated. We are not psychologists and don't pretend to know why one person's does and another's doesn't. We do know this, however: a big ego is a bad thing. Some great theologians have even said that there really is only one sin: pride. That every other sin is just a spin-off from pride.

Here's a rule of thumb. If you ever have an impulse that makes you want to be seen or adored or praised, it's probably an impulse you should suppress. Remember: God resists the proud (James 4:6).

Reflect: Proverbs 16:18 says, "Pride goes before destruction and haughtiness before a fall." Is there an area of your life where you have accomplished great things? To what degree do you struggle with ego? Have you ever been humbled? What are some things you can remember that will help you stay humble?

THE POTATO PLAY

IT HAPPENED IN Double-A ball. The Williamsport, Pennsylvania Bills, a farm club of the Cleveland Indians, were twenty-eight games out of first in August and looking for a way to liven up a bedraggled team and what few fans they had left. Catcher Dave Bresnahan came up with a play that will live in infamy.

With his teammate's knowledge and full support—but without telling the manager—he peeled a potato and carved it so that it would be perfectly round and about the size of a baseball. He waited until there was an opposing runner on third, then called time out, claiming his catcher's mitt was broken. He went to the dugout to retrieve another mitt, one that had the potato in it, and returned to his position. Without anyone noticing, he palmed the potato and held it down by his ankle. When the pitch came in, he caught the baseball and then stood up and threw to third in an apparent pickoff attempt, except that he threw the potato instead of the ball and intentionally threw it wildly into left field. Naturally, the runner broke for home, where Dave Bresnahan was waiting for him with the real ball. He tagged the runner for the third out and started trotting toward the dugout.

It took the umps a moment to realize what had happened. When they did, they allowed the run to score and kicked Bresnahan out of the game for unsportsmanlike conduct. It should be noted that players on both sides and the few fans that realized what had happened were doubled over in laughter.

The next day, Bresnahan was released.

We do not condone rule-breaking, but at the same time, we can only smile when we think about this story. Dave Bresnahan had a sense of humor, something far too many people in this world are lacking.

In a world where everyone seems mad and uptight all the time, a little more humor sure would be nice.

Reflect: Proverbs 17:22 says, "A cheerful heart is good medicine, but a broken spirit saps a person's strength." Have you ever pulled a crazy stunt to try to lighten things up? How was it received? Why do you think so many people are so serious all the time? What are some of the obvious benefits of humor?

DON'T ASSUME

ONE DAY, AT a fancy country club, a foursome was just starting its round. As a man in gray slacks and a white hat addressed his ball, a voice came booming out of the clubhouse PA system: "Ladies and gentlemen, respecting the rules of golf is essential to the health of the sport. Would the gentleman in gray slacks and white hat please respect the tee markers? Please move back behind the tee markers."

But the man in the gray slacks and white hat did not move his ball back. Instead he took his stance over the ball and prepared to hit it. So again, the voice came booming out of the clubhouse PA system: "We expect players on this course to respect the rules. Would the gentleman in the gray slacks and white hat *please* move back behind the tee markers?"

That's when the man in the gray slacks and white hat looked at his three playing partners and said, "Would one of you please go tell that guy that this is my second shot?"

It's never a good idea to assume, especially when dealing with people and situations you don't know.

There is a *Seinfeld* episode where Jerry is talking to an airport ticket agent who seems to be ignoring him. Finally, when she turns and looks at him, he says in complete exasperation, "Are you deaf?" She smiles and says, "Why yes, I am."

How many times have you judged someone harshly without knowing anything about him or her? Many people who look perfectly normal are fighting horrendous battles that you know nothing about. Our suggestion is to make grace your default attitude toward people who irritate you. If you want to assume something, assume there's a good reason for their off-putting behavior. Then cut them some slack.

Reflect: In Matthew 5:7 Jesus said, "God blesses those who are merciful, for they will be shown mercy." Have you ever had a *Seinfeld* moment where you embarrassed yourself by making a false assumption? Has anyone ever assumed something about you that was far from the truth? Why is it so hard for people to make grace their default attitude toward others?

THE FORGOTTEN VIRTUE

ROY FIRESTONE TOLD about the time Muhammad Ali heard about a Jewish old folks' home in New York that was going to be torn down, depriving numerous residents of a place to live. This bothered Ali, so he put up the money for a new home to be built. When it opened, Ali went to visit the residents. When he walked in, a very elderly man was sitting by himself in the corner. As Ali approached, the elderly man put up his fists like he wanted to spar. Bundini Brown, Ali's trainer, saw the man put up his dukes and said, "Do you know who this is?" The old man replied, "I sure do. He's the greatest ... the champ. He's Joe Louis."

Bundini started to correct him, but Ali grabbed his arm and whispered in his ear, "If it makes him happy to meet Joe Louis ... if that's who his hero is, let's not confuse him."

We love that story because it's a beautiful illustration of kindness. In a world where so many people are cynical and sarcastic and disrespectful to anyone who disagrees with them, simple kindness has become a rare commodity, a forgotten virtue. And the impact on our culture is telling. More people than ever before are emotionally wounded. More people than ever before are seeking counseling. More people than ever before are committing suicide.

We urge you to work harder at being kind, not just to people you like and agree with, but especially to people that you feel need correcting. And if you need an example to follow, try Jesus. The multitudes loved him for many reasons. One of the big ones was that he was so kind.

Reflect: Micah 6:8 says, "This is what he requires of you: to do what is right, to love mercy, and to walk humbly with your God." Can you name an act of kindness that was directed toward you that had a profound influence on you? Why do you think kindness is so hard for some people? What are some of the blessings you could reap from being kind to others?

AUGUST 5

NO QUITTERS ALLOWED

(PAT) JUST AFTER I completed the eighth grade, I tried out for a youth baseball team in our town. I made the cut. The problem was that I was the youngest player on the team by far. I didn't know how much I would get to play or how the older boys would treat me.

We were on our way to the first game. My mother was driving, and my grandmother was sitting in the front passenger seat. I was in the back, thinking out loud about my situation. At one point I said, "If things don't work out, I can always quit."

My grandmother whirled around, glared at me, and jabbed her finger in my chest. "You ... don't ... quit!" she said. "Nobody in this family quits!"

That was a huge moment in my life, and one that has motivated me for many years to persevere. Obviously, there are times when quitting is the right thing to do. For example, when you learn that you're involved in something unethical, or when you realize you're being taken advantage of. But generally speaking, we should never go into any endeavor with an attitude that says, "If it doesn't go well, I'll just quit."

One of the reasons quitting is such a terrible idea is because very, very few of history's greatest accomplishments happened on the first try. Some of the greatest contributors to human progress—like Thomas Edison— **DON'T BE AFRAID TO FAIL.** tried and failed for years before their ideas finally clicked. Some of the greatest authors were rejected by publishers dozens of times before their work landed in the right person's hands.

Don't be afraid to fail. *Do* be afraid to quit. Quitting could be the thing that keeps your dream from coming true.

Reflect: Romans 5:4 says, "Endurance develops strength of character." Have you ever quit something you were involved in and regretted it later? What are some reasons (besides the one listed in this devotion) why quitting is often a terrible idea? Why is quitting an especially bad idea for young people?

STAYING HOME

FOOTBALL, MORE THAN any other sport, is a game of deception. No play illustrates this more than the reverse. The ball is snapped, and the entire offense begins to flow to the right, causing the defense to flow to its left. Then a single offensive player—usually a speedy wide receiver—reverses direction and comes flying through the backfield to the left, against the grain. The quarterback hands him the ball, and at that point it's a footrace. Can he get around the corner before the defense recovers? If he can, it will be a big gainer.

There are two ways to beat a reverse. One is for a lineman or a linebacker to get penetration into the backfield. He can blow the play up by forcing the wide receiver too deep, giving the defense time to reverse itself and stop the play.

The other way is for the backside defensive players who are responsible for containment to "stay home." Too often, however, they get caught up in the flow of the play and end up being out of position.

There is a sense in which the same thing can happen to Christians. They can get caught up in the flow of what other people are doing and end up out of place. In an office, for example, conversations can flow in an ungodly direction, and if the Christian in the room isn't careful, he or she can get carried along, laughing at a vulgar joke or gossiping about a mutual acquaintance. And just as it is in football, by the time the mistake is realized, the damage is already done. The Christian's witness is tarnished.

We encourage you to understand your assignment as a Christian and "stay home." Stay in your place, take care of your responsibility, and don't let yourself get carried along with other people.

Reflect: Hebrews 10:23 says, "Let us hold tightly without wavering to the hope we affirm, for God can be trusted to keep his promise." Have you ever gotten caught up in the flow of what other people were doing and ended up regretting it? Why is even a momentary lapse in judgment dangerous for a Christian?

DO YOU KNOW WHERE YOU ARE?

IT'S A SIMPLE QUESTION, RIGHT?

Arnold Palmer would disagree.

Before the 1989 British Open, Arnold Palmer was playing a practice round at Royal Troon. A photographer approached him and asked if he would mind posing beside the plaque that commemorated his first British Open victory in 1961. Arnie, an affable sort, happily agreed. The problem arose when he and the photographer started looking for the plaque. They walked all around the clubhouse grounds and couldn't find it. Finally, Arnie called his caddie, Tip Anderson, and asked if he knew where the plaque was. Tip informed him that the plaque was four hundred miles away on a different golf course. He'd won his first British Open at Royal Birkdale, not Royal Troon.

No doubt Arnie was embarrassed. We're sure everyone got a laugh out of the situation. What isn't so funny is when Christians don't realize where *they* are, not physically but metaphorically.

When you look at adult websites, do you realize where you are? You're in the internet's red-light district, a place where lives and marriages and families are routinely destroyed.

When you sit in front of the TV and play video games for hours on end, do you realize where you are? You're in an imaginary world your lonely wife or children have no access to.

When you go to a bar with friends after work, do you realize where you are? You're in a place where Satan's elixir (alcohol) flows freely, enabling him to do some of his best work.

Where you are physically can be very different from where you are metaphorically. We urge you to stop every day and think about where you are, and if where you are is where God would want you to be.

Reflect: Deuteronomy 6:12 says, "Be careful not to forget the Lord." Have you ever suddenly realized you were in a place that was dangerous for you as a Christian? How did you end up there? Why do you think so many Christians end up going where they shouldn't? Even if you're committed to the Lord, what's the danger of losing track of where you are?

TRAINING CAMP

AS WE WRITE these words, football training camps are in full swing on college campuses and in NFL practice facilities all across America. In the early days of camp, you'll see plays being run without pads. Receivers will run perfect routes and quarterbacks will put the ball on a dime. Running backs will rip through holes in the line like flour through a sieve.

A few days later, the players will run the same drills in pads, which means real blocking and tackling. And yet players never forget that they are tackling their own teammates. No linebacker wants to put his starting running back on the injured list. No D-lineman wants to knock his starting quarterback into next week.

Eventually the season will start, and players will be facing players on the *other* team. If you think the intensity will pick up, you're right. If you think caution will be thrown to the wind, you're right. If you think some players are going to get their bells rung, you're right.

But here's the thing: players get hurt in those early padless drills, just like they do in real games. Ankles and knees get twisted, hamstrings get pulled, fingers get jammed. When you put on a pair of cleats and walk onto the gridiron, something bad can happen at any moment.

The same is true of life. Even when you think you're in a safe place (no pads), you can get hurt. Take church, for example. If we could line up all the people who've been hurt in church, the line would stretch around the world!

Don't be fooled. This side of heaven, there are no perfectly safe places. Don't let this fact scare you; let it impress upon you the importance of putting on the full armor of God.

Reflect: Ephesians 6:11 says, "Put on all of God's armor so that you will be able to stand firm against all the strategies of the devil." Have you ever suffered a deep hurt in a place that was supposed to be safe, such as church? How did that experience affect your faith? Why do you think church is often a more dangerous place than it should be?

HEART HEALTHY

WOULD YESTERDAY'S ATHLETES be able to compete with today's? Or today's with yesterday's?

Would Steph Curry and Anthony Davis be as good if they were playing against Oscar Robertson and Wilt Chamberlain? Would they be better? Would Ted Williams hit .400 in today's MLB with so many flamethrowers topping out at over 100 mph? Would Babe Ruth hit 714 homers? Would Jack Nicklaus win eighteen majors if he had to compete against today's generation of young golfers whose strength and skill are unprecedented?

This debate has raged forever and will continue for generations to come. We think it brings up another interesting question: Would yesterday's Christians be as faithful as today's? Or today's as faithful as yesterday's?

Would today's megachurch pastor, who has the big TV ministry, be able to face that fiery furnace or den of lions with the same faith and courage as Daniel and his buddies, Shadrach, Meshach, and

Abednego? Would young Timothy be able to survive in ministry if he had to contend with an unending barrage of attacks from social media in addition to his troubled church members?

We don't know about the athletes, but with regard to believers, we believe a faithful believer would be a faithful believer in any generation. Why? Because unlike sports, faithfulness is a heart issue, not a talent issue or a size or strength or equipment issue. A person with a true heart for God will be faithful no matter what he or she faces.

This is why it's so important to take good care of your heart. Proverbs 4:23 says, "Guard your heart above all else, for it determines the course of your life." We think this just might be the most undervalued verse in the Bible.

Reflect: Psalms 51:10 says, "Create in me a clean heart, O God. Renew a loyal spirit within me." Christians in this generation are often said to be soft. How do you think you would measure up if you had to face the trials and persecutions that believers in Bible times had to face? What, specifically, are you doing right now to guard your heart?

PRESSURE

IT'S AMAZING HOW much smaller a basketball hoop looks in a tie game than when you have a twenty-point lead. And it looks even smaller than that in a tie game with one second on the clock.

And how about that three-foot putt? On a Saturday afternoon with your friends, you'd step right up and knock it in. But on the final hole of the US Open, when missing that putt will cost you the championship, that hole will shrink to about the size of a quarter.

There are athletes that thrive under pressure and others who don't. Reggie Jackson earned the nickname "Mr. October" because of his outstanding play in the World Series. By contrast, Clayton Kershaw, a future Hall of Famer, has had his struggles in October.

So what's the secret of performing well under pressure? If we knew that, everyone would tap in and be great at crunch time. But there are a few factors that are worth mentioning.

One is confidence. Shooting, putting, hitting, field goal kicking … they're all done better when the player is full of confidence.

Another important factor is preparation. The gym rat who stays after practice and shoots five hundred extra free throws is always going to be better than the lazy dude who runs out of practice as soon as it's over because he has a date.

One more often-overlooked factor is the simple realization that no matter what happens, life will go on. If you miss that free throw or that putt, you're not going to be taken out and executed. Many people, in sports and in life, put too much pressure on *themselves* by placing far too much importance on the outcome of a single task.

We urge you to keep things in perspective. Win, lose, or draw, God and your friends will still love you. Life will go on, and you might even get a chance to try again someday.

Reflect: 2 Timothy 1:7 says, "For God has not given us a spirit of fear and timidity but of power, love, and self-discipline." Up to this point in your life, how have you done under pressure? Do you have a tendency to put pressure on yourself when no one else is pressuring you? What do you know about God and about failure that should help you relax?

HOW TEN MINUTES CAN LAST A LIFETIME

(PAT) SEVERAL YEARS AGO the manager of the ESPN Club in Orlando told me that they had Roger Clemens in to sign autographs. As you might expect, there was a long line of people hoping the line would go fast. But things ground to a halt when a little boy of about ten asked Roger how to throw a fastball. Roger could have brushed him off with a quick answer. Instead he knelt down and spent the next ten minutes showing the boy how to throw every kind of fastball: the four-seamer, the two-seamer, the cutter, and even how to make it rise or sink. Obviously, the boy was too young to go out and throw those pitches. And there were no doubt lots of people farther back in the line who were getting antsy. But Roger Clemens understood that those things were beside the point. The goal was to give that little boy a memory he would cherish the rest of his life.

Time is a wonderful gift. Even just a few minutes.

Every year at Christmas, people open elaborately wrapped gifts that their loved ones spent a lot of money on. I can't help wondering how many of the people receiving those gifts would gladly exchange them for a little time spent with that loved one. How many kids of workaholic fathers would rather go fishing or play ball with their dads than anything else in the world? How many wives would give up their fancy cars and wardrobes in return for their husband's undivided attention just two evenings a week?

Lots of people are starved for time and attention. Who in your life is secretly longing for a little time and attention from you?

Reflect: Ecclesiastes 4:11 asks, "How can one be warm alone?" Have you ever felt starved for someone's time and attention? Is there someone in your life that may be silently suffering because you have not given enough of your time and attention? How do you discern a real need with what could be a controlling, manipulative spirit?

THE DAY A LOSER GOT A STANDING OVATION

STANDING OVATIONS ARE generally reserved for champions, or at least for people who offer up a heroic effort in defeat. Back in 1963 a standing ovation was given to a golfer who performed horribly at the US Open, shooting 76 and 77 on the first two days.

That golfer was Jack Nicklaus, twenty-three years old at the time, who was the defending champion and had already won the Masters and two other tournaments that year. Everyone expected him to defend his title successfully, but after making bogeys on the first three holes of the tournament, he just wasn't able to get anything going.

So why the standing ovation?

It happened after the second round. Jack bogeyed the eighteenth to miss the cut by one stroke. You can imagine how steamed a great champion would be. Everyone expected him to clean out his locker and head for the parking lot. Instead he went to the press room and patiently answered every single question without showing even a hint of the anger everyone knew he felt. When he was finished, the press corps gave him a standing ovation for doing what they believed most players would not have done.

Many moments in our lives slide by without anyone taking notice, but everyone notices those moments when we have reason to be angry. The people around us take a step back, cringe, hide their children's faces, just waiting for the explosion. When it doesn't come, they are amazed.

THE AMOUNT OF RESPECT PEOPLE HAVE FOR YOU WILL BE LARGELY DETERMINED BY HOW YOU ACT WHEN SOMETHING GOES WRONG.

Here's a simple truth: the amount of respect people have for you will be largely determined by how you act when something goes wrong. We think it's our worldly successes that earn people's respect, but often it's the way we handle ourselves when one of those worldly successes slips through our fingers. Anyone can pout and throw a fit. It takes a true champion of character to calmly move on.

Reflect: James 1:19 says, "You must all be quick to listen, slow to speak, and slow to get angry." Have you ever exploded in anger and later been embarrassed by your words or actions? When do you believe showing some anger (within reason) is appropriate? In your mind, what are the keys to keeping yourself under control?

AUGUST 13

DON'T BELIEVE EVERYTHING YOU HEAR

KANSAS CITY ROYALS great George Brett loved to talk during games. He talked to teammates, opposing players, and especially to umpires. One day, Ron Luciano was umping third when Brett walked over and said, "You know, I've been meaning to tell you that you're my favorite umpire." Luciano was new in the league and felt honored to be respected by such a great player. He couldn't wait to tell his fellow umps after the game what Brett said.

After the game, Luciano was just about to mention Brett's comment when the first base umpire said, "You know, something happened out there today that made me feel really good. George Brett told me I was his favorite umpire." To which one of the older umps replied, "You can't pay any attention to him; he tells all the umpires that. He's just trying to get on your good side." Luciano laughed along with the group and never mentioned that he had fallen for Brett's schtick too.

Throughout the course of your life, you're going to have a lot of people tell you things that aren't true. They're going to try to woo you, manipulate you, and trick you. It will happen a lot in relationships, business, politics, and religion. People with agendas have figured out that the masses are completely gullible, so they have crafted pitches to suck them in and manipulate them.

This is why the Bible talks so much about discernment. Discernment is the ability to see through to the heart of a matter. It's a by-product of wisdom, and wisdom is available from God. Every day when you pray, you should be asking God for wisdom and discernment. There are a lot of entities out there trying to manipulate you.

Reflect: James 1:5 says, "If you need wisdom, ask our generous God, and he will give it to you." Have you ever been made a fool of by a con artist? Why do you think you didn't recognize the con? How has that experience changed the way you interact with people?

MIRROR, MIRROR, ON THE WALL

ROB EVANS WAS THE head basketball coach at Ole Miss from 1992 to 1998 and at Arizona State from 1998 to 2006. For twenty-four years before that, he was an assistant coach who was passed over again and again for head coaching jobs. Once he was passed over for a job he thought he would be perfect for. Angry, he poured out his frustration to his wife. She gave him a stern look and challenged him to do what he tells his players to do when they don't come out on top: look in a mirror and ask themselves, "What more could I have done that I didn't do?"

Rob did that. As a result, he spent the next year talking to athletic directors, getting a better feel for what they were looking for, and putting together a game plan. One of his next interviews was with Ole Miss, and he got the job.

Of all the inventions in the history of mankind, the mirror may be the most important. No, it doesn't cure diseases or make fuel to run our machinery or keep people from starving, but it does help people see themselves as others see them, which is often the first step toward a better life.

Almost every day you will encounter someone who lacks self-awareness … someone who is his own worst enemy … someone who continually undermines his own goals and desires because of a trait or attitude that is self-defeating but that he doesn't see in himself because he has never really looked in a mirror. And sometimes that clueless person you encounter is you!

If things haven't been going well for you lately, you could whine and complain and shake your fist at the powers that be. Or you could look in a mirror. Only one of those choices will help you.

Reflect: Lamentations 3:40 says, "Let us test and examine our ways." Have you ever suddenly learned that you were undermining yourself with an attitude or trait that others found off-putting? Why do you think you didn't see it at first? What are some ways you can keep that from happening again?

DEFENSE WINS CHAMPIONSHIPS

OR DOES IT?

This is a debate that has been raging forever. The opinions you get will probably depend on whether you're talking to an offensive or defensive player or coach. Offensive personnel will fall back on their eternal theme, "You have to score to win the game." And they are right, of course. But defensive personnel will counter by saying, "In playoff and championship games, both teams are going to have great offenses and are going to score. It's the team that can hold the great offense down below their usual output that is going to win." And history backs this up. If you look at a list of championship winners in any sport, you will see one great defensive team after another.

The problem is that defense isn't as glamorous or entertaining as offense. People love to see the scoreboard light up. They love to see home runs and touchdowns and rim-rattling slam dunks. But it's on defense that countless games are won or lost.

Defense is critical in our spiritual lives too. 1 Peter 5:8 says, "Stay alert! Watch out for your great enemy, the devil. He prowls around like a roaring lion, looking for someone to devour." Specifically, what kind of person is the devil looking for? The person whose defenses are weak. The person who hasn't been in the Word, who hasn't been praying, who hasn't been in fellowship with other believers. It's the same logic burglars use today. They look for homes with cheap locks and no security system.

Our advice to every serious-minded Christian is to be serious about defense. Offensive moves like preaching and teaching witnessing and tithing are important, but without good defense, you're in trouble.

Reflect: Ephesians 6:11 says, "Put on all of God's armor so that you will be able to stand firm." Think about times when you have been under attack spiritually. Have the outcomes of those events varied according to the strength of your spiritual defenses? What is the current state of your defenses? Is there an area you need to improve upon?

SHOW 'EM HOW IT'S DONE

(PAT) **DURING MY CAREER** as an NBA executive I have overseen the creation of five NBA team mascots. They are Benny the Bull (Chicago Bulls), Harry the Hawk (Atlanta Hawks), Big Shot (Philadelphia 76ers), Hoops (Philadelphia 76ers), and Stuff (Orlando Magic).

Hoops was our second 76ers mascot, and he wasn't taking off. We tried a few different people, and no one was making him come alive. I thought, "This can't be that difficult." Finally, exasperated, I decided to put the suit on and do a game myself to show people how it was done.

That night the fans had no idea that their general manager was in the Hoops suit. Neither did my friend Lenny Wilkins, who was coaching our opponent, the Seattle Sonics. During one time-out I sauntered over to the Sonics' huddle and listened in right next to Lenny. He thought it was some kid in the suit and gave me a shove to get me away from the huddle. I never did tell Lenny it was me. I'm sure he would have gotten a kick out of it.

That night I acted like a nut. If a grown man had acted like that on the street, he would have been carried off for observation. But in a mascot suit, you can get away with just about anything. The point is I made sure everybody knew what I was looking for in that job. Nobody had any questions after that night.

Far too many people in leadership positions rely on words alone. They give instructions and then criticize if things don't go well. Sometimes they yell and scream when they don't get what they want. In such cases, you have to jump in and show people what you want. It's called leading by example.

Christians understand this as well as anyone. We preach, we teach, we testify, but we also understand that it's critical to show people what godliness looks like. Words are important, but words alone won't cut it. Be what you teach!

Reflect: Titus 2:7 says, "And you yourself must be an example to them." Can you think of a time in your life when someone's example made all the difference for you? What is it about an example or a demonstration that is so powerful? Is there someone you're trying to lead right now who needs more than verbal instruction?

GOING OUT IN STYLE

IF YOU WERE a professional athlete, how would you like to end your career? How would you like your last play to go down?

If you were a basketball player, would you want to hit a three-pointer at the buzzer to win the game? If you were a football player, would you want to break off an eighty-yard touchdown run or kick a sixty-yard field goal to win the game? If you were a baseball player, would you like to crank a bottom-of-the-ninth grand slam to win the game?

Kansas City Royals great George Brett was once asked this question. He shocked everybody when he said that he'd like to hit a hard ground ball to second. Stunned, the interviewer asked why. He said he wanted to close out his career running as hard as he could to first base so every young player in the dugout could see how the game is supposed to be played.

We love this story because there are so many people who don't know how to finish. A lot of people, as they approach retirement, start to coast. They lose their passion and their energy. In some cases, they figure they deserve to be able to take it easy after all they've done. Sadly, they don't stop to think that there are young eyes on them seeing an awful example. They don't stop to think that, by coasting, they are compromising their integrity by drawing a full paycheck but not giving a full effort. They are doing the very thing a young employee would never be allowed to get away with.

At some point, we're all going to step down from our life's work. It can be a great moment in life. A time of fulfillment and accomplishment. But it's important to do it right. It's important to run out that last ground ball as hard as you can. People are watching. Show them how to go out in style.

Reflect: In 2 Timothy 4:7, Paul said, "I have fought the good fight, I have finished the race, and I have remained faithful." Have you ever watched someone finish poorly? How did it affect you? Why do you think so many people feel entitled to slow down and take it easy at the end instead of stretching for the tape?

PLAYING TO WIN

THERE ARE TWO TYPES of players on the PGA Tour: those who play to make a living and those who play to win.

The guys who play to make a living are not to be criticized. They work hard at their games, spending hours on the driving range and the putting green. They think of their families and their kids and their mortgages and their car payments. They are determined to provide a good life for their families. There's nothing at all wrong with this. However, it is generally not from this group of players that the great champions emerge.

Great champions generally emerge from that group of players that is obsessed with one thing: winning. Such players don't care what the purse is or how the money is divvied up at the end of the tournament. They never think, "All I have to do is finish in the top twenty-five, and I'll make a good check." The only question that crosses their minds is, "What do I have to do to win?" These players may or may not be more talented than the rest, but they do have an intangible quality that elevates them ever so slightly. And sometimes that's the difference between winning and making a nice check.

Something similar can happen in our spiritual lives. There is a type of person who wants to be good, to stay out of trouble, and to live a respectable life. There is another type of person who is determined to reach his full potential in Christ. The first type of person does what he's supposed to do; the second type of person goes beyond what most people would expect.

Both individuals will be well thought of by others, but only the person who is determined to reach his full potential in Christ will experience the deepest riches of God's blessings.

Reflect: 1 Corinthians 9:24 says, "Don't you realize that in a race everyone runs, but only one person gets the prize? So run to win!" Have you been content with just being a good, well-respected person? How might your life change if you made up your mind to reach your full potential in Christ? What changes would that decision require?

SHOW UP READY TO PLAY

AS STATED IN the opening devotion of this book, Cal Ripken put together a streak of 2,632 consecutive games played. According to Cal, his dad, Cal Sr., gets a lot of the credit because he taught Cal at a young age to show up every day at the ballpark ready to play. Don't be tired, don't be hung over, and don't be distracted by personal problems. The manager is going to put the guys in the lineup that he thinks give the team the best chance to win. Show up at the ballpark being one of those guys.

During Cal's streak, his managers were Earl Weaver, Joe Altobelli, Cal Ripken Sr., Frank Robinson, Johnny Oates, Phil Regan, Davey Johnson, and others. Day by day, month after month, year after year, those men looked at Cal and said, "This man can help us win today." Not once did Cal pressure them to play him. Not once did he remind them of the streak. If at any time they had seen fit to let him sit out a game, he would have done it with no complaints. Cal never tried to influence the manager's decisions; he just showed up ready and eager to play.

Showing up ready and eager is something we need more of in this world. As leaders of people for many years, we both have seen far too many individuals who are lazy, tardy, or who feel entitled. They show up late or sometimes not at all. They walk in yawning or complaining or focused on something other than the task at hand. They show up not to win but just to draw a paycheck.

DON'T BE THAT PERSON WHO JUST SHOWS UP. BE THAT PERSON WHO SHOWS UP READY TO PLAY AND READY TO WIN.

Don't be that person who just shows up. Be that person who shows up ready to play and ready to win.

Reflect: 1 Thessalonians 5:6 says, "So be on your guard, not asleep like others. Stay alert and be clearheaded." Do you have a problem with tardiness? If your boss or coworkers were to evaluate you, would they say that you consistently show up ready and eager to perform your best? Have you grown less diligent over time as you have gotten more comfortable?

OWN IT

IN 2009, R.A. DICKEY was pitching for the Minnesota Twins. In his first appearance after a stint on the disabled list with a sore elbow, he came into a tight situation with the bases loaded. His manager, Ron Gardenhire, told him not to throw his signature knuckleball because he was afraid of a wild pitch. Dickey didn't say anything but was angry. He felt his manager had taken his best weapon away from him and set him up for failure. Nevertheless, he attacked the hitter with his fastball and slider as instructed. Predictably, the opposing hitters jumped on those pitches, and the Twins lost the game.

Later, Gardenhire approached Dickey and apologized for what he realized was a dumb move. "I'm sorry I put you in that position. I should've known better." R.A. later gave this incident as a reason why Ron Gardenhire was such a good manager and so loved by his players … he always took responsibility for his mistakes.

Far too many people in this world hide from responsibility. They pass the buck, make excuses, or play dumb when something goes wrong. Or, in the case of politics, they blame the other party. This is one of the biggest reasons why so many dysfunctional systems in our society, from government institutions to schools to businesses, never get fixed. It's also why a lot of troubled marriages and even churches never get fixed.

We urge you to own your mistakes for two reasons. One, everybody probably knows you blew it anyway. And two, they will respect you more if you are man or woman enough to admit it. It's the people who *don't* own their mistakes, who try to pass the buck, that eventually become despised.

Reflect: Proverbs 28:13 says, "People who conceal their sins will not prosper, but if they confess and turn from them, they will receive mercy." Why do you think buck passing is so common when almost everyone agrees it's a bad choice? Besides earning people's respect, what are some other reasons why admitting your mistakes is wise?

REAL STEEL

(PAT) ONE DAY I went to visit Peter Vegso at his horse farm in Ocala, Florida. In case you're not familiar with Peter, he is the publisher of the *Chicken Soup for the Soul* books. When I arrived, his horse trainer was exercising some of the beautiful animals in his care. One was named Real Steel.

As Peter and I stood there and watched, Peter explained to me how flaky the horse was. He said, "Watch him carefully as he trots around the track. You'll see that every little thing distracts him. See that shadow on the track? That'll spook him. And look at that tractor over in the next field. He'll hear it and get all agitated." Then Peter said, "Real Steel will never be a winning horse because his attention is all over the place."

This principle is true in so many areas of life. Have you ever noticed that restaurants that try to serve every kind of ethnic food generally aren't very good? The best Mexican restaurants, for example, don't try to serve Italian and barbecue and burgers. And the best burger joints don't try to serve Mexican and Italian and barbecue. They tend to home in on one thing and do it right.

What about your life?

Do you have too many irons in the fire? Is your attention divided by so many things that nothing is getting enough attention? I've known people who owned businesses and had wives and children and pursued hobbies and served on boards and committees. They were pulled in so many different directions they couldn't do a very good job with any of their responsibilities.

Always remember: it's better to do a couple of things really well than to do a half-dozen things poorly. Whatever two or three things you focus on, make sure one of them is your family.

Reflect: Proverbs 4:25 says, "Look straight ahead, and fix your eyes on what lies before you." Make a list of the major responsibilities in your life. If your list is longer than three or four items, there's a good chance one of them is not getting the attention it deserves. If that's the case, what do you need to do to rectify the situation?

THE POWER OF INSPIRATION

(MARK) FOR QUITE A few years, I coached youth baseball. One year I had a team of twelve- and thirteen-year-olds that was very good—good enough to make it to the championship game of our league tournament. Our opponent that night was another outstanding team. I felt we were evenly matched, and I racked my brain to try to think of something that would give us an edge.

Our game was at six thirty, so I had the boys come to my house at four thirty in uniform. I gave them a little pep talk, and then I said, "We're going to just hang out here as a team and eat some snacks and watch some TV." The snacks I fed them were of the sugary variety, a calculated move to fill them with energy. And what we watched was a video cassette of the highlights of the St. Louis Cardinals' 1987 season, a season in which they won the pennant. On that video was one spectacular play after another: clutch home runs, diving catches, and late-inning comebacks. The boys hooted and hollered as they watched the video. I could see them getting fired up.

By the time we got to the field, those boys were nothing if not inspired. They took the field at a dead run and hustled like never before. They were all over the field defensively and dashing around the bases with abandon. To my surprise, we overwhelmed our opponent in a laugher.

I've never forgotten that night because it was such a powerful example of the power of inspiration. I'm convinced that if those boys had been laying around their houses watching cartoons or playing video games, they wouldn't have played with that kind of energy.

Most of us do a much better job when we're inspired.

Reflect: Psalms 16:8 says, "I know the Lord is always with me. I will not be shaken, for he is right beside me." Why does inspiration fade so quickly? What are some different ways a Christian can stay inspired? Do you feel that inspiration can become negative if it is seen as a substitute for hard work and preparation?

LIFE ABBREVIATED

IN A GENERATION when life spans are increasing, the life span of a major-league baseball has gotten shorter. Perhaps you've noticed that if a pitched ball hits the dirt, the catcher throws it out and asks for a new baseball. If the batter hits the ball and it touches the dirt, more often than not it is thrown out in favor of a new baseball. Foul balls and home runs hit into the seats also effectively end the life of a baseball. People who study such things are now saying that the life span of a baseball is five to seven pitches.

People sometimes live short lives too. Probably every person who reads this book will be able to think of someone—an acquaintance or loved one—who died young. It's especially painful when a child dies, or even a baby. Stroll through a cemetery sometime and look at the dates on the headstones. You'll see a surprising number of children and teenagers and people in their twenties.

Sometimes the death of a young person triggers a faith crisis in the survivors because it seems so unfair. I (Mark) have counseled a lot of parents who simply could not understand why God allowed their children to die. In one town I lived in, four teenagers were killed in a car that was hit by a train on the night of their high school graduation.

Anyone who tells you they can explain why such things happen is a liar. But here's one thing we do know: because life is so uncertain, we mustn't fail to teach our children about Jesus. Some parents say, "We're not going to try to influence our kids. We're going to wait and let them figure out what they believe when they get older."

Please don't do that.

If there are young people in your life, do everything in your power to make sure they know Jesus and have a personal relationship with him. You never know what a day might bring.

Reflect: James 4:14 says, "Your life is like the morning fog— it's here a little while, then it's gone." Has your life been touched by the death of a young person? How did it affect your faith? Even if you're not a teacher or a youth worker, are there some ways you can have an impact for Christ on the children in your world?

BLING!

PLAYERS TALK ABOUT winning a ring. Often fans and sportswriters judge them by how many rings they've won. Sometimes there's controversy over who should get a ring, especially if a player or coach was on the team but didn't finish the season. In 2019, Kelly Bryant was not given an NCAA championship ring by the Clemson Tigers because he left the team after four games and transferred to another school. The decision raised some eyebrows because Bryant definitely helped the team win those first four games.

What most people don't realize is that officials often get rings too. Theirs come a little easier, however, because they don't have to actually win the game or the series. That's why their rings are not nearly as expensive or flamboyant as the players'. Currently, the most expensive Super Bowl ring is the New England Patriots' ring from Super Bowl XLIX, ringing up at a mere $36,500 each.

As Christians we get some bling, too, when we finish the race of life and stand in the victor's circle. James 1:12 says, "God blesses those who patiently endure testing and temptation. Afterward, they will receive the crown of life that God has promised to those who love him."

A key word is "endure." We love that word because it has such hope in it. Notice James doesn't say you have to be perfect. He doesn't say, "God blesses those who pile up one victory after another when it comes to testing and temptation." Going to heaven is not like going to a sports Hall of Fame. To get into a Hall of Fame, you have to pile up mountains of victories, huge numbers that soar far beyond normal players. Heaven is not about works, so it's a different standard. You place your faith and trust in Jesus and then endure—hang in there—be faithful.

Jesus has already done the work.

Reflect: In 2 Timothy 4:8, Paul said, "The prize awaits me— the crown of righteousness ..." Do you live with a sense that you have to perform or endure in order to be saved? Do you feel guilty when you mess up, or do you ask forgiveness and glory in the grace of God? What could you do to be more aware of God's grace?

SHIPWRECK KELLY

ALVIN KELLY WAS born in 1893. As a young man who spent some time as a sailor, he became known as "Shipwreck" Kelly, but not because he'd been shipwrecked at sea. The name came from the fact that he'd been a not-so-hot boxer who was repeatedly knocked out. "The sailor has been shipwrecked again!" was a common statement heard at his fights.

As you might guess, Shipwreck Kelly decided to find another line of work, something a little less hard on the old noggin. Because he had no fear of heights, he was hired to work on a construction crew that walked the steel beams of skyscrapers. But even that wasn't his final career destination.

A Los Angeles businessman hired him to sit on top of a flagpole as part of a publicity stunt for the opening of a new theater. Shipwreck did it, pocketed a handsome fee, and realized it was the easiest money he had ever made. For the next twenty years, he made a handsome living as a flagpole sitter, claiming that he spent over twenty thousand hours in the sky.

We are not sure how much value there is in flagpole sitting. That Shipwreck Kelly made the world a better place is debatable. But we have to give him credit for not continuing to do something he clearly wasn't good at. Far too many people continue to grind away year after year at jobs they neither excel at nor enjoy. Often they look back and feel that they wasted their lives.

We urge you to chase your dreams. Pursue your passion. Do what you love and what you're good at.

We just hope it's something besides flagpole sitting.

Reflect: 1 Peter 4:10 says, "God has given each one of you a gift from his great variety of spiritual gifts. Use them well to serve one another." What talents or gifts do you possess? How did you come to realize what they were? Are you putting your efforts into those areas?

THE NBL

YOU'RE FAMILIAR WITH MLB.

And the NBA.

And the NFL.

And the NHL.

But do you remember the NBL?

Almost nobody does. The National Bowling League was born in 1961 and died less than a year later. Teams in New York, Dallas, Detroit, and seven other cities organized teams and competed like franchises in other professional sports. The owner of the Dallas Broncos even spent millions of dollars to build a six-lane arena for his team.

The problem was, almost nobody showed up to watch. Attendance was poor on opening night and got worse as the season went along. It became apparent very quickly that bowling, while a game people loved to play, was not a game they wanted to watch. At least not if they had to buy a ticket.

Have you ever watched what you thought was a great idea flop? It's not so bad if it's somebody else's idea, but if it's yours, it can be very painful. You might even harbor some resentment toward people for not supporting your idea or even badmouthing it. But great ideas generally survive, and bad ones generally don't. And God is certainly going to have a say in the matter.

The key, if you have an idea that flops, is to not let it keep you from continuing to dream. The world is full of authors, inventors, and businesspeople whose crowning life achievements were not their first ideas.

Reflect: Proverbs 19:21 says, "You can make many plans, but the Lord's purpose will prevail." Have you ever had what you thought was a great idea, only to see it fail? What did you misread about the situation? How did that disappointment affect your creativity or your willingness to chase new dreams?

WHEN YOU FEEL CHEATED

IF WE TOLD YOU there was once an NBA player who averaged 50.4 points a game and 25.7 rebounds a game during an entire season, would you believe us? Those sound like video game numbers; we agree. But they really were posted by a full-time, everyday player in 1962.

Now, what if we told you that after posting those numbers, that player did not win the league MVP? Sounds unthinkable, doesn't it? But it happened. Wilt Chamberlain is the guy who posted the numbers, and Bill Russell is the guy who won the MVP. Bill averaged 18.9 points a game and 23.6 rebounds.

There are times in life when we feel cheated.

NO ONE EVER SAID LIFE WOULD BE FAIR. THE CHALLENGE FOR ALL OF US IS TO NOT BECOME BITTER.

You work harder for your company than anyone in the department, but the other guy gets the promotion.

You treat the guy you love like a king, but he runs off with the girl who's only using him to get what she wants.

You sacrifice energy, time, and money to build your church or ministry, only to have a charismatic newcomer waltz in and win the people's affection.

No one ever said life would be fair. The challenge for all of us is to not become bitter. One way to do that is to use the disappointment as fuel to do even better. And to realize that your hard work and outstanding performance is its own reward. Whether other people recognize and appreciate you or not, the good job you did can hold much satisfaction.

Above all, keep in mind that even if there are some people who don't seem to appreciate your outstanding efforts, there will be many who will. Perhaps your greatest joy and satisfaction is to be found with someone you will meet in the future. Just keep on being awesome!

Reflect: Psalms 43:1 says, "Declare me innocent, O God! Defend me against these ungodly people." Have you ever felt cheated? How did you handle it? What did you learn through the experience? Have you since moved on and found vindication and appreciation elsewhere?

HANDSHAKES

WHEN KIDS START OUT in youth sports, they're taught to line up and shake hands with their opponent after the game. The tradition carries on as they get older too. Watch a college basketball game, and you'll see the coaches meet at half court as the buzzer sounds and their teams fall into line behind them. Even in college and professional football, where there's no official handshake line, players still make their way across the gridiron and greet one another. The only sport where opponents don't shake hands after a game is Major League Baseball, which begs the question ... What's wrong with those baseball players?

But there's another question that bears asking: Is all this postgame handshaking an exercise in hypocrisy? Are we supposed to believe that the losing players really want to line up and congratulate the team that just clobbered them? If you watch some of those handshake lines, you'll see about as much enthusiasm as you see water in the Sahara Desert. Could it be that the baseball guys, while seeming a bit unsportsmanlike for not shaking hands, are actually being more honest by shaking hands with their own teammates instead of their opponents?

We say, "Long live the postgame handshake!"

Good sportsmanship is never a bad thing. And no, you're not always going to feel like shaking hands, but the universal sign of maturity is doing things you don't necessarily want to do. You are a bigger person if you can look the guy who beat you in the eye and say, "Congratulations."

You might also want to smile and wink and say, "I'll be back, so don't get too comfortable."

Reflect: Proverbs 24:17 says, "Don't rejoice when your enemies fall." Think of times when you have been in fierce competition, either in sports or business. When you came out on the short end, how did it affect your attitude and behavior? What are some reasons it is important to remain positive and upbeat when you lose?

IGNORANCE

(MARK) I'VE WATCHED thousands of baseball games, but last night, as I was watching the Cardinals play the Royals, I saw a rule come into play that I didn't know about.

The bases were loaded with one out in a close game, so the infield was playing in. The Cardinals' hitter smacked a ground ball to the left of the shortstop. He dove and missed the ball. Just behind him, Yadier Molina was breaking for third. The ball hit Yadi's heel and rolled into short left field. When the ball was recovered and time was called, the Royals were screaming that Molina should be out. Everybody knows that a runner in fair territory that is struck by a batted ball is out.

Not so fast.

The rule states that the runner must be in front of the fielder. If the fielder is in front of the runner, the rule doesn't apply. In this case, the shortstop was playing in and was about three feet in front of Molina. The umpire called Molina safe, and the Royals flipped their lids. They didn't know that little-known aspect of the rule any better than I did.

It strikes me that much of our heartburn in life comes from ignorance … the things we don't know. God gave us the Bible, our rule book for life: sixty-six books loaded with information that will help us get through this very difficult world in pretty good shape. As Psalms says, the word is a lamp for our feet (Psalms 119:105). But if we don't know what the rule book actually says, we're bound to have times of anger and frustration. I wonder how many times God would look at us the way that ump looked at the Royals' skipper and say, "Simmer down. It's in the book. You can look it up!"

The more you know of God's word, the more life is going to make sense.

Reflect: Psalms 119:104 says, "Your commandments give me understanding …" How much do you read and study the Bible? Do you have a set routine? Are you into the Bible more or less than you were a couple of years ago? How often do you consult the Word when you come to a difficult situation in life?

ADDING LIFE TO YOUR YEARS

IT'S A WONDERFUL thing when people with disabilities play sports. Margaret Waldron was a case in point. She didn't let the fact that she was legally blind keep her from playing golf. She couldn't stand on the tee box and see the green or the flag because of macular degeneration, but her husband would describe the layout of the hole to her and help her get lined up.

We know what you're thinking.

You're thinking, "Aw, that's really nice, but she probably had a very difficult time getting the ball in the hole." You might be surprised. Margaret is the only person we've ever heard of—seeing or blind— who made holes-in-one on the same hole on consecutive days. It happened on Amelia Island's Long Point course, hole number 7, an eighty-seven-yard par three. She used a 7-iron and an old Ultra golf ball. Oh, and did we mention she was seventy-four-years-old?

And in case you're wondering, yes, there were witnesses. The National Hole-In-One Association confirmed everything.

Margaret Waldron was the best kind of person. And we don't mean she was a golfer. We mean she was a person who refused to make excuses and talk about what she couldn't do. She loved golf, so she played. Probably ninety-nine out of one hundred people in her situation would have said, "Play golf? I'm blind. How could I play golf?" Margaret just grabbed her clubs and headed for the course.

There's an old saying that instead of adding years to our lives, we should be adding life to our years. Margaret epitomized that, and because she did, she accomplished one of the rarest feats in sports.

Reflect: Ecclesiastes 11:8 says, "When people live to be very old, let them rejoice in every day of life." How are you doing with this idea of adding life to your years? Are you working too much and failing to have fun? Are you allowing your age or other disabilities to keep you from doing what you enjoy?

UNWRITTEN RULES

IF YOU WANT TO start a fight in baseball, just violate an unwritten rule. There are several of them. One would be bunting in the late innings to break up a no-hitter. If you do it, you can expect to get a fastball in your ribcage the next time you face that pitcher.

Now, you might ask, "But what's wrong with bunting for a base hit if your team is only down by a run or two? Aren't you trying to win the game? Should it matter what inning it is?" In our view, these are excellent questions with obvious answers.

Another unwritten rule is that you don't do a big bat flip when you hit a home run and hotdog it around the bases. You just put your head down and run.

But again, what if the tension is so thick you can cut it with a knife? What if the fans are on the edge of their seats? What if it's an epic moment in a playoff game? Isn't a guy allowed to show some emotion? We've sure seen enough pitchers pump their fists on a key strikeout.

Our view is that unwritten rules shouldn't be a thing. When rules are unwritten, people's opinions come into play, and when that happens, you've got trouble.

This brings to mind the brilliance of God in giving us the Bible. He didn't leave us to try to sort out a million opinions as to how the Christian life should be lived. He saw to it that his perfect will was written down and passed down through the ages. Yes, religious people have come up with many unwritten rules, but we encourage you to ignore them. Just stick with the Bible. You'll never go wrong.

Reflect: 2 Timothy 3:16 says, "All Scripture is inspired by God and is useful to teach us what is true and to make us realize what is wrong in our lives." What are some of the unwritten rules religious people have come up with? To what degree do you pay attention to them? Do you happen to have some expectations of your own that might qualify as unwritten rules?

EMBARRASSING MOMENTS NEVER DIE

TIM KURKJIAN IS ONE of the best baseball analysts around. He tells the story about the time he was fifteen years old and taking a sociology class. During the class, the subject of circumcision came up. Tim didn't know what it was, so he asked the girl sitting next to him. She glared at him and told him to stop joking around. Puzzled, he asked her again, only to have her refuse more sternly. Oblivious but now wildly curious, he went straight home and looked it up and got the shock of his life. Thoroughly embarrassed, he suddenly understood why the girl was so irritated by the question.

Fast-forward twenty years.

Tim went to his class reunion and saw the same girl. Immediately, his embarrassing moment came to mind, but he thought, *No worries. Twenty years have passed. There's no way she'll remember.* But she did. As Tim said, "She remembered it like it was yesterday."[27]

Embarrassing moments have a way of sticking in people's minds. Therefore, you should try not to have them. Sometimes, as was the case with Tim Kurkjian, they're just harmless things that happen organically and turn out to be funny. But other times our embarrassing moments are those instances when we lose control of our emotions and say or do something unbecoming, often overreacting to something that isn't a very big deal. Later, when we come to our senses, we have to retrace our steps and apologize.

You hear a lot of people say, "Watch what you do, because everyone has a cell phone and they'll record you." We say watch what you do even when there are no cell phones around. It's not about trying not to get caught, it's about being a good Christian.

Reflect: 1 Thessalonians 5:6 says, "So be on your guard, not asleep like the others. Stay alert and be clearheaded." What was your most embarrassing moment? Was it just something funny that happened, or the result of your bad judgment or behavior? How impulsive are you? How can you reign yourself in so that you create fewer awkward moments?

WHAT'S COMING OUT OF YOUR MOUTH?

THE VERY FIRST baseball game was played in Hoboken, New Jersey, on June 19, 1846. Something happened in that game that has happened in countless games since: a player got mad at the umpire. Then something else happened that has happened a lot since then: the player cursed. Then something else happened that *never* happens today: the player got fined six cents for cursing.

If players in any sport were going to get fined for cursing today, most of them would be flat broke, even with the salaries they make. Your humble authors once attended a big-league game together and sat in the third row, by the home team's dugout. There just happened to be a controversial play at the plate, and boy did our little ears get assaulted. Some of the curses that were flying through the air could peel paint off a wall!

Times have changed a lot since we were young. We grew up in an era when movies and TV shows and books weren't filled with profanity.

Now they are, plus social media is a cesspool of horrendous language. And my (Mark) daughter, who works in the school system, reports that you can hear every bad word conceived in the mind of man in your local middle school.

We hope you don't curse, but if you do, please stop. You might have to work to break the habit, but please do. There are too many junk words in the world already without you adding to the total. But the greater issue is your witness as a Christian. If praises and curses both are coming out of your mouth, no one is going to take you seriously. And Christ will be dishonored, which is the greatest tragedy of all.

Reflect: Ephesians 4:29 says, "Don't use foul or abusive language. Let everything you say be good and helpful, so that your words will be an encouragement to those who hear them." Do you swear? If you say, "Occasionally" or "Only when I get angry," it's likely that you curse more than you think. What do you need to do in order to break that habit completely?

THE LONG HAUL

THOUGH THEY ARE NOT recognized sports, a number of remarkable feats of physical strength and endurance that almost defy imagination are remembered in history.

For example, in 1900, Johann Huslinger walked 871 miles, from Vienna, Austria, to Paris, France, in fifty-five days. That in itself is quite a feat. But then consider that he walked all that distance on his hands.

In 1891, Silvain Dornon, a baker from France, walked from Paris to Moscow, a distance of 1,546 miles, in fifty-eight days. He didn't do it on his hands like Johann Huslinger, but he did do it on stilts.

In 1977, Matthew Hullfish rode a bicycle from San Francisco to Atlantic City, New Jersey, a distance of 3,606 miles. The feat becomes even more impressive when you realize that Matthew was only eight years old.

And then there's the interesting case of Walter Nilsson who, in 1934, traveled 3,306 miles from New York City to San Francisco while riding an eight-foot-tall unicycle.

In all of these cases, there must have been times when the temptation to quit was very strong, much like it can be for Christians. We are not walking on our hands or riding unicycles, but we are contending with countless struggles. Solomon warned that people who grow old will have to deal with "many dark days" (Eccles. 11:8). This is especially true of believers, who will always find the secular world aligned against them.

THE POINT IS NOT TO BE PERFECT EVERY DAY. THE POINT IS TO BE FAITHFUL OVER THE LONG HAUL.

We encourage you to take the long view of life. Don't let a bad moment or a bad day or a bad week discourage you. The point is not to be perfect every day. The point is to be faithful over the long haul.

Reflect: 1 Corinthians 15:58 says, "So, my dear brothers and sisters, be strong and immovable." How long have you been following Christ? Have there been lapses when you have not been as faithful as you should have been? What are the challenges that make endurance the hardest? What are the truths that inspire you?

KNOW THE FISH

THERE IS AN aspect to bass tournament fishing that is extremely counterintuitive. Let's say a tournament is being held on a lake that you, an amateur fisherman, fish all the time. Fishermen from all over the country are coming in to fish a lake they're not familiar with, prompting you to think that you could probably outfish a lot of them. You're on the lake all the time. You know where the hot spots are. You can get in your boat and drive to a dozen spots where you've caught a stringer of fish.

Sounds logical, right?

But the truth is, a professional fisherman who doesn't know a lake will outfish a local amateur fisherman who does know a lake almost every time. Why? Because, when fishing, it's more important to know the fish than it is to know the lake. An amateur fisherman knows the lake. He knows his favorite spots. But a professional fisherman knows the fish and can evaluate nuances in water, cover, wind, weather, and a dozen other factors which will help him catch fish no matter what lake he happens to be on.

There is a strong parallel to this in evangelism, or what Jesus called "fishing for men." You have to know the fish. You have to know people. Far too many would-be evangelists end up driving people away by, for example, being too pushy. Or by trying to manipulate people with guilt. Or by casting judgments on their lifestyle. Such approaches to evangelism are usually taken by people who "know the lake" but not the "fish." They've read their Bibles and know everything lost people are doing wrong, but they have no understanding of how to connect and relate to the person.

We encourage you to share your faith with lost people. But don't just pepper them with verses and clichés. Get to know them. Find out what they're dealing with. And then show them how Jesus can make a difference.

Reflect: In Matthew 4:19 Jesus said, "Come, follow me, and I will show you how to fish for people." How much effort have you put into witnessing? If your answer is "not much," why? Do you feel unqualified? Have you had a bad experience? Think of someone you know well who doesn't have a relationship with Christ. What could you say that might open the door to a conversation?

EXERCISE

THERE ARE THREE TYPES of people: those who exercise, those who don't exercise and feel guilty about it, and those who don't exercise and don't feel guilty about it. Here are some statements that have been attributed to some famous people in that last group:

Henry Ford: "Exercise is bunk. If you are healthy, you don't need it. And if you are sick, you shouldn't take it."

Neil Armstrong: "I believe every human has a finite number of heartbeats. I don't intend to waste any of mine running around doing exercises."

Rita Rudner: "I've been doing leg lifts for fifteen years, and the only thing that's gotten thinner is the carpet where I've been doing the leg lifts."

Mark Twain: "I take my only exercise acting as a pall bearer at the funerals of my friends who exercise regularly."

As humorous as these statements may be, we recommend that you not adopt such a mindset. The Bible talks about our bodies being the temple of the Holy Spirit, about all of us having a "treasure" in these earthen vessels. Exercise is one way to take care of the temple and protect the vessel. Some might say, "But we don't see Jesus exercising in the Gospels." Oh yes, we do! Jesus walked everywhere he went. Combine that with a diet of fish, fruit, and vegetables, and Jesus was probably as physically fit as anybody you know.

Don't be a couch potato. Get up and move. Take care of that temple. You've got an honored Guest living there.

Reflect: 1 Corinthians 6:19 says, "Don't you realize that your body is the temple of the Holy Spirit, who lives in you and was given to you by God?" How much do you exercise? Are you consistent with it? In addition to better health, what are some of the other benefits exercise can bring into your life?

LET YOUR LIGHT SHINE, BUT NOT IN SOMEONE'S EYES

FRANK MARTINEZ WAS a Mets fan. Nothing wrong with that. But even the Mets didn't approve of a stunt he pulled to try to help the team. In 2007, he brought a powerful flashlight to a game at Shea Stadium. From his seat behind the plate, he proceeded to shine the light into the eyes of the opposing pitcher and infielders. Naturally, the players complained, prompting security to conduct a search for the source of the light. They found the flashlight in his backpack and promptly escorted him from the stadium, adding a three-year ban from the stadium to his eviction. What makes his actions even dumber is that his offense occurred in an April game, when the Mets were already down by seven runs!

Mr. Martinez is a good example of a fan doing more harm than good for his team. Sometimes Christians who are fans of Jesus do more harm than good. For example, not long ago there was a street preacher on a corner in Orlando. On a sunny, ninety-five-degree afternoon, he was dressed in a white shirt and tie, holding a big sign about God's judgment and screaming into a microphone that was hooked up to a portable amplifier. I (Mark) watched as he confronted passersby. None of them stopped to talk to him. One young mother looked truly frightened as she took her youngster's hand and guided him away from the man she must have thought was a nut.

There's a right way and a wrong way to represent Christ. Letting your light shine doesn't mean shining it in people's eyes. If people are refusing to talk to you and even avoiding you, you might want to consider the possibility that you're doing something wrong. The love of Jesus is winsome and inviting, not frightening and off-putting.

Reflect: In Matthew 5:14 Jesus said, "You are the light of the world." Have you ever had a believer drive you away by acting in a way that was off-putting? What are some ways you let your light shine for Christ? Where do you draw the line between being open about your faith and being off-putting to others?

YOU ARE WANTED

HAVE YOU EVER heard of a baseball player named Harry Chiti? We didn't think so.

But he does hold a pretty interesting distinction. In 1962, the New York Mets got Chiti in a trade with the Cleveland Indians for "a player to be named later." We'll give you one guess who that "player to be named later" was.

If you said "Harry Chiti," you get the prize.

Yes, Harry Chiti was actually traded for himself.

Setting the oddity of the situation aside for a moment, think about how ole Harry must have felt about that. We're pretty sure it must have been pretty painful, knowing that both teams wanted to get rid of him.

People who are not ballplayers can feel unwanted too. Many are let go from jobs they love. Some are put up for adoption as children. Lots of married people are abandoned by their spouses. And more than a few businesspeople are left high and dry by associates who suddenly get a better offer from a competitor.

Feeling unwanted hurts. Happily, as Christians, we have a source of comfort we can turn to when that particular feeling strikes. It's the story of Jesus as told in the Gospels. You can't read it without getting one message loud and clear: he wants everybody. Watch him as he welcomes crooks, paupers, lepers, beggars, criminals, adulterers, and a host of other misfits that polite society would have rejected.

Believers are human and feel the sting of abandonment and betrayal just like everybody else. But we can never say we are unwanted.

Reflect: In John 3:16 Jesus said, "For this is how God loved the world: he gave his one and only Son …" Have you ever felt unwanted? What precipitated that feeling? If you have worked through it, who or what helped you? Moving forward, what can you do to prevent that feeling from coming over you again?

FAKES

SECURITY AT MAJOR SPORTING events is better now than it was a few decades ago. A case in point would be Super Bowl XIII, where a man nobody knew got into the locker room. Steve Sabol was interviewing Mean Joe Greene when a man walked by that Sabol had never seen before. "Who's that?" Sabol asked Greene. "I don't know," was Joe's answer. This was particularly disturbing because the man was naked and walking out of the shower soaking wet.

As he was getting dressed, he even fielded a few questions from the media. After he was dressed, he walked out of the locker room without a single soul asking him who he was. He never came forward either, and to this day, nobody knows the man's identity.

Anybody who loves Jesus knows a little something about fakes. We meet people all the time who look like believers at a glance. They go to church and have the Christian lingo down pat. They give the appearance of being interested in spiritual things. But a closer look reveals that something is off. Maybe curse words pepper the person's speech, or evidence of a grudge surfaces in a conversation, or the person is caught in a lie. Everybody sins, and it is not our business to judge, but Jesus said, "You will know them by their fruits." Today, we would call this "the eyeball test." Sometimes things just don't look right.

We urge you to live in such a way that no one will have any reason to wonder if you're a fake.

Reflect: 1 John 3:18 says, "Dear children, let's not merely say that we love each other; let us show the truth by our actions." Have you ever encountered someone who gave every indication of being a fake Christian? What are some ways insincere believers damage the cause of Christ? Since everybody sins, what are the keys to being a real Christian?

YOU KNOW UNO

THE CARD GAME known as Uno is not a sport, but it can produce as many hoots and hollers as any football game when you gather the family around the kitchen table.

Uno was invented in the 1960s by Merle Robbins, who was a barber in Cincinnati, Ohio. One day he played the game with an acquaintance named Bill Apple. Bill Apple loved the game and played it with his two brothers-in-law, who also loved it. In fact, they loved it so much they decided to buy the rights to it. They paid $100,000 for all the rights in 1972 and started to develop the game to sell to the public. After one year, they had made a whopping fifty-four dollars. Split three ways, they had earned eighteen dollars apiece.

Working hard to try to break through with what they thought was a great game, they went to Bentonville, Arkansas, and pitched it to Walmart. Sam Walton happened to walk in during the pitch and decided to place an order. The rest is history.

Sometimes it doesn't take much to turn a struggle into a raging success. You can be right on the edge of a breakthrough and not know it, like that moment just before Sam Walton walked in and made Uno one of the most popular card games in history. Or like that moment when the Children of Israel thought they were hopelessly trapped at the Red Sea, and suddenly the waters parted.

This is why it's so important never to give up hope. Even when a situation looks hopeless, it can be one instant from turning completely around.

Reflect: Jeremiah 29:11 says, "For I know the plans I have for you … They are plans for good and not for disaster, to give you a future and a hope." Have you ever been in what looked like a hopeless situation, only to see it turn completely around? Why do you think so many people lose hope? What are some ways to keep hope alive?

GET LOCKED IN

KEN VENTURI ALMOST did something that has never been done. No amateur has ever won the Masters, but in 1956, while still an amateur, Ken was leading going into the final round. The conditions were difficult. The wind was whipping the course, yet Ken played well from tee to green. The record shows that it was his putting that failed him. What the record doesn't show is another factor that likely came into play.

Shortly before the final round began, Venturi was talking to a friend who was trying to encourage him by talking about all the great things that would happen to him if he could just hang on and win. Though still an amateur, he knew very well that successful golfers must have ironclad concentration. Nevertheless, he let his mind drift to thoughts of what it would be like to be a millionaire and what kind of house he might like to build for his parents. Later, he was haunted by the likelihood that his poor putting day was caused by his wandering mind and lack of focus.

Focus is important for Christians too. When Paul was writing to his protégé, Timothy, instructing him on how to be an effective leader in the church, he laid out several challenges and then said, "Give your complete attention to these matters" (1 Tim. 4:15). Often the difference between great results and marginal results is focus.

But focus is important for another reason too. Satan is looking for someone to devour, and it stands to reason that an attractive target for him would be a believer who isn't paying close attention to the spiritual disciplines. Too distracted to pray? Too preoccupied to spend time in the Word? Too busy to serve? If so, you can expect Satan to show up on your doorstep.

Get locked in. Focus. Concentrate. You'll never be a great putter or a great Christian until you do.

Reflect: Proverbs 4:25 says, "Look straight ahead, and fix your eyes on what lies before you." How locked in are you on the spiritual disciplines? If you're lacking in this area, what are some of the reasons why? What can you do to improve your focus on the things of God?

PERFECT GAMES, PERFECT LIVES

(MARK) LAST NIGHT I watched an interesting baseball game. It started out like any other game but gradually took on greater significance because the pitcher was throwing a perfect game into the fifth inning. Fifteen batters up and fifteen batters down. Of course, the fifth inning is a long way from the ninth inning, but still the announcers and fans knew what was happening, and even sitting at home in my recliner, I could sense the tension.

Then came a base on balls, and the perfect game was kaput. However, the no-hitter was still intact, so plenty of tension remained.

Then in the eighth, a batter dropped in a bloop double. Goodbye, no-hitter. However, the shutout was still intact, so there was still a very nice accomplishment to root for.

The final result was a 3–0 one-hitter. A truly wonderful game for the home team, but somehow everyone felt a little disappointed. The announcers, while happy about the result, were lamenting what might have been. "We were only a couple of pitches away from perfection!" they said.

We've found that far too many Christians worry too much about perfection. They feel bad and berate themselves for small mistakes. They talk about how important it is not to judge others, while often judging themselves unmercifully. We believe this breaks God's heart, because he never said we had to be perfect to please him; he only said we needed to accept his Son. Accepting Jesus as Lord and Savior is the perfect response that fixes all imperfections.

Reflect: Hebrews 10:14 says, "For by that one offering he forever made perfect those who are being made holy." Are you a perfectionist? Do you have a tendency to beat yourself up when you make a mistake? Where do you think this thought process comes from? Why is it unhealthy for you to think this way?

GET A GRIP

IN SPORTS, GRIPS ARE EXTREMELY IMPORTANT.

If you've ever taken a golf lesson, the first thing you were taught was how to grip the club properly. If you ever see a bad golfer spraying shots all over the place, look at his hands, and you will likely see that he has a horrendous grip.

NFL quarterbacks, running backs, and receivers often wear gloves to help them grip the ball because one fumble is all it takes to lose a ballgame.

Many a basketball player has fumbled the ball out of bounds at a key moment because he or she "lost the handle."

And baseball players, especially pitchers, depend totally on their ability to grip the baseball for success. Sliders, cutters, curves, four-seamers, two-seamers, sinkers, knucklers ... they all start with the right grip. And the rosin bag is always there to help as well.

Did you know that a good grip is important in the Christian life too? In Philippians 2:16 the apostle Paul said, "Hold firmly to the word of life; then on the day of Christ's return, I will be proud that I did not run the race in vain and that my work was not useless."

Judging by the number of people who drop out of church and drift far away from God, "holding firmly" is a problem for many. We suspect one of the main reasons for this is unreasonable expectations. People expect the Christian life to be easier than it is. They are shocked when they discover that the world has disdain for their commitment to Christ. They are dismayed when they find themselves facing problems that were never an issue before they accepted Jesus.

Let there be no confusion on this point. The Christian life is not easy. Sometimes it boils down to just getting a grip and holding on.

Reflect: 1 Timothy 1:19 says, "Cling to your faith in Christ, and keep your conscience clear." As a Christian, has your grip on your faith in Christ ever slipped? What caused it? Were you able to get it back, and if so, how? What are some steps you could take to keep it from slipping again?

THE CEREMONIAL FIRST PITCH

VERY FEW PEOPLE are asked to throw out the ceremonial first pitch at a Major League Baseball game. Of those who are, a good percentage are former players who have no trouble with it. There are people, however, who by virtue of some newsworthy accomplishment or celebrity status, are asked to do the deed without a shred of athletic ability. This has produced some of the most hilarious video clips in sports history.

Mariah Carey's voice might be able to soar into the heavens, but the ceremonial first pitch she threw in Japan in 2011 went straight into the ground.

Olympian Carl Lewis also threw the ball into the turf, bouncing it to home plate, and then added to the debacle when he decided to try the throw again and fumbled the ball when it was rolled back to him by the catcher. He finally, comically, chased it down behind the pitcher's mound.

Photographers, emcees, and various other bystanders have been drilled by the wild arms of first-pitch throwers. Sometimes it seems the safest person on the field is the catcher!

What a vivid reminder that we all need to operate within the boundaries of our giftedness. There are millions of people, many serving in churches, who are doing things they're not good at. Sometimes it may be because of a shortage of help, but often it's because they don't recognize their limitations. Even worse, it can be because they desire some degree of glory that comes with a particular role.

YOUR GREATEST CONTRIBUTION TO THE KINGDOM OF GOD WILL ALWAYS BE IN THE AREA OF YOUR GIFTEDNESS.

Your greatest contribution to the kingdom of God will always be in the area of your giftedness. If you venture out of it, you could even do more harm than good.

Reflect: 1 Corinthians 12:7 says, "A spiritual gift is given to each of us so we can help each other." Do you serve God in the area of your giftedness or outside it? How confident are you that you have properly assessed your gifts? In your opinion, is it better to do a job poorly or not do it at all until a gifted person comes along?

DR. J.

(PAT) **JULIUS WINFIELD ERVING** II was the premier basketball player of the 1970s and early 80s, the most recognized athlete of that time. We acquired his contract when I was the general manager of the 76ers, and fan mail poured into our offices. The letters were addressed to Dr. J., The Doctor, or simply Doc.

Dr. J. was a scintillating athlete. At only six feet six, he could soar through the air with the kind of grace rarely seen. His hands were so large that palming a basketball was no harder than holding a tennis ball. His quickness and agility allowed him to improvise breathtaking moves that other players wouldn't even attempt. Several times in every game, he would do something that would make the fans gasp.

But the greatest thing about Dr. J. was his makeup. No one worked harder than he did in practice. And he was completely dedicated to the task at hand. Never did he allow himself to get drawn into the silly dramas that can break out in the middle of competition. He didn't trash talk his opponents; he simply dominated them. His mental toughness and clarity of purpose made him larger than petty theatrics.

Mental toughness is often what separates the successful from the mediocre. We tend to rate people according to their physical abilities, but often it's what's between their ears that elevates them above their peers. This is especially true in the Christian life. We live in a world that is hostile to our faith. We have an enemy that is always trying to trick us and bring us down. This makes right thinking critical and petty dramas a waste of time. Many capable athletes and Christians have been defeated because they didn't police what was going on between their ears.

Reflect: Proverbs 24:10 says, "If you fail under pressure, your strength is too small." How would you rate your own mental toughness? Do you have a tendency to wilt under pressure? Do you allow yourself to get caught up in petty dramas that fill your head with distractions? What can you do to take more control of your mind?

UNSPECTACULAR

IN SPORTS, IT'S THE spectacular athletes that get most of the attention. We all know there's a need for unspectacular athletes, too, players who grind it out and help the team but don't score a lot of points or make awe-inspiring plays. But most of the time, the cameras find and the announcers talk about the superstars.

Enter Brad Johnson.

Brad Johnson will never be listed among the NFL's greatest quarterbacks. Put him up beside Dan Marino or Peyton Manning or Joe Montana or Tom Brady, and the gulf seems immeasurable. Asking him to scramble out of the pocket like Fran Tarkenton would be like asking him to flap his arms and fly. We're not talking about a spectacular athlete here.

But one day Brad Johnson went to a card-signing show in New Jersey where he appeared with Magic Johnson, Emmitt Smith, Ronnie Lott, and Marcus Allen. In relating the experience, Brad said that every one of those great superstars said the same thing to him: "Congratulations, champ!" Yes, Brad Johnson, one of the most unspectacular quarterbacks in NFL history, led the Tampa Bay Buccaneers to the 2002–2003 Super Bowl and won it.

Mark it down: spectacular is overrated.

Oh yes, we love to see the superathletes perform their mind-bending feats. We love those ESPN highlights that rock our world. But success is more about steady than spectacular.

The same is true in the kingdom of God. Spectacularly talented people are amazing and certainly make a contribution, but it's those unspectacular believers who just go out and honor the Lord consistently every day that make the biggest difference. Part of their effectiveness is their consistency. But a huge part of it is the fact that they are relatable. You may find it hard to relate to that spectacular singer or speaker, but that neighbor who is always submissive to the Lord no matter what happens helps you truly understand what real faithfulness looks like.

Don't worry if you lack spectacular talent. Just be faithful.

Reflect: Proverbs 28:20 says, "The trustworthy person will get a rich reward." Do you ever feel overshadowed by people with big talent? Do you ever find yourself wishing you had greater gifts and abilities? Why do you think most people are more enthralled by talent than faithfulness?

HUMANISM? NO THANKS!

WE TAKE YOU to Faurot Field on the campus of the University of Missouri. The date is October 6, 1990. There are 46,856 fans in the stands. The host and unranked Tigers are playing the number twelve team in the country, the Colorado Buffaloes. The Buffs are a prohibitive favorite.

Unexpectedly, the game is close. The lead changes hands several times. All around the country, the eyebrows of sports fans are raised as the lead changes are reported. Surely Colorado wouldn't lose to ole Mizzou, would they?

The game comes down to the final series. Almost unbelievably, Missouri is leading 31–27. Colorado gets the ball down close to the goal line but is rebuffed by the Mizzou defense once, twice, three times.

And this is where we step into the twilight zone.

The referees miscount the downs. When the Mizzou defense stops the Buffs on fourth down, the refs think it is third down and allow another play, an illegal fifth down, on which Colorado scores a touchdown and wins the game.

Howls of protest fall on deaf ears. Hours of ridicule on sports shows go ignored. It is still considered one of the greatest injustices in the history of the sport, especially when you consider that Colorado went on to win the national championship with a win on their record that was actually a loss.

It's one thing when people face complex challenges and make mistakes, but even a child can count to four. It's not that hard.

This is why we are not humanists. Humanism says that humans are this world's best hope. Really? Seriously? Um, no thanks. We'll stick with God.

Reflect: Romans 3:23 says, "For everyone has sinned; we all fall short of God's glorious standard." Humanism is a predominant philosophy in our culture. Given man's propensity to fail, why do you think that is? Considering that we have to trust people for some things, where do you draw the line between trusting people and trusting God?

ONE HUNDRED HOLES IN A DAY

(MARK) A COMMON FUNDRAISER is the golf marathon. For years, I'd been asked to participate in one to raise money for various missionary endeavors. Finally, in a moment of insanity, I agreed. The idea was to play one hundred holes of golf in a day and find sponsors that would donate a specific amount of money per hole to the mission.

We teed off at the crack of dawn. My body was stiff, as I would normally be in bed at that time of day. I could barely see the ball through the haze, and my shoes were soaked with dew before I even swung the club one time. I thought, "What am I doing here?"

Eight hours later, I dropped my clubs in the trunk of my car with calluses on my hands, sore feet, and an aching back. I remember speaking out loud to myself, which is something I rarely do. "Mark, you are a complete idiot." When I got home, my wife cheerfully asked, "Did you have fun?" I said, "If I ever even mention participating in one of these things again, you have my permission to haul off and slap me. *Please* knock some sense into me." It took me a week to recover. My back hurt so bad I could barely get up and down out of a chair.

Golf marathons are a stark reminder of the importance of moderation. Golf is a beautiful game that I love, but not one hundred holes in one day. Work is important, but not if it steals the time you should be spending with your family. Eating is a source of great pleasure, but not to the extent that it makes you obese and unhealthy. Shopping is great fun, but not if you're buying things you can't afford.

Sometimes it's not what you're doing that's so bad; it's how much you're doing it. Use a little common sense.

Reflect: Proverbs 25:16 says, "Do you like honey? Don't eat too much, or it will make you sick." Is there something you love to do that occupies a large part of your time and attention? Are there indications that you might be overly committed? What are they? How can you bring some reason into the picture without giving up your participation all together?

DR. STRANGEGLOVE

BACK IN THE 1960s, Dick Stuart was a first baseman for the Pittsburgh Pirates and a guy who made opposing pitchers nervous. He was a slugger deluxe who popped twenty to thirty homers a year and drove in over a hundred runs. His best season was in 1963 when, for the Red Sox, he hit 42 dingers and drove in 118.

But Dick Stuart had a problem that kept him from being one of baseball's all-time greats: he couldn't catch the ball. In '63, when he had his best hitting season, he piled up an astonishing twenty-nine errors, which was seventeen more than any other American League first baseman. The next year he had another monster offensive season, but led the league in errors for the seventh straight year with twenty-four. It was about this time that someone called him "Dr. Strangeglove," a nickname he was never able to shake.

It's said that Stuart was playing first base in Pittsburgh on a windy day. A hot dog wrapper blew past him, and he reached out and grabbed it, prompting a standing ovation from the fans. Many said it was the first thing they'd ever seen him catch.

An important fact about Dick Stuart is that he never worked on his defense. He believed his offense was so good that it more than made up for his defensive shortcomings. Managers disagreed, of course, including Johnny Pesky, who ranted about Stuart's lackadaisical attitude.

It's one thing to be bad at something, but the least you can do is try to get better. As Christians this is especially true. Do you have a weakness? Fine, we all do. But acknowledge it and work on it. With God's help you could actually turn it into a strength.

Reflect: Colossians 3:5 says, "Put to death the sinful, earthly things lurking within you." Do you have a glaring spiritual weakness? If so, how long have you known it? What have you done to try to grow stronger in that area? Why is being lackadaisical about our weaknesses dangerous?

THE GOLDEN VIRTUE OF THOUGHTFULNESS

IF YOU'RE READING this devotional, you probably at least like sports, and there's a better than fifty-fifty chance that you played organized sports at some point in your life. For those of you who didn't play organized sports, you likely still had to play some sports in high school PE. It is in high school PE that one of the most traumatic childhood experiences happens. Perhaps not so much anymore, but many of the readers of this book will remember when it was common.

The PE teacher would choose two team captains for, let's say, a softball game, and then he would flip a coin to see which captain got to pick first of the remaining students to fill out the teams. The horror of horrors for any kid was to be picked last, or next to last, or anywhere near the end of the line. Without verbalizing it, the captains were saying, "I don't want you."

It would have been so much better if those old coaches had just counted everyone off—one, two, one, two, one, two—and then let the ones play the twos. Perhaps the coaches were clueless because they themselves were good athletes, were always picked first in such situations, and therefore never suffered the indignity of being picked last. We'll give them the benefit of the doubt.

There are many great attributes a person can have, but we believe one of the best is simply to be thoughtful with regard to other people's feelings. James 1:19 challenges us to be "quick to listen, slow to speak, and slow to get angry." These eleven words taken to heart will go a long way toward keeping you from hurting people's feelings. Listen, keep your mouth shut, and keep a lid on your anger.

> THERE ARE MANY GREAT ATTRIBUTES A PERSON CAN HAVE, BUT WE BELIEVE ONE OF THE BEST IS SIMPLY TO BE THOUGHTFUL WITH REGARD TO OTHER PEOPLE'S FEELINGS.

Reflect: Philippians 2:3 says, "Be humble, thinking of others as better than yourselves." Did you ever suffer the indignity of being picked last or next to last? How did it affect you? Have you ever hurt someone's feelings without meaning to? What did you say or do that you should have thought more about? How did it change the way you interact with people?

AFRAID TO LOSE

JOE MONTANA, NICKNAMED "Joe Cool," was a pretty good quarterback in the NFL. We are being facetious, of course. He was arguably one of the greatest two or three quarterbacks of all time. Consider this partial list of accomplishments: four Super Bowl victories, three Super Bowl Most Valuable Player awards, two National Football League Most Valuable Player awards, two Associated Press Male Athlete of the Year awards, and Sports Illustrated Sportsperson of the Year. The guy has more hardware than Home Depot.

Just before his San Francisco 49ers took the field to play the Denver Broncos in Super Bowl XXIV (1989), which would be his last Super Bowl, he sat down and talked with his old friend Joe Theismann. Theismann thought he seemed restless and unsettled, so he said, "Joe, you can't possibly be scared." Montana's response was, "If you're not scared of losing, then losing means nothing."[28]

As Christians, we're not supposed to live in fear of losing confrontations with Satan because we have God's grace to cover our sins. But perhaps there are other reasons to be afraid of losing spiritual battles. One is that we might cause someone else to stumble. Another is that we would almost certainly give unbelievers a reason to ridicule God's people. A third is that our sin might cause pain to our families and other innocent loved ones.

The fear of losing is part of what made Joe Montana such a great champion. Maybe we need a little more of it ourselves.

Reflect: 1 Timothy 6:11 says, "But you, Timothy, are a man of God; so run from all these evil things." Have you ever been adversely affected by someone else's spiritual failure? Did that affect the way you thought about your own sin? Do you believe it can be healthy to have a little fear of failure for the reasons mentioned above?

BETTER LATE THAN NEVER

TUG MCGRAW WAS a promising pitcher in the New York Mets organization. Like a lot of young ballplayers getting their first taste of life as a professional athlete, he got involved with a young woman and made some less-than-stellar decisions, one of which resulted in the birth of a baby. Unfortunately, Tug wanted no part of being a father, and the young woman took the baby and moved away.

It turned out that the baby was gifted musically, so gifted that he ended up moving to Nashville and becoming a country music superstar. Tim McGraw, though extraordinarily successful, still felt a yearning to know his father. He knew who his father was and followed his very successful baseball career from afar. But there was a wide gulf between the two men and, apparently, no bridge over that gulf.

The story got even more tragic when Tug got brain cancer. But they say the night is darkest just before the dawn. The diagnosis melted Tug's heart and caused him to seek out his son. The two became close at the end of Tug's life, and Tim even ended up paying for his father's cancer treatments.

There's an old saying: "Better late than never." There are a million reasons why something good that needs to happen doesn't happen. Anger, bitterness, distance, misunderstanding, and a host of other things can keep people from taking important steps to do what's right. If that's where you are right now, stuck in a bad place and needing to do something important, don't ever think it's too late. It's never too late to do what's right.

Reflect: John 9:4 says, "We must quickly carry out the tasks assigned to us by the one who sent us." Have you ever been late to do something you needed to do much sooner? What held you back? What emotions did you feel when you finally did the right thing? Is there something right now that you need to do but have been putting off?

THE HUMAN BEING BENEATH

(PAT) **A FEW YEARS** ago, I was coaching third base in a major-league old timer's game. The American League's third baseman was Wade Boggs, which means we were standing just a few feet apart, close enough to have a conversation. I've never been one to let such opportunities slip by, so I asked Wade which of the managers he played for had the biggest impact on his life. He didn't hesitate. He said, "John McNamara. One season my mother was dying, and he was so thoughtful and sensitive to what I was going through. I've never forgotten it."

I, of course, was expecting him to answer from a purely baseball perspective: Who was the best leader? Who was the best strategist? When he didn't, it taught me something. Even when we are involved in high-stakes, career-related endeavors, it's the personal side of life that touches us the most deeply. Wade Boggs was making millions of dollars on his job, but it was concern for his mother's health that was filling his heart and occupying his mind.

This is something we Christians must never forget. The world looks at people through the lens of their career. Wade Boggs was a baseball player. I was a sports executive. My cowriter, Mark, was a pastor. Actually we were always, first and foremost, human beings with very human struggles, hopes, disappointments, dreams, failures, and successes. Some people never see past the title or the reputation to the human being beneath. John McNamara did for Wade Boggs, and Wade never forgot.

Who in your life right now might be longing to be seen as a human being? Your boss? Your pastor? Your professor? The cop sitting at the table next to you? Be that person who sees people, not just professions.

Reflect: Romans 12:15 says, "Be happy with those who are happy, and weep with those who weep." Have you ever sensed that people saw you only through the lens of your profession, forgetting that you are human? How did that make you feel? What are some specific things you can do to keep from making that mistake with people you know?

PAY ATTENTION

(MARK) I WAS COACHING junior Babe Ruth Baseball in southeast Missouri. My team was playing our archrivals. I was coaching third in the late innings of a tight game. Our fastest player was on first. I was pretty sure he could steal second, so I gave him the sign to go on the next pitch, but he wasn't paying attention and missed it.

Swallowing hard, I gave the sign again, and he missed it again.

Feeling the heat rise on my neck, I gave the sign again, and he missed it a third time.

Finally, I'd had it. As soon as the pitcher went into his windup, I screamed at the top of my lungs, "*Go!*"

Everyone on the field and in the stands froze and looked at me, including the pitcher, which, of course, was a balk. I looked at the umpire and said, "That's a balk. Runner goes to second." The opposing coach flew out of the dugout and started accusing me of yelling at his pitcher to cause the balk. I explained that I wasn't yelling at his pitcher; I was yelling at my runner, which is not a violation of any rule.

He took his hat off and threw it on the ground. The ump jerked his mask off and started yelling at me. Fans in the stands were screaming horrible things at me, the nicest of which was that I was a bad sport. It was one of the biggest baseball rhubarbs I was ever a part of. I honestly thought someone might try to beat me up in the parking lot after the game. And it all happened because my player wasn't paying attention.

A large percentage of the problems we have in the world are sparked because someone isn't paying attention. Do yourself and everyone around you a favor. Pay attention.

Reflect: Psalms 119:71 says, "My suffering was good for me, for it taught me to pay attention to your decrees." Have you ever gotten into trouble or caused a problem because you weren't paying attention? Have you ever been victimized by someone else's failure to pay attention? Why do you think so many people have a hard time concentrating?

THE STRANGE CASE OF JOHN MONTAGUE

IN THE EARLY 1930s, a man named John Montague showed up in Hollywood, California, and made a name for himself as a golfer. Playing several area courses and often pairing up with celebrities, he demonstrated a level of skill that blew people's minds. Time and time again, people asked him why he didn't pursue golf as a career, but he always dodged the question, giving vague responses and refusing to talk about his background.

One day Grantland Rice played a round with Mr. Montague and was so impressed that he wrote an article about him that appeared in *Time* magazine. The article featured a picture that a freelance photographer had taken. Three thousand miles away, a New York police inspector named John Cosart saw that picture and thought John Montague looked familiar. It turned out that the mysterious John Montague was actually LaVerne Moore, who was wanted in connection with an armed robbery case Cosart was investigating in New York.

No wonder he didn't want to talk about his past.

Montague was arrested and did eventually stand trial. In what most people believe was a gross miscarriage of justice, he was acquitted when his mother and sisters—surprise, surprise—gave him an alibi. They said he was home sleeping in his bed when the crime occurred.

Of course we can't say if John Montague was guilty, but we *can* say there is a lot about his case that seems very fishy. Above all, his story reminds us that the truth has a way of hunting a person down. Moving thousands of miles away and changing his name didn't prevent him from being identified as a suspect.

Every day, people from all walks of life discover how hard it is to hide from the truth. The better option is always honest confession. The instant you confess, your problem becomes a part of your past. As long as you're hiding, it's a part of your present and your future.

Reflect: Numbers 32:23 says, "You may be sure that your sin will find you out." Have you ever gone to great lengths to hide something you did, only to have it come out anyway? Has anyone ever hidden something from you that you found out about later? How did you feel, knowing there was an attempt to deceive you?

J-MAC FOR THREE!

JASON MCELWAIN HAD THE HOT HAND.

He came off the bench in the fourth quarter to play guard for his Greece Athena High School basketball team. He missed his first two shots but didn't miss again, nailing six three-pointers and another jumper to rack up twenty points in just four minutes.

Sound impressive? Wait till you read this:

Jason McElwain was born with autism and was the team's equipment manager. Just before the final game of his senior year, the coach tossed him a jersey and told him to put it on. With the team having a comfortable lead in the fourth quarter, the coach put him in to let him realize a lifelong dream. Perhaps God smiled on him that day, allowing him to have a red-hot shooting touch, filling up the bucket from all over the floor. When the final buzzer sounded, the fans, who were already going crazy, rushed the floor and mobbed the kid they affectionately called "J-Mac."

In our view, the hero of this story is the coach, Jim Johnson. Just having the idea of letting Jason have a memorable moment like that is impressive. It shows that he understood an important truth that we wish every coach understood: sports is about more than sports. It's about people.

This is true of every walk of life. On the surface, it's about winning or selling or building or healing or writing or filming or whatever. But unless you live in a cave in the middle of nowhere, you are interacting with people, which makes what you do a people business. Wherever we go and whatever we do, we should be asking ourselves, like Jim Johnson did, what we can do to profoundly touch the lives of the people around us.

Reflect: 1 Corinthians 16:14 says, "Do everything with love." Do you have any great memories that are the direct result of someone being extraordinarily kind or thoughtful? Have you ever given such a memory to someone else? Can you think of someone close to you right now who could use a special blessing?

EXCUSES BLOWN

ANTHONY ROBLES WAS born with one leg. At the age of three, he threw aside his prosthetic leg and refused to wear it. As he got older, he was determined to make up for his missing limb by strengthening other parts of his body. When he was in the sixth grade, he set a record for push-ups at his school. When he was in the eighth grade, he started wrestling. As a freshman, he struggled with balance and leverage, but his exceptional upper body strength exceeded just about every opponent he faced. By the time he graduated, he had figured out how to make his body work effectively on the mat and went 96–0 his junior and senior years.

He was just getting started.

At Arizona State he excelled, earning All-American honors three times and winning the Pac-10 three times in his weight class. In his final year of eligibility, he went 36–0. And to prove that Anthony didn't allow himself to deteriorate physically after his eligibility was used up in 2011, he set a world record for the most pull-ups in one minute at a New York Jets game in 2018. He did sixty-two!

The world needs people like Anthony Robles to remind us what can happen when a person has determination. So many people are so soft nowadays. They wilt in the presence of any challenge that looks the least bit difficult. Or they take a disability far smaller than the one Anthony Robles has and use it as an excuse every time they come face to face with an uphill climb.

Thank you, Anthony, for exploding our excuses.

Reflect: Isaiah 50:7 says, "I have set my face like a stone." Do you have a ready-made excuse that you could—or perhaps have—used to justify yourself? What are some of the reasons why excuse-making is so tempting? Why do you think excuses are so tempting?

AN NCAA TOURNAMENT STAR

EVERY YEAR SOMEONE unexpected seizes the spotlight at the NCAA tournament. In 2018, it was a ninety-eight-year-old woman.

Sister Jean Dolores Schmidt last dribbled a basketball in competition in the 1930s, but she came up with a huge assist in the 2018 tournament as the chaplain and unofficial head cheerleader of the Loyola of Chicago Ramblers. Decked out in maroon and gold and sitting in a wheelchair, Sister Jean became America's darling as the Ramblers made an unlikely run deep into the tournament. After every victory, Loyola players filed by and gave her a big hug. And the media couldn't stay away either, seeking her thoughts on the team's play and their prospects for the next game. She made no bones about the fact that she thought God was smiling on her team, and considering the upsets they were pulling off, no one dared argue. Not surprisingly, a bobblehead was commissioned in her honor, and she was invited to appear on the *Today* show.

If you are a young person reading this book, we urge you to enjoy your youth. We remember how wonderful it was to bounce out of bed every morning with no aches or pains, ready to take on the world. Use the energy and good health you have to do something significant. Make your life count for something.

USE THE ENERGY AND GOOD HEALTH YOU HAVE TO DO SOMETHING SIGNIFICANT. MAKE YOUR LIFE COUNT FOR SOMETHING.

If, on the other hand, you have significant mileage on you like your humble authors, we *still* urge you to enjoy life. Maybe you won't be bouncing out of bed in the morning like you once did, but you can still do important, worthwhile things with the wisdom and experience you have acquired over the years.

Reflect: Job 12:12 says, "Wisdom belongs to the aged, and understanding to the old." How has your age affected your productivity? Have you ever used your age as an excuse? In what ways have you found it to be an advantage or disadvantage? What are some of the advantages of growing older?

THINK TWICE

THE NATIONAL ANTHEM is performed before every major sporting event in America. We support this. We believe players ought to stand and put their hands over their hearts. We are a couple of staunch national anthem guys. We do wish, however, that the song wasn't so frequently butchered by those who are privileged to sing it.

Yes, we know it's a difficult song to sing with a wide range and lots of odd intervals. And those words ... we've all heard them a million times, but when you start singing them, they can become blurry in your mind. We get it. But it seems to us that a lot of singers try too hard, seizing the opportunity to sing it because they want to demonstrate their vocal chops to the world rather than pay tribute to our country.

Perhaps you remember Fergie's rendition at the 2018 NBA All-Star Game. She offered up a slowed-down, jazzy version of the song that was completely inappropriate (and so bad) that it had some of the players fighting the giggles. She later apologized.

We have noticed that in our current culture, fewer and fewer people seem to have a sense of what's appropriate. Want more examples? Go to the mall and look at the way people dress. Go to a kids' sporting event and listen to the parents scream and curse at the officials in front of their kids. Show up at a department store on Black Friday and watch people rudely elbow others out of the way to get what they want.

It's tempting to say that people don't stop and think, but that's not true. The problem is they don't stop and rethink. Often, our first impulses are based on emotion or some primitive desire, like wanting to be noticed. It's our *second* thoughts that are often clearer and more sensible. So don't just think ... think twice! You might be surprised how many fewer embarrassments you'll have.

Reflect: Proverbs 29:20 says, "There is more hope for a fool than for someone who speaks without thinking." Have you ever embarrassed yourself because you didn't give enough thought to what you were doing? Why do you think so many people today seem to have no grasp of what's appropriate?

STEPPING UP

WHILE WE'RE ON the subject of the national anthem, there are moments worth remembering too. In 2003, eighth grader Natalie Gilbert won a competition that allowed her to sing the national anthem before an NBA game. Her opportunity came on April 25, before the third game of the playoff series between the Oklahoma City Thunder and the Portland Trailblazers. Perhaps because of her youthful nerves, and perhaps because she'd been suffering from the flu, Natalie faltered on the second line of the song and covered her face in shame. That's when Oklahoma City assistant coach, Maurice Cheeks, stepped to her side, placed his hand on her shoulder, and sang along with her.

Later, Cheeks said, "I was brought up the right way by my mother and father. We didn't have the best life, but they instilled in us to treat people the right way. That's all it is. It's no secret. It's no recipe to it. It's just treating people correctly, and if you do it correctly, it'll come back to you."[29]

We couldn't agree more. How many times a week, or even a day, do we find ourselves in a situation where someone in our presence needs a little help? From the single mom struggling to handle both her groceries and her toddlers to the elderly gentleman looking a little lost in an airport. So often we're oblivious to such people because earbuds are blasting music into our heads or our eyes are glued to our cell phones.

We urge you to be more alert to what's going on around you. Probably every time you get out among people, you'll encounter someone who could use a helping hand. Jesus would surely be quick to help such people. One way we can be like him is to be ready ourselves.

Reflect: Philippians 2:4 says, "Don't look out only for your own interests, but take an interest in others too." Can you think of a time when you needed a helping hand and someone stepped up at just the right moment? How aware are you of what's going on around you when you're out in public? Are there ways you could cut down on distractions and be more aware?

SEPTEMBER 30

DOING THE WAVE

THE UNIVERSITY OF Iowa Hawkeyes play their football games at Kinnick Stadium, which has a seating capacity of 69,250. That's a lot of screaming fans. But if you ask the players and coaches, they'll tell you that it's not the fans inside the stadium but the fans in the building next door that mean the most to them. The building next door is the Stead Family Children's Hospital, the top floors of which look down onto the Kinnick Stadium field. Every time there's a home game, many of the young patients and their parents gather at the windows to enjoy the competition.

A couple of years ago, someone suggested on Facebook that the fans and players should wave to the sick kids. The idea took hold and has now become one of the most heartwarming traditions in college sports. At the end of the first quarter of every home game, fans, players, and coaches turn and wave. And of course, the kids wave back.

We love this tradition for one big reason: it keeps things in perspective. Football is a game that we often take too seriously. Some people act like the future of human civilization depends on whether or not their team wins. Looking up and seeing those sick kids is a great reminder that, in the grand scheme of things, football is not all that important. A child being able to walk and breathe and overcome cancer is what's important.

We don't know if the architect of that hospital built it so tall intentionally so that the kids and their parents would be able to watch the games. If not, it surely was a happy accident.

Reflect: Psalms 127:3 says, "Children are a gift from the Lord; they are a reward from him." Do you sometimes lose perspective and treat sports or other hobbies like they're more important than they really are? What's the craziest thing you've ever done to support your favorite team? What are some practical things you can do to keep things in perspective?

THE WISDOM OF R.E. LITTLEJOHN (PART 1)

(PAT) **FOR THE NEXT** few days here at the beginning of October, I am going to tell you about R.E. Littlejohn, a man who had a tremendous impact on my life. He was the owner of the Spartanburg Phillies, a minor league affiliate of the Philadelphia Phillies. I met him when I was twenty-five and was hired to run his ball club. As a protégé of Bill Veeck, I had some big ideas, some of which were a little crazy, and Mr. R.E. gave me the freedom to implement them. Along the way, the club set attendance records because of our constant promotions. But at the end of it all, I can honestly say that Mr. R.E. did more for me than I ever did for him, as I will relate in the coming days.

There was, however, a point during my work for the Spartanburg Phillies that I began to wonder about the value of what I was doing. The season had ended, and I was reflecting on all the promotions we had run. Did they really mean anything? I mean, getting people to attend baseball games is not exactly on par with seeking a cure for cancer.

Troubled, I called Bill Veeck and told him how I was feeling. He said, "How many people came to your games this season?" I told him our attendance was 125,000. He said, "How many of them had a good time?" I told him that I was pretty sure all of them did. Then he said, "Pat, you never have to apologize for putting smiles on people's faces. This is a tough world; people need reasons to smile."

That was exactly what I needed to hear. And I believe it's true, even more so now as our world has become more and more complicated. So, guilt-free, I rededicated myself to my career there in Spartanburg and followed wherever the Lord led. My life has been about two things: showing Christ to the people I meet and giving them reasons to smile.

Reflect: Ecclesiastes 3:4 says, "There is a time to cry and a time to laugh." Have you ever been confronted by the notion that Christians should be serious minded and not have too much fun? Have you ever felt guilty for enjoying activities that some very narrow religious groups would frown upon? How would you describe your theology when it comes to having fun?

THE WISDOM OF R.E. LITTLEJOHN (PART 2)

(PAT) MR. R.E. WAS as fine a man as I have ever known, a down-home southern gentleman who was charming and soft spoken yet a hard bargainer when it came to business. But he understood people. He treated them well and knew how to cultivate loyalty. The way we negotiated my salary every year is a case in point.

On New Year's Day, Mr. R.E. and his wife, Sam, would have me over for a traditional southern New Year's meal of roast pork, black-eyed peas, and turnip greens. Then we would sit down and watch football. At some point, it would be time to address my salary for the coming year. Mr. R.E. would give me a slip of paper and a pen and ask me to write down what I thought my salary should be. Then he would write down what he thought my salary should be on his own slip of paper. It was an unorthodox way of doing things, but it worked because the salary he wrote down was always higher than the one I wrote down, which made me happy, of course, and made me want to run through a wall for the man. It is no accident that Mr. R.E. had the lowest employee turnover rate of any business I've ever heard of.

How many people do you know who love their jobs and constantly praise their boss? I'd be surprised if you know more than one or two. That's because the art of dealing with people has been all but lost in our dog-eat-dog world. I'm grateful to Mr. R.E. for teaching me that people are more important than things.

Reflect: Matthew 7:12, often referred to as the Golden Rule, says, "Do to others whatever you would like them to do to you." Have you ever felt mistreated or taken for granted by someone in authority over you? How did you respond to that? How has it shaped the way you treat people? What's the most important thing a person can do to make you feel appreciated?

THE WISDOM OF R.E. LITTLEJOHN (PART 3)

MR. R.E. WAS a dynamic Christian. When I was in my twenties, I couldn't nail down what it was about him that made me think this. I just knew he was very different from anyone I'd been associated with before, and I wanted to be like him. One day, thinking I was paying him a compliment, I said, "You know, I think Jesus must have been a lot like you." Mr. R.E.'s face took on a pained expression as he gently said, "Pat, no man can compare with the Lord Jesus."

I realize now what a dumb thing I said, but at the time I was a clueless twentysomething young man who was simply reacting to what I was seeing in front of me every day. I was around this incredible man who was so kind, so considerate, so righteous that he made me think of Jesus. Since then, I have tried to conduct myself in a way that people can see a little bit of Jesus in me.

It's been many years now since the "WWJD?" (What would Jesus do?) movement died out. I can't remember the last time I saw one of those bracelets. And no, I'm not suggesting that we bring them back. But there is something about that idea that I long for. Christians today seem to have lost sight of the idea of simply trying to be like Jesus. Instead there seems to be a Christian stereotype our culture has created that they are content to adopt: go to church, care about social justice, be politically conservative.

It's true that no person can compare with Jesus. But every person can reflect Jesus in his day-to-day life. And every person should.

Reflect: 1 John 2:6 says, "Those who say they live in God should live their lives as Jesus did." Think of some of the most dynamic Christians you have known. What was it about them that stood out to you? As you live your life, can you honestly say you are reflecting Christ and not just fitting a stereotype our secular culture has created for Christians?

OCTOBER 4

THE WISDOM OF R.E. LITTLEJOHN (PART 4)

(PAT) MR. R.E. was an exceptionally wise person. You could talk to him for five minutes and know that he had a unique understanding of how life works and what it takes to excel, personally or profession-

CONTROL WHAT YOU CAN AND LET GO OF EVERYTHING ELSE.

ally, without compromising your Christian values. Over the next six days, I want to share his six wisdom principles.

The first is to control what you can and let go of everything else. As a young executive, I tried to control everything, and if I couldn't control it, I worried myself to death about it. Like the weather, for example. If we had a big promotion planned, I would sweat bullets if a dark cloud happened to form on the horizon. There was nothing I could do except worry, so that's what I did.

Mr. R.E. taught me to focus on things I could control, like how clean the ballpark restrooms were or how good the food was that was coming out of our concession stands. It was an important lesson that has served me well for years. It has kept me from wasting a lot of emotional energy on futile concerns.

How about you? Do you fret and stew over things you can't change? Maybe there is someone close to you, a friend or family member, who repeatedly disappoints you. You've said and done everything you can think of to help that person change, but nothing works. So now you're beating yourself up and feeling like a failure.

Stop it.

You can't control other people any more than you can control the weather. You can love them and pray for them and be available to them and encourage them, but you cannot control them. Control what you can, and cut yourself some slack on everything else.

Reflect: Isaiah 55:9 says, "For just as the heavens are higher than the earth, so my ways are higher than your ways and my thoughts higher than your thoughts." Have you ever overestimated your own ability to control things? Are you doing it right now? Why do you think so many people worry about things they have no control over?

THE WISDOM OF R.E. LITTLEJOHN (PART 5)

(PAT) THE SECOND OF Mr. R.E.'s wisdom principles is to be patient. When I was in my twenties and just getting started in my career as a sports executive, I was Mr. Impatient. I was a bubbling cauldron of ideas, and in my own estimation, they were all brilliant. I wanted to implement them today and have them bearing fruit tomorrow. The reality was that not every idea I had was a good one, and even the good ones needed planning and tweaking. I needed to tap the brakes. I needed to find the happy medium between trusting my impulses and being impulsive.

The years have taught me that I'm not the only one who tends toward impatience.

Young people often rush their romantic relationships along much too quickly, ending up in bed together before they really know each other. Married couples that run into trouble often split up rather than face a lengthy and painful program of counseling. Corporate climbers who are desperate to get to the top feel mistreated if a coveted promotion goes to someone else. Even some pastors have been known to bail on their slow-to-change churches in favor of a congregation that they think promises faster results.

Jesus is perhaps the greatest example of patience. The Bible never pictures him running, even though he was doing the most important work in the world. He didn't start his ministry until he was thirty. He took three years to train his disciples. Very few people would have unfolded such a ministry so slowly. While most people obsess over doing things quickly, Jesus apparently only cared about doing them right.

There may be some instances when "quickly" and "right" are compatible, but often the two ideas are at odds.

Reflect: Galatians 6:9 says, "So let's not get tired of doing what is good. At just the right time, we will receive a harvest of blessing if we don't give up." How would you rate yourself with regard to patience? What evidence can you offer to substantiate your rating? Why do you think so many people are in such a rush to do everything?

OCTOBER 6

THE WISDOM OF R.E. LITTLEJOHN (PART 6)

(PAT) THE THIRD OF Mr. R.E.'s wisdom principles is to pay your dues, which is appropriate since we just talked about patience. Impatient people don't want to pay their dues. They want to move ahead as quickly as possible, even if it means skipping key stages of development. Anything to reach their goals as quickly as possible.

When I was in Spartanburg, I understood that I was not in the center of the baseball universe. We played in the Western Carolinas League. It was the first stop for a lot of recently drafted players, many of whom would never see a day of big-league action. Our home field, Duncan Park, was not exactly Yankee Stadium. But it was real, professional baseball, and the team needed someone to run it. By working in what was little more than a remote outpost in the world of sports, I learned how to do the things I would eventually get paid to do at the very highest levels of that same world of sports.

I think about Jesus's disciples.

In remote, out-of-the way places, they watched and listened as Jesus taught and interacted with people of all kinds: commoners, religious leaders, wayward sinners, Roman soldiers. Years later, they would be taking upon their shoulders the responsibility of leading the early church, which was one of the greatest leadership challenges in history. That three-year period of training in the outposts of Judea would have been invaluable.

If you investigate the lives of highly successful people, you'll see that they have a few key things in common. One of them is that they are well prepared when the big opportunity is thrust upon them.

Pay your dues.

Reflect: Matthew 5:1–2 says, "Jesus went up on the mountainside and sat down. His disciples gathered around him, and he began to teach them." How teachable are you? Why do you think so many people are not teachable? What are some of the things you have to give up in order to be teachable?

THE WISDOM OF R.E. LITTLEJOHN (PART 7)

(PAT) THE FOURTH of Mr. R.E.'s wisdom principles is to keep it simple. This is so important for smart, talented people to remember. When you're very bright, your mind operates on a little higher level than the average person. The danger is that as you're waxing eloquent about your grandiose theories and ideas, your listeners' eyes are glazing over. Who hasn't been trapped in a lecture or a church service or a business meeting where you had no idea what the speaker was talking about? Talk about a morale killer! Nothing bleeds the energy out of people like unnecessary complexity.

Once again, a great model for keeping it simple is Jesus. If anyone ever could have pontificated, he could have. Instead, he spoke to the masses with simple stories called parables. They were short, sometimes not more than a few sentences. And they all focused on everyday situations that even the commonest commoners would have understood, such as farming, animals, and family relationships. By contrast, the

Pharisees spat out a tedious mixture of self-righteous theology and unreasonable expectations that were all bound up in hundreds of rules that they expected their listeners to follow, or else. Is it any wonder why the common people chose to follow Jesus?

Whether you're running a ball club or a church or raising a family, you'll be much better off if you strip every task down to its basic essence: this is what we're doing, this is why we're doing it, and this is how it's done. Not only will your business or organization run more efficiently but your people will be happier and more energetic. Everyone loves simplicity!

Reflect: 1 Corinthians 14:33 says, "For God is not a God of disorder but of peace, as in all the meetings of God's holy people." How do you react to complexity when you encounter it? Have you ever chosen complexity over simplicity if you had a choice? Why do you think people have a tendency to overcomplicate things?

THE WISDOM OF R.E. LITTLEJOHN (PART 8)

(PAT) THE FIFTH of Mr. R.E.'s wisdom principles is to attack your problems. Most people see problems as bad things, but I never have. I've always seen them as opportunities for me to prove myself. In fact, this is one of the key factors in the development of my career as a sports executive. I gained a reputation as a problem solver. And it's not that I was smarter than everyone else; it's just that when other people were backpedaling, I was diving in head first. The biggest key to problem solving is just not being afraid to tackle the thing. Remember this: It's already a problem. You're probably not going to make it much worse if you try to solve it, and you just might fix it.

I do need to offer a word of caution here, however. If you make up your mind to be a problem solver, you can easily get sucked into your work to a point that is unhealthy. When I arrived at Spartanburg, I found myself doing everything. I mowed grass. I painted restrooms. I met with the town council to drum up support for the team. I sold all the ads in our program; I organized all the game night promotions and got the brooms out for the postgame cleanup crew. I even drove the receipts to the night deposit at the bank after the game! I may have been solving problems, but I was also killing myself!

Being a problem solver doesn't mean doing everything yourself. Not only is it OK to delegate, it's wise! Problem-solving is mostly an exercise of the mind. It's figuring things out, finding answers, plugging holes. From there, it's healthier for both you and your organization if you get other people involved.

Reflect: Proverbs 12:24 says, "Work hard and become a leader." How would you rate yourself as a problem solver? Do you tend to dive in or back away when problems arise? How are you with delegating? Do you feel the need to do everything yourself? If so, how does your thinking need to change so that you can free yourself from that obsession?

THE WISDOM OF R.E. LITTLEJOHN (PART 9)

(PAT) THE SIXTH of Mr. R.E.'s wisdom principles is to take care of the little things. One of my heroes was Coach John Wooden. It was my privilege to spend quite a bit of time with him, and on one occasion I asked him the simplest, most basic question I could think of: "Coach, in one sentence, what is success?" He answered, "It's a lot of little things done well." There's nothing I have ever read or experienced that would lead me to believe he was wrong.

At Spartanburg, we had some good players come through. In 1966, we had a double play combination of Larry Bowa and Denny Doyle. That year we had a record of 91–35, which caused that team to be selected as one of the top one hundred minor league baseball teams of all time. But what I came to understand was that, good team or not, the restrooms still needed to be clean. The trash cans still needed to be emptied before they started to overflow. The concessions still needed to be tasty and reasonably priced. Just because our team on the field was great didn't mean we could let the little things go. The fans wouldn't have paid money to come into our park and have an unpleasant experience.

It's true in one's personal life as well. You may be great at your job, but do you pray? Are you nice to the overworked server who's a little late with your refill? Do you make it a point to be home with your family at dinnertime? Many people blow these things off as being inconsequential. What I've learned is that in many cases, the smaller a thing seems, the more important it is. Or we could just say it this way: There really are no little things.

Reflect: In Luke 16:10 Jesus said, "If you are faithful in little things, you will be faithful in large ones." Can you think of an experience you had where a lack of attention to little things ruined your experience? When you are drawn to a restaurant or some other type of business, is it the big things or the small things that make the difference?

CAN, NOT CAN'T

LET US INTRODUCE you to Ibrahim Hamato.

He is not a household name, but he should be. As a child, he lost both arms in an accident. You might think that would have crushed any dreams he might have had to compete in any kind of sports, but it didn't. In 2016, he went to Rio and competed in the Paralympics as a table tennis player. If you're wondering how he manages to play, he serves the ball with his feet and holds the paddle in his teeth. It's true that he lost both of his matches, but so did other players who had two arms.

Britain's David Wetherill defeated Ibrahim but had an interesting take on the proceedings. He said, "In table tennis it is skill versus skill, and I know I won today, but I think he has demonstrated far more skill than I have just now."[30]

But it's not Ibrahim's skill that impresses us the most. We are enthralled by the kind of determination that makes a person with no arms say to himself, "I can play table tennis." We live in a world where the word "can't" is used far too often.

"I just can't get along with him."

"I just can't pay my bills."

"I just can't find the time."

"I just can't quit smoking."

On and on the "can't" statements go, rolling off of people's tongues like slobber off of a baby's chin. Really, we ought to be ashamed. May Ibrahim Hamato's determination shame us and cause us to buck up and do those important things we have so flippantly said can't be done.

Reflect: Hebrews 12:1 says, "Let us strip off every weight that slows us down ..." What weights have slowed you down in the past and put the word "can't" on your lips? Is there something right now that you need to do but have convinced yourself is out of reach? What's keeping you from at least giving it a try?

FROM LAST TO FIRST

HOW MANY TIMES have you been watching a sporting event that was so lopsided you knew that nothing short of a complete catastrophe would give the underdog a victory? At the 2002 Winter Olympics in Salt Lake City, the one-thousand-meter speed skating competition featured just such a scenario.

The Australian skater Steven Bradbury was not exactly a contender. In the first race, he was in fourth place behind two previous medalists and another skater who'd been in the Olympics before. Two of those skaters collided and fell to the ice, which enabled Bradbury to skate across the finish line in second place.

In the next race, his competition was tougher. Bradbury was in fifth place (out of five) and looked to have no shot at a medal. Suddenly, the Chinese skater fell and tumbled every skater in the race to the ice like bowling pins ... except for Steven Bradbury. With skaters strewn all over the ice, he sailed through them and across the finish line, becoming Australia's first gold medalist in the winter Olympics.

Mr. Bradbury's story reminds us of what Jesus said about the last being first and the first being last. He was talking about Judgment Day and how those who ruled the secular world—who were in "first place" in the world's estimation—would find themselves at the back of the line when they stood before God. And those in last place in the world's eyes would be escorted to the front of the line.

No slips. No stumbles. No runners' bodies strewn all over the ground. This reversal will happen because of the faith and obedience (or lack thereof) of the competitors. God will never be impressed by our standing in the world. He looks at the heart.

Reflect: In Matthew 20:16 Jesus said, "So those who are last now will be first then, and those who are first will be last." Have you ever been made to feel second rate by our secular culture? Have you ever been shoved aside or discounted in some way because you were a Christian? How do you believe God would want you to handle that situation?

THROW LIKE A GIRL

WANT TO INSULT a guy? Tell him he throws like a girl.

Or maybe it would be a compliment.

Back in 1931, a seventeen-year-old girl named Jackie Mitchell pitched for the Chattanooga Lookouts, a class AA minor league team. She was a terrific athlete who had been tutored as a pitcher by Dazzy Vance, who led the National League in strikeouts for seven straight seasons.

That year the Yankees ended their spring training with a couple of exhibition games against the Lookouts as they worked their way back north. Everyone wondered if the Lookouts' manager would put Jackie in to pitch. Some sportswriters made jokes about the possibility, suggesting that there would be more "curves" than usual on the mound.

Well, the manager did indeed put Jackie in to pitch. She appeared in relief and faced perhaps the three greatest sluggers to ever appear consecutively in any lineup: Babe Ruth, Lou Gehrig, and Tony Lazzeri. If you're thinking Jackie must have gotten crushed, think again. In one of the most astonishing moments in sports history, she struck out Ruth and Gehrig before walking Lazzeri.

If you're a guy, the next time someone says you throw like a girl, thank him. And then share the story of Jackie Mitchell.

We love stories like this where people stretch beyond the stereotypes that our culture has carved out for them. Our view is that you should chase whatever dream is in your heart, even if it doesn't fit with people's expectations. There are a lot of walls and barriers that need to be broken down, and who better to do it than someone with a burning passion? Don't let people put you in a box.

THERE ARE A LOT OF WALLS AND BARRIERS THAT NEED TO BE BROKEN DOWN, AND WHO BETTER TO DO IT THAN SOMEONE WITH A BURNING PASSION?

Reflect: Psalms 37:4 says, "Take delight in the Lord, and he will give you your heart's desires." Do you have a dream you've never chased because it seemed too unconventional for someone like you? Have others discouraged you? If so, how? If you never chase your dream, do you feel you will regret it someday?

FIVE MORE MINUTES

BOXING IS A dangerous sport. You can put the biggest, softest gloves you can find on a man's fists, but if he hits you square in the head with a powerful blow, he can do damage. So imagine how dangerous bare-knuckle boxing was. We say "was" because it's a sport that is almost nonexistent today, except for the occasional Saturday night bar fight between a couple of drunks. Boxing with no padding whatsoever on the hands was popular in the 1700s. Amazingly, quite a few bare-knuckle boxers had long careers. Jem Mace, for example, fought for almost forty years, stepping into the ring for the last time at the age of seventy-eight.

What caught our attention was a bare-knuckle fight that took place on December 3, 1855, in Australia between James Kelly and Jonathan Smith. This was at a time when the idea of having fifteen three-minute rounds hadn't been thought of yet. Fighters basically slugged it out until one of them dropped or gave up. This fight is said to have lasted six hours and fifteen minutes and only ended because Smith threw in the towel.

We have some questions.

What kind of shape was James Kelly in when Jonathan Smith quit? He, too, had been bare-knuckling it for over six hours. Surely Smith had landed some blows along the way. Could it be that Kelly himself was ready to quit and Smith simply beat him to it? If Smith had fought another five minutes, would Kelly have been the one to throw up his hands in surrender?

Our research didn't turn up any answers to these questions, but this story is a reminder that sometimes victory is all about hanging on just a little longer. We usually picture victory as being a glamorous thing, the result of a superlative performance. But sometimes it's just managing to stay on your feet for another five minutes. This is especially true in the Christian life.

Reflect: Galatians 6:9 says, "So let's not get tired of doing what is good. At just the right time, we will reap a harvest of blessing if we don't give up." Have you ever thrown in the towel and wished later that you didn't? Have you ever resisted the temptation to quit and been glad that you did? What are the basic differences between a quitter and a winner?

OCTOBER 14

DON'T MESSIE WITH HESSIE

WHILE WE'RE ON the subject of boxing, we'd like to introduce you to Hessie Donahue. Born in 1874, she was married to the owner of a boxing school in Worcester, Massachusetts. In 1892, John L. Sullivan, a heavyweight boxer known as the "Boston Strong Boy," went on a tour of the United States doing boxing exhibitions in theaters. Hessie's husband was his partner in this endeavor, so she went along.

At some point on the tour, they had the idea of letting Hessie be part of the act. Sullivan would announce that he had been challenged by a woman, and Hessie would bound onto the stage wearing feminine attire and a pair of boxing gloves. The two would dance around and spar until the curtain came down.

One night, things went horribly wrong.

Sullivan accidently popped Hessie a good one right in the nose. Stunned and angered, Hessie hauled off and put everything she had behind a punch that Sullivan wasn't expecting. It caught him flush on the jaw and knocked him out cold. The crowd went wild, and Hessie became the only woman to ever knock out a bona fide heavyweight champ. By the way, the crowd reaction was so great that they left the knockout punch in the act, only they faked it from then on.

Hessie's legendary punch was an instantaneous reaction to the punch she took, which is understandable. There's something in us that makes us want to hit back when someone hits us. We've all experienced it. But Jesus challenges us not to strike back. His command is for us to turn the other cheek. Difficult? Yes! But it is the fastest and best way to deescalate conflict. And in a world where conflict is exploding all around us, the message seems more important than ever.

Reflect: In Matthew 5:39 Jesus said, "Do not resist an evil person! If someone slaps you on the right cheek, offer the other cheek also." Have you ever been attacked, either physically or metaphorically? What was your reaction? Was it a gut reaction, or did you take the time to think it through? What are the benefits of obeying this very difficult command of Jesus?

THE LONG SLOG

(MARK) IT'S ALREADY BEEN established in this book that my coauthor is a marathoner and I am not. When I listen to Pat talk about his many marathons, I begin to suffer from deep feelings of inferiority. What's wrong with me? Why can't I get out there and run like that? I will continue to seek God's peace on this issue.

While I'm doing that, I would like you—and Pat—to know about James Saunders. He was a British ultrarunner who, in 1882, entered a twenty-four-hour race put on by the American Institute in New York. The race had no finish line. It was just a test to see how far you could run in one day. Mr. Saunders turned in a distance of 120 miles and 275 yards.

Let that soak in.

120 miles would be roughly the distance from the east coast to the west coast of Florida. The big advantage Saunders had was that he didn't have to deal with tourist traffic around Disney World. But still. His

mark of 120 miles still stands over a hundred years later as the amateur world record for running distance in a twenty-four-hour period.

In Scripture, the life of faith is pictured as an endurance test. Not a sprint. Not a feat that you train for and then execute in a moment. It's a long slog through, up, over, and around all kinds of obstacles, some of which can badly wound or even kill you. This might sound like bad news, but it's actually good news. It means your journey isn't ruined just because you have a bad moment, day, week, month, or year. The race goes on. You can repent, confess, and keep going.

Remember, no one runs a perfectly clean race.

Just keep those legs churning and thank God for his grace.

Reflect: In 2 Timothy 4:7 Paul said, "I have fought the good fight, I have finished the race, and I have remained faithful." Are there times when the "long slog" of faith wears you down and makes you think about giving up? What kind of circumstances are most likely to produce that feeling? What are some ways you can fight that feeling?

HOW ABOUT A GAME OF ...

GAMES GENERALLY EVOLVE. Basketball, for example, was played for years using a peach basket instead of a hoop. (Finally, they got tired of climbing up and lifting the ball out of the basket.) But there is one popular game everyone has played that has evolved perhaps more than any other sport. Among other things, it's been called, gossima, whiff-whaff, pom-pom, pim-pam, netto, and clip-clap.

Today, we just call it ping-pong.

Or table tennis.

And the name isn't the only thing that's evolved. The first game is reported to have been played in England using cigar boxes as paddles and champagne corks as balls. And they didn't bat the corks back and forth over a net ... they batted them back and forth over stacks of books.

As Christians, we say we don't believe in evolution. That isn't true, of course, except when it comes to creation. In every other area of life, we not only believe in evolution, we thank God for it.

Aren't you glad helpless humans evolve into self-sufficient humans?

Aren't you glad teenagers evolve into adults?

Aren't you glad bumbling new employees evolve into efficient pros?

Aren't you glad inexperienced interns evolve into world-class surgeons?

Here's something most people never think about: we're all evolving. Or perhaps devolving. No one stands still in life. We're all either going forward or backward. The challenge for every individual is to determine what kind of change is happening and whether it's good or bad. The Bible calls this self-examination. It can be a painful exercise at times, but it must be done if we hope to steer clear of trouble.

Reflect: 2 Corinthians 13:5 says, "Examine yourselves to see if your faith is genuine. Test yourselves." Are you evolving or devolving spiritually? What evidence would you offer to support your answer? How often do you test yourself? Name some specific ways you are different now than when you first started seeking the Lord.

CONTROL WHAT YOU CAN

EVERY FISHERMAN UNDERSTANDS that there are a lot of things he can't control, such as the weather, the location of the fish, whether the fish hits the bait, where the fish chooses to go if he does hit the bait, etc. However, the good fisherman understands that there are many things he can control, such as the quality of his equipment, the sharpness of his hooks, and the tightness of his knots. The most important thing the fisherman controls is what he does when a fish bites his lure.

Some fishermen are good at hooking fish but not good at landing them. One of the most common mistakes fishermen make when bass fishing is not letting the bass run. When he realizes he's hooked, a bass will take off in a straight line. The inexperienced fisherman will jerk on the line, which will stress the line and possibly cause it to snap. A hard jerk will also turn the fish, possibly causing it to head for underwater cover that could also tangle or break the line.

Something similar happens when we fish for men. We get a "bite" (someone shows some interest), and we get excited and try to jerk them into the boat (church). It's so much wiser to let the person we're witnessing run: to let him or her have some time to carefully work through all the new ideas and find the answers to lingering questions.

There's so much about evangelism we can't control, such as the influences a person faces when he or she isn't in our company. That makes it all the more important to use good judgment when it comes to the things we *can* control. Remember: don't jerk on the line!

Reflect: 2 Timothy 2:15 says, "Work hard so you can present yourself to God and receive his approval. Be a good worker, one who does not need to be ashamed and who correctly explains the word of truth." When you share your faith, do you get frustrated when the person you're witnessing to doesn't respond quickly? What are the benefits of taking it slow?

OF PING-PONG BALLS
AND POPULARITY

(PAT) IT'S REALLY VERY easy to make people dislike you. All you have to do is win the NBA draft lottery two years in a row. This is what the Orlando Magic did in 1992 and 1993.

The first time, in '92, everyone was happy for us. We were a young expansion franchise and people kind of felt sorry for us. "Let the poor Magic have the number one pick. They need it." So we took Shaq, who, as you know, turned out to be a halfway decent player.

It was the next year that we turned into villains.

Going into the draft lottery, we had one of sixty-six ping-pong balls. One of sixty-six! We didn't expect to get the number one pick, and no one else expected us to either. But the world is a strange place at times, and lo and behold, our lonesome little ball was sucked right out of that conglomeration as pretty as you please. That ball turned into Chris Webber, and then into Penny Hardaway, who paired with

Shaq and gave us the two star players we needed to become an NBA heavyweight.

The commissioner, David Stern, was not happy. Nor were the other NBA teams. Suddenly the Magic was the most resented team in the league by everybody except Magic fans. So what did the league do? It changed the rules of the lottery. Now, only the three worst teams in the league have a chance at the number one pick. They call it "The Orlando Rule."

Sometimes people decide they don't like you for no reason except that you have been blessed. You got what they wanted, and they don't like it. This is a great test of your character. Do not bear resentment. Do not flaunt your blessings. Do not find satisfaction in other people's jealousy. Instead stay humble, realizing that all earthly blessings are temporary.

Reflect: In Luke 14:11 Jesus said, "For those who exalt themselves will be humbled, and those who humble themselves will be exalted." Have you ever been resented because of your success? What kind of challenge did that present to your character? Have you ever been jealous or resentful of someone else's success? How did you work through that feeling?

MANAGE YOUR MISSES

YOU MIGHT LOOK at the title of this devotion and think it has something to do with having multiple girlfriends. Wrong! It was actually inspired by the reputation of five-time PGA champion Walter Hagen.

Mr. Hagen was an outstanding golfer, to say the least. But as good as he was, he knew he would still hit some bad shots on every round. He figured he would average six clunkers off the tee or the fairway for every eighteen holes he played. So, if you believe you're going to hit six bad drives or irons on every round, what do you do? Most people would probably say, "Practice your drives and irons more," but Mr. Hagen had a different answer. He decided to practice more on his short game.

Counterintuitive, but very wise.

Basically, Mr. Hagen decided that no matter how much he practiced his drives and irons, he would still slice or hook one now and then. It happens to everybody, even the very best players. So why not learn to manage those bad shots better than everyone else? Learn how to chip out of the rough and hit a great sand shot and make solid contact on a sidehill lie and let that be your advantage over your opponent. He did just that, and it made him one of the toughest match play competitors in history. People marveled at his ability to escape trouble unscathed.

Just as golf is a game of misses and mistakes, so is life. The key to success is not eliminating those misses but learning how to manage them. For the Christian, it all starts with acknowledging sin … confessing it honestly to the Lord and then repenting. There may be other needed steps too. Perhaps an apology will be in order, or even restitution. But there *always* must be confession and repentance.

Reflect: Proverbs 28:13 says, "People who conceal their sins will not prosper, but if they confess and turn from them, they will receive mercy." How do you handle your spiritual "misses"? Shrug them off? Beat yourself up? Feel guilty? Besides forgiveness, what are some of the other benefits of confession and repentance?

WHERE DID YOU PUT IT?

RAISE YOUR HAND IF, when you were a kid, you asked your mom where something was, and she said, "Where did you put it?"

Thurman Thomas was an outstanding running back for the Buffalo Bills. In 1991, he piled up 2,038 yards from the line of scrimmage and helped his team make it to the Super Bowl. You can imagine how shocked everyone was when he didn't start the game. Announcers and fans alike were completely puzzled by his absence. Later, it was revealed that he wasn't in the game because he couldn't find his helmet.

As the story goes, Thurman had a certain place he put his helmet before every game. That place was near the thirty-four-yard-line. But on Super Bowl Sunday, things were different. His favorite spot was in the way of some equipment that needed to be put on and taken off the field so Harry Connick Jr. could sing the national anthem. Someone obviously moved the helmet out of the way, setting off a frantic search that lasted until after the game started. In case you're wondering, Thurman Thomas had a horrible day, rushing for only thirteen yards on ten carries, and his team lost.

With all due respect to mothers everywhere, the question "Where did you put it?" isn't always the right question. It wouldn't have helped Thurman Thomas at all. Still, a football player is responsible for his own helmet.

In life, there are certain things we are responsible for, like our choices and our attitudes and our associations.

PEOPLE WHO LIVE TROUBLED AND DYSFUNCTIONAL LIVES GENERALLY SPEND ALL THEIR TIME EXPLAINING WHY THEIR PROBLEMS ARE SOMEONE ELSE'S FAULT.

We might like to whine and make excuses when things go sideways, but when all is said and done, we are responsible. The happiest, most successful, and most godly people accept that responsibility, even when doing so is painful or embarrassing. People who live troubled and dysfunctional lives generally spend all their time explaining why their problems are someone else's fault.

Reflect: In Matthew 12:36 Jesus said, "And I tell you this, you must give an account on judgment day for every idle word you speak." How are you doing with accountability? Do you accept it when you should or make excuses? How do you react when people refuse to accept responsibility for their actions? What are some of the negative results of excuse making?

THE MAKING OF A HERO

WE LOVE THE STORY of Rumeal Robinson.

He was playing basketball for the University of Michigan in 1989. In a game against the University of Wisconsin, he had a chance to sink two free throws for the win. Michigan was behind by one point, and there were only 2 seconds left, so if he made one free throw, the game would be tied, and if he made two, in all likelihood, Michigan would walk away victorious.

But he missed both free throws.

That day in the locker room, he apologized to his teammates and promised that for the rest of the season, he would stay after every practice and shoot one hundred extra free throws. And that's what he did.

And if you know your college basketball history, you know the rest of the story.

That year, Michigan ended up making it to the championship game of the NCAA tournament. The game went into overtime, and with three seconds left, Rumeal Robinson stepped to the free throw line with a chance to win the game for his team. The tension was almost unbearable, but it was no problem for Rumeal. Both free throws swished through the net.

What a beautiful picture of a guy taking full responsibility for his failure and then doing everything in his power to keep it from happening again.

We'll all come to that moment, sooner or later … that moment when we've messed up and have to decide how we're going to respond. May we all handle that moment the way Rumeal Robinson did. Admit it, apologize, and do what it takes to keep it from happening again.

Reflect: Isaiah 57:15 says, "I restore the crushed spirit of the humble and revive the courage of those with repentant hearts." Have you ever had a monumental failure that let other people down? How did you respond to it? Did that failure change the way you live your life? If so, in what ways?

THE PARTY YOU MUST NEVER THROW

WITH RUMEAL ROBINSON'S story fresh in our minds, let's look at the other end of the spectrum.

Steve Little was a placekicker for the University of Arkansas, an All-American football player who once kicked a sixty-seven-yard field goal. He was drafted in the first round of the NFL draft, which is rare for kickers, but he never achieved greatness in the pros.

One day, he missed a short field goal that could have won the game for his team. The fans booed him unmercifully, and he walked off the field feeling humiliated. That night, he decided to throw himself a pity party.

He went out to a bar and got roaring drunk. On his way home, he crashed his car into a concrete retaining wall going seventy miles an hour. Surprisingly, he didn't die in the crash. But he did end up being paralyzed from the neck down. He was twenty-four years old at the time.

Steve Little died in 1999 at the age of forty-three, which means that for the last nineteen years of his life, he wasn't able to move anything from the neck down ... all because he decided to throw himself a pity party.

Pity parties have destroyed a lot of lives. Psychiatric and medical professionals will tell you that self-pity can lead to depression, drunkenness, drug abuse, reckless sexual behavior, relationship problems, and yes, even suicide. Self-pity is never a good choice. Humbling yourself before God and submitting to his will is the only choice that guarantees a good outcome.

Reflect: Psalms 43:5 says, "Why am I discouraged? Why is my heart so sad? I will put my hope in God!" Have you ever thrown yourself a pity party? Can you name one good thing that came from it? How long did it take you to come out of it, and what triggered your recovery? Why do you think self-pity is so easy to fall into?

IT'S ALL IN YOUR HEAD

GARRY TEMPLETON WAS one of the most talented baseball players ever to lace up a pair of spikes, and that's not just our opinion. Hall of Fame manager Whitey Herzog, who managed numerous Hall of Famers, said Templeton was the most gifted player he had ever managed. Herzog also grabbed Templeton and shoved him up against the dugout wall, suspended him, and traded him the first chance he got.

Why, you ask?

Because Templeton gave the St. Louis fans the finger.

He'd been dogging it on the field, going through the motions, refusing to hustle, and Cardinals fans could see it, so they let him know what they thought with a chorus of boos. Not an unreasonable response, considering that those fans paid hard-earned money expecting to see their favorite players compete to the best of their ability.

Herzog, an old-school baseball guy if there ever was one, was livid. He shopped Templeton to other teams and finally made a deal to send him to the Padres for a light-hitting shortstop named Ozzie

Smith, who ended up in the Hall of Fame. Templeton had a decent career but never lived up to his potential and never lived down that one shameful moment.

Garry Templeton is the classic example of a guy who let his attitude undermine his ability. He is our reminder that it doesn't matter what you can do with your hands or your feet; it's that area between your ears that will determine your level of success. The world is full of incredibly talented people who are their own worst enemy. Don't be one of them!

Reflect: Philippians 2:14–15 says, "Do everything without complaining and arguing so that no one can criticize you." Have you ever known a super talented person who undermined himself with a bad attitude? What are some signs a person might see in himself that indicate a bad attitude? Why do you think it's so hard to improve a bad attitude?

PERSEVERANCE

AS YOU READ THIS, somewhere there is a child dribbling a basketball, dreaming of playing in either the NBA or the WNBA. Visions of screaming fans are going through that child's head as shot after shot flies toward the driveway hoop. Eventually, many of those children will grow out of those dreams, realizing they just don't have the physical ability it takes to make them come true.

One guy who never did grow out of that dream is Andre Ingram. He played his college ball at American University, scoring 1,655 points for his career. In 2007, he was drafted into the NBA Developmental League, a place for young players who aren't quite NBA ready to work on their games. The key word being "young." You go to the developmental league, you give it your best shot, and see what happens. What you don't do is make a long career out of playing in the developmental league. Except that happens to be exactly what Andre Ingram did. He played in the developmental league for eleven years.

And then it happened.

He signed to play the last two games of the 2017 season with the Los Angeles Lakers. What's even better is in his first NBA game, he hit four three-pointers and scored nineteen points.

It's refreshing to hear a story like this because we live in a snowflake culture, where many people wilt at the first sign of difficulty or disappointment. No, we're not suggesting that you should never give up on a dream. Some dreams just aren't meant to be. But far too many people give up too soon. We urge you to persevere. Understand that sometimes it takes a while for circumstances to align, for doors to open. You don't want to live your life wondering what might have happened if you'd just hung on a little longer.

Reflect: Hebrews 10:36 says, "Patient endurance is what you need now so that you will continue to do God's will. Then you will receive all that he has promised." Have you ever given up on a dream? What caused you to make that decision? Why do you think people in our generation give up so easily?

ONE FINAL ORDER

DEAN SMITH WAS ONE of the most successful basketball coaches in history. He led the North Carolina Tarheels to 879 wins against just 254 losses. He won two NCAA championships and went to the Final Four eleven times. He was a four-time National Coach of the Year and an eight-time ACC Coach of the Year.

Not bad. Not bad at all.

But in our opinion, the most impressive thing about Coach Smith had nothing to do with basketball. He was well known for having great relationships with his players and staying in touch with them after they graduated. He knew where they lived, what careers they were involved in, and even the names of their wives and kids. Even more impressive is the fact that when Coach Smith died, he stipulated that a $200 check from his estate be sent to every one of his former players with a note telling them to take their wives or significant others out to dinner.

(Pat) I was once talking to basketball great Bobby Jones, who played at UNC. He told me that one former UNC player said, "But what if I don't want to take my wife out to dinner? What if I want to spend the money on something else?" Bobby said, "You *better* take your wife out to dinner. It's Coach Smith's final order."

There are so many lessons in this story, but we want to focus on what it means to be genuine. There are people who will take an interest in you and help you and treat you well because it serves *their* best interest. But when you're gone, they forget about you. Genuine caring and concern doesn't stop just because circumstances separate people. When you really care about someone, you think more about what you can do for them than what they can do for you.

Reflect: Romans 12:9 says, "Don't just pretend to love others. Really love them." Have you ever been hurt by someone who pretended to care about you and then proved by his (or her) actions that he didn't? What are some ways you can gauge the genuineness of someone who seems to care about you? How genuine are you in your interactions with others?

MAKE IT EASY ON PEOPLE

YEARS AGO, WHEN Sparky Anderson was managing the Detroit Tigers, he was standing around the batting cage during a spring training workout. The great Ted Williams was visiting that day and approached Sparky. He stuck out his hand and said, "Hi, Sparky, I'm Ted Williams." Sparky smiled and said, "You didn't have to tell me who you are. I knew." To which Ted Williams replied, "Well, I just like to make it easy on people in case I meet someone who doesn't know."

That made such an impression on Sparky Anderson that for the rest of his life, whenever he would speak to someone, he would always start by saying, "Hi, I'm Sparky Anderson." He loved the idea of making it easy on people.

(Mark) This story means a lot to me because of a certain uncomfortable experience I've had many times. As a pastor, I meet countless people and can't possibly remember them all. I've had people approach me in a restaurant or a grocery store and say, "Do you know who I am? I met you at your church." Talk about awkward! What's worse,

I've even had people say, "You don't know who I am, do you?" And I can tell from their sly smile that they're enjoying my discomfort.

Here's an idea: Make it easy on people!

Do what you can to put people at ease, to save them embarrassment. I promise you they will appreciate it. Things like this are a matter of simple courtesy, which is something that ought to emanate from a Christian like a fragrant aroma.

Reflect: In Matthew 7:12 Jesus said, "Do to others whatever you would like them to do to you." Can you think of a time when someone seemed to delight in putting you in an awkward situation? How did that make you feel toward that person? What are some other common ways you can show courtesy to the people you meet?

OPENING DAY

THESE WORDS ARE BEING written on the opening day of the 2019 NFL season. All week long the crescendo has been building. Every sports talk show has been focusing on matchups and roster moves and injuries. Every sprained ankle is being scrutinized and analyzed and hyperbolized. Prognosticators are picking scores and point spreads. Fantasy football geeks are drafting their teams. And even restaurants are getting into the act. Our in-boxes are full of advertisements about deals on chicken wings and party platters.

Every sport makes a big deal out of their opening day, which is fine. However, opening day is probably the least important day of the season if you think about it. Teams grow and evolve (or devolve) throughout the season. The team you put on the field on opening day may not even resemble the one that ends the season. And even if the players are the same, there's a good chance that injuries and adjustments to playing time will change the team's complexion.

This is true of the life of faith too. When you first accept Christ, there is excitement aplenty. You feel so much joy you almost think you're going to explode, which is great. But things are going to change. Stuff is going to happen. Life is going to get messy. Bad days are going to come. Just as sports teams have opponents that are trying to beat them, so we Christians have an enemy who is trying to undermine our faith.

JUST AS SPORTS TEAMS HAVE OPPONENTS THAT ARE TRYING TO BEAT THEM, SO WE CHRISTIANS HAVE AN ENEMY WHO IS TRYING TO UNDERMINE OUR FAITH.

If you happen to be a new Christian, welcome to the family! You made a great decision! But don't let that "opening day excitement" trick you into thinking it's all going to be easy. It isn't. The good news is that God's grace is more than sufficient for whatever is waiting for you down the road.

Reflect: Hebrews 4:16 says, "So let us come boldly to the throne of our gracious God. There we will receive his mercy, and we will find grace to help us when we need it most." How did you feel when you first became a Christian? At what point did you realize the Christian life was going to be hard? How does God's grace impact your day-to-day life?

SOME ROADS WILL SURPRISE YOU

AS WE COLLABORATE on this devotion, I (Mark) must tell you that there is some pain involved for me. And I (Pat) want you to know that I am grinning ear to ear.

(Pat) My son Jimmy studied sports management at Seton Hall. He wanted to follow in dear old Dad's footsteps as a sports executive. And he got off to a good start, landing an internship with the New York Yankees. He worked for them for two years, hoping to land a permanent position, but it didn't work out. His next job offer was another internship, this time with the Boston Red Sox. Jimmy was disappointed. He didn't want another internship. He wanted a permanent position somewhere. But I said, "Son, take the job. You never know what might happen."

Jimmy took the job. The year was 2004, the year the Red Sox won the World Series for the first time since 1918, sweeping the St.

Louis Cardinals. And so today my son Jimmy is the proud owner of a World Series ring, something any sports fan would love to have.

(Mark) As a lifelong Cardinals fan, it pains me to think of that 2004 series. But as Pat and I collaborated on this devotion, I at least found a small measure of peace in hearing about Jimmy. And what a great lesson it is for all of us, that sometimes the roads that look the least appealing bring the biggest blessings into our lives.

They say, "Don't judge a book by its cover." Don't judge an opportunity by its appearance either. It may not be exactly what you're looking for, but God might have something hidden in that opportunity that will bless you beyond your wildest dreams.

Reflect: James 1:17 says, "Whatever is good and perfect is a gift coming down to us from God our Father, who created all the lights in the heavens." Can you think of a choice you made that led to unexpected blessings? Why do you think we so often judge people and opportunities by appearances?

INKY HANDS, WARM HEART

(PAT) I ONCE ATTENDED an event at Tropicana Field in St. Petersburg, Florida, where several former major leaguers were signing autographs. They had several tables set up, and all of the lines except one were moving pretty quickly. I walked over to see which line was stalled, and it belonged to Cal Ripken Jr. But it's the reason why his line was moving so slowly that made an impression on me.

He was taking the time to talk to every person, and I don't mean just saying hello. He was asking kids where they went to school and what sports they played and talking to the adults about their jobs and families and what team they rooted for. And I noticed one other thing: before Cal signed his name, he was thoughtful enough to wipe the tip of his pen so that it didn't leave a glob of ink on the item he was signing. And he didn't have a piece of paper to wipe it on, so he was wiping it on his hand! The entire palm of his hand was black, but he didn't seem to care.

What I saw in Cal that night was a guy who was fully engaged. He wasn't going through the motions. He wasn't distracted. He wasn't giving the slightest indication that he would rather have been somewhere else. I will guarantee you that, of the men who were signing that night, Cal was the one people talked about on the way home.

We live in a multitasking world of constant distractions that no doubt explains why so many of our social interactions are so shallow and our relationships so tenuous. Let me urge you to fully engage when you interact with people. Put the phone down. Look people in the eye. Really listen to what they're saying. Treat people like they are important … because they are!

Reflect: Philippians 2:4 says, "Don't look out only for your own interests, but take an interest in others too." Are you in the habit of doing other things while interacting with someone? Are you always on your phone? Do you have conversations while watching TV? If you were to engage more with people, how might you and they benefit?

WHAT OFFICIALS AND PASTORS HAVE IN COMMON

(MARK) WHEN I WAS in my twenties, I decided I wanted to be a basketball official. I took all the classes, jumped through all the hoops (no pun intended), and got my striped shirt and whistle. I thought I was pretty hot stuff.

My first job was as an official in a league for eight to ten year olds. I absolutely hated it. Seriously, I could have called a foul or a violation every ten seconds. To keep from blowing our whistles constantly, my partner and I decided to call only the most egregious infractions. Those games were an absolute mess.

Then I was asked to do a high school game. I really didn't have enough experience, but the money was better, and the basketball was a much higher level. It was *real* basketball, so I said yes. That night I was yelled and screamed at by coaches and fans like I had never been yelled and screamed at before. Did I make some bad calls? No doubt.

But you would have thought I pushed a little old lady down a flight of stairs and stole her walker.

That was the end of my officiating career. I thought, *I don't need this.*

Sadly, I've known pastors who have quit the ministry for the very same reason. Some Christians—and even some churches—have a talent for chewing up pastors and spitting them out. I don't think any pastor goes into ministry thinking he'll never be criticized, but most of them are surprised by the level and the frequency of it.

Please be thoughtful about how you treat your pastor. Don't make a tough job even tougher. He or she won't be perfect (and won't claim to be), but if the effort is there and the attitude is right, that should be good enough to garner your support.

Reflect: 1 Thessalonians 5:12–13 says, "Honor those who are your leaders in the Lord's work. They work hard among you and give you spiritual guidance. Show them great respect and wholehearted love because of their work." If you're in ministry work, how has harsh criticism made your job harder? How can you tell just criticism from unjust criticism?

SEE THE WHOLE COURT

A REGULATION NBA basketball court is ninety feet by fifty feet. There are two types of players: those who see the whole court, and those who only see what's happening where they happen to be standing at a given moment. By far the greatest players are those who have an ability to see the whole court. But they are very few and far between.

Magic Johnson was one.

In the 1980s, Magic played point guard for the LA Lakers, and there are those who say he had an almost supernatural sixth sense, an uncanny ability to know exactly where his teammates and opponents were at a given second: in front, beside, and even behind him. He could look one way and pass another and hit his teammate right in the chest. He knew when a defender was coming up behind him. He could zip a pass through a tight window simply because he spotted a defender with his head turned for a split second.

Numerous investigations have concluded that Magic does not have eyes in the back of his head, though some of his opponents still wonder.

In life, it's also important to be able to see more than just your own little area. In fact, having a broad vision of the world around you can make you a much healthier person, spiritually and emotionally. It will keep you from getting all wrapped up in your own problems. It will also make you aware of how blessed you are as you see the struggles of other people.

So lift up your head and look around. Don't be that person people are talking about when they shake their heads and say, "He lives in his own little world." That statement is never a compliment.

Reflect: Proverbs 20:12 says, "Ears to hear and eyes to see—both are gifts from the Lord." Do you sometimes have a tendency to get wrapped up in your own problems to the point that you don't realize what others are going through? What are some things you could do to make yourself more aware of the world beyond your bubble?

WHEN WAS THE LAST TIME YOU CRIED?

LOU HOLTZ IS ONE of the most successful and humorous college football coaches in history. But not every day was a good one. In his second year as the coach of the Notre Dame Fighting Irish, his team got spanked by Texas A&M in the Cotton Bowl. Coach Holtz had expected his team to win and was crushed when they didn't. However, what really disturbed him was the cavalier, lighthearted attitude his players had after the loss. For the most part, they didn't seem to be bothered by the whipping they'd taken.

When Coach Holtz walked into the locker room, he spotted one player sitting with his head in his hands, sobbing. That player was a second-string defensive tackle named Chris Zorich. Right then and there, Coach Holtz decided that Chris Zorich would be a team captain the following season and that he would only allow players on his team who cared as much about winning as Zorich did.

By the way, Chris Zorich went on to become a consensus All-American in college and an All-Pro in the NFL.

We find it troubling how few people seem upset by their moral and spiritual failures. "Oh well, it happens. Nobody's perfect!" is a common refrain. While true, it doesn't reflect a spirit of remorse and repentance that a person needs to keep from repeating the same mistakes again and again. It's our view that not enough tears are being shed over sin and its devastating consequences. If there's sin in your life right now, don't just shrug it off and say, "Oh well." See it for what it is: something deadly that Satan will try to use to separate you from God.

Reflect: 2 Corinthians 7:10 says, "For the kind of sorrow God wants us to experience leads us away from sin and results in salvation." Have you ever wept over your own sin? If so, how long has it been? Are there sins in your life that don't bother you as much as they once did? If so, what does this say about your spiritual growth?

THE POWER OF WORDS

"**IF YOU'RE NOT PRACTICING,** just remember: someone, somewhere is practicing, and when you two meet, given roughly equal ability—he will win."[31]

These words were spoken at a youth basketball camp by Easy Ed Macauley, a forward for the St. Louis Hawks. One of the young campers who heard the words was Bill Bradley, from nearby Crystal City, Missouri. Many years later, after a long and decorated career in the NBA, Bill Bradley recalled those words and wrote about how they impacted his life.

He said that, starting when he heard those words, he began practicing like he'd never practiced before. He practiced three to four hours a day, four days a week, often shooting jump shots and free throws until his arms were sore. He ran untold miles over railroad tracks and along the banks of the Mississippi River with weights strapped to his ankles. He had a pair of glasses made that prevented him from looking down so he could learn to dribble without looking at the ball. He even stacked chairs seven feet high in front of the basket so he could practice shooting over tall obstacles. All of that was triggered by a twenty-two-word sentence spoken by Ed Macauley.

If you think words don't have power, think again.

The thing is, they have power for good and bad, which is why we always need to be very thoughtful about what we say. Say the right thing, and you can launch a person to a better life. Say the wrong thing, and you can crush somebody's spirit. It's our view that most of us are too careless about the things we say. We urge you to think before you speak. And then think again, just to make sure.

Reflect: Psalms 141:3 says, "Take control of what I say, O Lord, and guard my lips." Has anyone ever said something that either crushed you or sent you soaring? How much does the identity of the speaker add or detract from the power of the words? What are some practical ways you can guard your speech?

OVER AND OVER AND OVER AGAIN

ATHLETES WHO EXCEL at sports are generally very gifted. However, even a gifted athlete will not become elite without hard work. And hard work for an athlete generally means repetition. When you see a right-handed hitter stroke a low-and-away curveball into the right center-field gap, you know it's because that hitter has seen thousands of curveballs and learned how to go with the pitch. If you see a basketball player toe the free throw line and swish two in a row to win the game for his team, you know it's because he's shot thousands—maybe hundreds of thousands—of free throws and perfected his form.

But it's not just sports. I (Mark) have a good friend who is a professional magician. One of his specialties is sleight of hand. He can do things with a ball or a rope or a deck of cards that you would swear can't be done. You can stare right at his hands and not see what he's actually doing. And you know it's because he has practiced those sleight-of-hand moves thousands of times.

Repetition is the number one way to build any skill, and that goes for a skill like witnessing. So many Christians are nervous about sharing their faith with someone. You know why? Because they rarely, if ever, do it! People say, "I just feel uncomfortable talking to people about religion." Of course they do! You can't do something once every three years and expect to feel comfortable.

IF YOU WILL START WORKING YOUR FAITH INTO CONVERSATIONS YOU HAVE WITH THE PEOPLE YOU MEET, YOU'LL FIND THAT IT WILL GET EASIER AND EASIER TO DO.

We'll make you a promise. If you will start working your faith into conversations you have with the people you meet, you'll find that it will get easier and easier to do. Furthermore, when you get some favorable reactions from people who are seeking, you'll find yourself looking forward to those conversations. Eventually, you'll find that you're really good at sharing your faith. Repetition is the number one way to build any skill.

Reflect: Romans 1:16 says, "For I am not ashamed of this Good News about Christ. It is the power of God at work, saving everyone who believes—the Jew first and also the Gentile." When was the last time you were intentional about sharing your faith? Do you shy away from doing it because of discomfort? What are some nonthreatening ways you bring faith into a conversation?

CRUISE CONTROL

NO, WE'RE NOT TALKING about that button on your steering wheel that allows you to take your foot off the gas and relax a little. We're talking about something that happens in competitive sports that relies on conditioning. Like basketball, for example.

It's been said that the team with the most talent will win, and talent is critically important. But a fantastically talented person can be bested by a marginally talented person if that marginally talented person is in better shape. A player that is in better shape can run his opponent ragged and cause him to become frustrated and/or distracted by his fatigue. One of the best at this was John Havlicek of the Boston Celtics. He would run all over the court, cutting and slashing through the defense, not because he was executing a play but just to wear his defender down. Then when his defender was laboring, he would make his play toward the bucket.

Simply put, when you're cruising and your opponent is laboring, you can control what happens. Thus we call it "cruise control."

Here's the thing to remember: this kind of superior conditioning must happen long before the game begins. If you don't do your duty in the gym when no one is looking, you'll never have the advantage when it really counts. The same is true in the life of faith. It's in your private prayer, worship, and devotional life that you condition yourself for spiritual success. Satan is hoping he can run you ragged and distract and discourage you. You have the final say on whether he will be successful.

Reflect: Mark 1:35 says, "Before daybreak the next morning, Jesus got up and went out to an isolated place to pray." How much time each week do you spend conditioning yourself to be successful against Satan's attacks? Do you find it difficult to have a private devotional life? What are some things you could do to remove the obstacles that hinder you?

STEP UP

SAY THE NAME "Shane Spencer" to any Yankees fan, and we guarantee you'll get a smile. It was in 1998, as the Yankees were pressing toward the playoffs, that their most effective outfielder Darryl Strawberry got sick and couldn't play. The Yanks brought up Shane Spencer, a twenty-eighth-round draft pick and an eight-year minor leaguer. No one thought they were bringing up the second coming of Babe Ruth, but for a while, that's who he turned out to be. Mr. Spencer hit eight home runs and knocked in twenty-one runs with a .421 batting average in his first thirty-eight at bats. He even hit three grand slams in a span of ten days. Those, friends, are monumental, Hall of Fame numbers.

Granted, it didn't last. Shane Spencer wasn't really another Babe Ruth. But when the Yankees needed help, he stepped up and made a huge contribution that helped the Yankees win the World Series.

Both of us have been in leadership positions, and we know what a wonderful thing it is when a need arises in the organization and someone steps up and fills it. In fact, we've both seen situations where it seemed like a person was made for that particular moment. Before and after, that individual twinkled like a star in a faraway galaxy, but in that moment of great need, he or she exploded like fireworks in the sky.

Someday there will come a time when your church, school, company, or organization will have a need. Many will sit back and wait for someone else to fix it. Some will gripe and complain that the need isn't being met fast enough. Hopefully, eventually, someone will step up and do what needs to be done. We hope that person will be you.

Reflect: Romans 12:11 says, "Never be lazy, but work hard and serve the Lord enthusiastically." What is your attitude when a need arises in your church or company? Do you hide? Keep quiet? Hope no one thinks to ask for your help? What kind of blessing could you be to people if you stepped up and volunteered to fill that need?

IS IT TIME TO CALL AN AUDIBLE?

IF YOU WATCH a lot of football, you know that calling an audible—or changing the play at the last second—is sometimes the best way to prevent disaster. If either the quarterback or the defensive captain sees the opposing team line up in a way that is contrary to what was expected, he can quickly shout out a change in alignment or a different play. The players will quickly adjust and, hopefully, be better equipped to succeed on that particular play.

Audibles are called in every game. Often they work, but sometimes they don't. It's possible to call the wrong audible, or sometimes your opponent will adjust to your audible and do something to counteract it. This is why quarterbacks and defensive captains have to be smart and know the playbook frontward and backward. When the teams are lined up, there's no time to think through options; they have to react instantly to what they see.

Audibles are sometimes necessary in life too. Sometimes a situation arises that calls for a change in what we're doing. A good example would be when a man realizes he's been working too much and neglecting his wife and kids. Nothing short of a change in routine will fix such a problem, but so many guys plow right on ahead without changing a thing, opting for excuses or rationalizations. Then they wonder what happened when their family blows apart.

We encourage you to call an audible when needed. Don't be stubborn. Don't think that problems will just magically fix themselves. It is the nature of problems to get worse if ignored, not better. If what you're doing isn't working, do something different.

Reflect: Ecclesiastes 3:6 says, "There is a time to keep and a time to throw away." Have you ever been stubborn about making changes when things weren't going well? If so, what makes you not want to change? Do you think it's sometimes good to change things even when nothing is going wrong?

THE KEY TO RESPECT

AT THE 1995 US Open played at Shinnecock Hills, Tom Kite had a one-foot putt on the last hole of the third round for a bogey. He addressed the ball, then stepped away and readdressed the ball before tapping it into the cup. No big deal, right?

Except that Tom thought he saw the ball move—just barely, which is why he stepped away. By rule, he should have replaced the ball. Failure to do so was a two-stroke penalty. Tom, sensing that he might have broken a rule, mentioned his failure to replace the ball to an official before he signed his scorecard. The official assessed the two strokes and turned his bogey into a triple-bogey.

Here's why we love this story. Other than Tom, not one soul on the face of the earth knew the ball barely moved. If Tom hadn't said anything, he could have avoided the penalty. And remember, we're talking about the US Open. His decision to self-report his mistake stands as one of the greatest examples of integrity in the history of sports.

Integrity is the number one way to earn respect. Far too many people think they can earn respect by being successful or earning lots of money. In fact, the desire to be respected is what drives a lot of people to work seventy hours a week. They think accomplishment will bring them approval and acceptance. Everyone eventually learns, however, that respect and poor integrity are mutually exclusive. You can work yourself half to death and achieve great heights in the world's eyes, but if you don't have integrity, no one will respect you. They might fear you. They might obey you because they have to. They might show you a surface respect out of politeness. But if you don't have integrity, they won't respect you.

Reflect: Proverbs 11:3 says, "Honesty guides good people; dishonesty destroys treacherous people." Think of someone you respect, and someone else you don't respect. What are the differences between these people? Do they have mostly to do with character traits or success? How flexible or inflexible is your integrity?

WHAT TO DO WITH AN OBSTACLE

THERE'S A STORY we love about the Miami Dolphins' great Larry Csonka, a member of both the college and pro football Halls of Fame. A bull of a man, he was known as one of the toughest ball carriers in the NFL. His coach, Don Shula, called him one of the most competitive and determined players he ever coached. These qualities once produced a play that Coach Shula had never seen before.

Csonka was carrying the ball down the sideline when a tackler approached. Many players in that situation would get as much yardage as possible and go out of bounds. No point in absorbing a huge collision if you don't have to. But Csonka had other ideas. He lowered his shoulder and blasted the oncoming tackler with a forearm shiver, sending him flying out of bounds. As Csonka continued on down the field, a yellow flag soared through the air. Larry Csonka was called for unnecessary roughness as an offensive against a defensive player, something that almost never happens.

We do not condone forearm shivers, but we love Larry Csonka's attitude toward the obstacle he faced. He simply did not allow it to intimidate him. It's our view that more people need to have that kind of attitude. Far too many slam on the brakes and look for alternative routes when they see an obstacle. Here's why that's such a bad idea: many of the obstacles we face look more fearsome than they really are. They are like a movie set, plywood panels painted to look like concrete buildings. You could literally walk up and push them over, but not if you convince yourself there's no point in trying.

Obviously, some obstacles *are* invincible. But not nearly as many as people think. The next time you come to one, get your Larry Csonka. You might be surprised at how easily you can send it flying.

Reflect: Isaiah 57:14 says, "Clear away the rocks and stones so my people can return from captivity." Why do you think people are so easily intimidated by obstacles? Have you ever been surprised at how easily you overcame what seemed to be a big obstacle? Are you currently facing an obstacle that has slowed you down? How do you plan to deal with it?

THE SLUMP

NO, WE'RE NOT talking about posture. We're talking about that time in your life when nothing seems to be going right. When everything seems way harder than usual. When the results you're used to getting just aren't happening. For a baseball player, it's that period when he can't buy a hit. For a basketball player, it's that period when the hoop seems about as big as a wedding ring. For a golfer, it's that period when the fairway seems as wide as a bowling alley.

Writers can go into slumps. It's called writer's block. So can preachers and teachers and students and salespeople and, well, just about anybody who is expected to produce something. There are times when things just don't click.

Here are three observations about slumps.

One, everybody has them, so don't beat yourself up when you do.

Two, slumps test the mind more than they do one's ability. Ask anybody who's been through a prolonged slump, and they will tell you that their biggest challenge was between their ears: keeping their thoughts positive and their confidence up.

Three, slumps sometimes speak to us. A friend in the publishing business once said that prolonged writer's block might be your project's way of telling you it's no good. A prolonged sales slump might be a wake-up call regarding your attitude or work ethic. The hard part is knowing if a slump is just a slump or a sign that something is in need of fixing.

Our advice is to hang in there and keep plugging. Ask a trusted and knowledgeable friend if he or she notices something out of kilter. And go back to basics. Chances are your slump will end just like it began—for no apparent reason.

Reflect: Romans 5:4 says, "Endurance develops strength of character." Have you ever been in a prolonged slump? How did you handle it mentally and emotionally? Did you change something or just keep going with what you'd been doing? In what ways did you benefit from the experience?

GATORADE SHOWERS

WE'VE ALL SEEN IT. At the end of a championship win or a monumental performance, the winning coach or heroic player gets a cooler of Gatorade dumped on him from behind. Everyone agrees the custom started in the 1980s, but various players seem to want to take credit for it. The New York Giants and Chicago Bears have both claimed to be the originators of the custom. We will let others figure all of that out.

What interests us is an incident with Don Shula on the day he won his 325th game, surpassing George Halas for the most coaching victories of all time. A couple of players grabbed the Gatorade cooler and started to make their move. Then some others stepped in and stopped them. They reasoned that Coach Shula was going to be interviewed on TV, and they didn't want him looking like a drowned rat. So they came up with a better plan. They hoisted him onto their shoulders and carried him like a conquering king.

There is an exuberance to sports that is endearing. You won't find many Gatorade showers in the corporate boardroom or the retail store or the church office. Employees may deliver outstanding performances in such places, but they probably won't be hoisted up on anybody's shoulders and paraded through the hallways. In many cases, they will barely be acknowledged. Sports teaches us many things, and this is another one: we need to celebrate each other more. When somebody does something positive, we ought to acknowledge it. When somebody does something great, we ought to celebrate it. If we did, perhaps fewer people would hate their jobs and feel unappreciated.

SPORTS TEACHES US MANY THINGS, AND THIS IS ANOTHER ONE: WE NEED TO CELEBRATE EACH OTHER MORE.

It's called affirmation, and everybody needs it now and then.

Reflect: 1 Thessalonians 5:11 says, "So encourage each other and build each other up." Have you ever felt unappreciated by the people you were serving? Are there people serving you who might be feeling unappreciated? What are the dangers of allowing that to continue? What are some things you could do to fix that?

WHAT MIGHT HAVE BEEN

IN 1874, A PROFESSIONAL baseball pitcher had one of the worst days in the history of the sport. His name was Dan Collins, and he played for the Chicago White Stockings. In his first game, he was the winning pitcher against the powerful Boston Red Stockings. But in his second game, he reached levels of futility that have never been matched. His team was beaten by a score of 38–1. He gave up thirty-three hits and threw so many wild pitches that the scorekeeper quit counting. Finally, with hitters too scared to step into the batter's box, and with his catcher completely worn out from chasing all the wild pitches, a relief pitcher was brought into the game.

We actually have a lot of respect for Mr. Collins. After giving up thirty-three hits and throwing so many wild pitches they couldn't be counted, the fact that he was still in there trying and hadn't walked off the field in frustration is pretty impressive. He may have been a terrible pitcher, but at least he wasn't a quitter!

Quitting is epidemic in our culture. Every day, millions of people quit jobs, drop out of school, jettison relationships, cheat on their diets, and stop going to church. And we are not of the opinion that no one should ever quit. Quitting is sometimes the right choice. Our contention is that most people quit too soon, often when things get difficult, and never get to find out what might have been.

"What might have been" are four of the most mysterious words in the English language and, we think, four of the saddest. We have no doubt that millions of people throughout history would have seen blessings beyond their imaginations if only they hadn't given up too soon. Some were perhaps inches from a breakthrough, on the verge of seeing their hopes come to fruition. But they will never know.

Reflect: Romans 5:3 says, "We can rejoice, too, when we run into problems and trials, for we know that they help us develop endurance." Have you ever persevered through a difficult time and been rewarded by eventual success? Why do you think the temptation to quit is so strong? How can you tell when quitting is the right thing to do and when it isn't?

BY THE SKIN OF YOUR TEETH?

THE NORTH CAROLINA State Wolfpack won the 1983 NCAA basketball championship under the able leadership of coach Jim Valvano. And they did it by the skin of their teeth.

They finished third in the ACC and went into the conference tournament knowing they had to win it to get into the NCAA tournament. In a series of close games, they did.

In the first round of the NCAA tournament, they knocked off Pepperdine, but only because Pepperdine missed key free throws at the end of the game.

In round two, they beat UNLV by one point, again because of missed free throws.

In round four, they shocked a Ralph Sampson–led Virginia team by one point when Virginia's would-be winning bucket went through the net one second after the buzzer sounded.

And in the championship game, a put-back dunk at the buzzer on a missed shot gave State the win at 54–52.

That's four games they won by a total of six points.

Yet today when people talk about that season, no one diminishes the accomplishment, because the games were close. No one ever says, "NC State didn't really deserve to win. They only won because other teams missed free throws." Free throws are part of the game, and if your team hits them and the other team doesn't, that means, at least for that night, you were the better team.

We think this "by the skin of your teeth" idea ought to be retired once and for all. If you're a winner, you're a winner, whether you won big or in a cliffhanger. Your accomplishment should not be diminished because you scraped by. In fact, the scraping by might even mean you're deserving of more respect.

Here's one thing we know: No one is saved by the skin of their teeth. We are saved by God's grace, and it is more than abundant to cover our sins. Nobody barely gets into heaven. There is no "barely" when it comes to God's grace.

Reflect: James 4:6 says, "And he gives grace generously." When people ask you if you're saved, what do you say? Is your answer hesitant, based on your weakness, or confident, based on God's grace? What are some reasons why it is important to fully appreciate the power and the depth of God's grace?

CONSISTENCY

MANY THINGS MAKE SPORTS fandom stressful. One is the inconsistency of so many players that our favorite teams depend on. We say a player is "streaky" when he goes from hot streak to slump to hot streak to slump. There are pitchers who are unhittable at home but little more than glorified batting practice pitchers on the road. There are hitters who tear up left-handed pitching but flail helplessly against righthanders. There are basketball players who elevate their games when the crowd is friendly but tighten up in a hostile environment. Every coach or manager is looking for that player who can deliver good results consistently, regardless of the situation.

Perhaps the most consistent player in sports history was Stan Musial. Stan the Man finished his career with a .331 average and 3,630 hits, both extraordinary stats. But an even more impressive fact is that he had 1,815 hits at home and 1,815 hits on the road. It didn't matter what ballpark he was playing in. It didn't matter if the fans were cheering or booing. It didn't matter who was pitching. Stan just hit and hit and hit.

Consistency is important in the Christian life, too. We've all seen Christians who run hot and cold. They're on fire for God one minute and lukewarm the next. They're praising God and volunteering for ministries one minute and dropping out of church the next. Meanwhile, their inconsistency is interpreted by unbelievers as hypocrisy, which completely undermines our message.

We find it interesting that the primary metaphor the Bible uses for the life of faith is "walking" with God. Unlike running or sprinting, walking is the one thing we can do consistently for long periods of time. If you want to end your up-and-down, hot-and-cold inconsistency, learn to walk.

Reflect: Micah 6:8 says, "This is what the Lord requires of you: to do what is right, to love mercy, and to walk humbly with your God." How consistent have you been in your faith? Have you dropped in and out of church? Do you serve for a while and then quit? If so, what would it take for you to become more consistent?

THE BLOODY SOCK

IN THE 2004 ACLS, Boston became the first MLB team in history to come back from a 3–0 deficit. And while that was a huge accomplishment, there was another one in that series that was equally impressive. In game one, Boston ace Curt Schilling pitched with a torn tendon sheath in his ankle and was shelled. Before game six, the Boston medical staff came up with a procedure that involved suturing the tendon to the skin. The procedure was so unusual and, well, radical, that they tried it on a cadaver first.

If you remember that game, you'll recall that blood came seeping through Schilling's sock. The cameras showed close-ups of it, and the announcers couldn't stop talking about it. It may be the only time in history a professional athlete performed in a high-leverage game while bleeding from a surgical wound. But perform Schilling did, with his typically filthy splitter in top form. The Red Sox (pun intended) won 4–2.

The greatest athletes all play hurt. The greatest Christians all do too.

And yes, Christians do get hurt. It's been said that there are more former church attenders than church attenders in America. Think about all those gigantic megachurches running in the tens of thousands. There are even more people who used to go to church but quit. And the vast majority of those former church attenders quit because something bad happened and they felt hurt.

We are not here to minimize anyone's painful experience, but let's be honest: everybody gets hurt, sooner or later. God's people need to suck it up and keep playing. And if you find that hard, think about Jesus. He wasn't wearing socks as he played out his final hours, but if he had been, they would have been bloody. He had nails through his hands and feet.

Reflect: Matthew 24:13 says, "The one who endures to the end will be saved." Have you ever felt hurt by something that happened at church? How did you react? Why do hurts that we suffer at church seem more painful? What are some truths you need to remember when a brother or sister in Christ does something to cause you pain?

DECISIONS, DECISIONS

BEING A COACH or a manager of a college or pro sports team is an incredibly difficult job. For one thing, you have a whole host of personalities to manage, not to mention egos. Then of course, you have a fan base that will scream for your head if you don't win. And every one of those fans will second-guess you if you make a decision that doesn't work out. And, thanks to technology, they will scream for your head and second-guess you through the megaphone of social media.

But here's what we've learned about decisions: Just because one doesn't work out doesn't mean it was the wrong decision. If a manager brings in his virtually unhittable closer in the bottom of the ninth with a one-run lead, and that closer throws a home run ball for the loss, it was still the right decision.

The same is true in everyday life. If you marry someone in your twenties, and fifteen years later that person goes through a midlife crisis and has an affair, it doesn't mean you married the wrong person. It means the person you married committed a sin. No one can ever see the long-range outcome of a choice the moment it is made. You simply do the best you can with the information you have and then deal with whatever comes.

We offer one suggestion when it comes to decision making: figure out what your goal is and then make sure every decision fits that goal. If your goal is to win ball games, then make your decisions to win, not to make players happy. If your goal is to honor Christ, then make your decisions within the constraints of his will regardless of what the people around you are doing.

Reflect: Proverbs 4:26 says, "Mark out a straight path for your feet." Have you ever been burned by a decision you thought was a good one when you made it? What are some reasons why seemingly good decisions can turn out bad? What's the best way to deal with a decision that turns out bad?

WHO'S BACKING YOU UP?

IN 1999, JOE TORRE had prostate surgery, which meant that he would be unable to manage the Yankees from about the middle of spring training until the end of May. Someone had to fill that gap, and Joe was adamant that someone already on his staff should be chosen. The last thing he wanted was an outsider coming in and disrupting the culture. After some discussions, it was decided that a Yankee coach, Don Zimmer, would manage the club in Torre's absence.

> **THE KISS OF DEATH FOR EVERY LEADER IS TO TRY TO BE SOMEONE YOU'RE NOT.**

It worked out fine, but two things had to happen during this period in order for the move to be successful. First, Joe had to let go and not try to control things from his home. The fact that he was recovering from surgery made it easier to do that at first, but as he felt better and better, the temptation was stronger to reach out and meddle from afar. Second, Zim had to be himself and not try to be Joe Torre. The kiss of death for every leader is to try to be someone you're not. Most people, whether they play baseball or work in an office, can smell an imposter a mile away.

If you're a leader or in any position of responsibility, you need to think about who's backing you up. If you had a health crisis, is there anyone you trust to step in and take over? There should be. As any sports fan knows, it's often the bench—the backup players—that determine how successful a team is. One of the biggest misconceptions about organizational success is that it's all about the head honcho. Get the right leader, and your success is guaranteed. Talk to any successful head honcho, and he or she will explain why that is far from the truth.

Reflect: 1 Corinthians 12:12 says, "The human body has many parts, but the many parts make up one whole body." Have you ever played a backup role to someone else? Have you ever needed a backup to step in and help you through a tough time? In your opinion, what are the most important qualities a backup needs to possess?

THE BUNT

WE ALL GROW UP swinging from the heels, trying to hit the baseball as far as we can. But people who understand the game know that sometimes finesse is called for. And sacrifice.

Which brings us to the bunt.

Sometimes players bunt to try to get a hit, but mostly they bunt to try to advance a runner. The bunter may reach base, but that's not the primary objective. The bunter squares around to bunt knowing full well that he will probably be thrown out. If he's a team player, he doesn't care. He knows that advancing the runner is key and may end up being the difference between his team winning and losing.

Sadly, bunting is a lost art in MLB today. Very few players, maybe only one or two per team, are excellent bunters. Also, many players are so concerned about their personal stats that they don't want any part of sacrificing themselves. The game has evolved too. Now the home run is glorified and is the thing that brings the big contracts.

Once again, life imitates sports. Very few people want to sacrifice themselves for the good of the company or the organization. They don't want to do the dirty work. They don't want to step outside their job description just to help out. Above all, they don't want to do anything that isn't going to benefit them personally in some way. It's the age-old "look out for number one" mentality.

When Jesus chose his disciples, he made it clear to them that he was calling them to a life of sacrifice. Many of them gave up homes and jobs and businesses to go on the road with Jesus. And that was only the beginning. Eventually, they were all martyred because of their faith.

If you're not willing to sacrifice, you have yet to come close to being the person God has called you to be.

Reflect: Hebrews 13:16 says, "Don't forget to do good and to share with those in need. These are the sacrifices that please God." What's the biggest sacrifice you've ever made for God? Was it painful at the time? What happened as a result? Do you regret making it? Why is sacrifice so important to the kingdom of God?

GO WITH YOUR GUT

THE YEAR WAS 1982. North Carolina was playing Georgetown for all the marbles in the NCAA tournament. The game was coming down to the end, and Carolina was trailing 62–61, which put Coach Dean Smith in a strange situation. One of the tenets of his coaching philosophy was to always put the game in the hands of his most experienced players, his upperclassmen. In this case it would have been James Worthy or Sam Perkins.

But on this last critical trip up the floor, Coach Smith knew his upperclassmen would be heavily guarded. He felt it was very unlikely that either one of them would be able to get off a shot. His gut told him to get the ball into a freshman's hands, a kid named Michael Jordan. In the huddle during the time-out, he explained to his players what he wanted them to do, then he looked at his talented freshman and said, "Knock it in, Michael."

Of course, all these years later, giving the ball to Michael Jordan seems like a no-brainer. But this was before Michael Jordan was

Michael Jordan. That night he was just a college freshman—a good one, to be sure—but nowhere near the basketball superstar he would eventually become. Coach Smith's play call was a gut feeling, and it paid off. MJ followed his coach's orders and knocked it in.

We want to be clear about one thing: You should never go with your gut feeling in areas where God has spoken. But in other areas, your gut can be a reliable advisor. Why? Because that gut feeling you get doesn't just materialize out of thin air. It's a conclusion based on every shred of knowledge and experience you have acquired. God gave you the ability to reason intuitively, to draw on your knowledge and experience and process it all on the fly. Where God has not spoken, don't be afraid to go with your gut.

Reflect: Job 38:36 says, "Who gives intuition to the heart and instinct to the mind?" How reliable have you found your gut feelings to be? Do you sometimes find that you overthink things and that your gut feelings can be more reliable for that reason? In your opinion, what's the difference between going with your gut and being impulsive?

THE POWER OF A SIMPLE CONVERSATION

ON JUNE 2, 1932, something happened that is hard to imagine. A twenty-year-old Georgia farmer went to a shallow, one-acre lake with a bait-casting reel and tackle costing less than ten dollars and caught a twenty-two-pound four-ounce bass, which just happened to be the world record. He was floating in a homemade boat and using a Wiggle Fish lure that cost a dollar and a quarter.

The young man's name was George Perry. He supported his mother and younger siblings, and fishing was one way he put food on the table in very hard economic times. It took him and his family three days to eat all the meat his monster bass provided.

George Perry's bass record has held up for eight decades. Because it happened so long ago, some people began questioning it, especially considering the primitive equipment that was used. But in 2006,

George Perry's descendants produced pictures of him holding the fish and pretty much put a rest to the skepticism.

Since the 1930s, countless improvements have been made in fishing equipment and fishing techniques. It's not unusual for today's professional fishermen to go out on the water with six figures worth of technology and equipment, if you count the bass boat. But all of that has yet to surpass George Perry's ten-dollar rod and reel.

Here's a life truth: sometimes the old ways are the best ways. In an age of computers and blogs and podcasts and teaching videos and satellite technology, sitting down and having a simple conversation with someone can still be the best way to lead him or her to Christ. It worked for the apostles, and it will still work today. And no, we are not antitechnology. Such things can help. We are just pro-friendly, face-to-face contact. There's something about a smile and a heartfelt conversation that breaks down barriers and warms hearts.

Reflect: Acts of the Apostles 1:8 says, "And you will be my witnesses, telling people about me everywhere." What makes having a conversation with someone about Jesus so intimidating to Christians? When was the last time you had a conversation with someone about Jesus? What are some simple ways you could work Jesus into normal conversations without being overbearing?

SUCCEEDING VS. WINNING

IN SPORTS, THE ONLY thing that matters is winning. You've heard this, right? Some off-the-charts competitive person will say, "Winning isn't everything; it's the *only* thing."

But is that true?

Let's say you're a coach or manager and you have a mediocre roster, lots of young players who are still developing and no great superstar to carry the team. You know before the season starts that you're not going to win a championship. What do you do? Throw up your hands and conclude that the whole season is going to be a waste of time because the championship is the only thing that matters? Or do you decide that even though you won't win a championship, you can still have a successful year by developing your young talent, building a healthy culture, and identifying players you can count on for the future? The answer is obvious, isn't it?

With all due respect to the sports gurus who talk about winning being the only thing that matters, we say nonsense. Only one team can win the trophy, but many teams can improve and perhaps even position themselves to win the following year. Who in their right mind would say that doesn't matter?

This principle is applicable to life too. There are many times when we don't win. We don't get the job or the promotion or the account or whatever. But what if that experience teaches you what you needed to know to get it the next time? What if just being considered puts your name on the lips of influential people who could help you later on? There are millions of people in this world who are winners *because* they lost at some point. To minimize or trivialize those losses … to say they mean nothing and don't matter is crazy.

Reflect: Romans 5:3 says, "We can rejoice, too, when we run into problems and trials, for we know that they help us develop endurance." Have you ever suffered a loss that taught you what you needed to know to succeed later? Do you think there are some instances when a loss could actually be called a win? In what ways might a failure be more valuable than a win?

BENCHED

THERE ARE VERY few players in every professional sport who don't know what it's like to be benched. They are the truly elite super-stars who only find the bench when they need a little rest or are injured. Most other players are going to be benched at some point, either because of an attitude problem, lackluster play, or age. When it happens because of age, it can be extraordinarily difficult for the player. Most great players believe they still have it even when they don't. They see that young player—or young whippersnapper, in their minds—coming up, and they think, "This kid isn't ready. He doesn't have my experience. I'm still better than he is." But there comes a day when the kid really is better.

We have seen lots of grizzled veterans handle a demotion to the bench poorly. Sometimes they sulk. Sometimes they grumble to teammates or the media. Sometimes even in their facial expressions and body language, you can see their displeasure. And of course, this always hurts the team. At the least, this type of behavior is a distraction, and at the worst, it is poison to the team's culture.

Someday you may get a demotion that may or may not be fair. Whatever you do, don't taint your legacy by lashing out. Don't make people uncomfortable by pouting. Don't force your friends and coworkers to choose sides by bad-mouthing the boss. You don't have to like it, but don't let it define you. Move on to another company if you have to, but don't be that person who causes the air to hang heavy with resentment everywhere you go. You do not want to be remembered that way.

Reflect: Ephesians 4:31 says, "Get rid of all bitterness, rage, anger, harsh words, and slander, as well as all types of evil behavior." Have you ever been demoted or replaced at a time when you thought you were still the best person for the job? How did you handle it? What are some ways you can turn a demotion to your advantage?

BATBOYS

WE LOVE BATBOYS. Who works harder than the batboy? When his team is batting, he's running around like crazy, picking up bats and helmets, retrieving an array of pads and elbow and shin guards from players who reach base, taking new baseballs to the home plate umpire, and swapping out a new bat for one that might get cracked. And that's not to mention his duties before and after the game, which are considerable. We talk about the importance of hustle in sports. Nobody hustles more than a major-league batboy.

And he never calls attention to himself.

The batboy usually wears a uniform with no name on the back or the word "Batboy," as if people would not be able to tell him from the players. If you watch closely, you'll see that batboys move in and out of the dugout during the game; they weave in and out among the players, doing their jobs quietly, without ever calling attention to themselves. You rarely notice them, but they would be greatly missed if they weren't there.

How can you not love batboys?

Both of us have worked in leadership roles in organizations, and we can tell you that an employee with a "batboy mentality" is a wonderful blessing. Far too many workers are undisciplined, whiny, and self-absorbed. They seem to think the business, church, or organization is working for them rather than the other way around. They complain at the drop of a hat and act like they're being persecuted if they're asked to step even a quarter of an inch outside their job description.

> **AS A CHRISTIAN, YOUR WORKPLACE WITNESS IS FAR MORE IMPORTANT THAN YOU MAY THINK.**

As a Christian, your workplace witness is far more important than you may think. If people get a negative impression of you at work, it will undermine every other thing you say or do for Christ away from work.

Reflect: Colossians 3:23 says, "Work willingly at whatever you do, as though you were working for the Lord rather than for people." How is your attitude toward your job and the people you work with? If there's frustration, how do you process and handle it when you're at work? Is it possible that they are just as frustrated with you?

CHARACTER IS ESSENTIAL

MARVIN LEWIS WAS the longtime coach of the Cincinnati Bengals. He tells the story of how he learned the importance of surrounding yourself with high-character people. He was a college coach at the time and was made aware of a supremely talented junior college player who was being recruited by some of the bigger schools. He thought he might have a chance to land him, but an assistant warned him. He said the kid had character issues and would be nothing but a headache. But Marvin saw only the kid's talent and went after him anyway. Sure enough, the player repeatedly got into trouble and had a terrible influence on two younger players who started hanging out with him. Marvin said, "I learned then and there that while talent is important, character is essential."[32]

High-character people do three important things that are essential for any group dynamic.

First, they value the team. They never, ever do things that smack of selfishness or any kind of personal agenda. If it's not good for the team, it's not good period.

Second, they respect the decisions that are made by the people who are paid to make decisions. This does not mean they like every decision, but they understand and respect authority. And when a conversation needs to be had, they have it behind closed doors instead of in the public arena.

Third, they make those around them better. They know how to put people at ease and when to challenge or encourage a teammate.

By the way, what we've just shared is the way to make yourself successful in your career. You will be valued, promoted, and loved by the people on your team, and especially your boss. And your Christian witness will be powerful, which is even more important.

Reflect: Ephesians 4:16 says, "As each part does its own special work, it helps the other parts grow." If you are a part of a team, identify your best teammates and define what makes them so. Do you believe your coworkers would identify you as a great teammate? What does your team need right now that you could help contribute?

MOUTH THEOLOGY

WE LIVE IN a generation where healthy eating is encouraged, which has not seemed to slow the proliferation of sports bars and burger joints. Still, most of us know it's important to eat healthful food. Imagine the dilemma you would be in if you were a professional eater and your doctor told you your cholesterol was high. Just about every professional eating event features foods that are far from healthy.

For example, Don Lerman set a world record at the butter eating championships. How many pats, you ask? Oh, friend, we are not talking *pats* of butter, we are talking *sticks* of butter. Don put away seven quarter-pound sticks of salted butter in five minutes. (Mark) As a lifelong fan of butter, even I almost feel sick just thinking about such a feat.

Or how about Ukrainian Oleg Zhornitskiy? He is called the "undisputed world mayonnaise-eating champion" because he put down four 32-ounce bowls of mayo in eight minutes.

Healthy eaters everywhere will be aghast thinking about what these men put into their bodies. But Jesus made a very interesting comment about what we put into our mouths that is worth noting. He said it's not what goes into your mouth that defiles you; it's what comes out. No, I don't think he would condone eating butter by the stick or mayo by the bowl, but he seems to be much more concerned about what we say than what we eat. I believe he would remind us that you could have the perfect diet full of broccoli and kale and still be defiled if you lie or gossip or curse.

Isn't it interesting how the mouth figures prominently into both our physical and spiritual health? We urge you to be very careful about what goes in *and* what comes out.

Reflect: In Mark 7:15 Jesus says, "It's not what goes into your body that defiles you; you are defiled by what comes from your heart." Are you a healthy eater? Do you, by any chance, take pride in your healthy eating while not being careful at all about your speech? Why do you think Jesus was so concerned about how we talk?

THAT'S NOT WHAT I MEANT!

WHILE WE'RE ON the subject of talking, we need to make the point that even when you say the nicest things, even when you go out of your way to be positive and complimentary, someone can misinterpret and think the worst of you.

Linda Cohn, of ESPN fame, tells about the time she was doing *SportsCenter* at the height of the Beanie Babies craze. She was talking over a highlight which featured a player demonstrating amazing toughness in making a great play. In what she thought was a clever line, she said, "He's no Beanie Baby!" Meaning, of course, that he was not soft. You know, like a Beanie Baby. But many fans either apparently didn't know what a Beanie Baby was or somehow misinterpreted her meaning. They thought she was putting the player down and spared no energy in letting her know it. The backlash was tremendous.

Both of your fearless authors can relate. We have spent a lifetime making speeches and preaching sermons. We couldn't begin to count the times people have "heard" something we didn't say or completely misconstrued something we did say. We have been misquoted, lectured, and criticized and glared at, not because of bad communication but because of bad interpretation.

Our takeaway for you is to tap the brakes and give some extra consideration before you assume someone's ill intent. Think back to that time someone got angry at you, and you said, "No, no, that's not what I meant!" Then you desperately tried to explain what you *did* mean. If you don't like being put in that position, don't put other people in it.

And one more thing.

Even if the person *did* mean to be hurtful with a comment, your job as a Christian is to turn the other cheek and forgive.

Reflect: James 1:19 says, "Understand this, my dear brothers and sisters ... be slow to get angry." Have you ever been misquoted or misinterpreted in a way that made you look bad? How did you react? Do you think in such situations it's better to confront the person or let it go? How quick are you to assume the worst when someone says something that hits you wrong?

SHOCKINGLY KIND

(PAT) COUNTLESS WORDS HAVE been written about the greatness of John Wooden as a coach and a person. Quite a few of them have been written by me. One of my favorite Coach Wooden stories was shared with me by Swen Nater.

Swen stopped by Coach's hotel to pick him up. He went to the room and knocked on the door. Coach answered and told Swen he'd be ready to go in about five minutes and to please come in and wait inside the room. Swen sat down and watched as Coach Wooden tidied up the room. He collected the bathroom towels and folded them, stacking them neatly in the bathroom. He took the used filter out of the coffee maker and threw it away. He walked around the entire room and made sure there was no litter on the floor. Then he left a generous tip for the maid.

I doubt that one out of a thousand hotel customers would do such a thing. Most people would say that part of the fun of staying in a hotel is *not* having to lift a finger to clean up after yourself. But

Coach Wooden wasn't typical. He was kind to a level rarely seen. He was shockingly kind.

It's quite possible that the maid never knew who stayed in that room. To her, it was just another day, another room, another mess … except that this mess wasn't quite as bad. And the tip may have helped her buy a pair of shoes for one of her children.

Most of us are kind. We hold a door for someone or say hello to the next-door neighbor. How much more of a difference could we make if we decided to be shockingly kind … to go above and beyond what most people would even think of?

Reflect: 1 John 3:18 says, "Dear children, let's not merely say that we love each other; let us show the truth by our actions." Has anyone ever been shockingly kind to you? What impact did that kindness have on you? Do you look for opportunities to be shockingly kind to others? Think of someone right now who could use a good jolt of kindness. Are you willing to act?

STAY WITH IT

EVERY SPORT HAS a record book. Every now and then, one of the great all-time career records is broken, but it doesn't happen every day, and it's always done by a grizzled veteran. Young players can break single-game or single-season marks, but the career records are the exclusive domain of aging warriors.

Hank Aaron, for example, hit his five hundredth home run at the age of thirty-five. Think about that. Age thirty-five, and he still had well over two hundred homers to go to catch Ruth! People had their doubts that he would be able to pull it off. But in his next few seasons, he tallied 44, 38, 47, 34, and 40 big flies. Finally, at the age of forty, he tied and broke the Babe's record.

In an interesting side note, Hammerin' Hank ended the 1973 season just one home run short of Ruth's record of 714. He was quoted as saying that his biggest fear was that he might not live to see the opening of the 1974 season. Can you imagine a guy climbing that mountain and getting to within one swing of the record and not making it? Hank could imagine it! But he did make it to the top and beyond and became one of the most celebrated sports stars in history.

So the question arises: How do you achieve greatness?

The answer is, stay with it.

Keep showing up.

Keep swinging.

Day after day.

Year after year.

One day you'll wake up and be amazed at what you accomplished.

Reflect: Galatians 6:9 says, "So let's not get tired of doing what is good. At just the right time, we will reap a harvest of blessing if we don't give up." How would you rate yourself with regard to endurance? Do you tire easily? Do you have a track record of quitting? If so, why? What would it take for you to have more endurance?

A CAR BEATS A HORSE ANY DAY

THE THREE-POINT SHOT was introduced to college basketball in 1986. If you weren't around back then, you can probably still imagine how it changed things. For one thing, teams suddenly had a way to try to cut into a lead more quickly. Games became more exciting as coaches, players, and fans felt like games were never out of reach. Also, a whole new breed of player began to emerge: the long-range shooter. Shooters have always been valued in basketball, but suddenly teams were feverishly recruiting kids who could fill it up from downtown. Finally, coaches had to rethink their defenses. Packing it in the paint wasn't going to work anymore, as teams began sending more and more sharpshooters onto the floor.

The game is much better with a three-point shot, but at the time there were people who pooh-poohed the change. "The game is fine just the way it is!" they whined. "Why mess with a perfectly good game?" There are always purists who think any kind of change is bad.

Thankfully, there are more people who see the need for change and are always thinking of ways to improve things.

Henry Ford was one of those. In an Orlando restaurant, there is a sign on the wall that is a quote from him. He said, "If I had asked people what they wanted, they would have said a faster horse." The next time you jump into your car, give a nod of gratitude to ole Henry's vision and creativity.

We urge you not to be one of those people who resist and bellyache about change. No, you don't have to turn somersaults and shout for joy, but at least keep an open mind. If the change is bad, the idea will probably fail, and another, better change will likely come. But if it's good, then things will be better. So, in a sense, you can't lose.

Reflect: Isaiah 43:19 says, "For I am about to do something new. See, I have already begun!" Do you typically like change or dislike it? Can you name a change you encountered that you hated at first but later came to like? What are some reasons why change is important, even if it is uncomfortable?

STAY IN YOUR LANE

PERHAPS THE MOST tragic sports story of 2016 had to do with the death of Marlins pitcher José Fernández in a boating accident. That he had high levels of alcohol and cocaine in his system and was expecting the birth of his first child is heartbreaking and makes the loss feel even more tragic. In the first game after his death, something happened that will forever remain one of the most dramatic moments in sports history.

His teammate, second baseman Dee Gordon, led off the game for the Marlins. A left-handed hitter, he stepped into the box right-handed and took one pitch while mimicking José Fernández's batting stance. It was a tribute to his friend for everyone to see. Then he stepped over into the left-hand batter's box and hit the next pitch over the fence for a home run. Gordon, who is not a home run hitter, was crying as he ran around the bases and fell into the arms of his teammates when he returned to the dugout. We doubt that there was a dry eye in the entire stadium.

In the aftermath of Fernández's death, it became clear that he was deeply flawed and yet deeply loved. This is the case with so many people. They have goodness in them and earn the love of family and friends, while at the same time they are struggling with some kind of darkness that takes them to unthinkable places. José Fernández reminds us that people are very complicated and that it is always unwise to paint people with a broad brush. As the saying goes, "There is good in the worst of us, and bad in the best of us."

WE URGE YOU TO REMEMBER THAT IT'S GOD'S JOB TO JUDGE AND OUR JOB TO SIMPLY LOVE PEOPLE.

We urge you to remember that it's God's job to judge and our job to simply love people. Everything works better when we stay in our lane.

Reflect: 1 Peter 4:8 says, "Most important of all, continue to show deep love for each other, for love covers a multitude of sins." Why do you think people are generally so quick to judge others? What are some of the dangers of a judgmental attitude? Is it possible to take a hard stance against sin without being judgmental?

677

BYE-BYE, TACO BELL

WHEN ALEX RODRIGUEZ—better known as A-Rod—was a rookie, his team, the Seattle Mariners, played in Kansas City. If you know anything about how rookies are treated in Major League Baseball, you know that A-Rod was going to be called out by the veterans every time he stepped out of line.

On this particular day, he showed up a little late for early batting practice carrying a Taco Bell bag. He sat down in the dugout and was having a bite to eat when his teammate Jay Buhner, a grizzled veteran, walked up to him and said, "What are you doing?" A-Rod said that he was having some food, that he was starving. Buhner asked him if he had enough for the whole team. A-Rod handed him the bag and said that he would be glad to share. Jay Buhner took the bag, tossed it up in the air, and swung at it with his bat as hard as he could. The bat hit the bag and exploded, and tacos and nachos flew all over the place. Buhner looked at A-Rod and said, "Don't you ever be late for early BP again. Now get this stuff cleaned up."

There is no question that Jay Buhner got his point across. There is also no question that he could have found a gentler, less demeaning way to do it. This is often true of people in other walks of life: spouses, employers, teachers, coaches. Often, the offending party is crushed under the weight of an over-the-top rebuke. This should never be. You can get your point across without belittling, humiliating, or otherwise insulting someone. Even if the mistake is egregious, take a breath and think before you respond.

Reflect: Proverbs 15:1 says, "A gentle answer deflects anger, but harsh words make tempers flare." Have you ever been on the receiving end of an unreasonably harsh rebuke? How did it make you feel? What are some reasons why harsh rebukes, though effective in the moment, can ultimately backfire?

FELONY HIT AND RUN

ON THE FIRST DAY of the 1996 US Open, Phil Mickelson and his caddy, Jim "Bones" Mackay, were driving around the country club parking lot, looking for an empty space. Bones was driving and ever-so slowly came up behind a pedestrian who was walking to his car. Just as Bones pulled alongside the pedestrian, the man took a hard left turn and bumped into Bones's vehicle. He simply hadn't heard the car approaching and barely brushed against the front passenger-side fender. The pedestrian waved, apologized, and went on his way. No harm, no foul.

Later, about forty-five minutes before Mickelson was supposed to tee off, two police officers showed up and started interrogating Bones, telling him they had a report that he committed a hit and run on a pedestrian. They got out their handcuffs and threatened to haul him away to jail. Bones was frantic, trying desperately to explain what had happened and why he didn't deserve to be arrested. Then he looked the other way and saw his boss, Phil Mickelson, standing behind a tree, dying laughing. Mickelson had called the cops and set up the prank.

(Mark) When I was in college, our dorm was prank heaven. Hardly an hour went by without someone pulling a fast one on somebody else. My survival technique in this free-for-all environment was simple. I said, "If you prank me, I will prank you twice as bad. So proceed at your own risk." I still got pranked a few times, but I was true to my word. We had so many laughs.

I'm not advocating that you go out today and prank somebody, but I do long for the days when people weren't so uptight and sensitive— when you could actually play a joke on someone and everyone would get a good laugh. Today, many people would charge you with abuse and try to get you fired. Don't be that humorless grouch who can't take a joke.

Reflect: Proverbs 17:22 says, "A cheerful heart is good medicine." What's the best (or worst) prank that was ever pulled on you? Did it make you laugh or fume with anger? Are you a good-humored person or a grouch? Do people feel free to joke in your presence, or are they serious all the time? Why is it better to be good humored?

MORE THAN MEETS THE EYE

IMAGINE YOU'RE ORGANIZING a basketball camp. You're going to have a hundred kids under your supervision who are eager to sharpen their skills and become better players. Your job is to put a plan together, to create a schedule that will take the kids through a comprehensive overview of the game. The question is, where would you start? What's the very first thing you would do with the kids?

Want to know how John Wooden started his youth basketball camps?

He began by telling all the campers to take off their shoes and socks. Then he spent quite a long time talking about foot health, explaining how they must avoid blisters at all costs if they want to play basketball. Eventually, he gave them careful instructions on how to put their shoes and socks on.

The exercise had to do with shoes and socks and feet and blisters, but the main purpose was much deeper. Coach Wooden was emphasizing the importance of the seemingly small things that most people overlook. And by having every camper go through the exercise together, he was equalizing every kid, from the old to the young, from the hotshots to the beginners. They were all sitting there together, barefooted.

This is a reminder that there is often more going on than meets the eye. If this is true of a basketball camp, imagine how true it is of life circumstances, when God has things he wants to teach us. Often we wonder why he puts us through certain experiences, not realizing that we're being prepared, molded, shaped for some important moment in the future. It can be much later that we have our *Eureka!* moment.

The next time things don't make sense, trust that God is up to something, and that it will all make sense in time.

Reflect: Ecclesiastes 8:17 says, "I realized that no one can discover everything God is doing under the sun." Have you ever been mystified by your life circumstances, wondering what God might be up to? Did you later make some sense of the situation? Do you feel that God is always up to something, even when nothing unusual is going on?

TIME AND PLACE

HALL OF FAME quarterback Steve Young tells a story from his days with the Tampa Bay Buccaneers. He was in the huddle during the game when one of the referees pulled him aside and told him that he had a daughter going to BYU (Young's alma mater) and that he would like for Steve to meet her and take her out. Steve expressed an interest and redirected his attention back to the game.

Later in the same game, the Bucs were down 31–23. Steve was trying to lead a comeback when he scrambled out of the pocket and took an earth-shaking hit that caused him to fumble the ball. Naturally, the other team recovered the ball as Steve was lying on the ground, seeing stars and wishing someone would answer the phone. Suddenly a yellow flag landed beside him. The referee who had the daughter going to BYU had called a personal foul, which meant a first down for the Bucs. Steve got up, still wobbly, and walked back to the huddle. As he passed by, the ref whispered in his ear, "She likes Italian."

As fathers of daughters, we both understand the ref's desire to help his daughter find a good guy to marry. But there is a time and place for everything, and the middle of an NFL game was not the proper time to be playing matchmaker.

Time and place are important, especially when witnessing for Christ. People do not like to be put on the spot in front of friends or coworkers. They do not like to be asked personal questions or theological questions in front of a group. If you're going to witness to someone (and we hope you are!) make sure you give careful consideration to the proper time and place.

Reflect: Matthew 9:38 says, "So pray to the Lord who is in charge of the harvest; ask him to send more workers into his fields." Why do you think people feel self-conscious being witnessed to in front of others? What type of environment would be perfect for talking to someone about Jesus? Do you feel a planned approach or a spontaneous approach to witnessing is best?

JUST BE NICE

TED WILLIAMS WAS an amazing hitter, but he was not the nicest man who ever lived. He was often surly and difficult, causing people to steer clear of him.

One day he was checking into a hotel under a false name, a practice that is not unusual for celebrities who are seeking privacy. However, the hotel clerk thought she recognized him and said, "Aren't you really Ted Williams?" Ted said, "No, I'm not," and proceeded to engage the woman in a conversation about something besides baseball. When the conversation ended and Ted was ready to head off to his room, the clerk said, "I really thought you were Ted Williams. You look just like him. But now I know you're not him because he's not nearly as nice as you are." That should have been a wake-up call for Ted, but there's no indication that he changed his surly ways.

Just being nice is one of the most important things we can do to foster goodwill and happiness in people. Some folks live every day grouchy, irritable people, so when someone is nice to them, they feel almost euphoric. And being nice is so easy! Even a grouch like Ted Williams could do it when he wanted to.

As Christians, we should be the nicest people around. Hotel maids, restaurant servers, grocery store clerks, plumbers, lawn mowers … everyone we come into contact with should walk away saying, "He (or she) sure is nice." Especially when we have a complaint, we should be nice about it. Perhaps this is the single biggest thing that would improve the quality of life in our country: if everybody would just be nice.

Reflect: Ephesians 4:32 says, "Be kind to each other." Everyone is nice when it serves their needs, but how consistently nice are you? Are you nice even when something happens that causes you discomfort? Is there ever a time when you shouldn't be nice?

INFLUENCER MATH

KRISTI YAMAGUCHI HAS HAD quite a life. She is a 1992 Olympic figure skating champion, a Goodwill Games champion, a two-time world champion, a United States champion and, if that's not enough, the 2008 celebrity champion of *Dancing with the Stars*. "Champion" could be Kristi's middle name.

As a child learning to skate, Kristi's idol was Dorothy Hamill. She even had a Dorothy Hamill doll that she carried with her when she went to the rink. She wanted to be like Dorothy in every way. She copied her moves the same way young boys copy the batting stances or pitching motions of their favorite major leaguers. In 1992, just before she took the ice to try to secure her Olympic gold medal, Dorothy Hamill paid Kristi a surprise visit. She'd heard about Kristi's affection for her and wanted to meet the rising young star. Kristi was stunned but delighted. It was a moment that made her gold medal even more memorable.

Two observations:

First, it says a lot about Dorothy Hamill that Kristi Yamaguchi wanted to be just like her. When talented young people with high aspirations see you as a role model and look to you for inspiration, you must be doing something right.

Second, when Dorothy went out of her way to meet and encourage Kristi, she was giving a great gift. It may have cost her little or nothing in terms of time or money, but it was a pearl of great price to the young skater, a treasured moment she will always remember.

Motivational speakers and writers talk a lot about being a good influence, which is good. In a world of bad influences, we need more good influences. We love how this story about the influence Dorothy Hamill had on Kristi Yamaguchi reduces it down to a very simple math equation:

BEING GOOD AT WHAT YOU DO + BEING A GOOD PERSON = INFLUENCE.

Reflect: Titus 2:7 says, "And you yourself must be an example to them by doing good works of every kind." Think of someone who has influenced you for the better. What is it about that person that you like? Can you name someone that you know who, beyond any doubt, you've had a positive influence on? In general, do you feel your influence is substantial? Why or why not?

SO YOU THOUGHT IT WAS GOING TO BE EASY

WE WANT TO TAKE you back to 1983, to a game between the Baltimore Orioles and Toronto Blue Jays. The game went to extra innings, and the Orioles lost both their starting and backup catchers, leaving them no choice but to put a noncatcher behind the plate. Infielder Lenn Sakata was the manager's choice.

You can imagine what the Blue Jays' players were thinking in a tie ballgame: *If we get on, we can steal. There's no way Sakata will be able to throw us out.*

The first player to get on was Barry Bonnell. He was itching to steal. The pitcher, Tippy Martinez, picked him off of first.

The second player to get on was Dave Collins. He, too, was itching to steal. Tippy Martinez picked him off of first.

The third player to get on was Willie Upshaw. He, too, was itching to steal. Tippy Martinez picked him off of first.

Three batters, three base runners, three pickoffs. Oh, and one more thing … Lenn Sakata, the noncatcher catcher, hit a three-run homer to win the game.

Sometimes we get cocky. Sometimes we think things are going to be easy. More often than not, when we get such an idea in our heads, we are unpleasantly surprised.

Satan looks for cockiness and overconfidence as he works against us. And don't think he doesn't try to exploit it when he finds it. We urge you to stay humble. Don't take anything for granted. Pay attention, concentrate, and don't give the devil an opportunity.

Reflect: 1 Corinthians 10:12 says, "If you think you are standing strong, be careful not to fall." What are some moments when Christians are likely to feel overconfident? Have you ever stumbled when you least expected to? What tripped you up? How is staying humble different from being afraid of failing?

IT'S NOT A RACE

THERE'S A FUNNY story about Louis B. Mayer, the movie mogul and founder of MGM. Born in a Russian territory, he came to the United States with his family and began to acclimate himself to American culture. It wasn't long before he discovered golf, but he didn't quite get the point of the game. He hired two caddies, one to walk with him and another one to run on ahead and locate his ball so that Louis could hit it again as quickly as possible. When he finished his round, he checked his watch, judging his success by the amount of time it took him to play. It fell to one of his friends to inform him that golf is not a race—that success or failure is determined by how many strokes you take, not by the amount of time it takes you to finish.

You will often hear life referred to as a race. This is because the apostle Paul used the metaphor when talking about the importance of self-discipline. People who win races discipline themselves, he says. But life is *not* a race in the sense that we should be rushing through it, hurrying as fast as we can. Just as a wise golfer takes his time and weighs every swing carefully, so a believer should take his time and weigh every decision carefully. It's safe to say that much of the trouble people get into has to do with hasty, impulsive choices.

We encourage you to tap the brakes when you get that impulse to hurry. A few minutes to cool down before you speak … another day to think about that purchase … a few more months before getting married might spell the difference between a great life and a miserable life.

Slow down. It's not a race.

Reflect: Ephesians 5:15 says, "So be careful how you live. Don't live like fools, but like those who are wise." Can you think of an instance where you got into trouble because you didn't take the time to carefully think through a decision? Why do you think most people feel pressured to hurry? What are the benefits of going slow?

INCOMING!

CAN YOU IMAGINE a baseball player being hit by his own home run ball?

It actually happened.

It was during Giancarlo Stanton's first year with the Yankees. The Yanks were playing the Red Sox at Fenway, and Stanton popped his thirty-eighth home run over the Green Monster. A Red Sox fan named Andrew Lastrapes got the ball and did what so many fans do when they get an archrival's home run ball: he chucked it back onto the field like it was radioactive.

We don't know if Mr. Lastrapes ever played ball, but we do know he has quite an arm. He leaned back and fired the ball back toward the infield and, lo and behold, it hit Giancarlo as he was rounding second base. If he'd been trying to hit him, he probably would have missed by fifty feet. As it was, Mr. Stanton is probably the only player in history to get hit by his own home run ball.

But our interest in this story concerns the nutty custom of throwing back home run balls. You can attend hundreds of games as a fan and not get a single ball hit to you, fair or foul. Then when you finally get one, you're going to throw it back. *Really?* (Mark) Allow me to go on record right now. If I ever catch a home run ball, I'm keeping it. Yes, even if it's hit by a Cub.

We do, however, appreciate the show of loyalty. When you chuck a home run ball back onto the field, it's a clear statement about how much you love your team.

If we could only be as loyal to God as we are to our sports teams, then we might actually succeed in changing the world.

Reflect: In Matthew 26:33, Peter said to Jesus, "Even if everyone else deserts you, I will never desert you." If you caught an archrival's home run ball, would you keep it or throw it back? When was the last time you took a bold stand that demonstrated your loyalty to God? In today's culture, what are some things that could happen if you take a stand for God?

SHE AIN'T HEAVY; SHE'S MY SISTER

ALLOW US TO INTRODUCE you to Sara Tucholsky. In 2008, she was playing collegiate softball for Western Oregon. Though Sara was a senior, she'd never hit a home run. But on this day, in an important game with playoff implications, she caught one perfectly on the barrel and sent the ball flying over the fence.

That's when things got crazy.

In her excitement, Sara missed first base, so she stopped and turned back to touch it. But the turn was awkward; she wrenched her knee and ended up tearing her ACL. The pain was so excruciating she couldn't take another step. The umpire informed her that, by rule, if she couldn't make it around the bases, she would be awarded a single. Also, by rule, if any of her coaches or teammates touched her or assisted her, she would be awarded only a single.

That's when Mallory Holtman, a member of the opposing team, asked the umpire if she could help Sara. According to the ump, there was nothing in the rule book to prohibit the opposing team from assisting her, probably because no one ever conceived of a situation where such a thing would happen. So Mallory and a teammate, Liz Wallace, picked Sara up and carried her around the bases. The three women received an ESPY in 2008 for what still stands as one of the greatest acts of good sportsmanship in history.

Being competitive is great, but there comes a time when competition needs to be set aside for the greater good. Too often we root against the people we're competing with and secretly rejoice when they fall. These young women remind us that people are far more important than any game, and that winning is about much more than just scoring points.

Reflect: Galatians 6:2 says, "Share each other's burdens, and in this way obey the law of Christ." How competitive are you? Does it bother you if you don't win? Have you ever sacrificed your own advantage to help someone who was in competition with you? What are some things that take the joy out of winning?

WHAT MAKES A CHAMPION

IN 1989, LOYOLA MARYMOUNT, coached by Paul Westhead, hosted US International in an NCAA basketball game. When the teams took the floor, fans had no idea they were about to witness a record-setting contest, but witness one they did.

That night, more combined points were scored than in any previous NCAA game in history. The two teams averaged scoring a point every 7.3 seconds. There was virtually no passing or working the ball. Players were chucking the ball almost as soon as they came across the half-court stripe. And as for defense, well, those who watched the game said it looked like neither team had ever even heard the word "defense" and didn't know what it was. The final score was 181–150, with Loyola Marymount coming out on top.

Can you imagine scoring 150 points in a basketball game and still losing by 31? Imagine those players someday telling their grandkids about the day their college team scored 150 points. "Wow, Grandpa!

You must have really smeared the other team!" And Grandpa says, "Well, no. Actually, we got blown out by thirty-one points."

Reminds us of an old saying: "Offense makes you a star. Defense makes you a champion." This is true in the Christian life, too. Offense (being a great speaker or teacher or singer or writer) will get you lots of fans and social media clicks, but defense (steadfastly resisting Satan every day) will send him fleeing and bring you close to God.

We urge you not to become so enamored with offense and the glory it brings that you neglect defense. Don't be that person who scores all kinds of points for God but loses in the end because he didn't pay enough attention to keeping himself pure.

Reflect: 2 Timothy 2:21 says, "If you keep yourself pure, you will be a special utensil for honorable use. Your life will be clean, and you will be ready for the Master to use you for every good work." In sports or in life, why do so few people seem to love defense? What are some specific ways you can resist Satan?

SILENCE IS NOT ALWAYS GOLDEN

(PAT) IT'S 1995. The Magic are in the NBA Finals against the Houston Rockets. This is the great Rockets team with Hakeem "the Dream" Olajuwon and Clyde Drexler. But the Magic are positioned to win game one, with Nick Anderson going to the line in the closing seconds. Two free throws will put the game away. Nick is a good free throw shooter. We all feel great about our chances.

But Nick misses both free throws.

We all gasp, horrified, as the second one clanks off the rim, then cheer deliriously as somehow Nick gets the rebound and is fouled again, sending him back to the line. No way he will miss them this time!

But he does.

Clank.

Clank.

Seconds later, Kenny Smith hits a three-pointer for the Rockets, and the Magic lose.

At that time, Buzz Braman was our shooting coach and was on the bench. He told me years later that he saw a flaw in Nick's free throw form on his first trip to the line but chose not to say anything, thinking Nick, as an experienced player, would self-correct on his second trip to the line. It was a decision that has haunted Buzz ever since. If he'd spoken up, would the Magic have won the game?

IT'S PAINFUL TO SAY SOMETHING AND REGRET IT. IT'S ALSO PAINFUL TO *NOT* SAY SOMETHING AND REGRET IT.

Would it have changed the outcome of the series? We'll never know.

It's painful to say something and regret it. It's also painful to *not* say something and regret it. I encourage you to speak up when your heart tells you something needs to be said, especially if it's intended to be helpful. One observation, thought, or suggestion could change everything.

Reflect: Proverbs 15:4 says, "Gentle words are a tree of life." Can you think back to a time when you didn't speak up and regretted it later? What kept you from speaking up? What are some of the reasons why people hold their tongues when they have something important to say?

UNTAPPED TALENT

AN ART PROFESSOR died and went to heaven, where he and St. Peter became buddies. One day over lunch, the art professor said to Peter, "I spent almost my entire life on earth studying art and artists, from Rembrandt to Van Gogh, and I've always wondered who had the most talent. Can you tell me?"

St. Peter pointed at a man nearby and said, "See that guy? He had more painting talent than anyone who ever lived."

The art professor said, "You must be mistaken. I knew that guy on earth. He was a janitor at the university where I taught. He never painted a picture in his whole life."

To which Peter replied, "You didn't ask who the best painter was. You asked who had the most painting talent, and it was him."

We could relate this story to the world of sports. Could it be that somewhere out there is a person who's never swung a club but possesses Jack Nicklaus–type golf talent? Is there a Tom Brady–caliber athlete somewhere who is playing the cello and has never even tried to throw a spiral? Is there a woman who could have been Serena Williams's nemesis if only she had taken tennis lessons as a kid?

Possibly.

Which begs the question: Do you have talent that's never been acknowledged or tapped into? Have you spent your life doing what *other* people tell you to do, following the trail *they* have marked out for you, struggling to meet *their* expectations, while at the same time feeling a call, an urge, an itch to go your own way?

We believe there are lots of people in this situation. If you think you might be one of them, what's stopping you from finding out? Answer the call. Follow the urge. Scratch that itch. You might be surprised what's inside you. You might be surprised what is waiting for you.

Reflect: 1 Peter 4:10 says, "God has given each of you a gift." Can you honestly say that you have spent your life developing and using your greatest talents, or have you sacrificed them to make other people happy? Do you often feel a sense of unfulfillment? What are you not doing that you sense you should be doing?

NEXT-LEVEL KINDNESS

(PAT) DOC RIVERS COACHED the first game of his professional career for the Magic in November of 1999. Just before he walked onto the court, we passed in the tunnel. He commented that he saw me and my wife, Ruth, running a few days earlier. I told him that we were training for the New York City Marathon that weekend.

So that weekend in New York, we enjoyed the city. The weather was great; we ate at Mickey Mantle's restaurant and saw *Annie Get Your Gun* on Broadway. At 11:00 p.m. we returned to our room and got a huge surprise. We found a beautiful fruit basket with a card that said, "Good luck in the marathon —Doc Rivers." You should know that Doc had no idea where we were staying, but he went to the effort to find out.

There's kindness, and then there's next-level kindness.

Kindness is when you see someone in a hallway and wish them well in the New York City Marathon. Next-level kindness is when you go out of your way to send them a fruit basket with a note of encouragement. If Doc had only wished us well in the hallway, it would have been encouraging enough. The fact that he carried his kindness to the next level was profoundly touching and unforgettable.

There is kindness in the world. You see it everywhere. Someone opens a door for a total stranger. A driver slows down to let someone else into the line of traffic. But next-level kindness is rare. I believe our world needs more next-level kindness to counteract the next-level rudeness that has become so common. We need to step up our game. If you're looking for a way to really touch people in a positive way, this could be it.

Reflect: 1 John 3:18 says, "Dear children, let's not merely say that we love each other; let us show the truth by our actions." Can you think of a next-level act of kindness that was done for you? What did that act tell you about the person who did it? How does a next-level act of kindness benefit the person who does it?

HIGH HOPES

(MARK) I HEARD A funny story about Speedy Morris when he was the basketball coach at La Salle. He was upstairs shaving when he heard the phone ring downstairs. His wife answered, then walked to the foot of the stairs and called up to him: "Honey, it's *Sports Illustrated* on the phone for you." Speedy's adrenaline spiked, causing him to cut himself shaving. He thought, *Wow, my first major interview!* Then he practically broke his neck trying to get down the stairs to the phone as fast as possible. When he picked up the receiver, the person on the other end said, "Sir, for just seventy-five cents an issue, you can get the greatest sports magazine in the country sent to your house."

Have you ever had sky-high hopes or expectations that were dashed?

When I was very young, I interviewed with a church I really wanted to work for. The people I met with were super nice, thoughtful, and seemed like they would be a dream to serve with. When we left our meeting, they shook my hand and told me they would call me the following week with an offer. That was over forty years ago. I am still waiting for that call. I don't know what happened. Perhaps one of them will read this and call me and let me know.

It's great to have high hopes. People with high hopes are generally positive, upbeat people. But high hopes are still hopes, and hopes are not reality. So hope all you want, but don't count your chickens until they hatch. You'll be much happier and more successful if you live in the real world.

Reflect: Proverbs 27:1 says, "Don't brag about tomorrow, since you don't know what the day will bring." Think of a time when your high hopes didn't pan out. What did you learn from that experience? Did it affect your outlook on life? What are some ways you might be able to tell if what you're hoping for is realistic or foolish?

BE LIKE BOB

AS EVERYONE KNOWS, the sports world is populated by people with gigantic egos. I am particularly struck by the guy who roars like a lion and pounds his chest like a gorilla when he hits a home run even though he's sporting a .225 batting average and his team is losing by five runs and sits in last place in the division.

This is why we love Bob Uecker, the king of self-deprecating humor.

He was once asked what the highlight of his career was. He said it happened in 1967, when he played for the Cardinals. He walked with the bases loaded and drove in the winning run in an intersquad game in spring training.

On another occasion, he told about the time he signed with the Milwaukee Braves for $3,000. He said it was very upsetting to his father because he didn't have that kind of money, but he found a way to scrape it up.

And then there was the time he was asked, as a big-league catcher, for some tips on how to catch a knuckleball. He said he had perfected the technique. He just waited until it stopped rolling and picked it up.

There's a reason why everybody loves Bob Uecker.

People will love you, too, if you are humble and can laugh at yourself. Unfortunately, we live in a dog-eat-dog world where the name of the game is self-promotion. Even perfectly boring people use websites and social media to try to draw attention to themselves. Many of their self-serving posts and pictures are painfully awkward and reek of desperation.

We encourage you to be different ... to be like Bob. Put on humility. Laugh at yourself. Be self-deprecating instead of self-promoting. It's the difference between people simply seeing you and loving you.

Reflect: In Matthew 23:12 Jesus said, "But those who exalt themselves will be humbled, and those who humble themselves will be exalted." Do you enjoy being around people with huge egos? Why or why not? In your opinion, what is the difference between a healthy ego and pure arrogance? As Christians, should we have any ego at all?

FROM "OH, NO!" TO ALL-PRO

CORNELL GREEN WAS an All-Pro defensive back for the Dallas Cowboys, but most people don't know how he got his start.

Gil Brandt and the Cowboys' scouting department made it a point to look for athletes who were under the radar, that other teams were paying no attention to. No one was paying attention to Cornell Green because, even though he was a terrific athlete, he didn't play football before the Cowboys drafted him.

On one of his first days in uniform, he was moving with great difficulty and acting as if he was in pain. His defensive backfield coach asked him what was wrong, and he said he didn't think his pads fit right. He was told to drop his pants, and when he did, the coach saw that he had his hip pads on backward, and that the piece that was supposed to protect his tailbone was in front, pinching him in an area where no man wants to be pinched.

It's hard to imagine a man who doesn't know how to put on a football uniform becoming an NFL All-Pro, but that's what happened to Cornell Green. Which serves to remind us that it's not what a person is but what he or she can be that's important. Jesus understood this. When he chose his disciples, he picked guys who were not trained theologians but fishermen and tax collectors. He wasn't looking at what they were but what they could become.

If you are a leader, don't be too quick to write off that inexperienced, bumbling team member who doesn't seem to have a clue. If you provide some coaching and encouragement, that person could become more valuable to your team than either of you ever dreamed would be possible.

Reflect: Matthew 4:19–20 says, "Jesus called out to them, 'Come, follow me, and I will show you how to fish for people!' And they left their nets at once and followed him." Have you ever been given a chance even though you weren't qualified? How did that make you feel? What are some qualities that can be more important than experience?

DALKOWSKI'S UNDOING

STEVE DALKOWSKI.

Never heard of him, have you?

Very few people have, but in the late 1950s, he was the hardest-throwing pitcher in the minor leagues. Cal Ripken Sr. said he believed that if they'd used radar guns on pitchers in those days, Dalkowski would have hit 115 miles per hour. He threw so hard that he broke bones when he hit batters. One batter in particular had his forearm broken almost in two when he was plunked by a Dalkowski heater.

If you're thinking he was hard to hit, you're right. In fact, he was almost impossible to hit. The reason he didn't go on to become one of the greatest big-league pitchers of all time is because he had terrible control. In a game in Kingsport, Tennessee, Mr. Dalkowski struck out twenty-four, walked seventeen, hit four, threw six wild pitches in a row, and lost the game 9–8. Many believe that if the man had had even decent control, he would have been the greatest pitcher of all time.

A lack of control has been the undoing of a lot of people.

In the Bible, Samson stayed in almost constant trouble because he couldn't keep his eyes, his mind, and his hands off the ladies. His physical strength was superhuman, but his out-of-control desires rendered him as weak as a kitten in the presence of a conniving woman like Delilah. He might have been the greatest hero of the Bible (other than Jesus) if only he could have controlled himself.

If you struggle controlling yourself, make it a priority to change that. Learn to say no. Get a handle on your desires. If you don't, you will ruin your life.

Reflect: 1 Timothy 4:7 says, "Train yourself to be godly." Is there an area of your life where you find it difficult to practice self-control? Why do you think self-control is easy in some areas and hard in others? What are some specific things you could do to make self-control easier?

TOO MANY TAXIS

THE GREAT TED WILLIAMS was born in 1918 and died in 2002. During that time, he never saw the Boston Red Sox win the World Series. Of course, Ted played for the Red Sox, and he played in one World Series in 1947. But the Sox were beaten by the Cardinals in seven games. That was as close as he would come.

> IT'S TRUE IN EVERY BUSINESS, ORGANIZATION, OR CHURCH: YOU EITHER HAVE A COLLECTION OF INDIVIDUALS OR A TEAM.

That is not to say, however, that the Red Sox never had the talent to win the World Series. Ted Williams thought there were several years when they did. But he summed up those teams very succinctly: "Twenty-five guys, twenty-five cabs." What did he mean? Simply that on those teams, there was no chemistry, camaraderie, or sense of brotherhood. Guys played the games because that's what they were paid to do, but after the games they all got into separate cabs and went their own way.

It's true in every business, organization, or church: you either have a collection of individuals or a team. If you have a collection of individuals, you won't get far. Individuals care about themselves and can be counted on to do what will benefit themselves. Teams, on the other hand, keep the big picture in view and are happy to sacrifice for the greater good. "There's no *I* in team" may be a cliché, but it's both literally and figuratively true.

If you're reading this and thinking that your business or your church is a collection of individuals instead of a team, we challenge you to do two things. One, ask yourself if you're part of the problem. How many sacrifices have *you* made for the team? And two, ask yourself what you could do to improve the chemistry. Change has to start somewhere; why not with you?

Reflect: Philippians 2:4 says, "Don't look out only for your own interests, but take an interest in others too." Have you ever been a part of a dysfunctional collection of individuals? If so, did you try to change the culture? What are some of the blessings and advantages of true, unselfish teamwork?

PIOTR AND OLEK

(MARK) EVERY NOW AND then you hear about someone who totally gets it, whose priorities are spot-on, who makes you wonder what the world would be like if everyone was so clearheaded in their thinking. Piotr Małachowski is such an athlete.

A discus thrower, he won a silver medal in the Rio Olympics. We suppose most Olympic medal winners create a special place in their homes to display the memento that marks them as one of the best in the world. Not Piotr. He put his up for sale the very next day. He created an online auction and sold his medal to the highest bidder.

The reason he did this was because of a three-year-old boy he knew. Little Olek Szymanski had retinoblastoma and needed surgery to correct his sight, a surgery his family could not afford. Piotr considered what he could do to help, and the most significant thing seemed to be cashing in his silver medal. And yes, in case you're wondering, the money was eventually raised.

Selflessness is a very rare trait in our world. Most people never think any further than their own comfort. And even when they do discover someone in need, they have an uncanny ability to rationalize it away and absolve themselves of any responsibility to help. That's why Piotr's story is so inspiring. Something he worked so hard for many years to achieve wasn't as important to him as the health of a little boy.

We encourage you, if you haven't already, to step out of your bubble and notice the needs around you. Maybe you don't have a hunk of silver to sell, but surely there's something you could give to make someone's life a little better. It could be something big, but it doesn't have to be. Jesus said that giving a cup of water to a thirsty person is important. The key is caring enough to do it.

Reflect: Hebrews 13:16 says, "And don't forget to do good and share with those in need." How sensitive are you to the needs of others? How much of your time and money do you contribute to help others? When was the last time you made a significant sacrifice for someone else? Why do you think so few people are truly selfless?

ARMOR ALL

IT WAS A NORMAL day at the old ball park. The umpires came out before the first pitch, went over the ground rules with the managers, and took their places on the field. Then the home team took the field, the pitcher took his warm-ups, and the game began. It was as normal a game as you'd ever hope to see until, in the fifth inning, a batter hit a foul ball off of umpire Johnny Rice's knee. That's when Johnny realized that he had forgotten to put on his shin guards.

If you think that's crazy, try to imagine the night Ron Luciano was umping behind the plate. The pitcher was finished warming up and ready to throw the first pitch of the game. He went into his windup when suddenly the first base umpire came running in, shouting and waving his arms in the air. He'd noticed that Luciano had forgotten to bring out his face mask. Luciano realized it too just as the pitch was delivered, and he ducked down behind the catcher.

There are certain times when we need to be armored up. When umping baseball games is one. When living the Christian life is another.

In his letter to the church at Ephesus, Paul went into detail about our need for protection from the "fiery arrows of the devil" (Eph. 6:16). Then he itemized the various pieces of armor we should wear.

A word that is often overlooked in Ephesians 6 is "all." "Put on all of God's armor," Paul says in verse 11. Ask Johnny Rice or Ron Luciano how important it is to have *all* of your armor on. One soft spot, one vulnerability is all Satan needs to strike a devastating blow against you.

Reflect: Ephesians 6:13 says, "Put on every piece of God's armor so you will be able to resist the enemy in the time of evil." Is there an area of your life where you have proven to be especially weak? What steps have you taken to protect yourself in that area? What are some factors that keep people from armoring up as faithfully as they should?

DAVIDS AND GOLIATHS

UNDERDOGS AND FAVORITES. Or you could say Davids and Goliaths. They are what make sports so thrilling. More often than seems reasonable, the Davids rise up and smack the Goliaths, leaving them wondering what happened.

The Princeton University Tigers basketball team has been a David many, many times. They almost never get the best athletes coming out of high school. The nation's premier players generally flock to the Power Five conferences, certainly not the Ivy League. But the Tigers have still managed to pull off upset after upset, especially when Pete Carril was the coach.

Coach Carril had a system—some would say a slow, boring system—that brought out the best in his own players and completely confounded the opposition. In 1996, the Tigers drew the UCLA Bruins, one of the most celebrated programs in basketball history, in the first round of the NCAA tournament. It was a David and Goliath matchup for sure. Late in the game, the Tigers trailed by seven, but they stuck with their methodical offense and squeaked out a 43–41 win.

There are times in our lives when we feel overmatched, when we know we lack the talent or experience that others around us have. But in life, as in sports, chickens should never be counted before they hatch. Slings and stones still sometimes bring down armored-up giants. Don't ever think that you have no hope. Instead, knuckle down and do what you do best to the best of your ability. When the dust clears, you may discover that the stone you slung found its mark. It wouldn't be the first time.

Reflect: Ecclesiastes 9:11 says, "The fastest runner doesn't always win the race, and the strongest warrior doesn't always win the battle." Have you ever won when you thought you had little chance of winning? Have you ever lost when you thought there was no way you could lose? What are some reasons why upsets happen? What are some practical ways to prevent them?

DOWN BUT NOT OUT

IN 1990, JENNIFER CAPRIATI landed in the tennis world like a three hundred–pound belly flopper lands in a swimming pool … with a huge splash. That year, at age fourteen, she became the youngest tennis player to ever win a Wimbledon match. She also reached the semifinals of the French Open and became the youngest player ever to be seeded in a Grand Slam event. For the next two years, she was the talk of tennis, a marvel the likes of which no one had seen.

But when she was seventeen, her life unraveled. Many people believe she was too young to have so much pressure thrust upon her. Whatever the reason, she made some bad decisions and saw her career and her reputation come crashing down.

But this is not the end of the story.

In 2001, at the age of twenty-four, Jennifer was back. She'd worked through her problems and rededicated herself to the game she loved. At the Australian Open that year, she defeated Monica Seles,

Lindsay Davenport, and Martina Hingis, three of the biggest names in tennis, to win the title.

When your world comes crashing down, especially if it's because of poor choices, everyone's going to know it. They'll see you as a failure. The critical question is: How do you see yourself? Do you see yourself as down and out, or just down? If you see yourself as down and out, you're finished. But if you see yourself as down but not out, then a comeback will be a real possibility.

Never forget: with God you are never out. You may be down. You may be embarrassed and humiliated. But as long as you never give up on God, you're not out, because God never gives up on you.

Reflect: Jeremiah 29:11 says, "For I know the plans I have for you … They are plans for good and not for disaster, to give you a future and a hope." Have poor choices ever messed up your life? How did you process what happened? Did you give up hope? What role, if any, did God play in your path forward?

HOW DO YOU SPELL "RELIEF"?

JESSE OROSCO WAS A left-handed pitcher for nine different major-league teams. He broke into the majors in 1979 and didn't retire until 2003. That's twenty-four years of slinging baseballs at the highest level. During that time, Jesse made 1,252 appearances. It should also be noted that, of Jesse's 1,252 appearances, only four were starts. The vast majority of the time when he came into a game, it was to relieve another pitcher who was either in trouble or tiring.

Jesse Orosco was never a superstar. Relief pitchers almost never are. Most of the time, he sat on the bench and didn't work up a sweat. But the fact that nine different teams signed him to a contract and that he stayed employed for twenty-four years tells you what a valuable player baseball managers and executives thought he was.

There are times in life when we all need relief. We're floundering, fatigued, or frustrated and have lost our effectiveness. Many people, perhaps out of guilt, keep slogging forward anyway. God knew the need for relief would be very real for us, so he came up with a little thing called the Sabbath. He established in the Old Testament law that his people should rest on the seventh day of the week. As New Testament Christians, we're not bound by that law, but we ought to see the wisdom of the principle behind it. Whether it's taking a day or two off a week, going on a vacation, or taking a sabbatical, we all need to get some relief.

We urge you not to be one of those hard-nosed workaholics who scoffs at time off. You'll do better work and be more pleasant to the people around you if you take a breather now and then.

Reflect: Exodus 34:21 says, "You have six days each week for your ordinary work, but on the seventh day you must stop working, even during the seasons of plowing and harvest." Is it hard for you to stop working and take a breather? If so, why? What is behind the pressure you feel to keep going no matter what? In what ways has this relentless drive hurt you?

A LITTLE GIRL AND HER GRANDPA

MICK COLLINSON HAD a granddaughter. He also owned a toy store. Talk about winning the grandfather lottery! What kid wouldn't want a grandpa with a toy store?

One of the toys Mick gave his granddaughter was a set of plastic golf clubs. He also started taking her with him when he went to play golf on the weekends. When she was eight, he took her to the course with real clubs and coached her as she played her first full eighteen-hole round. It took her 152 strokes to finish.

Sixteen years later, that little girl was twenty-six and learned that her grandfather was seriously ill. She thought about jumping on a plane and flying home to see him but decided to stay where she was for one more day. On that one more day, as a tribute to her grandfather, she went out and won the LPGA Championship, becoming the youngest female golfer to complete the career grand slam. The girl's name was Karrie Webb.

She played the last day of the tournament as a tribute to the man who had taught her the game. When the last putt dropped, she broke down in tears. Her grandfather died before she could get home to see him, but she knew she'd done the right thing. She knew her grandfather would have been upset if she'd bailed out of the tournament with a chance to win.

We love this story because it's a reminder that the time you invest in a child is never wasted. Even if little Karrie Webb had never become a world-class golfer, the relationship she had with her grandfather was worth all the time and effort he invested in her. In our world, children are often afterthoughts for the busy adults in their lives. Don't be so caught up in your own pursuits that you fail to invest in the children God has entrusted to your care.

Reflect: Psalms 127:3 says, "Children are a gift from the Lord; they are a reward from him." When you were a child, who invested the most in you? If there are children in your life, how much are you investing in them? Why do you think so many adults and/or parents fail to invest in their children the way they should? What is the long-range effect of that?

MERRY CHRISTMAS

IN DECEMBER 1914, World War I was raging. British, French, and German troops were dug in within shouting distance of each other.

And singing distance.

The lead singer of the Berlin Imperial Opera, in an effort to bring some Christmas joy to the troops, visited the German front line and began singing Christmas carols. The French and British were listening from a short distance away and began applauding when the singer finished. Soon soldiers from all sides were emerging from their trenches, calling an unofficial truce for Christmas. They began mingling, sharing chocolate candy, and showing each other pictures of their families. When someone produced a soccer ball, it took only a moment for a friendly game to get started. Though we could not find any definitive evidence of the outcome of that game, legend has it that the British and French defeated the Germans 3–2.

There's no day on the calendar quite like Christmas. It has the power to cease hostilities, to make friends of enemies, to turn gunshots into laughter—if not permanently, at least for a day. What is the secret of December 25? It's the simple fact that it, more than any other day, is associated with Jesus, the Prince of Peace.

Is there someone you are at odds with? On this Christmas Day, let the Prince of Peace inspire you to soften your heart toward that person. Even if that individual is guilty of some terrible offense, ask yourself what you have to gain by harboring a grudge. Always remember: forgiveness is a gift you give yourself. It sets you free from bitterness and allows you to move forward baggage-free.

We wish you a merry—and peaceful—Christmas.

Reflect: Luke 2:14 says, "Glory to God in highest heaven, and peace on earth to those with whom God is pleased." Why is it so easy for people to hang onto grudges? What are some of the negative results a grudge can produce in a person's life? What are some of the benefits of forgiveness?

ALMOST

ANYONE WHO HAD an ounce of compassion in his or her soul found the seventy-second hole of the 1999 British Open excruciating to watch. A Frenchman, Jean van de Velde, stood on the tee box with a three-stroke lead. Here's how he played the hole.

His tee shot went fifty yards to the right of the fairway.

His second shot hit the grandstand and found the rough, forty yards short of the fairway.

His third shot landed in the water, which added a penalty stroke.

His fifth shot landed in a greenside bunker.

He pitched out with his sixth shot and sank a putt for a triple-bogey 7.

This horrendous turn of events landed van de Velde in a tie with Paul Lawrie and Justin Leonard. A playoff ensued, which Lawrie won, sending van de Velde home to ponder what might have been and almost was.

Almost.

It's a word a lot of us have to reckon with. Maybe you were on a short list to get your dream job … maybe you were head over heels in love … maybe you were up for a promotion that you more than deserved, but somehow the bottom fell out. Some people pile up a lot of "almosts" in life, and with every one, the frustration builds.

SO TAKE A DEEP BREATH AND SMILE. WHATEVER ELSE GOES WRONG, JESUS NEVER WILL.

So by way of encouragement, let us remind you of one thing where the word "almost" will never apply: the sufficiency of Christ's sacrifice for your sins. The blood of Christ will absolutely, positively, most assuredly wash your sins as white as snow. No worries at all. So take a deep breath and smile. Whatever else goes wrong, Jesus never will.

Reflect: 1 John 1:7 says, "The blood of Jesus, his Son, cleanses us from all sin." Have you suffered major disappointments in life? If so, has this made you more pessimistic? Do you ever wonder if your salvation is really secure? What are some things you could do to gain greater assurance of your salvation?

FLAPPING SHOELACES

AT THE 1997 New York City Marathon, John Kagwe of Kenya had a choice to make. Having finished fourth the previous year, he was clearly a contender and went into the race with high hopes. The race began in a steady rain and a stiff breeze. Kagwe built up a nice lead but suddenly noticed that his shoelace was untied. At miles three and ten, he stopped to tie it, but wouldn't you know, it came untied yet again.

Kagwe still had his lead, but it had shrunk because of the stops. Could he possibly stop and tie it a third time without blowing his lead and losing the race that he had worked so hard to win? He decided that he could not and decided to ignore the problem and run on. His shoelace flapped for the rest of the race. And yes, he had to be careful that he didn't trip on it. But because he ran on and let the shoelace flap, he won the race with a time of 2:08.12.

Do you have a flapping shoelace in your life? Perhaps some smallish thing that keeps demanding your attention, that keeps frustrating you, that keeps taking your attention away from where it needs to be? Maybe, like John Kagwe, you've tried to fix the problem, but it just keeps cropping up at the most inopportune times.

Sometimes in life we just have to let our shoelaces flap because there are more important things to focus on. In fact, don't overlook the possibility that Satan is behind all those little annoyances and frustrations that crop up in your life. He'd love to distract you from the bigger, more important things God wants you to be focusing on.

Reflect: Proverbs 4:25 says, "Look straight ahead, and fix your eyes on what lies before you." In general, are you easily distracted? Do you start things and not finish them? Do you find yourself getting tangled up in things of lesser importance? What keeps you from focusing the way you should?

THE COMEBACK

THAT'S WHAT IT'S CALLED: The Comeback.

Capital T. Capital C.

The Comeback.

Any football fan over a certain age knows that title was given to the outrageous turn of events that happened on January 3, 1993, when the Buffalo Bills fell behind the Houston Oilers 35–3. There were twenty-eight minutes left in the game.

At halftime, with the Bills looking like a bunch of hapless losers, Coach Marv Levy kept himself under control. He didn't yell and scream and curse at his troops. He did make one very penetrating statement before he sent his guys back onto the field: "Whatever happens out there, you guys have to live with yourselves after today."[33]

The Bills must have decided it would be easier to live with themselves if they played better. They marched out onto the field and scored twenty-eight points in the third quarter, then another seven in the fourth. The game ended in a tie, and the Bills kicked a field goal to win in overtime.

Marv Levy's comment to his players is one that every Christian should think about, especially when facing temptation. You have to live with yourself. Even if you're sneaky enough to hide your sin, even if there are no repercussions or public embarrassments, you still have to live with yourself. And if your conscience is functioning properly, that won't be easy.

It's been said that your conscience whispers during moments of temptation, goes completely silent as you're sinning, and screams its head off after you've sinned. One of the keys to a happy life is simply not giving your conscience a reason to scream. Do what's right, and you'll find yourself an easy person to live with.

Reflect: In Acts of the Apostles 23:1, Paul said, "Brothers, I have always lived before God with a clear conscience." Think of something you did that made you feel guilty. Did you find the above quote about your conscience whispering, going quiet, and then screaming to be accurate? Do you think it's possible to have a conscience that's too sensitive? Why, or why not?

THE BEST HEROES

IT'S FOURTH DOWN, ten yards to go for the Steelers.

They're down 7–6 to the Raiders, and time is running out.

Terry Bradshaw is trying desperately to lead the team into field goal range.

He fires a pass downfield to Frenchy Fuqua.

The ball arrives at the same instant the Raiders' Jack Tatum does.

The ball pops into the air, where the Steelers' Franco Harris grabs it off of his shoe tops and gallops into the end zone with five seconds left. The Steelers win on a play that has been known ever since as the "Immaculate Reception."

Franco Harris has said many times that he was just in the right place at the right time. When he saw his quarterback scrambling and lofting the ball downfield, he was going to block for whoever might catch the ball. He had no idea that *he* would be the one to catch the ball and score.

We think it's significant that Franco was just doing his job, and an unglamorous job it was. He was running to assist a teammate, to block for the receiver who, he hoped, would become the hero. But suddenly, the ball was in *his* hands, and *he* became the hero.

Some of life's greatest opportunities come to us suddenly and unexpectedly, as we are going about our business. How many times have you seen an "ordinary Joe" hero interviewed on the news and heard him say, "I'm no hero. I was just minding my own business." In our view, these are the best heroes: those egoless individuals who aren't looking to be glamorized or praised, but who are courageous and strong when life decides to test them.

Our advice is simple: don't go out looking to be a hero. Just take care of your own business, and be ready for anything.

Reflect: 1 Corinthians 16:13 says, "Be on guard. Stand firm in the faith. Be courageous. Be strong." Think of someone you know who has done something you consider to be heroic. Was that person seeking the big moment or just ready when it came? What qualities or traits do you think are the main ingredients of heroism?

WHERE THERE'S A WILL THERE'S A (STEVE) WAY

STEVE WAY IS a guy whose story we love. He is a long-distance runner and the holder of the British 100 km record. People who meet him today would never guess that as recently as 2007 he was extremely overweight and smoked twenty cigarettes a day. He started running to get fit and quickly realized that he needed to do more than run. He also needed to quit smoking and change his diet, which he did. Eventually, he was running 130 miles a week and starting to show real promise as a competitive runner. As of this writing, he is 47, the winner of numerous competitive races, and is considered an elite athlete.

How can you not love his story?

We suspect the only way you wouldn't is if you are currently where he used to be. What does your diet look like? Do you smoke? Are you a couch potato? If so, a story like Steve's probably makes you a little uncomfortable. Why? Because you know you could do what he did. Not that you could become an elite athlete, but you could make changes to your lifestyle that would improve your health and, in general, make you a better person ... but you haven't done it.

Here's the interesting thing: when Steve Way started running, he had no idea where the road was going to take him, metaphorically speaking. He just wanted to lose a little weight. But one thing led to another and the first thing you know, he was loving his new lifestyle and, in many ways, became a brand-new person.

If you're not living a healthy lifestyle, we encourage you to make some changes. You don't have to go crazy and start training to be a competitive long-distance runner, but if you could just eat better and start getting some exercise, you'll be surprised at how much better you'll feel, and how much better you'll feel about yourself.

Oh, and one more thing. Your witness for Christ will improve too.

Reflect: In 3 John 2, the apostle John said, "I hope all is well with you and that you are as healthy in body as you are strong in spirit." How seriously do you take your health? Do you have a weakness or a habit that keeps you from being fit? Is there a lifestyle change that would be both a boost to your health and your witness for Christ? If so, what's keeping you from making it?

WHERE SPORTS CAME FROM

BEFORE THE 1800s, there are very few references to sports. Some references to contests and games and other diversions can be found in the historical record, but sports as we know it didn't start to really blossom until the 1800s. There is a reason for this: Until the nineteenth century, the only people who had leisure time were the royalty and the rich. Normal people worked from sunup to sundown, seven days a week, just trying to survive. It was the industrial revolution, the creation of factories and assembly lines and labor unions that created a middle class and shortened the average person's work day.

Oh yes, and something else pretty cool was created: the weekend.

Gradually people adjusted to having their evenings and weekends free. In need of something to do that didn't feel like work, people began playing games. Sticks and balls and mallets and peach baskets and all sorts of other things were used to create fun. And now we are the beneficiaries of that. Americans spend $56 billion a year attending sporting events, and that doesn't include the number of people who play sports, either in the backyard or in some organized program.

We encourage you to get in on the fun, if you aren't already. Life is serious business, for sure. There are lots of difficult issues and problems to deal with, and God gives us what we need to be able to do that. But everybody needs to be able to enjoy some recreation. Even if you're not an athlete, find something to do that doesn't involve a computer or a phone. Get out and be active. And if possible, do it with friends or family. Putting some fun in your life will lower your stress level and make life seem more manageable.

Play ball!

Reflect: Ecclesiastes 3:12 says, "There is nothing better than to be happy and enjoy ourselves as long as we can." How active are you? How intentional are you about having fun? Do you find that you work too much, even when you tell yourself you're not going to? What can you do to get a better handle on how you balance your life?

A MESSAGE FROM PAT

THIS IS ONE of my favorite books I've ever been a part of. Working with my buddy Mark Atteberry was great fun. What's better than going out to lunch and talking about God and sports for two or three hours? We laughed and told stories and shared Bible verses as our iced tea glasses were filled again and again. We filled reams of paper with notes and scribbles that somehow turned into this book. For that part of the process, we owe a great debt of gratitude to the wonderful people at Advantage Media Group. Kristin Goodale and Carly Blake were particularly helpful. And, of course, publisher Adam Witty's support and belief in the project made it all possible.

You can contact Pat at pat@patwilliams.com. His phone number is 407-721-0922. If you are interested in booking Pat for a speaking engagement, you may call Andrew Herdliska at 407-969-7578.

A MESSAGE FROM MARK

FEW PEOPLE KNOW that Pat and I started writing this book back in about 2009. We got twenty-five devotions done and ran into a roadblock, so the unfinished manuscript was thrown into a drawer and forgotten about. When Pat was retiring from the Orlando Magic ten years later, he was cleaning out his desk and found the manuscript. He picked up the phone and called me. He said, "Mark, you'll never guess what I just found." He thought I might not even remember it, but I did. Pat said, "We ought to give this thing another shot." I agreed, and here you are, holding it in your hands.

I'm grateful to Pat for his many years of friendship and unfailing support of my work. He's one-of-a-kind, and every day we got together to work on this project was a great day filled with calories, laughter, sports talk, and serious conversation about God. I also appreciate the amazing team at Advantage Media Group. Adam Witty, Kristin Goodale, and Carly Blake are as good as they come.

Most of all, I'm thankful to you, the reader, for giving this book your time and attention. Pat and I have tried our best to honor God and create a tool you can use to grow in your faith. We hope it's a blessing to you.

Mark is available for speaking engagements and retreats. You can reach him at markatteberry@aol.com. For more information about his books, visit alittlestrongereveryday.com.

ABOUT THE AUTHORS

PAT WILLIAMS, long-time NBA executive and basketball Hall of Famer, is currently engaged in trying to bring Major League Baseball to Orlando. He is the author of well over a hundred books, many of them on the art of leadership. Pat is a highly sought-after motivational speaker and the father of nineteen children and grandfather to nineteen more.

MARK ATTEBERRY is the award-winning author of fifteen books, including *The Samson Syndrome* and *The Solomon Seduction*. He spent forty-six years as a pastor in the local church and now works as a full-time writer. He lives in Central Florida with his wife, Marilyn.

ENDNOTES

1   Pat Summitt, *Reaching for the Summitt* (New York: Broadway Books, 1998), 40.

2   Warrick Dunn, *Running for My Life* (New York: Harper Entertainment, 2008), 190–191.

3   Jim Murray, *The Great Ones* (Los Angeles: Los Angeles Times Books, 1999), 237.

4   Alonzo Mourning, *Resilience* (New York: Ballantine, 2008), 41–42.

5   Charles Barkley, *Sir Charles* (New York: Warner Books, 1994), 96.

6   Buzz Braman, "Nothing but the Net: Making the 3-Point Shot," in *Why a Curveball Curves*, ed. Frank Vizard (New York: Hearst Books, 2008), 87.

7   Mia Hamm, *Go for the Goal* (New York: HarperCollins, 1999), 42.

8   Bill Bradley, *Values of the Game* (New York: Artisan, 1998), 61–62.

9   *The Quotable ESPN* (New York: Hyperion, 1998), 30.

10   David Hudson Jr., *Basketball's Most Wanted* (Dulles: Potomac Books, 2005), 189.

11   Steve Riach, *Heart of a Champion* (Nashville: Broadman & Holman, 2001), 21.

12   Steve Riach, *Amazing Athletes, Amazing Moments* (Hallmark, 2005), 190.

13   A. Lawrence Holmes, *More Than a Game* (New York: MacMillan, 1967), 160.

14   Pat Williams, *Coaching Your Kids to Be Leaders* (New York: Warner Faith, 2005), 148.

15   Pat Williams, *Extreme Dreams Depend on Teams* (New York: Center Street, 2009), 53.

16   Marv Albert, *I'd Love to But I Have a Game* (New York: Doubleday, 1993), 159.

17   Carli Lloyd, *When Nobody Was Watching* (Boston: Mariner Books, 2016), 2.

18   Gary Mack, *Mind Gym* (New York: McGraw-Hill, 2001).

19   Seth Davis, *Getting to Us* (London: Penguin, 2019), 247.

20   Joe Buck, *Lucky Bastard* (New York: Dutton, 2016), 60.

21   George Peper, *Grand Slam Golf* (New York: Harry N. Abrams, 1991), 173.

22   Cal Ripken, *Just Show Up* (New York: HarperCollins, 2019), 63.

23   Eddie Einhorn, *How March Became Madness* (Chicago: Triumph Books, 2006), 106.

24   Phil Mickelson, *One Magical Sunday* (New York: Warner Books, 2005), 151–152.

25   Criswell Freeman, *The Book of Football Wisdom* (Nashville: Walnut Grove Press, 1996), 43.

26   Tony Dungy, *Quiet Strength* (Carol Stream: Tyndale House, 2007), 210.

27   Mike Greenberg and Mike Golic, *Mike and Mike's Rules for Sports and Life* (New York: ESPN Books, 2010), 238.

28   Jack Canfield, *Chicken Soup for the Sports Fan's Soul* (Deerfield Beach: Health Communications, 2000), 152.

29   Adrian Asis, "10 Heartwarming Sports Stories That Will Move You to Tears," The Richest, July 7, 2014, https://www.therichest.com/other-sports/10-heartwarming-sports-stories-that-will-move-you-to-tears/.

30   Laura Depta, "12 Amazing Recent Sports Stories You Should Know About," Bleacher Report, accessed September 2, 2021, https://bleacherreport.com/articles/2664619-12-amazing-recent-sports-stories-you-should-know-about#slide6.

31   Bill Bradley, *Values of the Game* (New York: Artisan, 1998), 29.

32   Pat Williams, *Souls of Steel* (New York: Faith Words, 2008), 241.

33   Les Krantz, *Not Till the Fat Lady Sings* (Chicago: Triumph Books, 2003), 72.

Printed in the USA
CPSIA information can be obtained
at www.ICGtesting.com
JSHW011420151124
73645JS00016B/563

9 781642 253146